Editors Torrance and McCall have assembled a first-rate cast of authors writing with unusually sharp insight about God, science, and the created realm. The great achievement of their book is to demonstrate how productive—rather than how contentious—classical Christianity and contemporary scientific investigation can be. The book is accessible, but deeply considered chapters make a stellar contribution.

MARK NOLL, Francis A. McAnaney Professor of History Emeritus, the University of Notre Dame

Andrew Torrance and Thomas McCall have brought together an outstanding group of philosophers, theologians, biblical scholars, and scientists to reflect on the notion of creation. The result is a deep examination from diverse points of view on the relation of religion and science that ought to be required reading for anyone interested in this important topic.

ELEONORE STUMP, Robert J. Henle SJ Professor of Philosophy, Saint Louis University

Torrance and McCall bring together leading scholars in theology, biblical studies, philosophy, and the sciences to offer intelligent and immensely accessible perspectives on creation. Anyone who cares about the future of Christian theology and its potential to reinvigorate the meaning and purpose of the sciences should read this volume.

ELAINE HOWARD ECKLUND, Herbert S. Autrey Chair in Social Sciences, Rice University

Knowing Creation brings together leading Christian thinkers to enrich our understanding of the relationship between Christianity and science. I found myself enlightened and encouraged in my faith and my thinking. I recommend this book with great enthusiasm to a broad readership.

TREMPER LONGMAN III, distinguished scholar and professor emeritus of biblical studies, Westmont College

This volume includes chapters that exemplify awareness of relevant areas of contemporary science and biblical scholarship. Other contributors set the topic firmly within an historical context. The uses of the concept of creation are carefully scrutinised by philosophers determined to identify and expose muddled thinking wherever it occurs. The result is a challenging book which will fully reward careful and critical reading.

MALCOLM JEEVES, emeritus professor, School of Psychology and Neuroscience, St. Andrews University, and past president, the Royal Society of Edinburgh

Knowing Creation is a rich collection of theologically informed essays. The authors engage an impressive array of conversations partners from Job and Moses, to Plato and Aristotle, from Luther and Calvin, to Derrida and Dawkins. This is a valuable contribution to the science and religion dialogue.

KARL GIBERSON, professor of science and religion, Stonehill College

Knowing Creation moves beyond jaded conflict narratives to innovative, substantive dialogue about creation. By assembling a team of scientifically savvy theologians, philosophers, and biblical scholars in conversation with theologically informed scientists, *Knowing Creation* breaks new ground in thinking deeply about the astonishing richness of God's creation.

JEFF HARDIN, Raymond E. Keller Professor of Integrative Biology, University of Wisconsin-Madison

Knowing Creation is a wide-ranging resource for those who want to think more deeply about the complexity and wonder of the created world. We are indebted to the authors of these essays for their stimulating—and often challenging—reflections about our knowledge of God's creation.

J. RICHARD MIDDLETON, professor of biblical worldview and exegesis, Northeastern Seminary at Roberts Wesleyan College

Knowing Creation

PERSPECTIVES *from* THEOLOGY,
PHILOSOPHY, *and* SCIENCE

ANDREW B. TORRANCE and
THOMAS H. McCALL, EDITORS

VOLUME

1

ZONDERVAN

Knowing Creation
Copyright © 2018 by Andrew B. Torrance and Thomas H. McCall

This title is also available as a Zondervan ebook.

Requests for information should be addressed to:
Zondervan, *3900 Sparks Dr. SE, Grand Rapids, Michigan 49546*

Library of Congress Cataloging-in-Publication Data

Names: Torrance, Andrew B., editor. | McCall, Thomas H., editor.
Title: Knowing creation : perspectives from theology, philosophy, and science / Andrew B. Torrance
and Thomas H. McCall, editors.
Description: Grand Rapids, MI : Zondervan, [2018]
Identifiers: LCCN 2017046169 | ISBN 9780310536130 (softcover)
Subjects: LCSH: Creation. | Creationism.
Classification: LCC BS651 .K59 2018 | DDC 231.7/65—dc23 LC record available at https://lccn.loc
.gov/2017046169

Cover design: Studio Gearbox
Cover photo: Pexels.com
Interior design: Kait Lamphere

Printed in the United States of America

18 19 20 21 22 23 24 25 26 27 28 /DHV/ 15 14 13 12 11 10 9 8 7 6 5 4 3 2 1

To Marilyn McCord Adams,
Pax et bonum

Contents

III. Philosophical Perspectives

IV. Scientific Perspectives

Acknowledgments

The editors would like to thank the *John Templeton Foundation* for its generous support of the *Scientists in Congregations Scotland* program, and the *Templeton Religion Trust* for its generous support of *The Creation Project*. It is out of these two programs that this volume has been developed. Also, we are indebted to the helpful feedback and encouragement from our editors at Zondervan Academic, Katya Covrett and Matthew Estel, which proved to be invaluable. Lastly, we are enormously grateful to Bethany Rutledge and Diana Verhagen for the hard work they did on the indexing for this volume.

Contributors

MARILYN MCCORD ADAMS†—was distinguished research professor of philosophy at Rutgers University.

DENIS R. ALEXANDER—is director emeritus of the Faraday Institute for Science and Religion at St. Edmund's College, Cambridge.

WILLIAM P. BROWN—is William Marcellus McPheeters Professor of Old Testament at Columbia Theological Seminary.

SUSAN GROVE EASTMAN—is associate research professor of New Testament at Duke Divinity School.

C. STEPHEN EVANS—is University Professor of Philosophy and Humanities at Baylor University.

MARK HARRIS—is senior lecturer in science and religion at the University of Edinburgh.

ROBERT C. KOONS—is professor of philosophy at the University of Texas.

THOMAS H. MCCALL—is professor of biblical and systematic theology at Trinity Evangelical Divinity School and director of the Carl F. H. Henry Center for Theological Understanding.

TOM MCLEISH—is professor of natural philosophy in the Department of Physics at the University of York. He is also chair of the Royal Society's education committee.

SIMON OLIVER—is the Van Mildert Professor of Divinity in the Department of Theology and Religion at Durham University.

CHRISTOPH SCHWÖBEL—is professor of systematic theology and director of the Institute of Hermeneutics and Cultural Dialogue at the University of Tübingen.

WILLIAM M. R. SIMPSON—is a research associate of the University of St. Andrews and a doctoral student in philosophy at the University of Cambridge. He also holds a PhD in theoretical physics from the University of St. Andrews.

ANDREW B. TORRANCE—is lecturer in theology at the University of St. Andrews.

PETER VAN INWAGEN—is John Cardinal O'Hara Professor of Philosophy at the University of Notre Dame and research professor of philosophy at Duke University.

JOHN H. WALTON—is professor of Old Testament at Wheaton College.

FRANCIS WATSON—is professor of biblical interpretation at Durham University.

RANDALL C. ZACHMAN—is professor emeritus of Reformation studies at the University of Notre Dame.

Introduction

Knowing Creation

ANDREW B. TORRANCE
AND THOMAS H. McCALL

Today, perhaps more than any time since the second and third centuries, the church is divided over the question of how we should understand the Christian doctrine of creation. In some instances, there is a profound neglect of the doctrine of creation; one need only to compare recent theological work on the doctrine of creation with many other traditional topics to see this. In other cases, however, Christians are sharply and deeply divided over issues related to the doctrine of creation. There are many contributing factors, but one of the foremost reasons is the divergence among the ways Christians attempt to juggle theological, biblical, and scientific perspectives on the nature of creation—particularly with respect to the relation between creation as a doctrine and evolution as science. As Denis Alexander points out, several major ways of thinking about creation and evolution have developed.[1]

(1) At one end of the "spectrum" are the *young-earth creationists*, who believe that the world was created in six twenty-four-hour days around 10,000 years ago. This group is committed to reading the Genesis creation narrative (and the genealogies) as providing an accurate historical record of the events that took place at the beginning of creation. Some young-earth creationists have been involved in the development of "creation science" (even building a "creation museum" and an accompanying marketing empire). Many young-earth creationists understand that their views stand against mainstream

---

1. Denis Alexander, "Creation and Evolution," in *The Blackwell Companion to Science and Christianity*, ed. J. B. Stump and Alan Padgett (Malden, MA: Wiley-Blackwell, 2012), 236–37.

science; some simply reject this science by appealing to the authority of biblical teaching, while others insist that the scientific evidence is actually on their side.

(2) *Old-earth creationists* are happy to embrace the conclusions of contemporary science about the age of the earth. However, like young-earth creationists, they believe that the diversity of life in creation is the result of a series of special events of divine action. So, while creation may have occurred very long ago, and perhaps even over a long period of time, nonetheless God acts directly to bring about the diversity of life. In particular, they often insist upon the direct agency of God in the creation of humankind, and they insist upon the uniqueness of humans. Not surprisingly, they tend to insist upon the historicity of the first human couple (the "Adam and Eve" of Genesis).

(3) There are those within the *Intelligent Design* movement who are convinced of the reality of "irreducible complexity," and they conclude that such complexity is most reasonably understood to be from the action of an intelligent designer. This group is distinguishable from young-earth creationists and from some old-earth creationists, yet they also deny a Darwinian account of evolution. They take a further step and call this intelligent designer "God," and in doing so they engage in a kind of natural theology that associates the emergence of complex features of the natural world with special (intervenient) acts of divine design. For them, such association can be facilitated by scientific observation, even without the guidance of Scripture. Many such theorists also believe in a historical first human couple (although not usually on scientific or natural-theological grounds).

(4) Lastly, there are various types of *theistic evolutionists* who believe that God creates an evolving creation. These theorists take themselves to be directly in alignment with the prevailing scientific understanding of evolution. For some of this group, God is providentially involved in guiding the process of evolution (and various theological proposals are offered for making sense of this). For others, especially those who hold to noninterventionist accounts of divine action, God does not actively violate or suspend natural laws (as they have been interpreted by scientific investigation).[2] According to the more extreme versions of this position, God creates the world with a particular set of natural laws and then leaves it to evolve for itself. Such a position is believed to account for the seemingly random mutations that lead to genetic

---

2. Some of those who hold this view would argue that God limits his activity to the quantum level, where quantum indeterminacy would allow God to act without breaking any natural laws.

variation. On other accounts, God might engage more directly with God's evolving creation at various points. While some (perhaps many or even most) theistic evolutionists find it difficult if not impossible to maintain belief in a "historical Adam and Eve," others see no contradiction and thus maintain commitment to this historic Christian belief.

When summarising these four broad positions, it is easy to caricature, and such caricaturing can easily turn a conversation into a quarrel. So it is worth acknowledging that there are more charitable ways of presenting the above positions—although, obviously, what counts as "more charitable" will vary depending on one's commitments.[3] It is also worth noting that when we survey the various ways in which Christians think about the creator-creation relationship, we find that there are many people who don't fit neatly into one of these four categories but would align themselves with more than one of the above groups. Nonetheless, the above descriptions are representative of some dominant strands within the four groups.

Regardless of how we construe the various understandings of the creator-creation relationship, at least two things are clear. First, in the conversation about science and religion, the term "creation" (particularly "creationism") has come to be associated with those positions that are most willing to sacrifice mainstream scientific consensus—be it for the sake of a particular reading of the Bible or a particular form of natural theology. This has meant that Christians who want to present themselves as being in line with contemporary science can sometimes feel a need to avoid using the term "creation," particularly in the company of fellow scientists. Second, when Christians actually do discuss the doctrine of creation, the all-too-predictable debates about "creation vs. evolution" can quickly dominate the discussion. Such debates often suck all the intellectual oxygen from the room—with the result that other doctrinal matters of great importance (e.g., *creatio ex nihilo*, the contingency of creation, the goodness of creation, etc.) are often overlooked or ignored.

In this book, we seek to challenge the suspicion surrounding the term by presenting a broad picture of creation that finds harmony with both contemporary science and orthodox Christian theology. To paint such a picture, we have gathered together a group of leading experts from the fields of theology, biblical studies, philosophy, and the sciences to offer a diverse range of perspectives on

---

3. For further discussion of these positions, see J. B. Stump, ed., *Four Views on Creation, Evolution, and Intelligent Design* (Grand Rapids: Zondervan, 2017).

what it means to know creation. We also work to reinvigorate consideration of the major and classical doctrinal themes.

That the doctrine of creation offers so much scope for bringing these various disciplines together is one of the things that makes it so special. Indeed, it is hard to think of another area of Christian theology that offers such potential. This is because it not only invites reflection on an intellectual concept; it calls for contemplation on the endlessly complex, dynamic, and fascinating world that human beings inhabit. Yet the opportunity for interdisciplinary engagement is rarely taken up, and Christian reflection on creation tends to find itself constrained by the boundaries of particular specialisms. The reason for this is that scholars tend to be under enormous pressure to stay within the boundaries of their field and avoid being distracted by the thinking of other disciplines—especially in the contemporary academy where there is so much emphasis on specialisation.

As history testifies, when theologians, philosophers, biblical scholars, and scientists silo themselves within their respective disciplines, they are likely to end up drawing conclusions that are not only distinct but also incompatible. When scholars do decide to venture outside their area of expertise, the potential for a wide-ranging discussion can often be undermined by scholars talking past one another. There is a tendency for scholars from one field to expect scholars from other fields simply to conform to their own orthodoxies, regardless of whether such orthodoxies run into tension with the orthodoxy of the other fields. If disagreement persists, it can be all too easy for interdisciplinary conversations to conclude with the various parties agreeing to disagree before returning to their independent silos—perhaps more reluctant than ever to participate in interdisciplinary conversations.

As we can see from the above list of views on the creator-creation relationship, this dynamic has proven to be particularly problematic when it comes to thinking about creation. Too often theological interpretations of creation end up being at odds with scientific interpretations. One way to try to resolve such tension is to accept Stephen Jay Gould's view of nonoverlapping magisteria: scientific claims belong to one domain of enquiry, which concerns itself with the "hard facts" of reality, and theological claims belong to a very different domain, which is concerned about discerning a sense of value and meaning. The problem with this approach, however, is that Christian theology not only has things to say about value and meaning but also about the very nature of creation. So it is possible for theologians and scientists to draw conclusions that are not only different in kind but also directly incompatible with one another. This makes it vital for theologians and scientists to be in conversation, a conversation that benefits greatly from the input of philosophers and biblical scholars as well.

At the end of the day, there should be nothing about a Christian theology of creation that necessitates competition with the mainstream consensus of modern science. It is true that scientists can misinterpret the reality of the natural world; when they do, it is also true that their conclusions are not going to track with a true theology of creation. At the same time, such misinterpretation is so rare in the contemporary world that theologians should be hesitant to resist allowing their views to be challenged by the (scientific) conclusions of natural scientists.

That said, it is the case that persons can sometimes confuse empirical science with a kind of pseudoscience—a form of "science" that unwittingly draws conclusions that are not simply informed by empirical science but also by metaphysical assumptions about the nature of things. Thinkers such as Richard Dawkins and Lawrence Krauss have overestimated the ability of "science" to challenge theological claims about the nature of the cosmos. As such, it can be important for Christian thinkers to be able to recognise the difference between science and pseudoscience, at one level, and between physics and metaphysics, at another level.

So, on the one hand, when it comes to knowing creation, it is going to be a problem for the scientist if a Christian theologian concludes that evolution isn't true (e.g., perhaps because of an overly literal reading of the Genesis creation stories). On the other hand, it is likely to be a problem for the Christian theologian if a (pseudo)scientist claims that science can tell us that there is nothing beyond the natural order guiding or setting up the evolutionary process (e.g., because of an overconfidence in science's ability to discern the lack of a teleology).

When such disagreement occurs, it is important for both the Christian theologian and the Christian scientist to be willing to listen to one another and be open to changing their minds—depending on the validity of the conclusions that are being drawn by the other. This interrelationship, however, need not only be critically evaluative; it can also be one of mutual upbuilding.

Christian theology can help the scientist to have a greater confidence in the order and regularity of the cosmos, which enables it to be intelligible for science. According to Christian theology, the order and regularity of creation is not simply assumed but affirmed. Additionally, Christian theology can help the scientist appreciate that there is such a thing as objective truth, logic, and reason. Further, it can allow her to recognize, when faith requires, that certain occurrences and arrangements are to be associated with special divine action.

The sciences can help give theology an accurate understanding of the history and mechanisms of the natural order, which can, in turn, help theologians develop a deeper understanding of the genres of Scripture—that is, to help them appreciate the more poetic nature of the Genesis stories. Science can help theologians to develop a better understanding of what it means to be human, which can make a difference to many areas relating to theological anthropology. And science can help us develop a better understanding of what it means for Christians to look after our ecosystem and the flora and fauna that share it with us.

For many reasons, it is critical that the plurality of Christian scholars talk to and listen to one another when it comes to knowing creation. By being open to learn from the voices of other disciplines, Christian scholars are not only capable of broadening each other's horizons but also keeping one another accountable.

The Aim of This Volume

At a time when the doctrine of creation has been disparaged due to its supposed association with antiscientific dogma, and theological offerings sometimes risk appearing little more than reactionary exercises in naïve apologetics, ill-informed by science or distinctly wary of engagement with it, it is more important than ever to offer a cross-disciplinary resource that can voice a positive account of a Christian theology of creation and do so as a genuinely broad-ranging conversation about science and faith. Accordingly, this work aims to demonstrate that there is, assuredly, a more fruitful way to know the natural order *as* creation. This way forward requires mutual attentiveness to the conclusions of theologians, biblical scholars, philosophers, and contemporary scientists. By listening to one another, we can begin to develop a more balanced understanding of creation. And such understanding has an immense amount to offer the church, academy, and wider society, as that society grapples with debates about religious education, the funding and ethics of scientific research, the nature of religious commitment, and the relationship of private belief and public practices in a pluralist context.

To be clear, it is not a part of our endgame to encourage Christian scientists to start mentioning the created order in scientific journals. We are not hoping for the term "creation" to be introduced into science textbooks, nor do we expect Christian science teachers to always refer to the natural order as creation. The fact that Christians participate in a pluralist society means that it will often be best for Christians to opt for more neutral terms like "natural order" when we participate in the scientific world. This is especially true since the term "creation" has come to be associated with a whole host of theories that defy modern science.

So in the world of modern science Christians should follow the advice of Paul in Romans 13 and subject themselves to the leading authorities and their scholarly peers. As the success of the scientific world has proven, the leaders in the contemporary scientific world are not a terror to good science, but to bad. And, for reasons that are both understandable and justifiable, the leading figures in mainstream science have deemed it inappropriate to employ theological language. As we shall consider, there are not only good scientific reasons for this judgement but also good theological reasons.

At the same time, we also want to make it clear that the use of the term "creation" should not necessarily be a problem for the Christian scientist. Equipped with an accurate theology of creation, and living in a world where a Christian worldview is universally accepted, there should be nothing wrong with the term "creation" appearing in the world of science—because, as the Christian knows, that's what the natural world is. While it may be appropriate for Christian scientists to avoid using theological language in the lab, this does not mean that such omission should encourage a forgetfulness of the createdness of creation in the name of science.

It is worth asserting that it is not part of our objective to encourage Christian theologians to ground their theology of creation in the natural sciences. While we think that contemporary science can complement and thereby help Christians with some of the second-order details in understanding creation, we also think it is beyond the scope of science to make judgements concerning more foundational theological claims, such as those about the nature of the Creator, God's reasons for creation, God's act of creation and God's purposes for creation.

The Chapters

This volume gathers together a group of eminent scholars from theology, biblical studies, philosophy, and the natural sciences who are committed to furthering constructive dialogue between their respective disciplines. Together, they offer a challenge to some of the problematic ways in which we have come to know creation. But, more important, they also offer a constructive way forward for thinking about creation in a more holistic manner.

In the first part, we turn to the world of theology to ground our volume in an understanding of what the Christian faith teaches us about the doctrine of creation. For our interdisciplinary conversation to be Christian, it is important to begin by addressing what is distinctive about a Christian vision of creation. This is primarily a theological question—albeit one that needs to be informed by reading the Bible, to which we turn in the second part.

In the first chapter, Simon Oliver gets the volume underway with a careful consideration of how we should think about the interrelationship between nature and culture in light of the doctrine of creation *ex nihilo*. He shows how an appreciation of the givenness of creation can help the human world develop a more conservational and respectful relationship with the rest of the natural world.

Chapter 2 sees Christoph Schwöbel thinking about what it might mean to know creation as a speech-act of the triune God. Turning to Luther's lectures on Genesis, he offers an extended reflection on the metaphor of God speaking creation into existence. This leads him to consider the constructive ways in which this metaphor encourages us to think about creation as a web of communicative relationships.

In chapter 3, Randall Zachman presents John Calvin in a light that will be unfamiliar to many and surprising to some: as a theologian utterly devoted to the sciences—or to "natural philosophy" as it was called at the time. By exploring his theology of creation, Zachman makes the provocative case that, for Calvin, every Christian should seek to become a scientist, that is, someone who is constantly in pursuit of a deeper understanding of creation.

In the fourth and final chapter of the theology section, Andrew Torrance challenges two approaches that can serve as obstacles for the task of knowing creation: "methodological naturalism" and "methodological atheism." After assessing why these approaches have come to be associated with the scientific method, he argues that the Christian should not feel a need to associate science with philosophies (naturalism or atheism) that are incompatible with a knowledge of creation *as* creation.

In part 2, we look to the Bible as the primary resource for informing a theological understanding of creation. As these chapters dig into the text, they also consider how we ought to approach Scripture in a way that does not put the Bible and science into competition with one another and considers how they might be able to serve and complement one another.

This part begins with two chapters that address our approach to the Genesis accounts of creation. In chapter 5, John Walton offers some guidance on reading Genesis as an ancient text in the context of our modern scientific world. He shows that when we interpret the early chapters of Genesis with an attentiveness to their original context, there is no reason to read them as competitive with contemporary science and, in particular, evolutionary theories of creation.

Going beyond the ancient context in which Genesis was written, Francis Watson takes us into the nineteenth century to consider why Genesis came to be read in competition with the natural sciences. According to Watson, the reading of Genesis that conflicts with the scientific world is not appropriate to the text itself but one that obscures the text by reading it through the lens of modern science.

In chapter 7, William Brown reflects on the nature of creation by drawing on what, on first hearing, would appear to be two very strange bedfellows: the book of Job and astrobiology. By turning to Job, Brown reminds us that, in the midst of creation, human beings are in a wilderness that is not the anthropocentric cosmos it is so often imagined to be.

In the final chapter of this section, Susan Eastman considers how the apostle Paul envisages the epistemic relationship between Creator and creature. For Paul, she demonstrates, God relates to us as whole persons who are embodied within the materiality of creation. This prompts her to turn to the worlds of neuroscience and psychology to see what these disciplines can tell us about the nature of human beings as essentially relational creatures.

In the third section, four leading philosophers give us their take on what it means to know creation. Marilyn McCord Adams opens with a lucid introduction to some of the key things to keep in mind when it comes to knowing creation. As she reflects on some of the distinctively Christian features of the doctrine of creation, she helps us to see why creation is not simply a material order but a place of life that is defined by a holiness and love that, in relationship with God, enables it to surpass the value of its mere material composition.

In chapter 10, Peter van Inwagen offers a theological meditation on a passage from Julian of Norwich's *Revelations of Divine Love*. In this meditation, van Inwagen draws on Julian's words to illuminate the power, grandeur, and love of the triune God who creates.

In chapter 11, C. Stephen Evans asks whether human beings have been created with an innate ability to know that God exists. He argues that there are natural signs within creation pointing to God's existence that we have been hardwired to recognise as pointing to God and that provide a foundation for reasonable belief in God. Further, he turns to some recent conclusions in cognitive science and evolutionary psychology to consider whether they provide further support for his position.

In the next two chapters, a philosopher and a scientist each respond to one of the most complex questions in the conversation about science and faith: How should we think about the nature of creation in conjunction with a modern scientific worldview? By drawing on the Aristotelian tradition, they both challenge the modern tendency to be overly reductive in our analysis of the natural order by continually reducing wholes to a coordination of fundamental material parts—parts that are microscopic.

In the first of these chapters, Robert Koons turns to Aristotle's philosophy of nature as a key resource for helping us to think about the natural world from both a scientific and Christian perspective. More specifically, he considers the ways in which the quantum revolution of the last century has created exciting new opportunities for thinking about what Aristotle's thought can contribute towards a Christian understanding of creation as well as a new philosophy of nature.

In the second chapter on the theme of knowing nature, we hear from one of our four scientists, William Simpson, who turns to Aristotelian hylomorphism as a way forward for understanding the place of living things within the material order. For Simpson, this philosophy provides a third way to think about the nature of life in the context of contemporary science, a way that is neither overly mechanistic and reductive nor dependent upon a theory of emergence.

Moving on from our discussion of nature broadly understood, molecular biologist Denis Alexander contemplates the relationship between creation, providence, and evolution. Alexander demonstrates convincingly that the scientific theory of evolution is in no way a threat to the Christian doctrines of creation and providence. Moreover, he shows that evolution testifies to the orderliness of the universe, as it has been established by God's creative and providential activity.

In the penultimate chapter, physicist and scholar of science and religion Mark Harris offers a reflection on Isaiah 55:12, thinking about what it might mean to recognise the nonhuman features of creation as praising the Creator. According to Harris, there is a sanctity to nature that bespeaks an intimate relationship between God and the whole of creation and that invites a theology of nature according to which the natural order is defined by the praise to its Creator.

In the final chapter, physicist Tom McLeish argues that rather than talking about science and religion we should be thinking in terms of a theology of science. By so doing, he shows that we are much better positioned to develop a positive understanding of the interrelationship between the natural sciences and a Christian understanding of creation.

One thing to make clear is that each of the four parts is not siloed from the other parts. While we have gathered together representatives from each of the various disciplines, we did not require the contributors to approach the topic of knowing in a way that was confined by the practices of their particular disciplines. This is particularly the case when it comes to the scientists, who are not writing scientific papers but are reflecting on the doctrine of creation as persons whose primary expertise is in the field of science.

In putting together this volume, it is our hope that, by encouraging attentiveness to a wide range of voices, we can spark a more positive and constructive conversation about the natural order *as* a created order. If we are to overcome the controversies that so often surround this theme, it is vital to engage in such open conversation. By so doing, the doctrine of creation can perhaps once again be recognised as the cornerstone for a Christian conversation about faith and the natural sciences.

Chapter ONE

Every Good and Perfect Gift Is from Above

Creation *Ex Nihilo* before Nature and Culture

SIMON OLIVER

In the first account of creation in Genesis, humanity is created male and female in the image of God and is given dominion over the other creatures (Gen 1:26–28). The second account of creation describes Adam's formation from the dust in order that he might till the ground; he belongs to the earth and the natural order of creatures to which it gives birth (Gen 2:7–15). Combining these accounts, we can say that humanity bears the image of God in the midst of nature. Ancient Christian hymns such as the *Benedicite* similarly place humanity within the natural order of creatures. For medieval Christian thought, humanity lies at the heart of the cosmos as a microcosm of God's creation, sharing the spiritual nature of angels and the material nature of other creatures. The order of nature includes humanity at its centre.

What is nature? Christian theologians of the high Middle Ages were deeply influenced by Aristotle's understanding of nature when his thought was reintroduced into the Latin West in the twelfth century. Nature, according to Aristotle, is a difficult concept to define but is identified broadly as "the distinctive form of quality of such things as have within themselves a principle of motion, such form or characteristic property not being separable from the things themselves, save conceptually."[1] In other words, nature encapsulates those things that have *a nature*, by which Aristotle means an intrinsic principle

---

1. Aristotle, *Physics*, trans. P. H. Wicksteed and F. M. Cornford (Cambridge, MA: Harvard University Press, 1929), 2.1.193b5.

of change towards the actualisation or fulfilment of that nature. It is the nature of the girl to become a woman and the acorn to become an oak. Nature is contrasted with human artifice, in which the principle of change is not wholly intrinsic but also has an extrinsic source. To use Aristotle's example, the principle which brings about a bed is not a natural principle intrinsic to the material nature of the bed but lies extrinsically in the work of the maker of the bed as she fashions the timber. When Aristotle points out that "man is generated by man, whereas a bedstead is not generated from a bedstead," he makes a distinction between natural things which are generated and works of human artifice which are made.[2] The bed comes about from a cause other than nature, namely a craftsman. Although nature is thereby distinguished from human artifice, the two domains are intimately linked because "art imitates nature."[3] In other words, art must work with what is given by nature. Human artifice is teleological—that is, purposeful and meaningful—only because nature itself is purposeful and meaningful. In every aspect of human creativity, we only work with what is given in nature. The best human artifice works *with* the natures of creatures; at its best, art may even "carry things further than nature can."[4] Whilst nature and artifice are closely associated in Aristotle's thought in such a way that the latter participates in the former, the Christian inheritors of his natural philosophy could integrate the works of nature and the works of human culture even more intimately under the single category of "creation." All things owe their being to God, and every creature, human and nonhuman, is defined first and foremost by the reception of its existence from a divine transcendent source. All causation in the created order, including human artifice, is a participation in the primary causal power of God.

The vision of the unity of human culture and wider nature under the single category of "creation" undergoes a significant change in the seventeenth and eighteenth centuries. The identification of human culture as a separate domain standing over and against nature is often regarded as a characteristic feature of modern thought.[5] Human culture comes to be regarded as the

2. Aristotle, *Physics*, 2.1.193b12.

3. Aristotle, *Physics*, 2.8.199a15–a20.

4. Aristotle, *Physics*, 2.8.199a15–a20.

5. Bruno Latour, *We Have Never Been Modern*, trans. Catherine Porter (London: Harvester Wheatsheaf, 1993). See also Louis Dupré, *Passage to Modernity: An Essay in the Hermeneutics of Nature and Culture* (New Haven, CT: Yale University Press, 1993); and Richard L. Fern, *Nature, God, and Humanity: Envisioning an Ethics of Nature* (Cambridge: Cambridge University Press, 2002), ch. 5.

domain of free and creative subjects, whereas nature is understood as the distinct domain of brute animal instinct and necessity. We structure the modern university according to the division of nature and culture, with certain faculties having the natural world as their object of study (the natural and life sciences) whilst others concern themselves with the human cultural world (the arts and humanities, including law, business, and the social sciences). Intention, purpose, and freedom belong to the subjective human cultural realm. Nature is an objective domain governed by the laws of nature and the determinations of animal instinct.

Although the roots of the separation of nature and culture are contested, one can point to the post-Reformation period and the demise of the view that nature is a sacramental and symbolic realm encompassing human culture. Once devoid of any intrinsic meaning and significance, nature was reimagined as a separate domain and resource for human cultural use.[6] Moreover, the advent of a mechanical cosmology in the seventeenth century meant that the Aristotelian priority of nature over art was reversed. No longer was art thought to imitate or participate in nature. Nature was now thought to be akin to human artifice as creation was viewed as a divine artefact analogous to a clockwork mechanism.[7]

One area of contemporary debate which frequently assumes the separation of nature and culture is the environmental crisis. On the one hand, there are those who see the solution to global warming, climate change, and pollution lying in more nature via a retreat of human cultural interference. This means reverting to more "natural" forms of food production, energy, and transport, for example. The term "natural" is applied to anything from organic foods to biofuels and shampoo; it means little more than the relative absence of human manipulation and influence. This can reflect a romantic notion of a "pure nature" (an idea that has plagued Christian theology for other reasons) that is devoid of cultural infection. This is nature understood as unspoiled meadows and wild animals. On the other hand, there are those who see the solution to the environmental crisis lying in increased cultural intervention in the form

---

6. See Peter Harrison, *The Bible, Protestantism and the Rise of Natural Science* (Cambridge: Cambridge University Press, 1998), ch. 5.

7. See Michael Hanby, *No God, No Science?* (Oxford: Wiley-Blackwell, 2014), esp. ch. 4; Robert Spaemann, "What Does It Mean to Say that 'Art Imitates Nature'?" in *A Robert Spaemann Reader: Philosophical Essays on Nature, God, and the Human Person*, ed. and trans. D. C. Schindler and Jeanne Heffernan Schindler (Oxford: Oxford University Press, 2015), 192–210.

of strategic technologies for the enhanced control of nature towards more desirable environmental goals. Good examples are the genetic engineering of crops, industrialised farming, carbon capture and storage technologies, or punitive taxes levied against polluting industries.

Both strategies assume the distinction between nature and culture. Those who demand more *nature* argue that we should submit to nature and relinquish cultural manipulation, thus naturalising culture. Those who demand more *culture* seek ever more control over nature via enhanced use of technology and economic policies that direct the means of production to meet human material needs, whatever they may be. This latter approach has strong resonances with the post-Reformation Christian desire to have dominion over nature by returning it, via human intervention, to the perfection and order that belonged to the garden of Eden prior to the fall.[8]

Of course, nature has never existed in pure form outside the influence of human culture and activity. As the philosopher Bruno Latour has pointed out, modernity's desire to purify the domains of nature and culture has never succeeded because so-called "hybrids" of nature and culture constantly arise, hence "we have never been modern."[9] For example, is global warming a cultural or natural phenomenon? On the one hand, it seems to be caused by culture in the form of human industrial activity and consumption. This dramatic influence apparently begins with industrialization in the nineteenth century, yet scientists now refer to the "anthropocene" as a period of profound human influence on the environment, beginning as recently as the 1950s.[10] On the other hand, global warming is a phenomenon occurring within the natural domain in the form of climate change and environmental degradation. Others argue that global warming is an entirely natural phenomenon that occurs in cycles, regardless of human activity.

Understanding humanity's relation to nature and the environment through the separated domains of nature and culture therefore appears problematic. Appeals to increasingly natural forms of culture or cultural forms of nature assume the separation of these domains and seek the subjection of one to the

8. Peter Harrison, *The Bible, Protestantism and the Rise of Natural Science*, ch. 6; Harrison, *The Fall of Man and the Rise of Natural Science* (Cambridge: Cambridge University Press, 2007).

9. Latour, *We Have Never Been Modern*, ch. 1.

10. See Damian Carrington, "The Anthropocene Epoch: Scientists Declare Dawn of Human-Influenced Age," *The Guardian*, 29 August 2016, https://www.theguardian.com/environment/2016/aug/29/declare-anthropocene-epoch-experts-urge-geological-congress-human-impact-earth.

other. Can offering alternative resources from Christian theology overcome this dualism? This chapter will argue that the Christian doctrine of creation, in not severing human culture from the domain of nature, offers a different approach to our relationship to the nonhuman world, particularly through the understanding of creation as gift. Understanding creation as gift invests both nature and culture with intrinsic significance and value. It diverts us from thinking of nature merely as an objective resource for human use and points to the view that creation places moral demands on human agents because it establishes a relationship between giver and recipient.

In pursuing the understanding of creation as gift, this chapter will begin by examining the fundamental claim that God creates *ex nihilo*—"out of nothing." This distinguishes creation from any natural process and establishes its utterly gratuitous and dependent character as well as its unity, value, and purpose. Creation *ex nihilo* is the primordial gift because it simultaneously establishes both the gift of creaturely existence and the recipient of the gift, namely creatures themselves. There is nothing that stands outside the divine economy of gift because, as Saint Paul puts it, "What do you have that you did not receive? And if you received it, why do you boast as if it were not a gift?" (1 Cor 4:7).

Having identified creation as gift, the second part of this chapter will examine recent discussions of the theology, philosophy, and anthropology of gift that began in earnest with the work of Marcel Mauss in the 1920s. The gift is described by Mauss as bearing something of the giver to the recipient. Gift-giving is necessarily reciprocal and yet is not reducible to trade. It therefore establishes a different kind of gratuitous relation that bears ethical implications because gifts, including the gifts of creation, bear meaning. This chapter will conclude by pointing to the particular importance of the gift of food, a gift that explicitly unites the domains of nature and culture, for it is the fruit of the earth and the work of human hands. Genesis establishes food as God's first gift to creatures (Gen 1:29; 2:9). Prior to the fall and the requirement that Adam toil and labour (Gen 3:17–19), food is freely given. Genesis ends with another gift of food which effects Joseph's reconciliation to his starving father and the brothers who once sold him into slavery (Gen 39–50). Food is quintessentially natural and cultural, a reconciling gift that nurtures life, establishes the communion of nature and culture, and institutes the saving communion of God and humanity in the form of the eucharistic food. I begin, however, with the basic character of creation as gift.

Creation *Ex Nihilo*: The Gift of Being

The theology of creation was formulated in the early church in response to a crucial question: how is God to be distinguished from creation? The failure to answer this question with sufficient clarity would result in idolatry and confusion in every area of Christian thought. There was always a danger of construing God as part of creation, or creation as an aspect of God. The failure to begin with the doctrine of God and articulate the difference between God and creation was the mistake of the various gnostic philosophies encountered by early Christian theology.

By the fourth century, Christian theologians expressed the difference between God and creation in terms of the simplicity of God: God's essence and God's existence are one. In other words, it is of God's essence to exist. Unlike creatures, God's being is not composed or structured. Writing in the early fifth century, Augustine put it this way: "There is, then, a Good which alone is simple, and therefore alone immutable, and this is God. By this Good all other goods have been created; but they are not simple, and therefore are not immutable."[11]

In the thirteenth century, Thomas Aquinas was to give the doctrine of divine simplicity greater metaphysical precision. For Aquinas, if we are properly to distinguish God from creatures, we must refer to God as *ipsum esse per se subsistens*—self-subsistent being itself.[12] Unlike creatures, God is eternal, replete, and wholly uncaused. Moreover, God is not a type of thing, one amongst many, but absolute being itself or *ens per essentiam*—being by essence. On the other hand, it is not of the essence of creatures to exist. Creatures are contingent; they might not be. Whereas essence and existence are perfectly one in God, in creatures they are really distinct because existence is added to essence. In other words, existence is not of the essence of a horse or a tree because such creatures might not exist. So the being of creatures, in its contingency, always implies an outside source of existence from one that requires no explanation.

Because God is simple and "self-subsistent being itself," Aquinas shows that God is the source of *everything* that is *not* God. In other words, God is

---

11. Augustine, *The City of God against the Pagans*, trans. R. W. Dyson (Cambridge: Cambridge University Press, 1998), 11.10, 462.

12. Aquinas, *Summa Theologiae*, 1.4.2, co.

"the principle and cause of being in other things."[13] Whereas God exists by essence (*per essentiam*), creatures owe their entire being to God. Creatures exist not by essence but by participation (*per participationem*). Aquinas writes,

> Every thing, furthermore, exists because it has being. A thing whose essence is not its being, consequently, is not *through its essence*, but *by participation* in something, namely, being itself. But that which is through participation in something cannot be the first being, because prior to it is the being in which it participates in order to be. But God is the first being, with nothing prior to Him. The essence of God, therefore, is His own being.[14]

Such is the absolute difference between God and creation: God is "being itself" and exists by essence, whereas creaturely being is a composition of existence and essence. Creatures only exist by participation in God's being. This establishes a radical asymmetry between God and creation because there are not two foci of being, God plus creation alongside. Only God truly exists in himself and is therefore the sole focus of being. Everything that is not God—that is, creation—exists only by participating in God's existence.

The radical difference between God and creation led Christian theologians of antiquity to the conviction that God must be the mysterious source of all things, including matter, space, and time. God should not be thought to work on some preexistent material stuff in his creation of the cosmos because this would imply something—the material stuff—does not owe its existence to God. If God is the source of everything that is not God, this implies a fundamental principle or origin of creation. The scriptural witness, particularly the Septuagint's translation of the first verses of Genesis, implied a beginning (*archē*) to creation and described God as the source of all created existence (Rom 11:36; 1 Cor 8:6; Eph 3:9; Col 1:16; Rev 4:11). This led to a remarkable consensus amongst the theologians of the early church, one shared by Jewish theology and later by Islam, namely that if the absolute distinction between God and creation is to be maintained, as well as the utterly unique character of the divine creative act, God must be thought to create *ex nihilo*—out of

---

13. Aquinas, *Summa Contra Gentiles*, bk. 2, *Creation*, trans. James F. Anderson (Notre Dame, IN: University of Notre Dame Press, 1975), 2.6.1.

14. Aquinas, *Summa Contra Gentiles*, 1.22.9 (my translation and emphases).

nothing. Whilst implied by Scripture, this metaphysics of creation contradicted the Greek philosophical principle, traceable to Parmenides (fl. late sixth century BC), that *ex nihil, nihil fit*—out of nothing, nothing comes.[15]

What were the early Christian theologians attempting to articulate through the doctrine of creation *ex nihilo*? First, creation *ex nihilo* indicates the utterly free character of God's creative act. In human acts of making, we are constrained in some way by what is already given, namely the material with which we work. As the source of all created existence, including matter, space, and time, God is not so constrained. Moreover, when we create something, we realise something in ourselves. For example, in making a cabinet, the craftsman actualises his skill and thereby gains self-realization. Because God is eternally replete and fully actual, however, he cannot be said to gain anything by creating. The theologians of the early church recognised that God gains nothing and realises nothing in himself by creating because God's life is eternally complete and fully realised.

The second implication of creation *ex nihilo* is that God's act of creation is distinguished from any process *within* the created order because it is "the introduction of being entirely," to use Aquinas's phrase.[16] Creation *ex nihilo* is not a process—it is not one thing becoming another. This also distinguishes the theological and metaphysical doctrine of creation *ex nihilo* from scientific cosmologies because the natural sciences study processes. Even Big Bang cosmology does not describe the introduction of being entirely, but speculates on the origins of the cosmos in terms of a process or processes which gave rise to the Big Bang. For example, the Big Bang might be described as having emerged from the fluctuation of a quantum vacuum, but this is still a process within nature. A quantum vacuum is not "nothing" in the theological and metaphysical sense of that term.

The third implication of creation *ex nihilo* that should be noted is that creatures are nothing outside their relation to God. It is not simply that God created from nothing at the beginning of time and then stood back; every moment is equally "out of nothing" in the sense that God sustains creation

---

15. For wide-ranging discussions of the origins and implications of creation *ex nihilo*, see David B. Burrell, Carlo Cogliati, Janet M. Soskice, and William M. Stoeger, eds., *Creation and the God of Abraham* (Cambridge: Cambridge University Press, 2010).

16. Aquinas, *Summa Theologiae* 1.45, co. All translations of the *Summa Theologiae* are from *The "Summa Theologica" of St. Thomas Aquinas*, trans. Fathers of the English Dominican Province, 2nd ed., 10 vol. (London: Burns, Oates, and Washbourne, 1920–1922).

in being at every moment. Creation continually receives its existence through participation in a likeness of the divine.

The final implication of creation *ex nihilo* to be noted for present purposes is that the difference between God and creation is not akin to the difference between creatures. For example, consider the difference between me and the desk I am sitting at. The difference belongs to both me and the desk. It is a reciprocal difference. The form and matter of the desk mark it as a particular thing distinct from other things, including me. The matter individuates the desk just as my body individuates me; my matter is not the desk's matter and vice versa. Whereas the difference between creatures is reciprocal (creatures instantiate themselves qua individuals from other creatures), this is not the case with creatures' relation to God. Because God creates *ex nihilo* and establishes the being of every creature, the difference between God and creatures does not belong per se to creatures but is itself a gift of God. Whereas the desk holds itself as other than me, creatures do not hold themselves as other than God. It is God who, at every moment, holds creation as other than himself. So it is not the case that something exists to which God *subsequently* gives existence and life. God's first gift in creation *ex nihilo* is the gift of being other than God—that is, the gift of being with proper integrity. All other gifts of God presuppose this fundamental and primordial gift of "otherness" from God.[17]

These four implications of creation *ex nihilo* together point to the fundamental ontology of creation. Because God gains nothing by creating—there is no "ulterior motive"—there can be no reason for creation beyond the eternal gratuity of divine love. Creation is a wholly unmerited, gratuitous, and primordial *gift* that makes possible all intercreaturely relations characterised as self-donation. Every creature communicates its form and *gives* itself to be known by its very act of being. The act of being is the act of self-communication or self-donation of the creature predicated upon the primordial gift of created being in God's act of creation *ex nihilo*. According to John Webster, creation *ex nihilo* marks the basic ontology of creatures and is therefore a cardinal and distributed teaching—one which lies at the beginning of theological enquiry and influences every aspect of Christian doctrine.[18] The nature of creaturely

---

17. The difference between God and creation is not arbitrary. It is an expression of the eternal Trinitarian differences within the Godhead.

18. John Webster, "'Love Is Also a Lover of Life': *Creatio Ex Nihilo* and Creaturely Goodness," *Modern Theology* 29, no. 2 (2013): 156–71.

being is gift. Every creature is a gift of itself to itself by God, the Father of lights, from whom comes every good and perfect gift (Jas 1:17–18).

How does this creaturely ontology of gift further inform our understanding of intercreaturely relations and the relation of creatures to God? Can it offer an integration of nature and culture? We pursue these questions by focussing particularly on the nature of gift within the order of creation.

Creaturely Gifts

The category of gift has become increasingly important in recent theology.[19] One of the most significant writers on the theology and philosophy of the gift, John Milbank, points out that it is an all-encompassing theological category.[20] In addition to creation's fundamentally gifted nature *ex nihilo*, one can point to the importance of gift in other areas of Christian doctrine: Christ is God's gift of himself to creation in the incarnation; the Holy Spirit is known as the *donum* (the given) amongst patristic theologians (Isa 11:2–3; John 20:22); the church is the recipient of the Spirit's gifts and is therefore known as the community of the gifted (Acts 2:1–13; 1 Cor 12; Eph 4:11); grace is God's gratuitous gift for our salvation (Eph 2:8). The importance of the category of gift has been recognised in other disciplines, notably anthropology and history. The origins of this discussion can be traced to the work of the French sociologist Marcel Mauss and his publication of *The Gift* in 1923.[21] This is a comparative study in which Mauss uses published research on gift-giving in societies in Polynesia, Melanesia, and the American Northwest. He seeks to identify the common importance of gift-giving in the formation of societies which are otherwise extremely diverse. Mauss's conclusions are various and

---

19. For a brilliant and comprehensive treatment of the gift in Paul and his interpreters, see John M. G. Barclay, *Paul and the Gift* (Grand Rapids: Eerdmans, 2015).

20. John Milbank, *Being Reconciled: Ontology and Pardon* (London: Routledge, 2003), ix. Milbank's extensive publications on the gift include "Can a Gift be Given? Prolegomena to a Future Trinitarian Metaphysic," *Modern Theology* 11, no. 1 (1995): 119–61; Milbank, "The Soul of Reciprocity Part One: Reciprocity Refused," *Modern Theology* 17, no. 3 (2001): 335–91; Milbank, "The Soul of Reciprocity Part Two: Reciprocity Granted," in *Modern Theology* 17, no. 4 (2001): 485–507. Milbank is frequently in critical conversation with the Catholic philosopher Jean-Luc Marion, whose mature philosophy of the gift can be found in *Being Given: Toward a Phenomenology of Givenness*, trans. Jeffrey Kosky (Stanford: Stanford University Press, 2002).

21. Marcel Mauss, *The Gift: The Form and Reason for Exchange in Archaic Societies*, trans. W. D. Halls (London: Routledge, 2002). See also Harry Liebersohn, *The Return of the Gift: European History of a Global Idea* (Cambridge: Cambridge University Press, 2012).

complex, but perhaps the most important is that gifts involve reciprocity. Mauss's conclusion is that there is never a pure one-way, altruistic gift. To put the matter simply, authentic gifts are exchanged because a gift always prompts another gift in return. Such gift exchange is not merely concerned with the presents we give at Christmas and birthdays, but with any exchange of attention, time, skill, tenderness, and creativity that is not reducible to trade. Such is the dominance of market trade in contemporary Western democracies that we fail to recognise that every friendship, marriage, family, society, and institution requires a constant exchange of gifts that are not straightforwardly measurable in monetary terms—love, care, wisdom, experience, knowledge, and advice, for example, in addition to the material gifts that we constantly exchange without resorting to monetary debt and account, like preparing a meal for friends. Any action or gesture that provokes the return gift of gratitude is, in some sense, a gift.

Mauss also points to the meaning of gifts. For example, a married couple typically give and receive rings. These may or may not have a high monetary value. The significance of the rings, however, is considerable: through the symbol, they mediate the relationship between spouses. A wife looks at her wedding ring and is immediately reminded of her husband who gave it to her. This is also evocative of the constant round of gift exchange which constitutes a marriage. For Mauss, the gift not only mediates a relationship; it is also imbued with something of the giver's character or power. He writes, "It follows that to make a gift of something to someone is to make a present of some part of oneself."[22] This means that the significance and meaning of a gift can bear almost no relation to its monetary value. We treasure gifts of no economic value at all because of the relationship they mediate and the value of the person from whom they were received.

Mauss is clear that gift-exchange is a more primitive and important social and economic foundation than barter. The reciprocity of gift-giving, however, is always under threat from the possibility it will become merely market trade mediated by money. If I were to give you the gift of a Christmas present, would you feel obliged to give me a Christmas present in return? Would you not estimate the value of my gift and buy a return gift of roughly similar value so as to repay the "debt"? This leads some philosophers, notably

---

22. Mauss, *The Gift*, 16.

Jacques Derrida, to suppose that the category of gift could be understood as a market transaction. The giving of a gift could always be as much about achieving a benefit for oneself as the conferring of a good upon another. Even charitable gifts might involve economic exchange: I give to my former university to which I am in some sense indebted and, in return, receive a soothed conscience and the warm sense that I have benefitted others, as well as a welcome tax break. So an important question emerges: Can a true gift really be given, or are we always embroiled in trade? When I care for my elderly parents, am I simply returning a debt accrued when they cared for me in my childhood? More acutely for Christian theology, when I give the gift of myself in good deeds towards others, am I expecting some benefit from God in the form of a heavenly reward? These questions led Derrida to pursue the idea of a *pure* gift. Could there ever be a pure, utterly selfless donation? For this to be the case, Derrida surmised that such a gift would not feature reciprocity; it would be exclusively one-way and thereby avoid any suspicion of trade. Driving his argument to a theoretical extreme, he concluded that the pure gift must feature the death of the donor once the gift has been given because the donor is not then able to receive anything in return. Derrida therefore concludes that the true or pure gift marks "the impossible." All our gift-giving is, in a sense, compromised in some way. It is always tinged with trade and the sense that one is seeking self-benefit. Should we therefore abandon any notion of genuine reciprocity in our understanding of the gift, lest the purity of our gift-giving be compromised in such a way that our selflessness is tainted and we only trade with each other and God? Should we seek an ever-purer altruism? Or is the notion of reciprocity intrinsic to the notion of gift itself?

The nature of creation *ex nihilo* and the relation of creation to God makes the problem of reciprocity particularly acute for Christian theology. Given that God's life is eternally replete and God is the source of created being, what could a creature offer to God? How can any creature give to God what has not already been received from God? The utter dependence of creation on God suggests the complete impossibility of reciprocity (Rom 11:34–35). Despite this apparent impossibility, the Scriptures attest to God's gift of a reciprocal relationship with him through which we share in the divine life. This is expressed, for example, in the offering by King David on behalf of the people for the building of the temple and is recited at the offertory in many of today's eucharistic liturgies. "Yours, O Lord, are the greatness, the power, the glory, the victory, and the majesty; for all that is in the heavens and on the earth is yours; yours is the kingdom, O Lord, and you are exalted as head above all. . . . For all things come from you, and of your own have we given you" (1 Chr 29:11, 14).

Even creaturely relationships of profound asymmetry present a difficulty for reciprocal gift-giving. Consider, for example, a young child and his parents. Before they enter the labour market, children are entirely dependent on their parents or caregivers for housing, food, education, and clothing. Children have no economic power and are entirely dependent upon the daily gifts of those who care for them. At Christmas, this child's parents buy him a splendid present. The child, however, has no means of buying his parents a gift; everything he has, he has already received from his parents. The boy receives the Christmas gift with no means of reciprocating. Yet as he tears the paper from the gift on Christmas morning, he turns to his parents, smiles with delight, and says, "Thank you." The smile and the "thank you" are the reciprocal gift. In other words, for a gift to be truly a gift, it must be received and acknowledged as such, otherwise it becomes merely a useful or entertaining object and bears no *meaning*. The exchange of gifts—the Christmas present and the smile— cannot be reduced to trade because monetary exchange requires a degree of univocity—of sameness—in the goods traded so that they can be subject to a common currency. The value of the child's smile and "thank you" cannot be subject to that kind of measure. One cannot trade smiles and Christmas toys. Whilst the child's exchange with his parents is not trade (and we cannot imagine reducing our most important relationships to debt and account), it is an example of reciprocal exchange within a highly asymmetric relationship of dependence, one that points to the need for gifts to be recognised as gifts through thanksgiving, lest they become merely objects.

Nevertheless, reciprocal gifts, even within the most asymmetrical relations between creatures, are not the same as exchange within the uniquely asymmetrical relation between God and creation. Unlike a human parent, God does not give a gift to what is already present. According to creation *ex nihilo*, God gives the recipient being whereby it can be the recipient of further gifts: a gift of a gift to a gift. This leads Milbank beyond the contrast between unilateral and reciprocal gifts to the paradox of "unilateral exchange." There can only be reciprocity within God's Trinitarian life or between creatures, whereas the "unilateral exchange" between God and creation is only ever a matter of God's influx by which creation is given the power of receiving and returning to God. This has an important theological consequence: God's gifts to creation are never a matter of entitlement or right. Creation cannot make any claim on God because creation, as creation, is always in the mode of recipient. To be a creature is, first and foremost, before all else, to receive being. This is unilateral from God to creation. But to receive being truthfully—to be a creature—is to acknowledge the gift in thankfulness. Creation returns to God the gift of praise and thanksgiving and, in that return, receives itself most fully as created. All creatures, including humanity and its culture, are fundamentally themselves in the praise of God.

Beyond the gift of created being itself, the creation account in Genesis recognises a primary providential gift that is essential to sustain life. On the sixth day, God said,

> See, I have given you every plant yielding seed that is upon the face of all the earth, and every tree with seed in its fruit; you shall have them for food. And to every beast of the earth, and to every bird of the air, and to everything that creeps on the earth, everything that has the breath of life, I have given every green plant for food. (Gen 1:29–30)

Food unites nature and culture. It is a gift of God through nature, enjoyed by "everything that has the breath of life," yet humanity's food is also invested with deep cultural significance and is the product of human labour. How does the gift of food bear intrinsic meaning and value in addition to meeting our physical needs? To address this question, we turn from the first chapter of Genesis and the first gift of food to the final chapters of Genesis and the gift of food by Joseph to his estranged brothers.

Gift and the Meaning of Food

Joseph, the dreamer, was the favoured son of Jacob in his old age. Joseph's eleven brothers, mired in jealousy, sold him into slavery in Egypt. He rose to prominence in Pharaoh's court because he could interpret Pharaoh's dreams. In these dreams, God revealed that there would be seven years of plenty and seven years of famine. Pharaoh put Joseph in charge of agricultural and economic policy. Thanks to Joseph's prudence, reserves were accumulated during the seven years of plenty so that the lands could survive the seven years of famine. When the famine struck, people from the surrounding countries were forced to travel to Egypt, where Joseph sold them grain. Jacob and his remaining eleven sons were amongst those driven from Canaan to Egypt by their hunger. They encountered their brother Joseph in the Egyptian court. He recognised them, but they did not recognise him. Joseph's brothers were afraid that their plight was a direct consequence of what they had done to their brother, and they fought amongst themselves whilst Joseph looked on. After many years, Joseph's brothers remained deeply guilty over what they had done to their brother; this affected all their relationships. Physical hunger drove Jacob's sons to seek food in Egypt, yet there is also an emotional, spiritual hunger lying at the heart of this story: a desire for reconciliation and peace.

Joseph shared food with his brothers—the grain that he had stored from the seven years of plenty. However, Joseph secretly gave back the money his brothers had brought to pay for the grain (Gen 42:25). The food was therefore not traded; it was an unanticipated, secret gift from Joseph to his brothers. This becomes the meaning and use of the food Joseph had stored. The food was a gift that eventually effected reconciliation with his brothers and the unity of what were to become the twelve tribes of Israel. Joseph's reconciling gift to his brothers was a result of his grateful and measured reception of the gifts of God's creation. The implication is that Joseph's gift—to coin Mauss's phrase cited above—bore something of himself to his brothers: namely, his prudence and receptivity to God's will and providence, as well as his love for his brothers. Joseph's brothers returned with gifts (Gen 43:11–15), and Joseph offered further gifts of food to his brothers (Gen 43:16–25; 44:1). Reciprocity and communion were eventually restored in Jacob's blessing of his reconciled sons (Gen 49:1–27).

In the story of Joseph, the meaning and value of food, the fruit of cre was to be found in reconciliation and the celebration of commun' offering of gifts as expressions of thanksgiving and penance with of effecting reconciliation was similarly the basis of the ap' well temple sacrifice. In the temple in Jerusalem, the priestly f to God on behalf of supplicants as expressions of th restoration of communion. These took the form of as animal sacrifice. Rather than these sacrifices being given up or lost, they were often returned, sometimes in the form of food. This established a reciprocal economy of the gift within the elaborate system of temple rituals. Such reciprocity established the worshippers' fellowship with God. The worshipper was invited by divine graciousness to offer gifts to God which were returned to form a relational bond. Ritually, this was expressed in the form of a meal shared in God's temple using the gifts sacrificed on the altar. The return of sacrifices in the form of food, while certainly not an element of every temple sacrifice, was nevertheless an important expression of fellowship with God and amongst God's people. That reconciliation was mediated by the priestly families (Lev 7:1–10).

However, sin is the refusal of God's gifts and this reciprocal exchange was broken. The Letter to the Hebrews describes the elaborate and frequent temple sacrifice as inadequate to renew humanity's intimate relationship with God: "This is a symbol of the present time, during which gifts and sacrifices are offered that cannot perfect the conscience of the worshipper, but deal only with food and drink and various baptisms, regulations for the body imposed until the time comes to set things right" (Heb 9:9–10). How can the relationship of reciprocal exchange with God be restored in the face of human sin? As Anselm claims in *Cur Deus Homo*, because humanity has estranged itself from God, it is humanity which must offer sacrifice to God for the renewal of that reciprocal relation. However, any human action will be tainted by sin; it "cannot perfect the conscience of the worshipper." Only a divine action will be fully replete and perfect. Only a divine action can, once and for all, atone for human sin. The perfect once-and-for-all sacrifice can therefore only be offered by a divine humanity—namely, the incarnation of God himself in the person of Jesus Christ. So it is Christ's sacrifice of himself on the cross, as both fully divine and fully human, as both priest and victim, which brings the salvation of humanity and the reestablishment of reciprocity with God. Christ is a priest according to the order of Melchizedek, and in being replete and without sin, he offers himself, not over and over again but "once for all" (Heb 10:10). He is both priest and victim while also standing ~~in our~~ place. Christ represents all of humanity, yet this is, at one and the same ~~time, the~~ sacrifice of God.

~~How is t~~his sacrifice rendered reciprocal? In what sense is the sacrificial ~~gift offe~~red to the Father returned to the people? Is there any way in which, like the sin-offering, guilt-offering, and grain-offering described in Leviticus 6 and 7, the sacrifice of Christ is returned to the people as food? Is a relation of "unilateral exchange" between creation and God restored? The sacrificial offering of Christ, who is sinless yet represents every sinner, is returned to the people as food in the Eucharist in the form of the body and blood of the victim and priest (1 Cor 10:16). Whereas the reciprocity of the guilt-offering and sin-offering was enjoyed particularly by "every male among the priests" (Lev 7:6) or "all the sons of Aaron equally" (Lev 7:10), now the church is "a royal priesthood" (1 Pet 2:9–10), so everyone partakes in the reciprocity of Christ's gift of himself. The people of God are a priestly people in receiving the gifts of Christ's once-and-for-all sacrifice in the Eucharist. The priestly nature of the church is revealed by the particular priesthood that exercises the ministry of presidency at the eucharistic celebration. Whereas Joseph's gift of food to his brothers in the closing chapters of Genesis effects and expresses their reconciliation, the eucharistic meal demonstrates the ultimate meaning of food as communion with God who, as the ultimate source of every good and perfect gift, offers himself in the natural and cultural signs of bread and wine.

The psalmist expresses with great beauty the importance of the gift of food for all creatures:

> The eyes of all look to you,
>> and you give them their food in due season.
> You open your hand,
>> satisfying the desire of every living thing. (Ps 145:15–16)

What God gives in creation are not commodities for our consumption or a realm of nature fit for exploitation from which human culture is alienated. Creation is not simply a manifestation of divine ingenuity and power. God offers nothing less than participation in his own gratuitous life, and food is given for life. When that gift is refused, God restores the "unilateral reciprocity" in the sacrifice of Christ, mediated to us for our reconciliation in the nature and culture of the Eucharist.[23]

---

23. A further discussion of the Eucharist in relation to nature and culture is available in Simon Oliver, "The Eucharist before Nature and Culture," *Modern Theology* 15, no. 3 (1999): 331–53.

Conclusion

This chapter began by examining the modern separation of nature and culture and the subsequent distancing of humanity from the natural world. This distinction of the human realm from nature enhances our objectification of the environment. Insofar as human culture is regarded as a domain distinct from nature, we are able to conceive nature as a resource "out there" for our consumption, entertainment, or curiosity, even whilst in reality nature and culture remain intimately intertwined. In the Christian imagination of antiquity and the Middle Ages, nature and culture were bound together under the single category of creation. Understood theologically, creation's fundamental character is gift. Creation *ex nihilo* implies that nothing stands outside the divine economy of the gift, for even creation's otherness from God—its ability to be the recipient of God's good gifts—is itself a gift of God. This implies that the first mode of creaturely existence is receptivity—the receipt of being and life—which elicits in creatures the return gift of thankfulness and praise to God.

This chapter has argued that to understand creation as gift has important implications for human ethics. A brief reflection on the difference between gifts and functional goods helps to bring this ethics into focus. On my desk, I have a computer which I bought for work. It is a valuable and useful item which I would not be without. It does not, however, *mean* anything. Its value lies only in its function. I also have a mug on my desk, made for me by my youngest son when he was about two years old. I use it regularly and its monetary value is, of course, far less than the monetary value of my computer. Unlike the computer, the mug is more immediately identifiable as a gift. It bears something of my son to me; it reminds me of him and his love and character at a very precious age. The mug bears meaning and significance because it mediates a relationship. The gift of the mug calls forth a response from me: thankfulness, not simply for the gift of a mug, but most important for the gift of my son. In this way, gifts make demands on us in a way that functional items do not. I treasure the gift of the mug far more than the computer because the mug bears meaning and is irreplaceable. This is not mere sentimentality; it reminds us that value and significance may bear little or no relation to market worth or even usefulness. To understand creation as gift is to realise that all existence and life, precisely as gift, is called to thankfulness.

Within the economy of gift that binds nature and culture, Genesis teaches that God's first providential gift within the order of creation is food, given for the sustaining and nurturing of life (Gen 1:29–30; 9:3). All creatures, human and nonhuman, look to God as the source of food and life (Ps 145:15). Humanity's food "carries things further than nature can" (to coin an Aristotelian phrase) because food is invested with an even greater meaning exemplified in the Eucharist: the sharing in the divine communion of Father, Son, and Spirit.

A good portion of the environmental crisis concerns food production for a growing population and the grotesquely unequal distribution of food resources across the planet. Much economic policy assumes that food resources are inadequate to meet the unlimited wants of human beings, hence the problem of production and resource distribution. By contrast, the Jewish and Christian theology of creation and providence begins not with lack, but abundance. Leviticus commands the farmer not to harvest to the very edge of the field because there is enough: "When you reap the harvest of your land, you shall not reap to the very edges of your field, or gather the gleanings of your harvest; you shall leave them for the poor and for the alien: I am the LORD your God" (Lev 23:22). There is enough, because God's gifts are not only enough; they are abundant.

In the midst of the debate concerning the environment, the Christian doctrine of creation points to the meaning of creation and the first providential gift of creation in the form of food for life. As such, creation is not a set of natural resources set over and against human culture, but a pattern of gifts that form the unity and communion of the created order and provoke the return gift of thanksgiving. Such a stance draws culture into communion with nature once more, a communion that begins with thanksgiving and is exemplified in the Eucharist. To understand creation as a gift—from which creation derives its meaning and significance—is to call humanity to understand the relationship of gratuitous love mediated by the gift of creation, and therefore to treasure the gift, savour the gift, nurture it, and encourage its abundant sharing.

Chapter TWO

"We Are All God's Vocabulary"

The Idea of Creation as a Speech-Act of the Trinitarian
God and Its Significance for the Dialogue between
Theology and Sciences

CHRISTOPH SCHWÖBEL

This chapter explores the conceptual possibilities opened by understanding creation as a speech-act of the triune God. Starting with some reflections on the epistemological and ontological significance of metaphors, I take a closer look at the two metaphors that have dominated the relationship between theology and the sciences in the West: nature as a book and as a mechanical clock. With the help of Martin Luther's exposition of creation as a divine speech-act—presenting everything as a part of the divine vocabulary, connected by the rules of divine grammar—I develop some of the implications of such a view for knowing creation. Relating the view of creative divine speaking with the incarnation of the Word and the perfecting role of the Holy Spirit leads to an understanding of God as triune conversation. Thus, for the conversation between theology and the sciences, the task of knowing creation can be presented as listening to the dissonances and consonances between the two disciplines as they reflect the resonances of the triune conversation in creation.

Metaphors Matter

Our human language is pervasively metaphorical. It connects signs from one use of discourse to another and thereby creates a network of multilayered dimensions of meaning. There is a rich variety of metaphorical discourse, and not all metaphors conform to the same pattern. What they have in common is that they connect words associated with a field of meaning from one area of discourse to a reference associated with another area of discourse and another realm of our engagement with reality. In this way, metaphors expand the connections between particular functions of language by referring, predicating, and establishing meaningful associations between fields of signs and what they relate to in acts of signification. At first, metaphorical modes of communication can often evoke in the hearer or reader a moment of irritation about an unusual use of words that can seem to disrupt the usual flow of communication. But then, hopefully, an element of illumination will arise where, through the unusual use of words, connections of meanings appear that were not obvious at first glance. Once we become used to these connections, we automatically expand the field of metaphorical meaning further, becoming aware of implications or contradictions implied in metaphorical speech. Meaning is never atomistic but always potentially holistic. Ascribing meaning always implies a network of meanings that can be organized in distinct, variably cohesive fields; structured by affirmations, negations, similarities, and dissimilarities; and often expressed in analogies.

Such patterns of meaning not only affect the way we use language but also the way we engage with the world. Metaphors always show that the syntactic, semantic, and pragmatic dimension of every form of sign-use are intricately connected. We distinguish them only when we take a step back and focus on the sign-use itself. In this way, metaphors illustrate both how we do things with words and how things act on us through our use of words and signs. The relation between signs and what they signify is not a one-way street. Once things have been signified, they relate to the sign-users in different ways, affecting the way they use signs and engage with the realities signified. The relationship between signs and signs, signs and meanings, and sign-users and signs, identified by the three dimensions of a semiotic event, often appears more as a dialogue in the different dimensions of semiotic processes than a unidirectional act.

Metaphorical speech not only changes the way we talk about the world and ourselves but also the way we deal with the world in nonsignificative acts and how we experience the world relating to us. The meanings that metaphorical discourse suggest shape our view of the possibilities of action in the world and our view of ourselves as agents and patients who experience the agency of others on us. "Onward, Christian Soldiers" evokes different images of the Christian life than the petition "Make Me a Channel of Your Peace." The ways in which metaphorical discourse influences our relationship to the world and ourselves are ontologically significant. Metaphors do not simply add a coat of meaning to things which underneath remain what they are. They change the way things are for us and how we are to relate to them. One of the best ways to explore the scope and perspective of reality is to ask which possibilities of action it implies for us. The possibilities of action we perceive in our engagement with reality provide us with a clearer understanding of our ontological commitments than many formal presentations of our view of reality, delineating the structure of the world in formalized hierarchies of being. Looking at the possibilities of action (and passion) presents us with the being of ourselves *and* the world as our being *in* the world so that we have to start from the recognition of the way in which we are involved in the order of being. The fundamental relationality of this order is the first thing that impresses itself on us—and that is different from a theoretical view of reality. Yet this relationality, as it is presented to us in metaphorical speech, is not self-explanatory. It provokes our practical and interpretative activity to give an account of ourselves in relation to the world and ourselves in practical and in theoretical terms. Theory appears as one form of *praxis* which already presupposes our practical entanglement in what we are trying to grasp in theory.

In religious discourse, the enrichment of meaning inherent in metaphorical discourse can be grasped in all dimensions of a lived religion. It informs not only ways of speaking in religious situations but also our modes of acting in religious contexts. The enrichment and the irritation of meaning in lived religions and their metaphorical forms of discourse cannot be contained in these contexts but always spills over into all dimensions of life and confronts them with a new dimension of interpreting them, often in ways which become explicit in the religious use of language. Religious signs indicate the focus of the meaning-systems that provide orientation for our lives; they relate the ultimate significance of our lives to dimensions of meaning which thereby become penultimate. The use of metaphorical discourse in religions, as it spills over into all dimensions of life, serves as an illustration that religions indeed focus on the *ultimate concern*; they are anchored in that on which we hang our hearts. Religions deal with the first stories and the very last stories, stories about the primordial origin and ultimate destination of everything. They try to identify an ultimate dimension of reality and relate all other dimensions to it.

They envelop our actions and passions in every dimension of life in an ultimate framework in which everything is believed to find its meaning. Metaphorical discourse plays a crucial role in the way that religious believers frame reality in all its dimensions. The clarification of metaphorical discourse—in identifying the layers of meaning and testing out its interpretative and practical implications—is therefore not only a fundamental challenge within all religions but also in relation to religions, be it from another religious or a nonreligious perspective. The conversations between theology and the sciences are a good illustration of the range and the contentiousness of religious or quasi-religious forms of metaphorical discourse.

The Book and the Clock

In the history of the West, two metaphors have dominated the debates over how we understand reality in both theology and the sciences. These are the metaphor of nature as a book to be read or as a clock whose mechanical laws we are to follow. Seeing nature as a book to be related to the book of Scripture is a central element of Judaism, Christianity, and Islam. All three Abrahamic religions concur that the book of Scripture (the Tanakh, the Bible, or the Qur'an) enables us to read the world for what it is. Reading the book of Scripture implies an inherent summons to understand nature in such a way that it also becomes a book which we read in order to gain understanding and find guidance. Understanding creation as a fundamental speech-act of the Creator is an important element in the Hebrew Bible itself.

> By the word of the LORD the heavens were made,
>> And all their host by the breath of his mouth. (Ps 33:6)

The address of the Creator not only enables creation to respond to God and gives human beings the status of being accountable and responsible before God. It also invests creation with the capacity to respond to God in praise.

> The heavens are telling the glory of God;
>> and the firmament proclaims his handiwork.
> Day to day pours forth speech,
>> and night to night declares knowledge.

There is no speech, nor are there words;
    their voice is not heard;
yet their voice goes out through all the earth,
    and their words to the end of the world. (Ps 19:1–4)

Archaic as the powerful image of the heavens communicating the praise of God may seem, the text itself clearly indicates an understanding of the metaphorical character in which language is ascribed to the heavens and to God. Related to this, let us consider Psalm 33:9:

For he spoke, and it came to be;
    he commanded, and it stood firm.

This verse, which refers to God speaking creation into existence, offers precise criteria for distinguishing the speech of the Creator from all created speech. On the one hand, speech-acts that posit existence and meaning are a divine prerogative. On the other hand, all that God creates speaks to his glory, not only human beings but the whole of creation. For Paul, this means that nothing is without language (1 Cor 14:10b). Everything that exists testifies to the Creator who creates by performative and effective speech—through an activity that is communicative of God's glory. Being and meaning are never separated: God's work creates effects that have being and order, and God's work has to be understood as communicative action, even when it is not expressed as divine speech. The whole of creation is an ordered network of communicative relationships in which being and meaning are intrinsically connected.

Against this background, it is not surprising that the metaphorical forms of expressing the communicative capacities of creation as communicating the meaning which it had first received through the word of the Creator could be elaborated in the fully developed model of the book of nature which stands in a constitutive relationship to the book of Scripture. As in so many theological questions, Augustine's use of the relationship of the two books became the matrix for many versions of the view of creation as the book of nature which is consonant with the message of Scripture. He distinguishes between different ways of receiving the messages of the book of Scripture and the book of nature. The distinguishing mark of the book of nature is that it does not require literacy in order to be read by those who lack the skills only available to educated people.

"The divine page" (Scripture), he says, "shall be a book for you that you listen to. And the whole universe shall be a book to you that you see. In these codices (of Scripture) only those who are literate can read; while in the whole world even the uneducated can read."[1] The whole of nature becomes a meaningful whole. It is not a collection of unconnected facts, nor the actualization of forms, but contains in it meaning which connects the parts and the whole by intelligible structures which provide orientation to those who read their message.

For Augustine, the book of nature does not declare its own meaning and does not relate its own story. In order to be understood properly, as he explains in his exegesis of the creation story, it needs to be read with the other book, Scripture, in hand, which tells the readers that both books have one author.[2] While Augustine can see nature as a system of interconnected meaning, it is nevertheless Scripture for him that has the primary authority such that he views the firmament as a symbol of the all-encompassing and comprehensive meaning of Scripture. For Augustine, therefore, Scripture is the key to decoding the message of creation since Scripture identifies the unitary author of both books and so provides the hermeneutical key for reading the book of nature.[3]

The metaphor of creation as a book of nature, to be read in conjunction with the book of Scripture, has had a long history, flourishing in later medieval times.[4] Reflecting on this metaphor, Ingolf Dalferth notes, "Ironically, the Two-Books Model achieved precisely the opposite of what it set out to achieve; it began as an attempt to integrate nature, and the natural knowledge of the world, into the theological perspective, and it ended by freeing the study of the Book of Nature from domination of the Book of Scripture."[5] However,

---

1. *"Liber tibi sit pagina divina, ut haec audias; liber tibi sit orbis terrarum, ut haec videas. In istis codicibus non ea legunt, nisi qui litteras noverunt; in tot mundo legat et idiota"* (Augustine, *Enarrationes in psalmos*, Patrologiae Migne Latinae Elenchus 36, 518; on Ps 45, 7b. This reference can be found here: http://www.augustinus.it/latino/esposizioni_salmi/index2.htm).

2. Augustine, *De genesi ad litteram*, Migne Latinae Elenchus 32, 219–21.

3. Bonaventure emphasizes that while in paradise, Adam and Eve could read creation like a book, their fall makes the book of Scripture necessary to restore the meaning of creation and so guide human creatures to the Creator. Bonaventure, *Collationes in Hexaemeron*, ed. and trans. W. Nyssen (München: Kösel, 1979), XIII, 12.

4. This history has been charted with a wealth of scholarly detail by Hans Blumenberg, *Die Lesbarkeit der Welt* (Frankfurt: Suhrkamp, 1981). However, his somewhat mournful history of the loss of the notion that the world can be read, is dominated by his attempt to show that the thesis set forth by Karl Löwith in philosophy and by Wolfhart Pannenberg in theology that modernity is the secularization of the Jewish and Christian view of history is wrong and to argue for the legitimacy of the emancipation of theoretical curiosity from its religious roots.

5. Ingolf U. Dalferth, *Theology and Philosophy* (Oxford: Blackwell, 1988), 69.

what is described here as "freeing" has also proven to be a process of growing enslavement to seeing nature as a field of interaction of blind and dumb forces following mechanistic laws.

The great opponent of understanding the world as a book is the metaphor of the world as a clock—a clockwork machine that follows mechanistic laws. While the roots of this model can be traced back to Greek antiquity—to the atomism of Democritus and the materialism of Lucretius—and while its rediscovery in medieval times was still theologically motivated, the extension of this model to all spheres of reality is one of the hallmarks of early modern times.[6] And when the image of a mechanical machine started to become the dominant way that modernity viewed reality, the link that this image had with theology became increasingly tenuous. Together with the axiom that natural phenomena must be explained by natural reasons, the mechanistic metaphor had, from the beginning, the drive to displace the doctrine of creation in the scheme of things. The elaborate constructions of physicotheology, which focus on the teleological explanation of final causes for their theological import, present a view of God as the divine watchmaker who first sets up the mechanism and then takes early retirement—although some forms of world-explanation preserve a theistic element by assuming that the watchmaker is called back to correct mistakes and adjust the mechanism from time to time. Descartes (1596–1650) would still talk about the great book of nature, but this metaphor had become just a turn of phrase since the real world-explanations were seen to be discerned by way of calculation and experiment, through the observation of meaningless forces that were to be understood purely quantitatively. If the whole of the world is understood as *res extensa*—an extended thing, as opposed to the *res cogitans* of the reflective mind—then the world becomes devoid of qualities and must be accounted for in quantitative measurements. What is a philosophical program in Descartes becomes scientific procedure in Galileo (1564–1642), reducing every observation to quantitative properties so that mathematics can become the "language" of science. However, this language

---

6. It seems to me that the momentous spreading of this model has to do with the capacities of metaphors to transfer meanings from one area of experience to another. If one tries to describe the process of the extension of the metaphor, one is struck by the fact that it is not so much a picture of the world that impressed itself on human observers but rather the human engagement with the world in the development of constructing mechanical instruments that are employed to gain access to the understanding of the world. It is not science that makes us understand our engagement with the world, but our engagement with the world in developing craftsmanship and technology that makes us conceive of science as a world-disclosing enterprise.

does not say anything; it is merely the medium for transferring measurements in a mode of expression that can comprehend everything because it is compatible with everything.

Once the clock is established as the guiding metaphor for reality, its metaphorical influence envelops more and more of reality. The understanding of human nature as a machine, as in the title of La Mettrie's *L'homme machine* (1748), soon shapes the understanding of medical diagnosis and therapy. If humans can be understood as *automata*, humans can be viewed as mechanical apparatus in societies and states. Not only do the external relationships of humans come to be perceived as bodies of individuals that can be explained by mechanical laws, but also the internal relationships of the human person come to be interpreted as the workings of a sophisticated mechanism.[7] Once this step is taken, the field is open for every application of the mechanistic model in all areas of reality, including the workings of business, as in Taylorism—the ghost of which still haunts business studies and practice. Because of the suggestiveness of the metaphor of a mechanism or a machine, which facilitates its easy expansion from physics to political theory, this way of dealing with reality, be it of ourselves or of other beings, has survived its demise as a theoretical model in the sciences, made obsolete by more than a century of relativity theory, quantum theory, chaos theory, and evolutionary theory, among others. Even the developments overturning the clock as the dominant paradigm of perceiving reality still retain its metaphorical suggestiveness, as in "quantum mechanics" or "molecular genetic mechanics." The mechanics of the clock are still a widely used image for what makes the world and ourselves tick.

The chief characteristic of the clockwork view reality is the explanation of everything in terms of the interaction of noncommunicative forces, which are often understood as discrete entities externally connected by external relations. The specific difficulties of determinism, whether rigid or statistical, and of

---

7. The introductory passage of Thomas Hobbes's *Leviathan* is a conspicuous example of the transfer of the metaphor: "Nature (the Art whereby God hath made and governs the World) is by the *Art* of man, as many other things, so in this also imitated that it can make an Artificiall Animal. For seeing life is but a motion of Limbs, the beginning whereof is in some principall part within; why may we not say, that all *Automata* (Engines that move themselves by springs and wheeles as doth a watch) have an artificiall life? For what is the *Heart*, but a *Spring*; and the *Nerves*, but so many *Strings*; and the *Joynts*, but so many *Wheeles*, giving motion to the whole Body, such as intended by the Artificer? *Art* goes yet further, imitating that most Rationall and most excellent worke of Nature, *Man*. For by Art is created that great LEVIATHAN, called COMMON-WEALTH, or STATE (in latine CIVITAS which is but an Artificiall Man . . .)" (Hobbes, *Leviathan* [1651; repr., Oxford: Clarendon, 1909]).

reductionism, not as a scientific method but as a way of explaining reality, are all connected to the persuasiveness of this metaphor. Meaning, information, address, resonance, and response are all external to the processes of nature themselves. Furthermore, the processes of mechanics are all reversible by virtue of the construction of the mechanism. Everything depends on the initial conditions. This raises several questions. Can the mechanistic view really make sense of the cosmic history of the universe, of the history of evolutionary processes, and of the historical structure of all process of life—a history which prompted Ernest Mayr to see biology as a historical science and so question the reduction of living systems to the laws of physics? Is there no better view attentive to the polydimensionality of reality, which allows for connected but not reductionist ways of communication processing?

Interestingly, however, with the rise of molecular genetics, we have seen a return to the communicative metaphor of reading. Geneticists think in terms of encoding and decoding—terms that recognise their subject matter as inherently characterised by the communication of active information. This indicates a different way of seeing nature where the attention shifts from the meaningless transmission of force to the communication of information—communication which may have very real effects by triggering processes of physical interaction. Moreover, the change of the guiding metaphor reduces what one looks for not to the classical laws of physics, as the interaction between defined physical entities, but to a wider network of communicative relations. In reflecting on the relationship between theology and the sciences, it might therefore be interesting to follow the possible implications for the conversations between theology and the sciences further by exploring a classic theological example of understanding creation as a divine act and as the created result, in other words in terms of communicative relationships.

God's Vocabulary and the Grammar of Creation

Towards the end of his life, Martin Luther spent ten years delivering lectures on one biblical book, the book of Genesis—lectures which survive in extensive notes from his students. Formerly regarded as a somewhat questionable source for Luther's theology, they are now seen as a reliable guide to Luther's mature theological thinking. In his exegesis of God's work on the first day, we find a striking passage on God's creative speaking:

Here attention must also be called to this that the words "Let there be light" are words of God, not of Moses; this means that they are realities. For God calls into existence the things which do not exist (Rom 4:17). He does not speak grammatical words; He speaks true and existent realities. Accordingly, that which for us has the sound of a word is a reality with God. Thus sun, moon, heaven, earth, Peter, Paul, I, you, etc.—we are all words of God (*vocabula Dei*), in fact only one single syllable or letter by comparison with the entire creation. We, too, speak, but only according to the rules of language; that is, we assign names to objects which have already been created. But the divine rule of language (*Grammatica divina*) is different, namely: when He says: "Sun, shine," the sun is there at once and shines. Thus the words of God are realities, not bare words.[8]

Luther's interpretation of the creation story in Genesis 1 emphasizes those elements which speak of creation by word and of creation as word. Luther asks, "What else is the entire creation than the Word of God uttered by God or extended to the outside?"[9] Theological language—rooted in the language of Scripture and its ultimate author, the Holy Spirit—is a specific language for Luther, comparable to the language of lawyers, physicians, and philosophers. These languages have their own relative integrity. Luther, therefore, states something like a principle of the mutual availability of these languages by means of a division of labour:

> Every science should make use of its own terminology, and one should not for this reason condemn the other or ridicule it; but one should rather be of use to the other, and they should put their achievements at one another's disposal. This is what craftsmen do to maintain the whole city which as Aristotle says, cannot be composed of a physician and another physician but of a physician and a farmer.[10]

---

8.   Martin Luther, *Luther's Works*, vol. 1, *Lectures on Genesis 1–5*, ed. Jaroslav Pelikan (St. Louis: Concordia, 1958), 21–22 (hereafter *LW*). For a detailed explication of this passage cf. Martin Wendte, *Die Gabe und das Gestell: Luthers Metaphysik des Abendmahls im technischen Zeitalter* (Tübingin: Mohr Siebeck, 2013), 397–407.

9.   Luther, *Lectures on Genesis*, 22.

10.   *LW* 1:48. The difference and connection is most clearly defined in Luther's *Disputation Concerning Man* (1536), *LW* 34:134–44. Luther seems to refer to Aristotle, *Nicomachean Ethics*, 5.5.

This is somewhat surprising if one remembers Luther's criticism of reason as a "whore" or his less than complimentary remarks about Aristotle which are pervasive in his works. Luther clearly has a regionalized understanding of the modes of knowledge in the sciences and becomes polemical where philosophy, for instance, oversteps the boundaries of its territory, the study of worldly things, and makes pronouncements upon divine being and work.[11] Only theology can claim a comprehensive perspective, albeit not in terms of any superiority of theology as an intellectual discipline but only in virtue of its subject-matter, God. This, however, also confronts theology with the task of critically integrating the insights of the other sciences.

The question then becomes: What does Luther's view—of the act of creation by word and of creation as the vocabulary of God, structured by the divine grammar—contribute to the dialogue of the sciences?

First, the view that God creates by creatively speaking particular realities into being, avoids the disjunction between meaning and being that is characteristic for much of modern science. The world of nature in all its dimensions cannot be understood as a set of data that appears meaningless unless meaning is ascribed to it. The metaphor of speaking creation into existence—creation as a divine speech-act—posits an indissoluble unity of being and meaning, which, in Luther's view, is only disrupted with the displacement of humans in the relational order of creation (the fall) when they attempt to be like God, to assume the place of the Creator in creation. Following Luther's view, the investigation of created reality cannot be reduced to causal explanation. From the beginning, it has a hermeneutical dimension. Causality is included in the framework of understanding creation as a divine speech-act. Explanation is therefore based on the modes of discovery and disclosure and does not arise by way of human invention. And so, knowing creation requires the observation of this unity of being and meaning, keeping epistemological and ontological concerns together. The knowability of the created order of being was invested

---

11. On the relationship between philosophy and theology in Luther's thought cf. Mark Mattes, "Luther's Use of Philosophy," in *Lutherjahrbuch* 80 (2013): 110–14. For the systematic implications of this highly differentiated relationship, cf. Wilfried Härle, "Reformatorische Rationalität. Luthers Verständnis der Vernunft" in *Rationalität im Gespräch—Rationality in Conversation*, ed. Markus Mühling (Leipzig: Evangelische Verlagsanstalt, 2016), 261–74. For the application of this relationship for the understanding of what it means to be human, cf. Christoph Schwöbel, "Like a Tree Planted by the Water: Human Flourishing and the Dynamics of Divine-Human Relationships," in *Flourishing in Christ: Essays in Honor of Miroslav Volf*, ed. Matthew Croasmun, Zoran Grozdano, and Ryan J. McAnnally-Linz (Eugene, OR: Wipf & Stock, forthcoming).

in creation from the beginning by God's creative speaking. Following from this first characteristic, theology's task in the conversations with the sciences would be twofold: to listen carefully where the sciences explain natural processes in terms of communication processes *and* to be a constant reminder of the dimension of meaning in all dimensions of reality.

Second, if creating by the creative word points to an original unity of being and meaning, this also avoids the initial disjunction of fact and value. Everything that is created by the word carries a particular dignity in virtue of being created as this particular being, a dignity that addresses all other creatures and calls for their respect for this invested dignity. The created dignity conferred in the act of divine speaking becomes intrinsic to created being. If one attempts to develop a view of reality inspired by Luther's account of creation, one cannot focus on mere facts in abstraction from all questions of ethical or even aesthetic value. The judgement by which God assesses the results of his creative speaking ("And God saw that it was good" [Gen 1:10, 12, 18, 25], culminating in the statement "God saw everything that he had made, and indeed, it was very good" in 1:31) connects fact and value in such a way that questions of ethics cannot be a matter to be considered after the facts have been established. The demand for value neutrality becomes in this context a call for value transparency in a situation where the focus on facts alone already implies a negative value judgement. From this perspective, knowing creation includes ethical and aesthetic questions from the start. If theology attempts to follow Luther's recommendation that the sciences should be "of use to one another," it will need to listen carefully when the sciences raise ethical concerns (e.g., in all ecological considerations) or aesthetic considerations come into play (e.g., references to beauty or elegance) and protest wherever ethical considerations are only brought in after the fact.

Third, Luther's view of created reality as God's vocabulary interprets cosmic realities (sun, moon, etc.), personal realities (Peter, Paul, you, and I), and in other places everything that exists as particular bearers of being and meaning.[12] This theological view of knowing creation, therefore, sees creation as the creation of particulars, each of which has a particular significance. Similarly, that which is conferred together with existence is never a generalization but always a particularly conferred meaning that requires a similarly

---

12. Cf. *LW* 1:49: "Therefore any bird whatever and any fish whatever are nothing but nouns in the divine rule of language [*grammatica*]."

particular response. Knowing creation is knowing creation in its particularity. If theology is to contribute something to the conversation with the sciences, it would be as an advocate of particularity.

However, created particularity is not the particularity of discrete isolated entities. Particularity is, *fourth*, always understood as relational particularity—namely, bound together by the grammar of God's creative speaking, which is one universal that includes everything there is. While Luther can explain God's creation as calling into existence particular beings that can be understood as nouns, these nouns that indicate particular beings are nevertheless connected by the rules of divine grammar. One has to keep in mind that grammar in Luther's time comprised more than the formal rules of language. It also included the semantic dimension, which is the basis for the operation of dialectics and rhetoric. This divine grammar operates both synchronically and diachronically. Synchronically, Luther can grasp the relational order of reality in creation as a system of concentric circles. Most famously, this form of relating synchronically appears in the exposition of the creedal statement "C" in the *Small Catechism*: "I believe that God has created me, together with all that exists," and the organizing of creatures in concentric circles in which God upholds my created existence.[13] The divine grammar also operates diachronically insofar as every creature is the beginning of a story that is supported through time by God's promise. This is most famously expressed in the *Large Catechism* with the statement: "He created us that he might redeem us and make us holy."[14] Every created thing exists in this network of synchronic and diachronic relations. On the basis of this account, knowing creation always means knowing creation in its God-given ordered relationality. It is a form of knowing that is always self-involving and understands created relationality as a holistic order that includes the creature's own perspective of knowing and being as an element of the order of creation. The perspectival character of knowing does not relativize the objectivity of knowledge. The objectivity rests in God's

---

13. *The Book of Concord*, ed. Robert Kolb and Timothy J. Wengert (Minneapolis: Fortress, 2000), 354. The original "Ich glaube, dass mich Gott geschaffen hat samt allen Kreaturen" avoids the problematic implications of "all that exists." The inner circle of divine gifts ("eyes, ears, and all limbs and senses; reason and all mental faculties"), which refers to the bodily and spiritual constitutions of humans as embodied sensitive and rational beings, is enveloped by the outer circle ("shoes and clothing, food and drink, house and farm, spouse and children, fields, livestock and all property"), which comprises the fundamental bodily needs, primary forms of sociality, and their material presuppositions. This is summarized in the formula, "All the necessities and nourishment for this body and life" (*The Book of Concord*, 354).

14. *The Book of Concord*, 439.

giving and in God's promising; the subjective receptivity of this objectivity is its appropriation to me in faith. Both the language of gift, so famously employed in Luther's expressions of God's Trinitarian self-giving, and the language of a divine conversation bridge the subject–object dichotomy by the reciprocal, though asymmetrical, character of personal relationships. Knowing creation is therefore always a form of personal knowledge. Theology's role in the conversations with the sciences will therefore be a constant attentiveness to the relational character of an entangled universe in which relationality connects particulars and universal rules.[15] Conversely, it will try to direct the attention of the sciences to the forms of rationality that point to alternatives—to the dichotomies of realism and idealism, cognitivism and functionalism—because of their relationality.

Fifth, one can ask which forms of rationality are implied in such a view of creation. This seems to be the ongoing debate that Luther has with philosophy in his *Lectures on Genesis.* Luther combats all necessitarian schemes that posit the necessity of worldly events, processes, and their subsequent rational expressions. However, he maintains the position he adopted in *On the Bondage of the Will* and in his debate with Erasmus: On the one hand, Christians are committed to maintaining the central distinction between God's work and human work. On the other hand, we must address whether God foreknows anything contingently or everything is a consequence of divine necessity. Luther's position has been under continuous discussion. With regard to the contingent character of the knowledge of creation that cannot be deduced from necessary principles, Karl Barth has drawn the conclusion that we know of contingents only by revelation (*nihil constat de contingentia mundi, nisi ex revelatione*)—in events of disclosure which are the basis for grasping the rationality of the contingent.[16] Luther would, I think, go beyond that. For Luther, we have to rule out the idea that God knows anything contingently because God's knowledge could then be seen as reactive towards human free will. If that were the case, human willing would somehow have an independent

15. For the state of the discussion between theology and the sciences, cf. John Polkinghorne, ed., *The Trinity and an Entangled World: Relationality in Physical Science and Theology* (Grand Rapids: Eerdmans, 2008).

16. Cf. Karl Barth, *Kirchliche Dogmatik* III/1, 4th ed. (Zürich: EVZ, 1970), 5. For a thoroughgoing discussion, cf. Thomas F. Torrance, *Divine and Contingent Order* (Oxford: Oxford University Press, 1981), 26–61. The principle can be traced back to the Lutheran dogmatician J. A. Quenstedt. For full documentation, see the chapter "Theologie der Schöpfung im Dialog zwischen Naturwissenschaft und Dogmatik," in my *Gott in Beziehung* (Tübingen: Mohr Siebeck, 2002), 131–60, esp. 154n53.

position over the will of the Creator who, according to Luther, alone possesses the freedom of will that defines necessity for all created things. However, he would also claim that we can only know divine necessity as the freedom of God's self-determination from revelation, only in Christ through the Holy Spirit and through the witness of Scriptures as authenticated by the Spirit. It is precisely because of this necessity—which is rooted in the freedom of God's love, on which the trust of faith rests—that God will never revoke his promises. In this sense, divine necessity is an expression of God's freedom of self-determination, which, for the Trinitarian God, must always have a form mediating self-relation and relation to the other and which seems to be required for any consistent doctrine of creation. If this is true (*de necessitate divina constat nihil, nisi ex revelatione*), it would open up a fruitful exchange on the issues of chance and necessity, of rule-governed processes and the emergence of novelty that have played a major role in the debates with the natural sciences from cosmology to brain research. On a theological view, both what appears as chance and what appears as necessity do not reflect an impersonal fate but the personal self-determination of the triune God.

The Incarnate Word: Knowing the Creator by Created Means of Communication

Luther transformed the metaphor of the two books into a metaphor of creation as a divine speech-act that is calling for a human response, and he receives additional support from his interpretation of the incarnation of the divine Word in Jesus of Nazareth. The incarnation of the divine Word makes the creative divine speech at the beginning accessible through the means of communication in the field of created experience. The point of the incarnation is that the form and content of God's creative speaking through the uncreated Word, giving meaningful being to the whole of creation, is communicated in creaturely forms of communication in the life-witness of Jesus Christ and his continuing presence in the church and the world.

The impact of the incarnation for knowing creation has rarely been more radically underlined than in Luther's Christology of the radical personal union of God and man in Jesus Christ and in his teaching on the sacraments. The scandal of the incarnation is that the fundamental rational structures of reality are disclosed in the medium of human experience and that the eternal is disclosed in the temporality of human life and death. Such scandal is radicalized by Luther's insistence that the personal mode of knowing creation in Christ is always in an embodied form, be it in Christ, in the church as the body of Christ, or in Holy Communion as the self-giving of the Lord who is the Creator-Logos and the Redeemer in the very materiality of a shared meal.[17] In Christ God's address takes the form of an embodied personal presence and upholds the church in this form of embodied personal presence. The very materiality of creation becomes, in Christ, the communicative medium of the disclosure of knowledge of creation and of its Creator, so that the Spirit's activity remains bound to these bodily forms of communication. The link here between created matter and the ultimate forms of creative communication remains breathtaking, both theologically in negating all dualisms between mind and matter, Spirit and flesh, and scientifically in offering the challenge of a link that unites the basic configurations of material reality with the most complex dimensions of reality and the most elaborate forms of organisation.

If we follow the line of Luther's thought, the incarnation deepens, not only the understanding of everything in creation as divine words (part of God's vocabulary, held together by the rules of divine grammar), but also the assertion that the creative Word speaks these words and the divine grammar arranges their relationships, all of which become accessible in the medium of created matter. As the continuing embodied address of God, Christ becomes the key to understanding all reality though the experience of reality. It is here that the metaphor of the book is in a most radical way subverted. The author of the book, who has made the book a meaningful whole, no longer stands outside the story but becomes a character within it. His life and death become the overarching plot. A Christian theology that takes the incarnation seriously in this sense will be an awkward conversation partner. It will constantly have to be self-critical with regard to theological modes of rationality that take the words of the book either as data from which knowledge about its author can be inferred or as sign-posts to the axiomatic rules of divine grammar from which as a first principle everything can be deduced. The epistemic direction is inverted, not from the book to the author or from the world to God, but from

---

17. Cf. Christoph Schwöbel, "*Tamquam visibile verbum*. Kommunikative Sakramentalität und leibhaftes Personsein," in *Leibhaftes Personsein. Theologische und interdisziplinäre Perspektiven: Festschrift für Eilert Herms zum 75*, ed. Elisabeth Gräb-Schmidt et al., Geburtstag, Marburger Theologische Studien 123 (Leipzig: Evangelische Verlagsanstalt, 2015), 197–210.

the author as the main character in the book to the other characters, from the Creator-Logos incarnate in creation to the structures of creation, and from the embodied address that is heard in creation to the creative address that called creation into being and invested it with meaning.

Yet taking the incarnation seriously in this way may also open constructive encounters between theology and the sciences. Questions which first appear as theology-specific, like the sixteenth-century debate between Lutherans and Calvinists whether heaven is a spatial concept, may have far-reaching consequences. For the Lutherans, the expression "at the right hand of the Father" did not refer to a spatial location but meant "everywhere," which played an important role in the acceptance of scientific discoveries in astronomy and their implications for a scientific worldview. It was this debate that led to the development of a relational concept of space which Leibniz later formulated for the physical sciences, fully aware of the concept's Lutheran heritage.

The Word made flesh encourages theologians and scientists to take the communicative structure of physical reality with utter seriousness. Not only is this mode of knowing one that is understood as embodied knowing, but the "object" of knowing can never be understood as a mere object but as a conversation partner in the very materiality of creation. It is the impact of the incarnation that is continued as the mode of Christ's presence in the preaching of the word and the administration of the sacraments, and in the community of the church that is in this way constituted that makes creation a conversation partner in the efforts of human creatures to know creation. From this christological perspective, the vision of the Roman Catholic Romantic poet Joseph von Eichendorff (1788–1857) acquires a new poignancy:

> A song sleeps in all things.
> Which dream on and on,
> And the world begins to sing
> If only you find the magic word.[18]

From a christological perspective, one would have to say: the Word has been found, and it is not magic.

---

18. This is, of course, a theological appropriation or, indeed, an illegitimate subversion of a poem titled "Divining Rod." However, it seems that the implications of the incarnation point indeed in this direction and make all divining rods redundant.

The Spirit: Freedom for the Future

If the divine speech-act is the beginning of a history characterized by the constant interplay between the creative communicative relationality of the triune God and the created communicative relationality of the created order, then a question arises—namely, what is the goal of this history? In the *Lectures on Genesis*, Luther rejects the idea of an instantaneous creation and insists on creation as a sequential process, expressed in the scheme of six days. The directionality of creation, which insists that nature understood as creation is not an iterative or reversible process as suggested by a mechanistic understanding of the world, raises the question of how this directionality is to be understood theologically. With various accentuations in the biblical writings, the different forms of Spirit-discourse seem to agree with the Nicene Creed's confession of the Spirit as the Lord, the life-giver who spoke through the prophets, who proceeds from the Father (and the Son), and who is worshipped and glorified with the Father and the Son. Life is the beginning of a story of existence, and prophetic speech is the announcement of a future that cannot be deduced from the antecedent conditions of the past. Luther's slogan that creation means always to make something new (*creare est semper novum facere*[19]) can be applied to the Spirit-dimension of creation. This would indicate that the possibilities for the actualization of novelty are not restricted to the possibilities contained in the past of creation and are thereby not restricted to the possibilities inherent in what has already been actualized. On this view, there is space for genuine novelty in creation, for forms of emergence which receive their intelligibility not from antecedent conditions but from subsequent fulfilments. Paul's language of the Spirit as the anticipation of what is to come, the one who liberates us from our bondage to decay (Rom 8:19–25), offers freedom that is not grounded in the past and liberation from the past and to the past. However, for Paul, the Spirit not only brings the promise of future glory but also the help needed to bring our futile suffering before God. The Spirit, who has enabled creation to respond to the word of the Creator since the beginning, is also the one who restores the capacity to respond to the Creator where our words fail (Rom 8:26–27). The discovery of phenomena that point to emergent novelty in the story of cosmic evolution, however, raises the issue of how novelty

---

19. Martin Luther, *D. Martin Luthers Werks*, 121 vols. (Weimar: Hermann Böhlau, 1883–2009), WA 46, 556, 26.

can be reconciled with the familiar processes of conditioning by antecedent conditions. As the Pauline view of the Spirit indicates, the promise of future glory requires a genuine reconciliation, the overcoming of all the futility and suffering to which creation is subject, and its liberation which will be revealed in the children of God (Rom 8:18–21).

It is here that the significance of the Trinitarian specification of talking about the Spirit in the Nicene Creed can be appreciated in its full significance. The Trinitarian framework identifies the Spirit as the one "who with the Father and the Son is worshipped and glorified." This points to the theological necessity and to the theological space of integrating eschatological novelty as freedom for the future with both a God who creates by speaking things into being and the presence of God in the incarnate Word. When we understand the Spirit as the perfecting cause of God's work, the work of the Holy Spirit becomes the goal of the work of the Father as the originating cause and of the Son as the creative cause of everything there is.[20] These different aspects must be compatible if one confesses the triune God. Every work of the Trinity is perfected in the operation of the Holy Spirit. In conversations with the sciences, the Trinitarian perspective offers a strong argument for nonreductionist integration. Can the integration that Trinitarian doctrine attempts—between unity and plurality, between the transcendence of the first speaker, the uncreated word, and the incarnate Word, between absolute beginning and absolute future—be reflected in the art of knowing creation?

God in Conversation and God as Conversation

These considerations show that our understanding of God is at the heart of knowing creation and, indeed, at the heart of the dialogue between theology and the sciences. Asking the big questions in the physical and life sciences always exercises a temptation to engage, whether polemically or constructively, with the biggest of all questions—the question of God. Is there an understanding of the God of Christian faith that can support an emphasis on communicative relationality in understanding (1) creation as a divine speech-act, (2) the incarnation as an encounter with the Creator-Logos in created, bodily, and historical forms of communication, and (3) the interplay

---

20. Cf. Basil, *On the Holy Spirit*, 16.38.

between order and freedom that the Spirit introduces between the Creator and creation?

In Luther's *Lectures on Genesis*, there is a consistent emphasis on creation as a triune speech-act. Immediately after Luther identifies every being as part of the divine vocabulary, he states, "Thus God reveals Himself to us as the Speaker who has with Him the uncreated Word, Through whom He created the world and all things with the greatest ease, namely, by speaking."[21] Soon thereafter he discusses Augustine's Trinitarian interpretation, with "He said" referring to the Father, the attribution of "made" to the Son, and the expression "sees" (when God sees that the creation he has spoken into being) to the Holy Spirit.[22] And then he mentions the appropriation of "mind" to the Father, of "intellect" to the Son, and "will" to the Holy Spirit,[23] but immediately qualifies these references to the tradition by saying: "They speak thus because we picture these matters to ourselves this way in order to remember and explain the doctrine of the Trinity."[24] When Luther states his own Trinitarian theology—based on the prologue to John's Gospel and the description of the Holy Spirit's role therein—he develops the metaphor of a conversation between the Father, the Son, and the Spirit. The metaphor of the inner-Trinitarian conversation points to the different personal particularities of the Father, the Son, and the Spirit and locates the divine essence precisely in the eternal communicative exchange.

> Thus, there are two distinct Persons: He who speaks and the Word that is spoken, that is, the Father and the Son. Here, however, we find the third person following these two, namely, the One who hears both the Speaker and the spoken Word. . . . All three, Speaker, Word and Listener—must be God Himself; all three must be coeternal and in a single undivided majesty. For there is no difference or inequality in the divine essence, neither a beginning nor an end . . . just as the Father is a Speaker from eternity, and just as the Son is spoken from eternity, so the Holy Spirit is the Listener from eternity.[25]

---

21. *LW* 1:22.
22. *LW* 1:50. Luther seems to refer here to Augustine's *De genesi ad litteram*, 2.6.
23. *LW* 1:50. This seems to be a reference to Augustine's *De Trinitate*, 10.11–12.
24. *LW* 1:50.
25. *LW* 24:364–65.

In his *Table Talk*, Luther can summarize his Trinitarian teaching almost epigrammatically, by identifying the Father as the grammar of the divine conversation, the Son as the dialectics giving order and intelligible structure, and the Spirit as the rhetoric who makes the divine speech lively and impressive so that it can conquer the hearts.[26]

What is gained by understanding God as the inner-Trinitarian conversation? For Luther, this is not mere metaphor but the ultimate ontological foundation for conceiving of reality in terms of an ontology of communicative relations as a conversation, which is demonstrated by his attempts to formulate the revisions necessary in metaphysics to account for the hypostatic identities of the three persons.[27] In the speech-act of creation, God begins a conversation with his creation that is continued in creation through the incarnate Son and perfected in the Holy Spirit. The conversation God *has* with his creation is ultimately rooted in the conversation God *is* in his Trinitarian being.

Resonances and Consonances

With these reflections, we have tried to explore some of the critical and constructive possibilities opened by understanding the act of creation as a divine speech-act: the whole of creation is a part of God's vocabulary and thus the bearer of being, meaning, and created dignity. By giving this understanding of creation a distinctive Trinitarian form, as Luther does, we can recognise that God's conversational relationship with creation is rooted in God's own communicative being as a Trinitarian conversation. As we have seen, Luther's reformulation of the metaphor of the book of nature offers a number of promising avenues for a conversation between theology and the sciences. The particular ontology of relations that can be developed on this basis is one where the whole multidimensional structure of reality could be seen as a highly differentiated and complex structure of resonances.

The German sociologist Hartmut Rosa has demonstrated the fruitfulness

---

26. *Luther's Works*, WA, Tischreden 1, 564, 2–7.

27. For a more detailed treatment of Luther's Trinitarian teaching cf. my chapter "Martin Luther and the Trinity" in the *Oxford Research Encyclopaedia of Religion* (Oxford: forthcoming). doi:10.1093/acrefore/9780199340378.013.326. For a systematic exposition of the understanding of God as Trinity, cf. Christoph Schwöbel, "God as Conversation: Reflections on a Theological Ontology of Communicative Relations," in *Theology and Conversation: Towards a Relational Theology*, ed. Jacques Haers and Peter De Mey (Leuven: Peeters, 2003), 43–67.

of such an approach for analysing the human relationship to the world.[28] It seems useful to recover the theological roots of the metaphor of resonance, which is particularly apt for exploring communicative relationships in both horizontal and vertical dimensions. And this metaphor can be extended, as Rosa does, to help explore the embodied character of human relationships in the social world and the natural world.

Many of the obstacles that have made conversations between the sciences and theology so difficult seem to be located, not in particular scientific discoveries, models, and theories, but in the metascientific assumptions often connected with the power of metaphors that can stand in the way of a fruitful and mutually enriching conversation. The discovery of the crucial significance of relationality, both in theology and the sciences, was an important step in the direction of a more constructive view of God and the world—a view unrestricted by adherence to the metaphysics of substance and to modern theories of subjectivity. The next step has to be a continuing conversation on the question of which understanding of relationality can be most fruitfully explored. The view of relationality as communicative seems to offer one way forward, and as it does so it not only informs the practice of theological thinking but also the most fundamental practices of Christian worship. Following this way, we can expect dissonance at every stage of the conversation. Yet, as in music, the very character of dissonances points to the fact that there is still a way towards a satisfying consonance. It belongs to the very character of both theology and the sciences that we have not yet reached that point. Such an approach, which we have explored a little further with the help of Martin Luther's theology, not only offers the hope of listening more attentively to the resonances of a universe of communicative relationships; it also calls us to hear the Word that called everything into being, as part of God's vocabulary.

---

28. Hartmut Rosa, *Resonanz: Eine Soziologie der Weltbeziehung* (Frankfurt: Suhrkamp, 2016).

Chapter THREE

Why Should Free Scientific Inquiry Matter to Faith?

The Case of John Calvin

RANDALL C. ZACHMAN

We have become accustomed to the question of whether a scientist can also be a believer. Those of us in what might be called mainstream churches have become comfortable with the assertion that there is no conflict, let alone war, between faith and science, but this too often leads to a state of peaceful coexistence; we no longer ask the further question of how scientific inquiry might relate more fruitfully to faith and piety. By looking at the example of a historical figure, in this instance John Calvin (1509–1564), I would like to explore this issue by posing the more provocative question: not whether a scientist can also be a believer but rather whether every believer should also seek as much as possible to become a scientist. Is there something in the nature of genuine piety that should lead every believer to become passionately interested in the scientific investigation of the universe? My hope is that by looking at Calvin's understanding of this question in the sixteenth century, we might learn something about this issue that could be applicable in our own day.

Science and the Knowledge of God the Creator

John Calvin locates this question in the context of the knowledge of God the Creator, thereby linking the self-revelation of God in the universe with scientific inquiry into the nature of the universe. According to Calvin, the knowledge of God the Creator is available to every human being, not just the pious, by means of God's works in the world.

> The final goal of the blessed life, moreover, rests in the knowledge of God [cf. John 17:3]. Lest anyone, then, be excluded from access to happiness, he not only sowed in men's minds that seed of religion of which we have spoken but revealed himself and daily discloses himself in the whole workmanship of the universe. As a consequence, men cannot open their eyes without being compelled to see him.[1]

The works of God portray the powers or perfections of God to us like a painting, so that even the unlearned can see the nature of God portrayed in the works they see before their eyes. "We must admit that in God's individual works—but especially in them as a whole—that God's powers are actually represented as in a painting."[2] Our experience of the powers of God portrayed in God's works in turn reveals God to us and teaches us piety. "For the Lord manifests himself by his powers, the force of which we feel within ourselves, and the benefits of which we enjoy."[3] Since all can see, feel, and enjoy these powers, regardless of the degree of their education, the self-revelation of God in the universe is, in principle, available to all human beings.

Calvin acknowledges that the learned penetrate more deeply into the powers of God portrayed in God's works, for they investigate these works with great care, skill, and attention.

> There are innumerable evidences both in heaven and on earth that declare his wonderful wisdom; not only those more recondite matters for the closer observation of which astronomy, medicine, and all natural science are intended, but also those which thrust themselves upon the sight of even the most untutored and ignorant persons, so that they cannot open their eyes without being compelled to witness them. Indeed, men who have either quaffed or even tasted the liberal arts

---

1. *Inst.* 1.5.1. Quoted from Calvin, *Institutes of the Christian Religion*, ed. John T. McNeill, trans. Ford Lewis Battles, 2 vols., Library of Christian Classics (Philadelphia: Westminster, 1960), 1:51–52; henceforth LCC.

2. *Inst.* 1.5.10, LCC 1:63.

3. *Inst.* 1.5.9, LCC 1:62.

penetrate with their aid far more deeply into the secrets of divine wisdom.[4]

The sciences arise out of this learned investigation into the works of God, and so they can be said to penetrate more deeply into the powers of God, due to the skill of their investigations.

The Need for the Spectacles of Scripture

However, Calvin insists that neither the unlearned nor the learned come to the true knowledge of God from their experience of the works of God in the universe.

> But although the Lord represents both himself and his everlasting Kingdom in the mirror of his works with very great clarity, such is our stupidity that we grow increasingly dull toward so manifest testimonies, and they flow away without profiting us. . . . Not only the common folk and dull-witted men, but also the most excellent and those otherwise endowed with keen discernment, are infected with this disease.[5]

The problem lies not in the works of God, but in human reason, which has a desire to know the truth, but which is incapable of staying on the right path to attain to certain knowledge of the truth. "Yet this longing for truth, such as it is, languishes before it enters upon its race because it soon falls into vanity."[6]

For this reason, Calvin insists that we need spectacles to correct our vision and to lead us onto the right path by which we might attain to the knowledge of God the Creator. These spectacles are found only in Scripture: "So Scripture, gathering up the otherwise confused knowledge of God in our minds, having dispersed our dullness, clearly shows us the true God."[7] Scripture corrects our misguided assessment of the works of God, so that we might rightly perceive the powers of God portrayed therein, and by our awareness of these powers come to the true knowledge of the Creator. "We must come, I say, to the Word, where God is truly and vividly described to us from his works, while these very works

---

4. *Inst.* 1.5.2, LCC 1:53.
5. *Inst.* 1.5.11, LCC 1:63–64.
6. *Inst.* 2.2.12, LCC 1:271.
7. *Inst.* 1.6.1, LCC 1:70.

are appraised not by our depraved judgment but by the rule of eternal truth."[8]
All right knowledge of God the Creator is born out of obedience to the Word
of God in Scripture, for this alone reveals the Creator to us from the works
God does in the universe. "For our wisdom ought to be nothing else than to
embrace with humble teachableness, and at least without finding fault, whatever
is taught in Sacred Scripture."[9] Hence it would seem that Calvin would not be
supportive of the investigations of the learned into the nature of the universe
because these would not be clarified by the spectacles of Scripture. Indeed, the
problem is compounded by Calvin's awareness that the natural sciences have
their origin in the unbelieving nations of Egypt and Babylon. "We find also
that heathen writers, when speaking of the origin of the sciences, trace them up
to the Chaldeans and the Egyptians; for with them, it is said, have originated
astrology and all the liberal sciences."[10] Would Calvin therefore agree with the
condemnation of Galileo in the next century, which claimed that scientific
inquiry leads to heresy when it arrives at conclusions that contradict Scripture?

The Liberal Arts and Sciences
Are Gifts of the Holy Spirit

We must begin our examination of this question by noting that even though
reason fails to arrive at the knowledge of God the Creator without the spectacles
of Scripture, this does not mean that it fails to arrive at any truth whatsoever.
Calvin claims that all human beings have a certain aptitude for the liberal and
mechanical arts.[11] Even though only a few can discover, develop, or transmit
these arts, the fact that they are found in unbelieving nations such as Egypt,
Babylon, and Greece shows that they are common to all people as natural
gifts, and are not limited to the pious.[12] When the pious read the investigations
of these authors, they cannot help but feel admiration for their insight and
wisdom. "Those men whom Scripture [1 Cor. 2:14] calls 'natural men' were,
indeed, sharp and penetrating in their investigation of inferior things."[13] Even

---

8. *Inst.* 1.6.3, LCC 1:73.
9. *Inst.* 1.18.4, LCC 1:237.
10. *Comm. Jeremiah* 10:3, *The Commentaries of John Calvin on the Old Testament*, 30 vols. (Edinburgh:
Calvin Translation Society, 1843–1848), 18:13; henceforth CTS.
11. *Inst.* 2.2.14, LCC 1:273.
12. *Inst.* 2.2.14, LCC 1:273.
13. *Inst.* 2.2.15, LCC 1:274.

though these are natural gifts, the pious cannot help but acknowledge that these writings are inspired by the same Spirit that inspired Scripture, for the Spirit is the source of all truth, even the truth of the nature of the universe. "If we regard the Spirit of God as the sole fountain of truth, we shall neither reject the truth itself, nor despise it wherever it shall appear, unless we wish to dishonor the Spirit of God."[14] Calvin will therefore insist that God revealed the natural sciences to us, to be used for our benefit. "God has revealed all that is necessary to be known by means of the arts and sciences, which he intended to be used, and of which he approves."[15] Since God revealed the arts and sciences to us by the Holy Spirit, it would be the height of ingratitude to neglect to study and use them ourselves for the benefit of piety. "But if the Lord has willed that we be helped in physics, dialectic, mathematics, and other like disciplines, by the work and ministry of the ungodly, let us use this assistance. For if we neglect God's gift freely offered in these arts, we ought to suffer just punishments for our sloths."[16] Since the arts and sciences have been revealed by God and are free gifts of the Spirit, the pious have the right and the duty to investigate these sciences for themselves, as God has revealed them for their benefit.

Distinguishing Genuine Science from Magical Arts

However, since both natural science and Scripture portray the works of God in the universe, what is the relationship between the two? And what happens when these two accounts either diverge or appear to collide, as happened in the case of Galileo and as many think is still happening in the case of Darwin? Calvin begins by distinguishing between genuine science and the magical arts of the Egyptians and Babylonians. He uses Daniel and Moses as examples of previous pious figures who could separate the magical arts from true science. "Since Daniel here speaks of literature, without doubt he simply means the liberal arts, and does not comprehend the magical arts which flourished then and afterwards in Chaldea."[17] This was a real issue at the time of Calvin. There were theologians such as Luther and Melanchthon who were devoted to a kind of astrology that Calvin regarded as magical, and he worked hard to distinguish

---

14. *Inst.* 2.2.15, LCC 1:273–74.
15. *Comm. Isaiah* 19:3, CTS 14:51.
16. *Inst.* 2.2.16, LCC 1:275.
17. *Comm. Daniel* 1:17, CTS 24:112.

the genuine science of astrology from its magical use. Calvin wrote a treatise in French distinguishing genuine astrology, which we now call astronomy, from judiciary astrology, which is reflected in the use of horoscopes and other "magical arts." He thought that this distinction could also be supported by the study of astronomy by Daniel and Moses. "Through discontent with genuine science, they corrupted the study of the stars; but Daniel and his associates were so brought up among the Chaldeans, that they were not tinctured with those mixtures and corruptions which ought always to be separated from true science."[18] Calvin appeals to the example of Moses to support this claim, for he also distinguished the genuine science he learned from the Egyptians from their superstitious and magical arts. "Daniel, therefore, might have learned these arts; that is, astrology and other liberal sciences, just as Moses is said to have been instructed in all the sciences of Egypt."[19] Following their example, it is possible for the pious today to be "content with the pure and genuine knowledge of natural things."[20] Calvin appeals to Daniel and Moses to defend his own exhortations to believers to be interested in true and legitimate science, over against those who oppose faith and scientific investigation, "even as, in the present day, the Anabaptists have no other pretext for boasting of being spiritual persons, but that they are grossly ignorant of all science."[21]

Using Science to Interpret Scripture

Calvin assumes that Moses, the author of the Torah, knew the true sciences of the Egyptians, and he also assumes that all authors of Scripture were as learned in the sciences as was Moses. Hence he takes for granted that the sciences can help determine the meaning of Scripture. For instance, Calvin appeals to the secular writers on astrology for his interpretation of Amos. When the prophet mentions Pleiades and Orion, Calvin faults the rabbis for not knowing these sciences. "There is no need of laboring much about such names; for the Jews, ignorant of the liberal sciences, cannot at this day certainly determine what stars are meant; and they show also their complete ignorance as to herbs."[22] When Ezekiel speaks

---

18. *Comm. Daniel* 1:17, CTS 24:112. See John Calvin, "A Warning against Judiciary Astrology," trans. Mary Potter, *Calvin Theological Journal* 18, no. 1 (1983): 157–89.

19. *Comm. Daniel* 1:4, CTS 24:92.

20. *Comm. Daniel* 1:4, CTS 24:92–93.

21. *Comm. Psalm* 71:15, CTS 10:91–92.

22. *Comm. Amos* 5:8, CTS 27:261.

of a rainbow placed in the cloud, Calvin appeals to the philosophers to point out that rainbows are not substantial, but are rather made up of refracted colors.

> If any one should ask if those colors are without substance, it is certain that colors arise from the rays of the sun on a hollow cloud, as philosophers teach. Therefore when the Prophet says, *a bow appears on a rainy day,* he simply means, exists or appears in the midst; not that the colors have any substance, as I have just said, but the rays of the sun, whilst they are mutually reflected on the hollow cloud, occasion the manifold variety.[23]

Calvin uses the same method when interpreting the meaning of various animals that appear in Scripture. When David says that their youth shall be renewed like an eagle's, Calvin first accuses the rabbis of ignorance, since "they know not even the first elements of any science," and then appeals to the philosophers for the true understanding of the nature of eagles. "But we may easily gather the simple meaning of the Prophet from the nature of the eagle, as described by philosophers, and which is well-known from observation."[24] When Jeremiah compares the unjust to partridges, Calvin again turns to the philosophers, over against the rabbis, to understand the nature of those birds. "But it is said of partridges with one consent, by Aristotle and Pliny, as well as by others, that it is a very lustful bird."[25] Assuming that Jeremiah knew the same science as Pliny and Aristotle, Calvin then derives the genuine meaning of the prophet. "I doubt not therefore but that the real meaning of the Prophet is this,—that while partridges so burn with love to their brood, they are at the same time led away by their own lust, and that while they conceal their eggs, the male cunningly steals them, so that their labor proves useless."[26]

Calvin not only appeals to classical science to clarify the meaning of Scripture, but also appeals to the scientific inquiries of his contemporaries to discover the genuine sense of biblical authors. When we read in Jonah that God prepared a fish for Jonah, Calvin asks whether God created a fish specifically for this purpose, and uses the study of the fish of the sea by his contemporary to argue that such a fish already exists in the sea.

---

23. *Comm. Ezekiel* 1:28, CTS 22:105.
24. *Comm. Psalm* 103:4, CTS 11:129.
25. *Comm. Jeremiah* 17:11, CTS 18:358.
26. *Comm. Jeremiah* 17:11, CTS 18:358.

And William Rondelet, who has written a book [in 1554] on the fishes
of the sea, concludes that in all probability it must have been the *Lamia*.
He himself saw that fish, and he says that it has a belly so capacious, and
mouth so wide, that it can easily swallow up a man; and he says that a
man in armor has sometimes been found in the inside of the Lamia.[27]

In order to understand what Paul means by speaking of false teaching as a
disease, Calvin appeals to his own personal physician to give him a genuine
understanding of the medical term used by Paul. "I have been told by Benedict
Textor, a physician, that this passage is badly translated by Erasmus, who, out
of two diseases quite different from each other, has made but one disease; for,
instead of 'gangrene,' he has used the word 'cancer.'"[28] Calvin then defends
his physician's claim by appealing to a whole range of medical scientists,
such as Galen, Paul Aegenita, Aetius, and Cornelius Celsius, to arrive at his
interpretation of Paul.

Since, therefore, "gangrene" is immediately followed by (νέκρωσις)
mortification, which rapidly infects the rest of the members till it end
in the universal destruction of the body; to this mortal contagion Paul
elegantly compares false doctrines; for, if you once give entrance to them,
they spread till they have completed the destruction of the Church.[29]

Scripture and Science Describe the Same Wonders

Calvin also appeals to the way both science and Scripture draw our attention
to wonders and miracles that take place every day before our eyes. One of his
favorite examples of this is the appearance and preservation of dry land, for
both science and Scripture point out that this goes against the nature of water.

And this, philosophers are compelled to acknowledge, that it is contrary
to the course of nature for the waters to subside, so that some portion of
the earth might rise above them. And Scripture records this among the

---

27. *Comm. Jonah* 1:17, CTS 28:73. For Rondelet's book on the fish of the sea, *Libri de piscibus marinis*
(Lugduni apud Matthiam Bonhomme, 1554), see https://archive.org/details/gvlielmirondelet00rond.
    28. *Comm. 2 Timothy* 2:17, *Calvin's New Testament Commentaries*, ed. David W. Torrance and
Thomas F. Torrance (Grand Rapids: Eerdmans, 1959–72), 10:314; henceforth CNTC.
    29. *Comm. 2 Timothy* 2:17, CNTC 10:314–15.

miracles of God, that he restrains the force of the sea, as with barriers, lest it should overwhelm that part of the earth which is granted for a habitation to men.[30]

According to the philosophers, water is lighter than the earth and therefore should seek a place of rest above the earth, making it impossible for dry land to appear. "Philosophers themselves admit, that as the element of the water is higher than the earth, it is contrary to the nature of the two elements for any part of the earth to continue uncovered with the waters, and habitable."[31] Moreover, the elements are spherical, which means that the sphere of the earth should be surrounded by the sphere of water, which is lighter and stands between the element of earth and the element of air.

> As these elements are of a spherical form, the waters, if not kept within their limits, would naturally cover the earth, were it not that God has seen fit to secure a place of habitation for the human family. This philosophers themselves are forced to admit as one of their principles and maxims. The earth's expanded surface, and the vacant space uncovered with water, has been justly considered therefore one of the great wonders of God.[32]

Hence both Scripture and science point to a miracle that occurs every day to show that the hidden power of God provides the only explanation of the dry ground on which we live.

> Now, if any inquires how this is, it must be confessed to be a miracle which cannot be accounted for; for the sea, we know, as other elements, is spherical. As the earth is round, so also is the element of water, as well as the air and fire. Since then the form of this element is spherical, we must know that it is not lower than the earth: but it being lighter than the earth shews that it stands above it. How then comes it that the sea does not overflow the whole earth? for it is a liquid, and cannot stand in one place, except retained by some secret power of God.[33]

---

30. *Comm. Genesis* 7:11, CTS 1:270.
31. *Comm. Psalm* 24:2, CTS 8:403.
32. *Comm. Psalm* 136:4, CTS 12:184.
33. *Comm. Jeremiah* 5:22, CTS 17:294.

Calvin appeals to a current event to show what would happen if God withdrew this secret power. Calvin does so to show that we should be grateful for this preservation every day of our lives, as both science and Scripture demonstrate. "The Baltic Sea, in our own time, inundated large tracts of land, and did great damage to the Flemish people and other neighboring nations. By an instance of this kind we are warned what would be the consequence, were the restraint imposed upon the sea, by the hand of God, removed."[34] We of course have a different physics than Calvin, but the point is that he thought science and Scripture could both point to wonders that should astound and amaze us, as well as lead us to be grateful to God.

> Again, if the waters are higher than the earth, because they are lighter, why do they not cover the whole earth round about? Certainly the only answer which philosophers can give to this is, that the tendency of the waters to do so is counteracted by the providence of God, that a dwelling-place might be provided for man.[35]

Scripture Is for the Unlearned, Science Is for the Learned

But what happens when science and Scripture describe the world in different ways, as happened in the case of Galileo? Would Calvin believe the testimony of Scripture instead of the observations of the scientists? Calvin directly addresses this issue in his discussion of the creation narratives in Genesis. The first contradiction appears when Moses says that there is water above the firmament. "Moses describes the special use of this expanse, to divide the waters from the waters, from which word arises a great difficulty. For it appears opposed to common sense, and quite incredible, that there should be waters above the heaven."[36] Calvin explains this contradiction by pointing out that Moses is not writing a learned scientific treatise but is rather writing Scripture in accommodation to his unlearned readers, who do not know the arts and sciences like he does. Hence, we should not read Scripture to attain a scientific understanding of the universe. "He who would learn astronomy, and

---

34. *Comm. Psalm* 104:9, CTS 11:151.
35. *Comm. Psalm* 104:5, CTS 11:149.
36. *Comm. Genesis* 1:6, CTS 1:79.

other recondite arts, let him go elsewhere. Here the Spirit of God would teach all men without exception; and therefore what Gregory declares falsely and in vain respecting statues and pictures is truly applicable to the history of the creation, namely, that it is the book of the unlearned."[37] Calvin is convinced that Moses learned astrology from the Egyptians, and so he knows he is not writing a scientific treatise but is rather describing the world the way the unlearned experience it. Hence Calvin believes it is not the intent of Moses that we should ignore what we know from astrology in order to believe what Moses says in Genesis. "The assertion of some, that they embrace by faith what they have read concerning the waters above the heavens, notwithstanding their ignorance respecting them, is not in accordance with the design of Moses."[38]

Calvin makes a similar point when he comes to the description of the moon later in Genesis. Moses does not distinguish between the different spheres the way astrologers do when he describes the planets and the stars. He also states that the moon is the second largest heavenly body, when Calvin knows that astrologers have shown that Saturn is in fact larger than the moon. "Here lies the difference; Moses wrote in a popular style things which without instruction, all ordinary persons, endued with common sense, are able to understand; but astronomers investigate with great labor whatever the sagacity of the human mind can comprehend."[39] Calvin is aware that this may lead some believers to condemn the science of astrology, as it arrives at conclusions that appear to contradict Scripture. He therefore defends the legitimacy of this science, as being worthy of pursuit by the pious.

> Nevertheless, this study is not to be reprobated, nor this science to be condemned, because some frantic persons are wont boldly to reject whatever is unknown to them. For astronomy is not only pleasant, but also very useful to be known: it cannot be denied that this art unfolds the admirable wisdom of God. Wherefore, as ingenious men are to be honored who have expended useful labor on this subject, so they who have leisure and capacity ought not to neglect this kind of exercise. Nor did Moses truly wish to withdraw us from this pursuit in omitting such things as are peculiar to the art.[40]

---

37. *Comm. Genesis* 1:6, CTS 1:79–80.
38. *Comm. Genesis* 1:6, CTS 1:80.
39. *Comm. Genesis* 1:16, CTS 1:86.
40. *Comm. Genesis* 1:16, CTS 1:86.

Calvin makes the same point when he discusses the wisdom Daniel learned from the Babylonians. "I always exclude superstitions by which they vitiated true and genuine science. But as far as the principles are concerned, we cannot precisely condemn astronomy and whatever belongs to the consideration of the order of nature."[41]

Scripture Reminds Science to "Rise Higher"

If the scientific descriptions of the universe should not be corrected by the teachings of Scripture, which are accommodated to the unlearned, does Calvin think that Scripture adds anything to the scientific understanding of the universe? According to Calvin, Scripture consistently asks the learned scientists to "rise higher" than the order of nature they are investigating so that they see the work of God in the works of nature. For instance, scientists understand the way childbirth takes place, and we all have experience of this in our own lives. However, this should not keep us from rising higher whenever we see a child born as we consider the tender care of God in this event.

> Although it is by the operation of natural causes that infants come into the world, and are nourished with their mother's milk, yet therein the wonderful providence of God brightly shines forth. This miracle, it is true, because of its ordinary occurrence, is made less account of by us. But if ingratitude did not put upon our eyes the veil of stupidity, we would be ravished with admiration at every childbirth in the world.[42]

In particular, Calvin wants the reader to be amazed that the child is kept alive in the womb even though it is surrounded by water as though it is in a grave. And when the infant emerges from the womb, it is extremely vulnerable and confronted by death at every turn. Thus, "Unless he fed the tender little babes, and watched over all the offices of the nurse, even at the very time of their being brought forth, they are exposed to a hundred deaths, by which they would be suffocated in an instant."[43] This does not mean that what scientists

---

41. *Comm. Daniel* 2:27, CTS 24:155.
42. *Comm. Psalm* 22:9, CTS 8:369.
43. *Comm. Psalm* 22:9, CTS 8:369.

tell us about childbirth is wrong; rather, we must rise higher in order to see the tender care of God in every birth.

We see the same concern to "rise higher" when Calvin considers meteorology. He pays a great deal of attention to the insights of the natural scientists regarding the origin of the wind, for example, and uses these insights to understand what Jeremiah means when he says that God brings forth the wind from his treasures.

> The philosophers also find out the cause why the winds arise from the earth; for the sun attracts vapours and exhalations; from vapours are formed clouds, snows, and rains, according to the fixed order of the middle region of the air. From the exhalations also are formed the thunders, lightnings, the comets also, and the winds; for the exhalations differ from the vapours only in their lightness and rarity, the vapours being thicker and heavier. Then from vapor arises rain; but the exhalation is lighter, and not so thick; hence the exhalations generate thunders as well as winds, according to the heat they contain. How, then, is it that the same exhalation now breaks forth into wind, then into lightnings? It is according to the measure of its heat; when it is dense it rises into the air; but the winds vanish and thus disturb the lower part of the world. These are the things said by philosophers; but the chief thing in philosophy is to have regard to God, who brings the winds out of his treasures, for he keeps them hidden.[44]

Calvin's detailed and intricate discussion of the origin of wind shows that Calvin completely accepts the philosophers' description of how the winds arise, but he also wants us to rise higher to see the work of God in the rising of the wind.

The same holds true for the origin of clouds and rain. "Philosophers discover the origin of rain in the elements, and it is not denied that clouds are formed from the gross vapours which are exhaled from the earth and sea, but second causes should not prevent us from recognizing the providence of God in furnishing the earth with the moisture needed for fructification."[45] The origin of rain is understood well by the philosophers, so there is nothing wrong with their description of how this happens. Calvin simply reminds us to rise higher and see in these events the work of God. "We see that vapours arise from the earth

---

44. *Comm. Jeremiah* 10:12, CTS 18:37–38.
45. *Comm. Psalm* 147:7, CTS 12:297.

and ascend upwards. Philosophers shew how this happens: but yet the power of God cannot be excluded, when we say that anything is done according to nature."[46] The phenomenon of rain also involves lightning, which contributes to the formation of rain yet combines the two opposed elements of fire and water.

> Did not custom make us familiar with the spectacle, we would pronounce this mixture of fire and water to be a phenomenon altogether incredible. The same may be said of the phenomena of the winds. Natural causes can be assigned for them, and philosophers have pointed them out; but the winds, with their various currents, are a wonderful work of God.[47]

The same phenomena that science describes so accurately must also be seen by the pious as the works of God manifesting the nature of God.

> Since then God thus mingles contrary things, and makes fire the origin and the cause of rain, is it not so wonderful that it is sufficient to move the very stones? How great then must be the stupidity of men, when they attend not to so conspicuous a work of God, in which they may see the glory of his wisdom as well as of his power![48]

We see the same concern to start with the scientific explanation of a phenomenon and then rise higher to God when Calvin discusses the nature of thunder. Again, his science seems quaint by our standards, but it remains true that he uses the scientific explanation as the starting point for the ascent to see the very same phenomenon as the work of God.

> Philosophers, it is true, are well acquainted with the intermediate or secondary causes, from which the thunder proceeds, namely, that when the cold and humid vapours obstruct the dry and hot exhalations in their course upwards, a collision takes place, and by this, together with the noise of the clouds rushing against each other, is produced the rumbling thunder-peal. But David, in describing the phenomena of the atmosphere, rises, under the guidance of the Holy Spirit, above the

---

46. *Comm. Jeremiah* 10:12, CTS 18:36.
47. *Comm. Psalm* 135:7, CTS 12:175.
48. *Comm. Jeremiah* 10:12, CTS 18:37.

mere phenomena themselves, and represents God to us as the supreme governor of the whole.[49]

The Danger of Separating God from God's Works

Calvin was aware, however, of a tendency in some philosophers to confine their attention entirely to the natural phenomena they studied, so as to exclude all consideration of God from view. The problem is not that their investigations of the universe are wrong, but rather that they fail to rise higher to the God who is revealed in the universe. They create a web of natural causality that eclipses the self-revelation of God in the works of God.

> Philosophers think not that they have reasoned skillfully enough about inferior causes, unless they separate God very far from his works. It is a diabolical science, however, which fixes our contemplations on the works of nature, and turns them away from God. If any one who wished to know a man should take no notice of his face, but should fix his eyes only on the points of his nails, his folly might justly be derided. But far greater is the folly of those philosophers, who, out of mediate and proximate causes, weave themselves veils, lest they should be compelled to acknowledge the hand of God, which manifestly displays itself in his works.[50]

Calvin identified Aristotle in particular as the philosopher who most directed our attention to natural causes only to leave God's work out of consideration. "Aristotle, in his book on Meteors, reasons very shrewdly about these things, in so far as relates to proximate causes, only that he omits the chief point. The investigation of these would, indeed, be both a profitable and pleasant exercise, were we led by it, as we ought, to the Author of Nature himself."[51] Calvin believes that Aristotle used his genius to try to create a veil of natural causes that would blind us to God's work in the universe.

> This caution is the more necessary, since we find that some of the greatest of philosophers were so mischievous as to devote their talents to obscure

---

49. *Comm. Psalm* 18:13, CTS 8:273–74.
50. *Comm. Psalm* 29:5, CTS 8:479.
51. *Comm. Psalm* 29:5, CTS 8:479–80.

and conceal the providence of God, and, entirely overlooking his agency, ascribed all to secondary causes. At the head of these was Aristotle, a man of genius and learning; but being a heathen, whose heart was perverse and depraved, it was his constant aim to entangle and perplex God's overruling providence by a variety of wild speculations; so much so, that it may with too much truth be said, that he employed his naturally acute powers of mind to extinguish all light.[52]

Beginning and Ending Our Investigations in Wonder

Calvin addresses this danger by introducing a theological principle into natural science itself. He hopes to prevent natural science from becoming an obstacle to the knowledge of God by discouraging us from rising higher. "If, then, we would avoid a senseless natural philosophy, we must always start with this principle, that everything in nature depends upon the will of God, and that the whole course of nature is only the prompt carrying into effect of his orders."[53] Calvin seems to be saying that unless God is introduced into the descriptions of the world by the scientists and philosophers, then their science itself is deficient.

> If we do not hold fast to this principle, however acutely we may investigate second causes, all our perspicacity will come to nothing. It is thus that Aristotle, for example, has shown such ingenuity upon the subject of meteors, that he discusses their natural causes most exactly, while he omits the main point of all, upon which the merest child, at least having any religion, has the superiority over him.[54]

But this raises a question: How does Calvin place the knowledge of God as the first principle of true science when doing so opposes his claim that God gave us the sciences by means of people from Egypt, Babylon, and Greece, people who did not know the true God? The sciences were revealed by God and may be used by the pious even though the writers who teach us these sciences were not themselves pious.

---

52. *Comm. Psalm* 107:43, CTS 11:266.
53. *Comm. Psalm* 147:15, CTS 12:301.
54. *Comm. Psalm* 147:15, CTS 12:301.

Calvin has another way of "rising higher" that does not make God the first principle of all natural science. This has to do with the phenomenon of wonder. Calvin sees all inquiry about the universe as being initiated by wonder, and such investigations are at their best when they also end in wonder. Calvin sees this wonder in the way that David marvels over his creation by God. "From this particular instance David is led to refer in general to all the works of God, which are just so many wonders fitted to draw our attention to him. The true and proper view to take of the works of God, as I have observed elsewhere, is that which ends in wonder."[55] Calvin was especially struck by the capacity of the science of astrology to awaken wonder in those who study it, since they encounter therein the wisdom, goodness, and power of God.

> And, indeed, astrology may justly be called the alphabet of theology; for no one can with a right mind come to the contemplation of the celestial framework, without being enraptured with admiration at the display of God's wisdom, as well as of his power and goodness. I have no doubt, then, but that the Chaldeans and the Egyptians had learned that art, which in itself is not only to be approved, but is also most useful, and contains not only the most delightful speculations, but ought also to contribute much towards exciting in the hearts of men a high reverence for God.[56]

However, Calvin was convinced that all our investigations into the nature of the universe should produce in us the kind of wonder that reduces us to nothing, not in light of what we do not know but precisely in light of what we have come to know and to understand.

> For though it may seem a light matter, when he says, that the world was constituted by the wisdom of God, yet were any one to apply his mind to the meditation of God's wisdom in the abundance of all fruits, in the wealth of the whole world, in the sea, (which is included in the world,) it could not, doubtless, be, but that he must be a thousand times filled with wonder and admiration: for the more carefully we attend to the consideration of God's works, we ourselves in a manner vanish into

---

55. *Comm. Psalm* 139:13, CTS 12:214.
56. *Comm. Jeremiah* 10:1–2, CTS 18:8.

nothing; the miracles which present themselves on every side, before our eyes, overwhelm us.[57]

All sciences should so fill us with wonder and astonishment that we are reduced to nothing, and so learn humility, as well as gratitude. This is why Calvin wanted every pious person to meditate on the works of God in the universe, and he thought that God established the Sabbath precisely to encourage us in such contemplation.

> This is, indeed, the proper business of the whole life, in which men should daily exercise themselves, to consider the infinite goodness, justice, power, and wisdom of God, in this magnificent theater of heaven and earth. But, lest men should prove less sedulously attentive to it than they ought, every seventh day has been especially selected for the purpose of supplying what was wanting in daily meditation.[58]

Conclusion

We can no longer insist that natural philosophy must start with the principle that everything in nature depends on the will of God, even though Galileo and Newton would have agreed with this statement. Science now insists that God cannot be brought in as a cause to explain natural phenomena. However, the investigations of science since the day of Calvin have done nothing to reduce the sense of wonder and astonishment we can experience in our increased understanding of the universe in which we live. And for the pious, this experience of wonder and astonishment increases and strengthens their awareness of the presence of God and creates in them the humility that is proper to genuine piety and, I would say, to genuine science. For this reason, Calvin not only claims that a scientist can be a Christian but also that every Christian should seek to become a scientist, for piety itself leads us to seek a deeper appreciation of the God who created this immense and astonishing universe.

---

57. *Comm. Jeremiah* 51:15–16, CTS 21:220.
58. *Comm. Genesis* 2:3, CTS 1:105–6.

Chapter FOUR

Not Knowing Creation

ANDREW B. TORRANCE

It is a truism to say that most scientists avoid reference to God when explaining the history, structure, and behaviour of the natural world. Natural-scientific research focuses on those things that can be studied directly within the created order. Accordingly, when scientists observe something that appears to present an anomaly (water turning into wine, walking on water, bodily resurrection), they do not jump to the conclusion that "God did it." Such a conclusion would function as a "science stopper"—that is, it would allow scientific investigation to give up too quickly when faced with curiosities contrary to the existing scientific worldview. So if a person appears to have been healed in a way that eludes medical explanation, contemporary science will not see "God answered our prayers" as a satisfactory alternative. Instead, such healing will invite further empirical, scientific investigation that might benefit others with similar illnesses.[1]

In order to challenge such an approach, one would have to provide evidence of the most extraordinary kind. It would have to be such that it generated a wide consensus within the scientific community not only that God exists but also that God can be recognised from within a non-Christian worldview to be actively impacting on the operations and applications of the laws of nature—laws that science assumes (and must assume) in order to function. Put simply, if the secular scientific community cannot find empirical evidence that God exists and is active in particular events, then it should not be expected to interpret anomalies as occurrences that have been made possible by special divine action.

---

1. As one of the editors of this volume, I should make it clear that my position in this chapter is my own and should not be taken to represent the views of any of the other contributors to this volume or the next.

Given the hiddenness of God,[2] it has become commonplace for scientists (both theistic and nontheistic) to go a step further to avoid the possibility of reference to God. They adopt methodologies that are committed to studying the world on the following suppositions or assumptions: (1) that God does not exist—*methodological atheism* (hereafter MA); and/or (2) that the reality of the universe, as it can be accessed by empirical enquiry, is to be explained solely with recourse to natural phenomena—*methodological naturalism* (hereafter MN).[3]

One of the things that we need to be clear about from the outset is that MA and MN only insist on atheism or naturalism for the purpose of "disciplinary method."[4] In this respect, they are distinct from metaphysical naturalism or metaphysical atheism, which insist on atheism or naturalism *tout court*—not only for the purpose of systematising scientific method. It is because the MNist or MAist (persons who adopt MN or MA) only assume naturalism or atheism for the purposes of scientific method that it has become commonplace for many Christians to view it as an appropriate methodology for the sciences as well as many other areas of scholarship. It is seen to be a helpful way to focus attention on natural phenomena, *while* bracketing out the Creator and createdness of these phenomena and, in particular, the irregular ways that such a Creator might act in creation (i.e., miracles).

Nancey Murphy, for example, asserts that we should embrace an approach to the natural sciences that is "methodologically atheistic," adding "Christians and atheists alike must pursue scientific questions in our era without invoking a creator."[5] More recently, in a chapter titled "Does Your God Need Stage Props? On the Theological Necessity of Methodological Atheism," Ronald Osborn argues that MA is necessary not only to protect science from religion but also

---

2. For the purposes of this chapter, the hiddenness of God refers to the fact that we cannot directly observe or experience God (*qua* God) or God's activity (*qua* God's activity) in the natural world.

3. I should acknowledge that there are many different definitions of MN, some of which are not open to some of the critiques that I shall be advancing. For example, there are some people, like Kathryn Applegate, who would seem to advocate a Christian version of MN. However, in the modern world, the term *naturalism* does not generally bring to mind a philosophy that is compatible with theism. For this reason, I would agree with scholars such as Alan Padgett and Denis Alexander that the best way forward is to stop using the term MN. See Alan Padgett, "Practical Objectivity: Keeping Natural Science Neutral," in *The Blackwell Companion to Science and Christianity*, ed. J. B. Stump and Alan Padgett (Malden, MA: Wiley-Blackwell, 2012), 96–97; Denis Alexander, *Creation or Evolution: Do We Have to Choose?* (Grand Rapids: Monarch, 2008), 185–87.

4. Paul De Vries, "Naturalism in the Natural Sciences," in *Christian Scholar's Review* 15, no. 4 (1986): 389.

5. Nancey Murphy, "Phillip Johnson on Trial," in *Perspectives on Science and Christian Faith* 45, no. 1 (1993): 33–34.

to protect theology from diminishment, trivialization, and manipulation by scientists.[6]

When one listens to the many Christian advocates of MA or MN, it becomes clear that there are some very understandable reasons for adopting MA or MN. In what follows, I shall consider some of these reasons. However, my primary endeavor will be to offer a critique of the Christian commitment to MA or MN, which is a key obstacle for the task of knowing creation *qua* creation in the conversation about science and religion. When a Christian commits to MN or MA in the name of science, she holds that, *in her capacity as a scientist*, she cannot know the natural order as creation. To recognise the createdness of the natural order, one's systematic approach must remain open to the possibility that there is something (or someone) beyond nature, which (or who) creates the natural order. This is precisely what atheism or naturalism rules out *a priori*.

In this chapter I argue that MN and MA are not methodologies a Christian scientist should adopt. I contend that the Christian should recognize that her faith in the Creator gives her a deeper, fuller, and more accurate understanding of the history, structure, and behaviour of the natural world—by providing, not least, a wider and more integrated "compass" for the process of interpretation. As such, this faith is something that she should continue to embrace in her capacity as a scientist, thereby allowing her to view science as a Christian vocation. I shall conclude that the Christian scientist should always endeavor to study the natural order as a Christian knowing creation.

Why Adopt MA or MN?

I do not have the space to examine every reason a Christian might have for endorsing MN or MA, so instead I offer a critical reflection on what I consider to be the three main reasons.

To Prevent Haphazard Reference to Special Divine Action

Perhaps the main reason for endorsing MN is to distance science from those who refer to God in ways that can undermine scientific progress by being too quick to "stop science" with the explanation "God did X"—like

---

6. Ronald Osborn, *Death Before the Fall: Biblical Literalism and the Problem of Animal Suffering* (Downers Grove, IL: IVP Academic, 2014), 72.

some within the Intelligent Design (ID) movement. Adopting MA and MN is a clear way to avoid such an approach.

While this is a valid concern, it is imperative for us to realise that MN and ID are false binaries. The Christian scientist is not faced with an either-or choice between the two. She could advocate a theologically humble approach. So, for example, if a fellow Christian scientist were to make haphazard references to special divine action,[7] a Christian could suggest that, for the purposes of their particular research program, they should assume that they are unable to discern such action because, if it is taking place, it is not discernible by way of their particular mode of empirical study. Such an approach can restrict explicit claims to special divine agency without excluding the existence and action of God: it is characterized by a theological appreciation of the limits of human perception rather than the *a priori* exclusion of an agency beyond nature. In this way, there is no problem with the Christian scientist continuing to embrace her belief in God in her capacity as a scientist—there would be no need to commit to MN.

To Respect the Transcendence of God

In a chapter subtitled, "On the Theological Necessity of Methodological Atheism," Ronald Osborn writes:

> The move to exclude "natural theology" from science was first championed not by Darwin but by Isaac Newton and Robert Boyle, who saw that the metaphysical mixing of modern empirical methods with religious teleology resulted not only in bad science but also in a corruption of true faith. God's transcendence *theologically* requires a radical distinction between God as Creator and the operations of the universe through secondary causes that can be empirically observed and tested through inductive and deductive methods. Methodological atheism was necessary,[8] Newton and Boyle maintained, not to protect science from

---

7.   Here, we could take "haphazard references to special divine action" to mean unbiblical references to an occasional divine action that would be more specific than references to the general providence with which God upholds the regularities of the natural order. There is a much bigger conversation to be had about the relationship between the natural sciences and special divine action. However, that would take us beyond the scope of this chapter.

8.   I must admit that I find it very difficult to see how a concern "to protect theology from diminishment, trivialization and manipulation by scientists" makes MA a necessity.

religion but to protect theology from diminishment, trivialization and manipulation by scientists.[9]

It is orthodox for a Christian to believe that God is transcendent and cannot be studied as a part of the furniture of the world—as a visible object that is "pegged out to view." This means that there are clear theological reasons for the Christian scientist to assume that it should be normative for her research to be characterised by a complete absence of specific theological reference. She should recognise that God's activity should not be confused with the regular and immanent processes of the natural world, and which are the subject-matter of normal scientific enquiry. If the world is not God's body and the laws of the created order are not to be identified with God's free agency, then the Christian should not see God as directly accessible to or the direct object of empirical, scientific study. As such, for some, MA or MN can be seen to be a way to avoid confusion between God and creation.[10]

While MN and MA might provide a straightforward way to avoid such confusion, it should be quite clear that they are not the only way to do so. An alternative would be to allow Christian commitment to God's transcendence to inform one's scientific method. By so doing, the Christian scientist could draw a clear line between her scientific practice and her theological understanding while continuing to allow her (in her capacity as a scientist) to study the natural world as creation. It also allows her to remain open to the possibility that the transcendent God may engage with creation in ways that can make a difference in how we understand the history of the natural order.

To Focus the Scientific Task

Another reason for MA or MN is quite simply the focused nature of scientific work. To select a field of scientific research in which one's analysis and experimentation will take place will inevitably involve censoring or selecting out of consideration areas of enquiry that do not pertain to the precise

---

9. Osborn, *Death Before the Fall*, 72. It is worth mentioning that Osborn risks being anachronistic here because he suggests that "MA" was maintained by Newton and Boyle three hundred years before the specific term "MA" (or "MN") was first formally used. See Ronald L. Numbers, "Science without God: Natural Laws and Christian Beliefs," in *When Science and Christianity Meet*, ed. David C. Lindberg and Ronald L. Numbers (Chicago: University of Chicago Press, 2003), 320n2.

10. In addition to Ronald Osborn, see also Kathryn Applegate, "A Defense of Methodological Naturalism," in *Perspectives on Science and Christian Faith* 65, no. 1 (2013): 37.

operations of one's study. For example, neuroscience, marine biology, and political science are unlikely to shed light on cardiothoracic research, so it makes sense for the person researching in this particular field to set aside the results of work done in these other fields. However, no scientist would dream of suggesting that one should, therefore, adopt a methodology that assumes that none of these disciplines have any bearing on the larger picture of the world within which one's particular form of science operates.

Just because a scientist focuses her attention on a domain where neither God nor God's activity can be directly known does not mean that her methodology needs to be naturalistic. Denis Alexander writes,

> We don't call Christian accountants "naturalistic" because of the absence of theological terminology as they check the company accounts, any more than we expect our doctor to use theological language when she tells us that we've got the flu, or the mechanic to refer to biblical texts when servicing our car. The absence of specific references to God does not render our lives suddenly "naturalistic."[11]

Again, would it not be more consistent for a Christian scientist to commit to a methodology that requires her to acknowledge the hiddenness of God rather than a naturalism that rules out *a priori* the possibility of recognising that there is a God to bracket out? If she wanted to be more neutral, she could simply call such a method "natural scientific method," which would be more neutral than MA or MN, and then elaborate precisely what she means by it. A term such as this would allow both the theist and the atheist to avoid reference to God while allowing them to maintain their different reasons for doing so.[12]

Why Not Adopt MA or MN?

While it may not be the case that a person needs to adopt MA or MN to address the above three concerns, a case could be made that MA or MN provide the most straightforward way to address them. Rather than expecting a Christian to have a nuanced theological understanding of the natural order

---

11. Alexander, *Creation or Evolution*, 186.
12. For the Christian, I would argue, these reasons would make her resistant to adopting a methodology that goes under the name "MA" or "MN."

and the Creator-creature distinction, one could argue that it is just more straightforward to expect the Christian scientist *qua* scientist to adopt a method that has the restrictions of naturalism or atheism. So it is important for us to be clear about some of the specific problems with MA and MN that face the Christian scientist who adopts them.

In this section, I consider three reasons why MN or MA might be problematic for the Christian scientist. I shall primarily be addressing MN because it is more popular than MA. Nonetheless, my arguments against MN also apply to MA.

Recognising God's Existence Matters for Understanding the Nature, Behaviour, and History of the Natural World

It is a part of Christian orthodoxy to maintain that there are actual occurrences that take place within the natural order that we need to explain with recourse to special divine action (e.g., the incarnation, the miracles of Jesus, the resurrection, and Pentecost). It is not only past events, however, that Christians explain this way. There is strong biblical precedent for thinking that the very recognition of the truth of the Christian faith requires special divine action. The New Testament suggests that it is in and through the creative and transformative presence of God that persons receive the eyes to see and ears to hear what flesh and blood cannot discern (Matt 16:17).[13] Still further, Christian orthodoxy maintains more general claims about the natural order that involve a recognition of God's activity: divine action explains why there is something rather than nothing, why there is order in the cosmos that is intelligible for science, and why there are particular creatures who reflect the image of God.

By believing in God the Creator, the Christian scientist can have confidence in the order and regularity of the world—it is not simply assumed but affirmed. This belief is able to help the scientist trust in the existence of objective truth, logic, and reason. Additionally, this belief can allow her to recognize, when faith requires, that certain occurrences and arrangements are the result of special divine action (which she can bracket out from her scientific consideration if she so chooses). In these respects, the Christian's faith can benefit her scientific study.

If the Christian consistently commits to MN, however, she needs to explain all of the above without recourse to any nonnatural being (at least while

---

13. See also, e.g., John 16:7–14; Acts 2:38; 5:32; Rom 8:5–16; Gal 2:20; 4:6; Eph 2:4–8; 3:16–17.

adopting MN). In the name of naturalistic science, no recourse can be made to a Creator who is hidden from scientific investigation to help us understand the natural world and its history for the simple reason that MN rules out any such reference. As Peter Harrison argues, MN is characterized by a "commitment to study the world as if God plays no part in the secondary causes of nature."[14] It is hard to see why such a position would not be problematic at least sometimes for the Christian scientist.

The selective practice of MN is inconsistent

But what if the Christian scientist were only to adopt MN when she believed that she did not need to refer to God—for example, when she is studying the behaviour of bacteria or black holes? Could MN not simply be a method to help scientists focus attention on natural phenomena *while* bracketing out the Creator and createdness of these phenomena? T. F. Torrance writes,

> The acceptance of the contingent, autonomous nature of the world called for the development of autonomous modes of scientific inquiry appropriate to it. This involved what might be called a "methodological secularism," i.e., an orientation in which science bracketed the world off from its relation to God, in order to investigate its nature for its own sake. That was certainly in line with the renewed stress of the Reformation upon God's creation of the world out of nothing, and of the primacy of his grace in which God turns toward the world he has made, which summons man to join him in that movement of his grace toward the world, and that had the effect of making natural scientific investigation of the world part of man's obedience to the Creator.[15]

In addition, Conor Cunningham asserts that MN "is the approach that science must take when it engages with the universe insofar as it will fail to make any progress unless it brackets out the divine. . . . [Therefore, a] certain methodological naturalism is commonsensical."[16]

Torrance and Cunningham seem to maintain that secularism or naturalism

---

14. Peter Harrison, "Introduction," in *The Cambridge Companion to Science and Religion*, ed. Peter Harrison (Cambridge: Cambridge University Press, 2010), 12.

15. T. F. Torrance, *Divine and Contingent Order* (Edinburgh: T&T Clark, 1998), 41.

16. Conor Cunningham, *Darwin's Pious Idea: Why the Ultra-Darwinists and Creationists Both Get It Wrong* (Grand Rapids: Eerdmans, 2010), 265–66.

have a key role to play when it comes to systematising scientific method. At the same time, they would both acknowledge that bracketing out God will not always be appropriate when it comes to understanding the behaviour, structure, and history of this world. They would want to limit the practice of MN (or methodological secularism) to the field of scientific enquiry, in such a way as to allow Christians to refer to God when it comes to a nonscientific understanding of reality. With Robert O'Connor, they would affirm that science can permit "further, nonscientific appeal to the divine as the ultimate and sustaining source, meaning, and purpose of all natural phenomena."[17] O'Connor elaborates,

> The goal of *natural*[18] science should be conceived as aiming toward an understanding of natural entities, processes, events, states of affairs, relationships, and such, a*s natural entities, processes, events, states of affairs, relationships, and such,* i.e., explaining those phenomena from start to finish in natural terms. This does not commit the scientist to the view that all phenomena can be given a *complete* natural explanation (or indeed any), but only to the view that scientific explanations account for natural phenomena as far as they can in *completely* natural terms.[19]

What O'Connor proposes is a conditionalising approach whereby the scientist determines to operate within a circumscribed domain, assuming that scientific explanation within that domain proceeds in "completely natural terms."[20]

O'Connor's account of MN is about as theologically sensitive as it is possible for it to be. He presents MN as a methodology that serves to interpret the natural order in its own terms. MN is the method of natural science, and God is not an object of natural science. Yet there appears to be an inconsistency in his account, which raises a question: Is he more theologically sensitive than a standard account of MN would allow him to be?

O'Connor suggests that scientific accounts like MN can permit "further, nonscientific appeal to the divine as the ultimate and sustaining source, meaning, and purpose of all natural phenomena."[21] However, to be clear, MN

---

17. Robert O'Connor, "Science on Trial: Exploring the Rationality of Methodological Naturalism," in *Perspectives on Science and Christian Faith*, 49 (1997): 16.

18. Emphasis mine on this word, but the rest of the emphasis in this paragraph is original.

19. O'Connor, "Science on Trial," 17.

20. O'Connor, "Science on Trial," 17.

21. O'Connor, "Science on Trial," 16.

is an approach to science that develops scientific accounts that are essentially naturalistic insofar as they have been developed by MN. To the extent that a scientific account is naturalistic, it cannot permit any appeal or reference to the reality of God. Moreover, when a scientist adopts MN, she is unable to recognise that there is a God to discount. This means that, contrary to what Torrance, Cunningham, and O'Connor suggest, *it is not secular or naturalistic science that brackets out God*. Rather, it is the theistic scientist who brackets out belief in God in order to practice science naturalistically (or secularly).[22] And only the scientist *qua* theist, who is not committed to MN, can make nonscientific appeal to God by moving from the domain of scientific understanding to the domain of theological understanding. However, since the scientific account of the MNist would be naturalistic and her theological account would be theological, the two would be incompatible with one another. What the Christian scientist can do, as O'Connor suggests, is reinterpret her scientific account within a larger theological framework. However, if she does this, she essentially changes the nature of her scientific account—it is no longer systematised by naturalism.

For the scientist who wants to adopt MN selectively, the supposed commitment to MN is contained within an overarching methodological agenda that is logically incompatible with MN. That is, MN would be subordinate to a more foundational Christian methodology that determines precisely when and where it is appropriate or inappropriate to bracket God out of the equation. This being the case, it is hard to see how such a scientist would be consistently practicing MN.

Having made this point, I do not think that a Christian scientist repositioning her scientific account within a theological framework will necessarily make any practical difference to the scientific account itself. Indeed, I would argue that it is extremely unlikely to make a difference—unless she is studying something that she believes requires reference to special divine action, such as Christ's incarnation, resurrection, or Christian conversion. That said, it does influence how the Christian understands her relationship to the scientific task. And there is no reason for the Christian scientist to commit to a methodology that is incompatible with her understanding of the natural order as creation.

---

22. To be clear, there is nothing inherently naturalistic about science. It is true that there are limits to the empirical sciences. It is also true that a scientist should be aware of these limits. However, an awareness of these limits should not require the scientist to commit to disregarding possibly significant factors beyond these limits, as is the case with MN.

It Is Not Scientific to Disregard Anomalies Because They Do Not Conform to Standard Scientific Method

The fact that MN can run into problems is not missed by many Christian advocates of MN. For example, when making a case for MN, Kathryn Applegate notes that "the Bible reveals a God who *normally* accomplishes his purposes through means such as natural processes or human activity."[23] She acknowledges that there are occurrences that take place within the history of the natural world that cannot be adequately explained by MN. For similar reasons, John Hare comments, "Methodological naturalism is reasonable for *most* of science, since we cannot put God in the lab."[24] The problem for the Christian MNist is that she is committed to a methodology that does not allow for the recognition of key events within the contingent order that she recognizes have profound significance (i.e., every single event that requires to be identified with God's involvement in human history).

So why precisely would this be a problem for a naturalistic scientific method? For most scientists, a methodology that rules out the possibility of providing an adequate account of certain occurrences (within the natural order) would not be considered an adequate methodology. A scientific approach should allow anomalies (that cannot be explained away or reduced to error) to challenge and thereby revise their interpretative models and methodology. Science cannot ignore or rule out anomalies simply because they do not fit with standard scientific practice. Of course, MN does not constitute a problem for metaphysical naturalists, since they rule out *a priori* any involvement of God in any facet of reality. Christians, however, do claim that reference to God is required to make sense of certain occurrences within the natural order. So under certain circumstances Christians will recognize that MN will undermine their interpretation of the history of the natural order.

To account for this, Applegate notes that science cannot "capture all of reality, including the possibility of God's direct action in natural history" and considers miracles to be "the blind spot of science."[25] The trouble with MN, however, is that it does not allow the Christian scientist *qua* scientist to recognize miracles as blind spots. MN requires the Christian scientist *qua*

---

23. Applegate, "A Defense of Methodological Naturalism," 38.

24. John Hare, "Evolutionary Theory and Theological Ethics," in *Studies in Christian Ethics* 25, no. 2 (2012): 247, emphasis mine.

25. Applegate, "A Defense of Methodological Naturalism," 41.

scientist to offer naturalistic explanations of these spots that are going to be inconsistent with her Christian understanding of creation. Again, therefore, the Christian would need to operate with an overarching methodology that would allow her to determine what counts as a blind spot and thereby avoid adopting MN when it would undermine her Christian understanding. If she were to take this approach, however, her scientific study would not consistently be characterized by MN. Rather, it would be characterized by a methodology that sometimes required her to employ to naturalistic criteria (e.g., when she believed that a Christian scientist was making inappropriate references to God) and, at other times, required her to employ nonnaturalistic criteria (e.g., when she believed that a miracle had genuinely taken place).

If this is the case, it is hard to see why a Christian scientist should not advocate a scientific methodology that permits her to maintain her Christian perception—a methodology that would never require her to misexplain the blind spots. Again, this would not mean that her interpretation of the natural order would need to appear any different from the naturalist most of the time—only when her Christian understanding requires this of her.

Am I Confusing MN with Metaphysical Naturalism?

One way an advocate of MN might respond to my concerns would be to say that I am confusing MN with metaphysical naturalism. I have already acknowledged that there is a difference between the two. At the same time, however, I suspect it is not as easy to separate the two as is often suggested. For instance, if a scientist is consistently adopting MN (methodological *naturalism*), there will be no difference between her explanations and those of the metaphysical naturalist. The only difference between the two is that the MNist may be committed to different metaphysical assumptions that she chooses to set aside in order to adopt MN and that determine when MN should and should not apply.

It is sometimes assumed that MN is metaphysically neutral because it is only concerned with the scientific practice of interpreting natural phenomena. But this is just not the case. The person who adopts MN assumes that naturalism is the most appropriate philosophy for systematizing scientific investigation—over against a philosophy that is compatible with theism. And that is not a metaphysically neutral assumption. When a person advocates a particular methodology for approaching a particular object, she will normally do so because she has metaphysical views about the nature of that particular object—about how that object relates to reality and the nature of the reality the object is in. For example, a scholar of literature is likely to have metaphysical reasons for not adopting methodological materialism to interpret Tolstoy. She is likely to believe, for example, that *War and Peace* has inherent qualities that transcend the materiality that makes up the pages of the book. Therefore, she is likely to believe that these inherent qualities make this book more valuable than a block of wood—even though a block of wood will be more effective at fueling a fire. To believe this is normally to acknowledge that there is more to reality than the purely material. As such, she has metaphysically informed reasons for thinking that it is inappropriate to interpret this book by adopting methodological materialism.

Similarly, I would argue that there should be metaphysical reasons for the Christian scientist to think that her Christian understanding is more appropriate for systematizing her interpretation of the natural order than a naturalistic understanding. At the very least, the Christian scientist should hesitate to think that her Christian understanding would undermine her scientific understanding of the world—to the extent that she feels the need to adopt MN.[26]

The Christian believes that the natural world is created, ordered, and maintained by a God who acts in its history in special ways. As I have been arguing, there is no reason for the Christian scientist (in her capacity as a scientist) to think that maintaining these beliefs would get in the way of the scientific task. Therefore, the Christian scientist *qua* scientist should commit to a scientific methodology that allows her to maintain her Christian convictions, even if they are not going to make any practical difference to her field of study. She should engage in the natural sciences with a humble awareness that God is hidden from empirical science rather than with the assumption that God has nothing to do with the natural order.

As Denis Alexander writes, there are good theological reasons for seeking to ensure "that the scientist does not invoke God as an explanation for things

---

26. A person does not commit to a methodology that discounts certain explanations unless she thinks that it is possible for such explanations to get in the way of her particular practice. If, for example, a person said that a scientist should commit to methodological vegetarianism, this would come with the suggestion that eating meat could somehow potentially get in the way of scientific practice.

in the course of his or her daily scientific research."[27] But for Alexander the Christian does not need to take up MN to do this; he is rightly concerned that MN comes with "the unstated implication . . . that the Christian will somehow leave their faith in God behind the laboratory door."[28] Reflecting on his own scientific practice, Alexander writes, "When I walk into my laboratory I do not suddenly stop believing in God—far from it, I go in as the Christian explorer looking forward to uncovering more of the wonders of God's world. The more we discover, the more we glorify God by revealing his thoughts in the created order. . . . Naturalism is the philosophy that there is no God in the first place, so only an atheist can provide truly naturalistic explanations for anything."[29]

By taking Alexander's approach, the Christian can view science as a Christian vocation and can assume the complete compatibility of her faith and scientific practice—she can study creation with an integrity of understanding. And if, for example, a (pseudo)scientific theory is advanced that is essentially incompatible with her Christian faith, because of its naturalistic assumptions, that same intellectual integrity can lead her to call this theory into question.[30]

From the other side of things, the Christian should be able to allow certain scientific discoveries to make a difference to her Christian beliefs (e.g., how she interprets the Genesis creation sagas). If the Christian believes that her Christian beliefs correspond to the reality of the natural world, then the Christian should not feel obliged to bracket out her Christian beliefs in order to participate in the world of science. As Tom McLeish writes,

> A theological tradition is all-encompassing. In Judaism and Christianity the universe itself carries theological weight as God's creation, it carries rational weight as our human environment—with both positive and painful consequences. Keeping science and theology at arm's length artificially limits their domains of discussion—and this is inconsistent with the range of both of them.[31]

27. Alexander, *Creation or Evolution*, 186.
28. Alexander, *Creation or Evolution*, 186.
29. Alexander, *Creation or Evolution*, 185–86.
30. For a discussion of such pseudoscientific theories, see my article "Should a Christian Adopt Methodological Naturalism?" *Zygon* 52, no. 3 (2017): 691–725.
31. Tom McLeish, *Faith and Wisdom in Science* (Oxford: Oxford University Press, 2014), 168.

To conclude this section, my argument is quite simple: the Christian scientist should consistently seek to interpret the natural world by embracing all that she knows. At the very core of the Christian faith is the claim that God not only exists but has brought this created order into existence as an intelligible reality. Furthermore, the Christian believes that God is actively involved in history, creating a faith that can serve as a witness to God's creative, providential, and redemptive activity. For this reason, there should be a difference between the way in which the Christian scientist and the naturalistic scientist approach and interpret the structure, behavior, and history of the natural world.[32]

Conclusion

When a Christian scientist commits to MN or MA, she commits to not knowing the natural world as creation—at least while committed to MN or MA. There are understandable reasons for making this move. However, MN and MA are not the only options. I have argued that there are clear Christian ways to systematise one's scientific method in a way that avoids the problems MN seeks to avoid. Moreover, I have made the case that the Christian should be able to see her faith as serving her scientific study of the behaviour, structure, and history of the natural world. This has led me to the conclusion that the scientific methodology of a practicing Christian should not be divorced from what she believes she knows or the fundamental ontological claims involved. Rather, the Christian scientist *qua* scientist should seek to study the natural world as a Christian studying creation.

To avoid leaving this chapter too open-ended, I shall now close with five points concerning the Christian's relationship to the natural sciences.

(1) Unless God surprises the world, it is hard to imagine that the scientific world is going to make a discovery that will lead to consensus within the scientific community that a special event of divine action has occurred.

---

32. Since MN receives so much support from Christian thinkers, it would be helpful to consider ways in which MN can become a problem for some Christians in practice. While I do not have the space to discuss this here, I do discuss this in my article "Should a Christian Adopt Methodological Naturalism?" Here I propose that there are three particular problems that MN causes for Christianity: (1) it encourages scientists to develop theories that are essentially incompatible with Christianity, (2) it creates or underpins a culture that perceives there to be a tension between science and Christianity, and (3) it can prompt Christians to disregard the reality of God or, at least, perceive the reality of God as something that should not be taken seriously in certain domains of intellectual discourse.

(2) Christians should acknowledge that it is unlikely that divine action will ever be deemed an appropriate explanation within the natural sciences—unless, perhaps, the natural sciences are a part of life in the new creation. Accordingly, the Christian scientist *qua* scientist should avoid using distinctively theological language. Again, the Christian does not need to turn to naturalism to do this; she can have theological reasons for doing so.

The only reason a Christian scientist *qua* scientist should offer a theological explanation in her interpretation of the natural world is if her faith clearly requires her to do so: for example, if she is asked to explain the record of the resurrection or a process of conversion (events which, if Scripture has any credence at all, involve special divine action). Moreover, if she is ever required to offer a theological explanation to better understand the natural order, she should qualify her position with the statement "I believe this is the case" to make it clear that her faith has played a role in her assessment.

(3) If, however, the Christian needs to make this qualification, she should also try to be clear that God is not simply the object of her own subjective, personal belief. As a Christian, she believes that God reveals himself within the history of the natural world. That is, she believes that the Holy Spirit has given her the eyes to see that she has been created by a God who makes himself known to creation, and who comes to be with creation in the person of Jesus Christ. This recognition happens within the life of the church, as it is shaped by the practices of prayer, the Eucharist, the witness of its members, and the history of discernment to which this faith gives rise. As such, she can add the further qualification that for her a scientific hermeneutic that does not allow for this recognition is insufficient for developing a complete understanding of the behaviour, structure, and history of the natural order (or, more precisely, the contingent order).

(4) The Christian should be aware that MN is only appropriate for the person who is a naturalist.[33] As we have seen, the assumptions of MN and the associated criteria are not metaphysically neutral. As such, the person who commits to MN assumes that naturalism is the most appropriate system of understanding for shaping scientific method. So it is not at all clear why a person would make this assumption unless she is committed to naturalism.

---

33. However, insofar as naturalism is a metaphysical position, there is an inconsistency in even the naturalist committing to naturalism (methodological or metaphysical). See Michael Rea, *World Without Design: The Ontological Consequences of Naturalism* (Oxford: Oxford University Press, 2002), 59.

By taking up MN, the scientific world commits itself to assumptions that are no less beyond the scope of scientific enquiry than the existence of God. Consequently, if scientists really are devoted to better understanding the nature of reality *a posteriori*, it is ironical that they should so confidently exclude *a priori* a way of understanding the natural world that has the level of explanatory power possessed by theism. (This is especially the case since, as Quentin Smith notes, "If naturalism is true, then [the naturalist's] belief in naturalism is accidentally true.")[34] By shackling itself to naturalism, science makes the possibility that God exists and makes himself known to human beings become a threat to the entire scientific enterprise. For this reason, the Christian scientist has a duty not only to God but to science itself to discourage a commitment to MN.

(5) At the very least, the Christian scientist should encourage the secular world to practice science in a way that is less constraining. Again, something like methodological agnosticism might be appropriate here for the secular world. According to this method, the scientist acknowledges that her study of the natural world does not allow her to make theistic or naturalistic assumptions. As the Christian can demonstrate, anyone who argues that there is no room for theological assumptions in the methodology of the natural sciences must also argue, for the sake of consistency, that there is also no room for naturalistic or atheistic assumptions. This would make it more difficult for science to develop in a way that oversteps its boundaries and generate theories on the basis of *a priori* premises that are incompatible with theism and thus the Christian faith.

So what should we say about the Christian's approach to the sciences? While the Christian might encourage the secular scientist to adopt a methodology that is more neutral with respect to theology, the Christian herself should not embrace such a methodology. The reason for this is that the Christian believes that the truth claims that are definitive of the Christian faith are objectively true—that God exists and is personally present to human creatures. Intellectual and academic integrity requires, therefore, her to adopt a methodology compatible with her Christian understanding. By so doing, she can take up her scientific work as a Christian vocation; she can practice what she preaches—albeit in a way that recognises the hiddenness of God in

---

34. Quentin Smith, "The Metaphilosophy of Naturalism," in *Philo: A Journal of Philosophy* 4 (2001): 195–215.

the natural order. The finer details of what such a Christian approach to the sciences might look like would require its own discussion.[35] However, whatever we might say about this approach, it must not be systematized by naturalism.

How, then, might we describe the scientist who is a Christian? Let us call her a witness. By faith, she has been given eyes to discern what naturalistic science cannot discern—whose reference is beyond the scope and immediate perception of science. She has been given to see that the universe is created and ordered by the triune God who acts and reveals himself in history. Accordingly, she has been given to speak prophetically about the nature of reality (both created and eternal) in ways that are not possible to the person who reduces reality to natural phenomena. By so doing, she not only speaks of amorphous spiritual truths but of the one "Truth," who undergirds every facet of creation: the God who creates the universe to be a proclamation of his handiwork, a declaration of his glory, and a voice of witness that cannot be silenced.[36]

The Christian, moreover, speaks of a kingdom that has dawned and resides among us, albeit in a way that goes unnoticed by academic pursuits whose objective is restricted to the contingent rationality of a contingent order. With theological humility, the Christian acknowledges that God is not a part of the contingently rational, so she recognises that her capacity to speak faithfully penetrates beyond the range of her unaided scientific voice. However, she also realizes that the two are inseparable from one another because she is a creature whose language will always be bound to the contingently rational. As such, she recognizes that being attuned to the sciences serves a critical role in enabling

---

35. As Michael Rea notes, "[It is notoriously] hard to say exactly what methods are supposed to count as *the* methods of science." Rea, *World Without Design*, 67. It is worth mentioning that, in this book, Rea offers one of the best treatments of naturalism. He proposes that naturalism is best understood as "a stable shared research program, even though one and the same individual research program might count as naturalistic at one time but not another" (67). He qualifies, "A research program is a set of methodological dispositions—a way of conducting inquiry. One counts as a naturalist to the extent that one shares the relevant dispositions and conducts inquiry in the relevant way" (66). At the same time, he also thinks that "if naturalism is indeed a research program . . . there is no basis at all for saying that it is the sort of program that everybody, or every intelligent or right-thinking person, ought to adopt" (7). I am in complete agreement with Rea's account of naturalism. In line with Rea, I would argue that the Christian scientist should be one of the right-thinking persons who does not adopt naturalism as a research program. This, however, would not necessarily prevent the Christian from being involved in scientific research alongside a naturalist. It would be possible for the Christian to operate with a certain theological humility that, for purposes of open scientific research, could allow her to function in the same way as that naturalist. However, rather than assuming that there is no God, she would assume that any special divine causality at work could not be directly seen in an empirical study of the natural world and therefore cannot be incorporated into scientific explanations.

36. See Pss 8; 19:1; 66:4; 148; Luke 19:40.

her, first, to communicate with those engaged at that level. But, second, she also recognises that the sciences can serve a role in testing the deliverances of her faith—in making sure she is not misguided and making false claims about the nature and history of the world. Still further, her scientific voice is inseparable from her faithful voice because she is committed to the pursuit of truth—truth that includes the nature and purposes of the Creator as well as the nature and purposiveness of the created.

When the scientific world tells the Christian scientist that natural science is incompatible with the language of faith because science is essentially naturalistic, she must deny this. Consequently, she must deny the adoption of MN, lest she allow herself to become caught up in a culture seeking to silence her discourse and blind her to what she has been given to recognise. By resisting this culture, her scientific study can track the regularities of creation, trusting that her study is characterized by reason, logic, and a pursuit of objective reality that is only possible in a universe that has been created good through the loving purposefulness of the triune God.[37]

37. Word limitations mean that this chapter is not as nuanced and in-depth as some might like. For a more detailed discussion of the theme of this chapter, see my article "Should a Christian Adopt Methodological Naturalism?"

Chapter FIVE

Origins in Genesis

Claims of an Ancient Text in a Modern Scientific World

JOHN H. WALTON

I n the modern dialogue regarding science and Scripture, it is sometimes claimed that the two offer ultimately competing claims about origins. Before we can legitimately defend that such a conflict exists, we need to be certain that we have accurately assessed the actual claims each makes. What follows is the result of an analysis of the biblical claims based on a close reading of the biblical text and a comparative study with what is known from the texts of the ancient Near East concerning how people in that time thought about cosmic and human origins. As readers of Scripture we are committed to being faithful interpreters, and therefore we must do all we can to ascertain that we are reading the text of Scripture without imposing our own worldview or meaning on it.

Metaphysics and Interpretation

When we consider the claims made by the Bible (and its resulting theology) and those made on the basis of modern scientific understanding respectively, our first task is to consider the sorts of claims each is capable of making.[1] Much has been written on the limits of science and its underlying episte-mology, and I shall leave others who have expertise in that area to address

---

1. Some of the material in this section originally appeared in "'Natural' and 'Supernatural' are Modern Categories, Not Biblical Ones," BioLogos, 28 April 2015, http://biologos.org/blogs/guest/natural-and-supernatural-are-modern-categories-not-biblical-ones/.

that issue.[2] In general, however, the claims made from a scientific perspective assume a distinction between metaphysical categories traditionally labeled "natural" (processes that follow traceable laws of cause and effect describable and comprehensible through scientific investigation) or "supernatural" (events or phenomena that transcend or defy scientific analysis, prove impervious to scientific explanation, and are presumed to bypass natural processes). In recent centuries the former is often assumed to be free of divine involvement, while the latter requires divine intervention in the natural world—the disruption of natural laws—and is therefore associated with the miraculous. For the most part, science focuses on the "natural" by either simply neglecting what is claimed to be supernatural or, more aggressively, deducing that God has no role to play even if he exists. Scientific claims, then, are typically premised on this metaphysical divide, with the idea that if a natural explanation can be offered, then any biblical claims about God's involvement can be disregarded. This metaphysical assumption has dominated the way that the conversation has been structured. Contemporary thinking has a decided bias toward materialism and assumes that ultimate reality and the nature of existence are purely material, not spiritual.

Specifically with regard to origins, the scientific consensus sets forth explanations involving big bang cosmology and evolutionary models as evidence that all can be explained by means of natural laws (at least eventually), while those who value biblical explanations contest those claims based on their belief in the teaching that God is the Creator and that origins (whether cosmic or human) need to be understood with recourse to God's activity. As we turn our attention to the Bible, however, particularly to the Old Testament where the biblical origins account is located (Gen 1–2), we ought to begin by asking about the metaphysical categories current in the ancient world in general and among the Israelites in particular. Do they classify phenomena into categories that comport with our distinction between natural and supernatural?

Those who are inclined to reject scientific claims based on their understanding of biblical claims sometimes do so on the basis of their belief that when the Bible says that God did something, that event must therefore be categorized as

---

2. A seminal study on the limits of science is Delvin Ratzsch, *Science & Its Limits: The Natural Sciences in Christian Perspective*, 2nd ed., Contours of Christian Philosophy (Downers Grove, IL: InterVarsity, 2000). On epistemology see Ian Hutchinson, *Monopolizing Knowledge* (Belmont, MA: Fias, 2011).

supernatural and by definition unexplainable to natural laws. In other words they have accepted the metaphysical divide that natural and supernatural are mutually exclusive—if science can explain something, then God did not do it. I would propose instead that such a distinction between natural and supernatural is foreign to the ancient perspective reflected in Genesis. We cannot claim the Bible says something that makes no sense in the original context; it cannot make a categorical distinction if it does not have the categories.

It is common for people today to understand God's creative action in Genesis 2 as entailing the claim that, since he is portrayed as acting, he bypassed natural processes. This traditional perspective presupposes that the interests, language, and/or metaphysical concepts of the ancient Israelite author recognize a distinction between natural and supernatural. Ancient Israelites, however, believed that God is always active in the world in numerous and often undetectable ways; they did not have the categories of natural and supernatural.[3] The operations of the world that we consider regular, predictable, and able to be described in scientific ways would have been considered no less the works of God in the ancient world.[4] "Natural phenomena were indicative of divine decisions made in relation to human life."[5] They believed that when they planted a grain of wheat, wheat would grow. But God would be no less involved in that than if barley grew instead. In the same way, we cannot infer from Genesis whether God created humans naturally (through a process capable of scientific description) or supernaturally (beyond the regular and predictable cause-and-effect processes) just because God is identified as taking an active role. They believed God always took an active role. Since the Hebrew language does not have words that classify levels of causation the way we do today, the language of the Old Testament can't be used to confirm or deny our way of classifying cause and effect as either natural or as being the result of divine action alone. Since Israelites do not acknowledge a metaphysical divide, the actions of God cannot be metaphysically distinguished with regard to whether they bypassed natural processes or not. In their view everything has a metaphysical aspect to it.

---

3. Evidence is ubiquitous throughout the Old Testament. One example is Ps 139:13, in which God is seen as responsible for the development of each child in the womb.

4. Eclipses for example.

5. Beate Pongratz-Leisten, "Bad Kings in the Literary History of Mesopotamia and the Interface between Law, Divination, and Religion," in *From Source to History Studies on Ancient Near Eastern Worlds and Beyond*, ed. Salvatore Gaspa et al. (Münster: Ugarit, 2014), 527–48 (quote on 527–28).

When the Old Testament describes God's extraordinary involvement in the world, it is not to specify a supernatural event that is in defiance of natural, scientifically describable cause and effect. In the ancient world they undoubtedly understood certain phenomena as usual, ordinary, or normal. But they would not have therefore considered them as natural (i.e., scientifically describable; no involvement of God). If they have no such category as natural, then they cannot negate it ("nonnatural"). Generally, the Old Testament identifies phenomena as "signs and wonders." These stand as demonstrations both of God's power to deliver his people and of his covenantal love for them. At times, the text also emphasizes that the God of Israel, not another god, is in control of the events. Consider the plagues of Egypt. These demonstrated that God's power was superior to the gods of Egypt. The Old Testament focuses on the fact that he could do what no other god could do. This does not at all imply a distinction between supernatural events (God bypassing scientifically describable processes) and natural events (God acting through natural processes).

God is certainly capable of bypassing normal causes, but it is not safe to infer that he did so just because the Bible reports that he acted. Only the logistics of the scenario could lead us to that conclusion. For example, in the New Testament when Jesus turned water into wine, he obviously bypassed natural processes. The wine undoubtedly had a chemical structure like naturally made wine, but Jesus's act must have bypassed the usual natural processes. Some insist we should also believe that God bypassed natural processes in creating Adam. We could do so if the text or the scenario made it necessary to do so. At the wedding in Cana there is clearly no time and no means for the normal process to have taken place. As such, it is the scenario more than the language of the text that demands we understand that normal processes were bypassed. In Genesis 2 there is neither a distinction being drawn by the language nor a scenario that rules out a scientifically describable process for the creation of human beings.

Today, when we make distinctions between natural and supernatural activity in Scripture, not only do we push our modern categories into the Bible, but we also limit God's action. Once we designate some acts as "special" or "supernatural," we imply that other events which can be explained by normal cause and effect are not the acts of God. This drifts toward deism (distancing God from the operations of the cosmos) by suggesting that God only acts some of the time. This kind of thinking is responsible, at least in part, for bringing about the divide between science and the Bible. It is not the way the Israelites thought and it would be flawed for Christians to think about God in this way today.

Having laid the theoretical foundation by which we understand what sorts of claims the Bible and science make, we will now explore the specific claims that the Bible makes in Genesis 1 and 2 respectively. Just as it is important to understand the metaphysics of the ancient world, we must also understand the details of the text in the context of an implied author and implied audience situated in an ancient world—at least as best as we are able. We can accept the idea that the Bible was written for us, but we dare not think that it was written to us. We must proceed with the assumption that the text made sense in that ancient context and that it was meaningful in that culture. Only by employing an overly subjective hermeneutic would a person feel free to read modern scientific meaning between the lines and into the words of the ancient text. Although such interpreters may claim that God would have had such a sophisticated meaning in mind, the fact remains that if God's intentions are not conveyed in Scripture, such claims are neither falsifiable nor verifiable.

A close reading is called for. Such a reading will seek to set aside any translations that may have been affected by our modern cultural ideas so that we might develop the poetics of ancient cosmological thought. Beyond ancient cosmological interests and the lexical semantics of biblical Hebrew, it is important to have a working hypothesis relative to the rhetorical strategy of the book of Genesis, which entails a discussion of its compositional history and its implied audience.

Composition and Audience of Genesis

Communication in the ancient world was hearing-based, not text-based. The impact of the orality of the ancient world on the compositional history of the Bible cannot be overestimated.[6] Traditions were preserved and transmitted orally and only reduced to written documents (not yet the literary sources popular in redaction-criticism) occasionally for archives and scribal schools.[7]

---

6. For extensive discussion and introduction to the massive literature on the issue see John H. Walton and D. Brent Sandy, *The Lost World of Scripture: Ancient Literary Culture and Biblical Authority* (Downers Grove, IL: InterVarsity, 2013).

7. For detailed discussion of these issues see William M. Schniedewind, *How the Bible Became a Book: The Textualization of Ancient Israel* (Cambridge: Cambridge University Press, 2004); Donald B.

Such documents were copied over the centuries and existed alongside the ongoing oral preservation of the traditions. In this way, the traditions were not only preserved, but they were interpreted to serve the needs of successive generations. Authority figures were often seen as the source of these traditions, and capable tradents passed them from generation to generation.

We have little to inform us about when these archival documents began to be gathered together into literary works, eventually taking the rhetorical shape that we have in the book of Genesis. The rhetorical shape could conceivably have been dictated by the needs and situation of the implied audience of that time, but it could just as well have carried many of the earmarks and influences of the long transmission process. In this way, the final biblical book that we seek to interpret may plausibly be considered both in relation to the authority figure(s) at the fountainhead of the stream of a tradition as well as to the compilers who constructed the book for their audience. At times we may catch a glimpse of the *Sitz im Leben* of that target audience, but we see it no less than the inherent reflections of earlier shaping in its history. It is appropriate that we respect the complexity and sophistication of this process by confessing our limitations to reconstruct it. Its final form reflects a shaping that undoubtedly took place over centuries rather than just being the literary outcome of the last redactors. Consequently, even if we could conclusively locate the implied audience of the book in the postexilic period, for example, that would by no means make the book the invention or even the product of that period.

Rhetorically, the book of Genesis embodies the traditions of Israel with particular theological objectives in mind. The covenant with Abraham clearly takes center stage once the text moves into chapter twelve, but the first eleven chapters demonstrate that the covenant should be seen as playing a role in a larger picture. We often think of Genesis 1–11 as somehow introducing the covenant, but an alternative view sees the covenant contributing to the larger issue set forth in 1–11. In brief, such a proposal would see Genesis 1–3 as introducing the idea that the cosmos was ordered as sacred space—God dwelling among his people—and subsequently that order fell into jeopardy in

Redford, "Scribe and Speaker," in *Writings and Speech in Israelite and Ancient Near Eastern Prophecy*, ed. Ehud Ben Zvi and Michael H. Floyd (Atlanta: SBL, 2000), 145–218; Dominique Charpin, *Reading and Writing in Babylon* (Chicago: University of Chicago, 2010); and Karel van der Toorn, *Scribal Culture and the Making of the Hebrew Bible* (Cambridge, MA: Harvard, 2007).

what we have come to refer to as the fall. God's presence was lost, and Genesis 4–11 traces attempts to reestablish order (e.g., the cultural developments in Cain's line) as well as demonstrate the effects of disorder (e.g., sons of God, the flood). The Tower of Babel account in Genesis 11:1–9 shows the builders trying to reestablish God's presence in sacred space as they provide a ziggurat on which he can descend and manifest his presence in his temple as patron of his city.[8] But their initiative is tainted by selfish motivations (making themselves a name rather than making God's name), and God inaugurates a counterinitiative in the covenant. The covenant is intended to develop a relationship that will eventuate in his reestablishing sacred space and access to his presence as he lives among his covenant people (in the tabernacle, then the temple).[9] In this model, the rhetorical strategy of the book is focused on God's presence in sacred space. It is this idea that is introduced in Genesis 1–2, gives direction to the rest of the book (and indeed all of Scripture if we continue to trace it though incarnation, Immanuel, Pentecost, and new creation), and has relevance as a compelling issue throughout the history of Israel—not least the exilic and postexilic audience but by no means restricted to that time.

Genesis 1: Cosmic Sacred Space Initiated

Due to the aforementioned inclination of post-Enlightenment audiences to consider ultimate reality to be material in nature, readers of the Bible (whether modern or postmodern) have been inclined to read Genesis 1 as an account of the material origins of the cosmos.[10] Ancient audiences, lacking such a priority on the material cosmos, were more inclined to construct cosmologies with a focus on ordering and establishing roles and functions. Sumerian and Babylonian texts speak of the decrees of the gods that set up the ordered cosmos. Existence begins with acts of separating and naming, as is also evident in Genesis.

It is very difficult for present-day readers to consider Genesis 1–2 as focused on anything but material origins. The fact that the relevant Hebrew

---

8. J. H. Walton, "The Mesopotamian Background of the Tower of Babel and Its Implications," *Bulletin for Biblical Research* 5 (1995): 155–75. For more detailed discussion of the rhetorical shape of Genesis 4–11 and the role of the Tower of Babel as a transition to Genesis 12–50, see John H. Walton and Tremper Longman, *Lost World of the Flood* (Downers Grove, IL: InterVarsity, 2018).

9. J. H. Walton, *Lost World of Adam and Eve* (Downers Grove, IL: InterVarsity, 2015), 164–68.

10. Some paragraphs of this section are adapted from Walton, *Lost World of Adam and Eve*.

verbs used to convey the creative activity of God are translated by English terms such as "created," "made," and "formed" leads a modern reader to think intuitively of material processes.[11] When we add in Aristotelian levels of causation, it is easy for us to understand these verbs to specify the nature or extent of God's involvement. We can easily overlook the implication that God's speech (the most common of the verbs of creation in Genesis) has for understanding this cosmology in terms of the decrees of destiny known in the ancient world.[12]

Once we recognize that this is an ancient text, which has little interest or focus on material origins, we can arrive at an understanding of the text that is more in line with the way an Israelite would have perceived it. If Genesis 1 is seen to focus on ordering the cosmos as sacred space as it establishes roles and functions for the various inhabitants of the cosmos, we might consider that it is less interested in the building of a (cosmic) house than in making the cosmos a home—a home functioning for people and designed to be a place where God can dwell in the midst of his people and be in relationship with them.

To use a modern analogy, we could benefit from thinking about Genesis 1 as providing God's vision statement and mission statement for the cosmos.[13] His vision for the cosmos is that it would become sacred space by virtue of his presence here dwelling in relationship to his people. His mission statement in Genesis 1 is to order the cosmos to function for people, who have been given the role of co-order-bringers. Created in his image, they then serve alongside him to subdue and rule. In this analogy, the cosmos has been prepared (perhaps over eons) to fulfill this vision and carry out this mission. But in Genesis 1 the time has come to articulate this vision and mission and so to give direction to humanity and the cosmos so that they understand their created purpose. In that sense, it offers an account of cosmic *identity* rather than an account of scientific origins.

---

11. Detailed semantic analysis of the Hebrew terms underlying these translations has been done elsewhere, demonstrating that they are not inherently material in nature, but often appear in contexts where ordering or establishing functions is addressed. For "create" (*bara'*), see J. H. Walton, *Lost World of Genesis One* (Downers Grove, IL: InterVarsity, 2009), 36–43; J. H. Walton, *Genesis 1 as Ancient Cosmology* (Winona Lake, IN: Eisenbrauns, 2011), 127–33. For "made" (*'asah*) see Walton, *Genesis 1 as Ancient Cosmology*, 133–39; or J. H. Walton, *Lost World of Adam and Eve*, 30–33, 39–43. For "formed" (*yatsar*), see Walton, *Lost World of Adam and Eve*, 71–72.

12. Walton, *Genesis 1 as Ancient Cosmology*, 168–69.

13. Obviously, such an analogy is etic rather than emic, but I use it only as an analogy to help present-day readers to be able to think beyond their intuitive inclinations.

The sacred space concept derives from the idea that God rests on the seventh day. The account of the seventh day itself only indicates that God ceases (*shabbat*) his ordering activities. But other texts (e.g., Exod 20:11) indicate that God's rest also includes engaging in rest (*nuah*). Texts from the ancient Near East have no parallel to the observance of a weekly Sabbath outside of Israel, but the concept of divine rest on which it is based is commonplace.[14] The biblical theology of rest points us to an accurate understanding of the implications of divine rest that also happens to coincide with the ancient Near Eastern concept.

When God offers the Israelites rest (*nuah*) from their enemies (Deut 12:10; Josh 1:13; 21:44; 2 Sam 7:1; 1 Kgs 5:4), that rest refers to their being freed from invasion and conflict so they can live at peace and conduct their daily lives without disruption. It refers to achieving a state of order in society. Such rest is the goal of all the ordering activities that they undertake to secure their place in the land. This same concept is reflected in the New Testament (Matt 11:28; Heb 4:10–11).

Ordered stability is characteristic of God's rest in the cosmos just as it is in the temple. Temples in the ancient world were not just places for divine residence—they were the control centers of the cosmos.[15] God has established order, and now he is exercising control over his creation. The point is articulated in Psalm 132, where the temple is identified as God's dwelling place as well as his resting place (vv. 7–8). In verse 14 he sits enthroned in this resting place. This rule of God is consummated in creation on the seventh day and continues in perpetuity. Ezekiel 43:7 reiterates: "Son of man, this is the place of my throne and the place for the soles of my feet. This is where I will live among the Israelites forever" (NIV).

The seven-day account in Genesis can therefore be seen as indicating that God has ordered the cosmos to function for people. The order in the cosmos is maintained by God's presence and sustained by his rule because order emanates from him. His presence creates sacred space.

---

14. Walton, *Genesis 1 as Ancient Cosmology*, 110–19; Walton, *Lost World of Genesis One*, 71–76; V. Hurowitz, *I Have Built You an Exalted House*, JSOTS 115 (Sheffield: JSOT, 1992); M. Weinfeld, "Sabbath, Temple, and the Enthronement of the Lord—The Problem of the *Sitz im Leben* of Genesis 1.1–2.3," in *Festschrift Cazelles*, AOAT 212 (Neukirchen-Vluyn: Neukirchener, 1981), 501–12.

15. J. D. Levenson, "The Temple and the World," *Journal of Religion* 64 (1984): 275–98; M. Weinfeld, "Sabbath, Temple, and the Enthronement of the Lord"; B. Shafer, "Temples, Priests, and Rituals: An Overview," in *Temples of Ancient Egypt* (Ithaca, NY: Cornell, 1997), 1–8; M. B. Hundley, *Gods in Dwellings* (Atlanta: SBL, 2013).

This sort of thinking is present throughout the ancient Near East, where temple and cosmos were related ideas. The temple was viewed as a microcosm, the palace of the deity, and the center of his control.[16] Cosmologies, generally constructed to show the deity bringing order to the cosmos, often included temple-building accounts.[17] Once we realize the relationship between cosmos and temple, the seven-day structure of the account becomes more meaningful. When temples were built in the ancient world, the construction process prepared a building for God's presence. But the structure did not become a temple until its initiation. Both in the Bible and in the ancient Near Eastern accounts, seven days is an appropriate length for these significant inaugural celebrations.[18] We can consequently understand Genesis 1 in that light and conclude that the seven days inaugurates ordered sacred space and has nothing to do with the age of the earth. The seven days could only pertain to the age of the earth if Genesis 1 were an account of material origins. In contrast, as an account of God ordering the cosmos to be sacred space, it makes no claims about the age of the cosmos.

If the seven days are related to the inauguration of the cosmos as sacred space, it represents the period of transition from the material cosmos that has been prepared over the ages to being the place where God is going to relate to his people. It has changed from space to a place. The seven days is related to the home story not the house story—the purposeful ordering and establishing of roles and functions, not the production of material objects.

As modern readers, we have an impoverished understanding of the seven-day account when we fail to understand that it is all about sacred space. Without a clear understanding of day seven, the other six days are meaningless. In this home story, God is not only making a home for people, he is making a home for himself. If God does not rest in this ordered space, the six days are meaningless. The cosmos is not just a house; it is a home. Rich theology

16. Walton, *Genesis 1 as Ancient Cosmology*, 100–19.

17. Examples include The Sumerian Hymn to E-engura, Enki's Temple at Eridu, The Founding of Eridu, A prayer on a foundation brick of a temple, and, of course, *Enuma Elish*, the Babylonian Creation Epic. See R. Clifford, *Creation Accounts in the Ancient Near East and the Bible*, CBQMS 26 (Washington, DC: Catholic Biblical Association, 1994), 59–66; J. Assmann, *The Search for God in Ancient Egypt* (Ithaca, NY: Cornell, 2001), 35–36; R. B. Coote and D. R. Ord, *In the Beginning* (Minneapolis: Fortress, 1991), 6; M. Smith, "Like Deities, Like Temples (Like People)," in *Temple and Worship in Biblical Israel*, ed. John Day (New York: Continuum, 2005), 3–27; Walton, *Genesis 1 as Ancient Cosmology*, 107–9, 178–84.

18. Hurowitz, *I Have Built You an Exalted House*, 260–61, 275–76, 280–82; Walton, *Lost World of Genesis One*, 86–91; Walton, *Genesis 1 as Ancient Cosmology*, 181–82.

emerges from reading the chapters this way that is obscured by reading the text as a house story (about material origins). We learn that even though God has provided for us, it is not about us. The cosmos is not ours to do with as we please but God's place in which we serve as his vice-regents. Our subduing and ruling are done in full recognition that we are caretakers. Whatever humanity does should be directed toward bringing order out of nonorder. Our use of the environment should not impose disorder. This is not just a house that we inhabit; it is our divinely gifted home, and we are accountable for our use of it and work in it.

Relationship of Genesis 1 and 2

The seven-day account in Genesis 1:1–2:4 and the Eden account in Genesis 2:4–25 are separated by a formula that is a common structural element in the book. The formula features the term *toledot* (variously translated "account" or "story"; traditionally "generations"). Since the formula statement occurs ten other times throughout the book, we can study its rhetorical use to discover the narrative relationships that it governs. Upon analysis, we discover that in three cases the section after the formula is recursive of the section before the formula (e.g., the genealogies of Ishmael followed by the story of Isaac). The rest of them serve as a transition between an account and its sequel. That means that we have no reason to think that Genesis 2 is a recapitulation of day six. Nowhere else does the formula lead to a recapitulation. If Genesis 2 is something like a sequel, we would conclude that it is not intended as an account of material human origins. Genesis 1 conceivably addresses the creation of corporate humanity rather than focusing on only two (this would coincide with all ancient Near Eastern accounts as well as with the Genesis account of the creation of birds, fish, and animals as populations). In fact, Genesis 4, on three occasions, implies that there are other people around besides Adam's family.[19] If Genesis 2 is not recapitulating day six, we should inquire into what other purpose the account in Genesis 2 might serve.

---

19. Such a view is known and was widely circulated as early as the seventeenth century in the work of Isaac La Peyrère; it is discussed at length in W. J. van Asselt, "Adam and Eve as Latecomers: The Pre-Adamite Speculations of Isaac La Peyrère (1596–1676)," in *Out of Paradise: Eve and Adam and Their Interpreters*, ed. B. Becking and S. Hennecke (Sheffield: Phoenix Sheffield, 2011), 90–107. La Peyrère saw evidence not only in Genesis 4 but in Rom 5:14 in Paul's reference to those "who did not sin by breaking a command (that is, not like the transgression of Adam), as did Adam (that is, not like the transgression of Adam)." For summary case, see Walton, *Lost World of Adam and Eve*, 63–69.

Genesis 2: The Garden

Traditionally, readers have concluded intuitively that Genesis claims the first man was uniquely formed by God from the dust and the first woman was uniquely formed from the rib of the man. It is easy to see how readers would come to those conclusions. Acquaintance with ancient Near Eastern accounts of human origins, however, leads us to plausible alternatives. In these accounts whenever ingredients are mentioned (and they often are), the ingredients reflect something that is archetypal and ontological.[20]

In Genesis 2 the garden is the focus. It receives the most attention, and Adam and Eve are given the task of caring for the garden. It serves them (for food), but more important, they serve it (v. 15). Modern readers, unaware of the cognitive environment in the ancient world, are more inclined to think of Eden as a lovely environment for human enjoyment. Ancient readers would have been overwhelmed by the sense of the sacred. Eden is the center of sacred space, the Holy of Holies for the cosmos. God is there.[21] The seven-day account was designed to show God ordering the cosmos to be sacred space functioning for people. But it did not indicate where the center of sacred space would be. In Genesis 2 we see that Eden is the center of sacred space, and even though it serves people, people serve in sacred space to preserve its sacred status. It is the place where God dwells and where people will be in proximity and relationship with him.

As in the ancient Near Eastern accounts, we will find that close attention to the biblical text will show that here too the focus is archetypal and ontological, particularly in relation to sacred space, rather than biological or material. In Egyptian reliefs, when the craftsman god Khnum is shown forming pharaoh on the potter's wheel, he is forming pharaoh's identity for his royal role. It is not a story of biological origins. A Neo-Babylonian creation text talks about the gods forming the king and describes all the archetypal qualities of the king.[22] This view is confirmed by Zechariah 12:1, where it is the human spirit that is formed, not the human body. Even Isaiah talks about how God formed the Servant in the womb to have a particular identity and serve in a designated capacity. These show the inclination for forming accounts to focus on archetypal and ontological issues. They pertain to forming human identity.

---

20. Walton, *Lost World of Adam and Eve*, 82–91.

21. Walton, *Lost World of Adam and Eve*, 116–27.

22. Translation in R. Clifford, *Creation Accounts in the Ancient Near East and the Bible*, 69–71; See discussion in Walton, *Lost World of Adam and Eve*, 85–86.

If the forming of Adam and Eve were to be seen as archetypal and onto-logical, the result would be that the elements of "dust" and "rib" were not unique to them, but express what is true of all of humans. First of all, we are all formed from dust. This conclusion is confirmed through an examination of the rest of the biblical text. In the very next chapter of Genesis we are informed that "dust" is related to mortality. Further support for this concept is found throughout the Bible (e.g., Ps 103:14; 1 Cor 15:47–48). We are all formed from dust—mortal and frail. This is not a statement of what is unique to Adam; it is the identity of all of us.[23] Yet God has made us more than what we are formed from—that is, ontology is not simply a byproduct of ontogeny (as is also true in any Christian understanding of evolution).

When we turn our attention to woman, we find that there is little semantic support for translating the Hebrew word *tsela'* as "rib."[24] Even Adam's speech refers both to bone and flesh. A more appropriate rendering would reflect that God took one of Adam's (two) sides and built the woman from it. This makes a statement about the ontological relationship between the genders with Adam and Eve serving as the archetypes for humanity. Womankind is ontologically equal to mankind; both are halves of a whole. I would propose that Adam is shown this in a vision (the result of being in a "deep sleep")[25] rather than thinking that he was involved in a surgical procedure.

The text then is not discussing the unique biological origins of the first two humans. It has adopted Adam and Eve as archetypes for communicating the ontological identity of humanity. Their role is not as the first biological examples of the species but as those selected for a specialized assignment in this newly established sacred space. Caring for sacred space is the focus, and Adam is given that task in Genesis 2:15. It is too large a task to handle on his own, so he is given an ally. The two verbs in 2:15 are priestly in nature.[26] The first can, in some contexts and collocations, refer to agrarian labor, but it also frequently refers to the work of the priests in sacred space. The second cannot easily be associated with agrarian labor but is well-suited to the role of the priests as they guard sacred space. Therefore, Adam and Eve should not be considered the first biological human beings but the first significant human

---

23. See discussion in Walton, *Lost World of Adam and Eve*, 70–81.

24. Walton, *Lost World of Adam and Eve*, 77–79.

25. M. Oeming, *TDOT* 13:338.

26. Walton, *Lost World of Adam and Eve*, 104–15.

beings by virtue of the assignment they are given as priestly representatives in sacred space. It is their designated elected role that sets them apart, not their material origin.

The biological origin of human beings was not a concern of the ancient Israelites or any of their neighbors. They did not have categories of causation to differentiate the level of God's activity in making Adam from the level of his activity in making us. God made Adam; God made all of us. In the Hebrew language, the same verb ('asah) can be used for both instances, and God is no less involved in one than in the other. Some may claim there is a distinction because we were conceived and born through a nine-month process, while Adam is described as being formed from the dust. Yet the Bible affirms that God is no less involved in each birth (Ps 139:13). And before we could conclude that this is an intentional distinction of a different type of material origin for Adam than the rest of us had, we would have to determine whether the text is claiming to address Adam's material origin. The evidence both in the biblical text and the ancient Near East suggests that it is not.

Is the text claiming that Adam was formed from dust by the very hand of God, while the rest of us are born from a woman after a nine-month gestation period? Many assume this is the case. But such a view implies that the text asserts a supernatural theory of human origins for which there is no natural explanation or process involved. Again, the text cannot be making such a distinction because the Israelites did not classify phenomena in terms of these competing categories.

If the Bible is not claiming that God bypassed scientifically describable processes in the material creation of human beings (since its authors and its intended audience had no such categories), Genesis may not be used to rule out scientific explanations for material human origins (such as evolution). Both the Bible and theology agree that God is pervasively involved in his world no matter what level of scientifically describable cause and effect we can detect. So it is not inconsistent with the biblical text to suggest that God created human beings over a long period of time through processes that operate according to recognizable cause-and-effect patterns. As such, evolutionary creationism would be a perfectly acceptable view for Christians who take both the Bible and science seriously. God's activity is not limited to what scientifically describable cause-and-effect processes fail to explain; he is engaged in working through all processes.

At the same time, every Christian should affirm that humans are not *merely* the result of scientifically describable processes. God has made us onto-logically distinct beings, regardless of the material processes involved. We are *more* than dust; and we are *more* than any phylogenetic ancestor. Furthermore, this ontological uniqueness cannot be simplified to the imposition of a soul or to the assignment as God's images. Unique human ontology can't be reduced to anthropological components because it concerns the fundamental nature of our being. We are more than what we are made of, and God is responsible for that. Identity is more important than biology.

Christian theology has no room for those who exploit science to defend a purposeless and meaningless view of humanity and the world. Furthermore, evolutionary creationism does not intrinsically call for minimal or occasional divine attention. It does not intend to remove God from involvement in creation. It does not replace God with science. Taking the Bible seriously involves not imposing modern categories on it that can conceivably lead to a misunderstanding of its message or teaching. The Bible cannot be interpreted to specify categorical distinctions it never had because it cannot be interpreted to say what it never said.

Conclusion

In investigating the claims made in the biblical text as understood in light of the Hebrew terminology and the conceptual world of the ancient Near East, we have suggested that their questions are not the same as ours would be. They are more interested in identity than in material origins. The biblical claims are therefore not in conflict with modern scientific models. The Bible's interest is in agency, not mechanisms, while science can only comment on mechanisms and offers no insight into agency.[27]

---

27. Distinction between agency and mechanism prompted by comments by April Maskiewicz. See Robert Asher, *Evolution and Belief: Confessions of a Religious Paleontologist* (Cambridge: Cambridge University Press, 2012).

Chapter SIX

How Did Genesis Become a Problem?

On the Hermeneutics of Natural Science

FRANCIS WATSON

Nothing should be more welcome than the extension of knowledge of any and every kind. . . . If geology proves to us that we must not interpret the first chapters of Genesis literally; if historical investigations shall show us that inspiration, however it may protect the doctrine, yet was not empowered to protect the narrative of the inspired writers from occasional inaccuracy, if careful criticism shall prove that there have been occasionally interpolations and forgeries in that Book, as in many others; the results should still be welcome. . . . The substance of the teaching which we derive from the Bible will not really be affected by anything of this sort.[1]

Such was the view of Frederick Temple, eventual bishop and archbishop but headmaster of Rugby School at the time of writing.[2] Not all of his readers were convinced by his reassurances. The volume that contains them, blandly titled *Essays and Reviews*, was published early in 1860, just a few months after Darwin's *Origin of Species*. Its seven authors found themselves at the centre of a storm of controversy involving a flurry of pamphlets, letters to the *Times*,

---

1. Frederick Temple, "The Education of the World," in *Essays and Reviews* (London: Parker & Son, 1860), 1–49, quote on 47.
2. On Temple, see Peter Hinchcliff, *Frederick Temple, Archbishop of Canterbury: A Life* (Oxford: Oxford University Press, 1998).

mass petitions, and recourse to the ecclesiastical courts. As critics were quick to point out, there is little that is original in this volume. As they did not point out, it is precisely this lack of originality that makes it a valuable source for understanding the age that produced it. It was in mid-Victorian England that the public came to perceive a fundamental conflict between two monolithic entities labelled "science" and "religion."

This public perception is with us to this day. Science, we still hear, has disproved religion; we live in an age of science and no longer in an age of faith. The age of faith gave way to the age of science when Darwin's theory of evolution was accepted and the rival Genesis account of the origins of life was discredited. Indeed, in current usage "Darwin" and "Genesis" can serve as surrogates for "science" and "religion." In 1860 the opposition to Genesis was still represented by "geology," and not yet by "Darwin" or "evolution," but otherwise the battle-lines were remarkably similar to the present-day ones. Equally familiar is the counterclaim that, as Temple puts it, the substance of the Bible's teaching remains essentially unaffected by modern scientific and historical knowledge. In the years after 1860, that counterclaim would be repeated again and again by Christian apologists, not least by Temple himself in his later Bampton Lectures on *The Relations between Religion and Science.*[3]

We must carefully examine the counterclaim that rejects the necessary antagonism between science (or modern knowledge more generally) and religion (or the Bible or Genesis). As represented by Temple, the counterclaim proposes a compromise. Three fields of knowledge are selected: geology, history, and criticism. Geology shows that we must not interpret the first chapters of Genesis literally. Historical investigation shows that the biblical text is not immune from factual errors. Criticism identifies later additions to the biblical text. Yet, according to Temple, the essential content of the Bible is in no way affected by these newly discovered limitations. With a few minor adjustments, modern knowledge and biblical teaching can coexist without difficulty.

That a mid-Victorian theologian should adopt such a compromise in the face of competing truth claims is entirely understandable, not least because views of this kind remain a familiar feature of contemporary discourse on the supposedly problematic "relationship" between science and religion. This, however, is precisely the wrong strategy. Its fundamental premise is that all

3. Frederick Temple, *The Relations between Religion and Science: Eight Lectures Preached Before the University of Oxford in the Year 1884* (London: Macmillan, 1884).

truths are alike and that it should be possible, with some necessary fine-tuning, to demonstrate their ultimate unity and harmony, at least in principle. But doing so overlooks the possibility that truths may be incommensurable with one another without necessary detriment to their truth status within the areas of their jurisdiction. A critical analysis of nineteenth-century debates can show how and why this potentially promising option was widely ignored.

Truth and Its Domains

We must look closely at the three fields of knowledge selected by Temple. The first and perhaps the most significant is geology, which "proves to us that we must not interpret the first chapters of Genesis literally."[4] How does geology do that? Temple's readers possess Bibles in which the date "4004 BC" is printed in the margin of the text of Genesis 1.[5] Scattered chronological references from the Bible and elsewhere were supposed to provide a date late in the third millennium BC for the birth of Abraham, and the two genealogies in Genesis 5 and 11 provide not only a list of Abraham's ancestors through nineteen generations but also, crucially, the ages at which each of those ancestors fathered his successor. Thus, Adam was 130 years old when he fathered Seth, and Noah was 500 years old when he fathered Shem, Ham, and Japheth. Adding up all these figures, we learn that 1,456 years elapsed from the creation of Adam to the birth of Shem, a century before the Flood, with a further 390 years to the birth of Abraham. By the mid-nineteenth century, this chronological scheme had lost all credibility. As another contributor to *Essays and Reviews* notes, "Almost all intelligent persons are [now] agreed that the earth has existed for myriads of ages."[6] People were convinced by geologists' claim that the shaping of the physical world is best explained by slow but inexorable natural processes still operative today. The physical evidence does not support the belief that the

---

4. On geology and Genesis in the nineteenth century, see my article "Genesis Before Darwin: Why Scripture Needed Liberating from Science," in *Reading Genesis after Darwin*, ed. Stephen C. Barton and David Wilkinson (Oxford: Oxford University Press, 2009), 23–37.

5. The date derives from the chronological researches of James Ussher, in his *Annales veteris testamenti a prima mundi origine deducti* (1650), translated as *Annals of the Old Testament Deduced from the First Origins of the World* (1658). See James Barr, "Why the World Was Created in 4004 BC: Archbishop Ussher and Biblical Chronology," *Bulletin of the John Rylands University Library of Manchester* 67 (1984–85), 575–608.

6. Benjamin Jowett, "On the Interpretation of Scripture," in *Essays and Reviews*, 330–433, quote on 349.

world came into being recently and instantaneously on the second and third days of creation or that fossil-bearing rock strata are vestiges of a universal flood. For such reasons as these, Temple notes that geology warns us against interpreting the first chapters of Genesis literally.

Temple also refers to "historical investigations" which show that even the inspired biblical authors were not immune from "occasional inaccuracy" and to "criticism," which ("occasionally" again) identifies "interpolations and forgeries" within the sacred text. These findings ought to be welcomed too, however disconcerting they may at first appear. Among these biblical "forgeries," Temple may possibly have included later chapters of the book of Daniel in which Near Eastern history following Alexander's conquests is presented as prophecy of a still distant future. A large-scale interpolation might be seen in the latter part of the book of Isaiah. Late dates for the later chapters of Daniel and Isaiah were commonplaces of nineteenth-century German biblical scholarship, and they were gradually gaining acceptance even in religiously conservative England.[7] Equally, he may have in mind smaller-scale instances such as the text-critical data that would eliminate the so-called "Johannine comma," the Trinitarian interpolation that occurs at 1 John 5:7 in the King James Bible, from the Revised Version of 1881.[8] As for the occasional inaccuracies demonstrated by historical investigation, Temple may have in view the apparent discrepancies between one biblical text and another. For example, Matthew has Jesus's parents initially residing in Bethlehem, while Luke transfers them to Bethlehem from Nazareth only to take part in a census. Has one or the other evangelist perpetrated an "inaccuracy"?[9] Unlike other essayists, however, Temple does not actually provide any examples. The point is to establish a principle: that a flawed and limited Bible remains religiously significant and that, conversely, religious significance does not stand or fall

---

7.   See John Rogerson, *Old Testament Criticism in the Nineteenth Century: England and Germany* (London: SPCK, 1984).

8.   "For there are three that bear record in heaven, the Father, the Word, and the Holy Ghost: and these three are one" (1 John 5:7 KJV). The authenticity of this Trinitarian testimony, along with that of the Greek *Textus Receptus* that contains it, were controversial topics in the nineteenth century. For a succinct summary of the text-critical evidence, see Bruce M. Metzger, *A Textual Commentary on the Greek New Testament* (New York: United Bible Societies, 1975), 715–17.

9.   Early translations of German critical literature that brought this problem (among many others) to the attention of English-speaking readers include F. D. E. Schleiermacher, *Luke: A Critical Study*, trans. Connop Thirlwall (1825; repr., Lewiston, NY: Edwin Mellen, 1993), 51–52, with an additional comment by the translator, 317; D. F. Strauss, *The Life of Jesus Critically Examined*, trans. Mary Anne Evans (George Eliot) (London: Chapman Brothers, 1846; repr., London: SCM, 1973), 184–90.

with the usual apparatus of infallibility and plenary inspiration.[10] Modern investigation in the fields of geology, history, and criticism has acquired a better understanding of certain realities than was available to earlier generations of readers, and new knowledge is always to be welcomed, never to be feared.

A Singular Truth

Like all the contributors to *Essays and Reviews*, Temple is in quest of a *via media* between the competing absolutisms of right and left. To his left there are those, already strident, for whom the credibility of the Bible and traditional religion has simply been destroyed by the rise of modern science. To his right are those for whom a flawed and fallible Bible is inconceivable; for such people the Bible remains the touchstone for all human knowledge, and true science will always be in harmony with it. These parties of left and right compete with one another to occupy the same space, the space of *fundamental knowledge*—knowledge of the basic constitution of the world and of our own existence within the world. Is fundamental knowledge to be acquired through the natural and historical sciences or through the Bible? Temple wants to persuade the religious right to abandon its claim to monopolize this sphere of fundamental knowledge. The Bible will retain an important role within that sphere, but it will not occupy the whole of it. In particular, its claim to tell the truth about the world's origins must be abandoned, for geology "proves to us that we must not interpret the first chapters of Genesis literally."[11] Here Temple exemplifies a traditional Anglican concern to maintain an authoritative role for reason *alongside* Scripture, although in harmony with it, in opposition to the monopolistic Bible of the Puritans.[12] In the nineteenth-century version of this position, the place of reason is now occupied by science, but the concern remains the same: to assert that the sphere of fundamental knowledge is not the sole preserve of the Bible and that, where there are tensions with the results of free human enquiry, accommodations and compromises must be found.

---

10. Temple's argument is indebted to S. T. Coleridge's *Confessions of an Inquiring Spirit*, ed. H. N. Coleridge (London: Edward Moxon, 1840, 1853), where an eloquent critique of the doctrine of biblical infallibility is short on examples of alleged scriptural errors.

11. Temple, "Education of the World," 47.

12. For a thorough though unsympathetic analysis of the origins of this Anglican emphasis, see H. Graf Reventlow, *The Authority of the Bible and the Rise of the Modern World* (London: SCM, 1984), 91–285.

Also characteristically (though not uniquely) Anglican is the related point that the sphere of fundamental knowledge is itself *singular*. Truth is one and indivisible; there can be only one true account of the world's origins. In the past the Bible appeared to provide a framework for that true account, but that role must now be taken over by geology. It is assumed that there cannot be more than one true story of the world's origins. It does not occur to Temple—or to any of his fellow-essayists—that geology and Genesis might have their own distinct and incommensurable perspectives on the world's origins.

For participants in the mid-Victorian debate, the indivisibility of truth is axiomatic. It could hardly be otherwise in the context of an established church, a "Church *of England*" that identifies itself with the entire national community. Truth is one because church and state are one. Oxford and Cambridge Universities played a key role in the maintenance of this *status quo*, for it is at these two institutions that the future ministers of church and state prepare for their life's work. Frederick Temple and his fellow-essayists are all closely associated with the two universities, especially with Oxford. He himself was a fellow of Balliol College and had lectured in mathematics and logic. The other contributors include the Regius Professor of Greek, the Savilian Professor of Geometry, a former Rawlinsonian Professor of Anglo-Saxon, and a tutor—soon to be rector—of Lincoln College.[13] These five Oxonian essayists were all Church of England clergy, members of an educational institution open only to Anglicans. Mid-nineteenth-century Oxford produces and imparts an increasingly diverse range of knowledge, but the ethos within which this occurs is still distinctively Anglican. The particular domains to which this diversified knowledge belongs are parts of a greater whole, a single truth grounded ultimately in the one God.

The Pluralist Option

In this intellectual context, it is impossible to envisage two true yet incommensurable accounts of the world's origins. However, that is not a logical impossibility. It is entirely possible to speak truthfully of the same entity from incompatible perspectives. In the early modern period a geocentric universe

13. Respectively, Benjamin Jowett ("On the Interpretation of Scripture"), Baden Powell ("On the Study of the Evidences of Christianity"), Henry Bristow Wilson ("Séances Historiques de Genève. The National Church"), Mark Pattison ("Tendencies of Religious Thought in England, 1688–1750").

gives way to a heliocentric one, yet the sun continues to rise and set as before. In a heliocentric universe, the moon is visible only insofar as it is illuminated by the sun, but no one proposes to remove the term "moonlight" from ordinary language because it implies that the moon produces its own light just as stars produce starlight and the sun sunlight. The two perspectives on the same reality—the sun, moon, and Earth in their relationship to one another—are not in competition with one another. Rather, they operate in different spheres—one in the sphere of general human experience in which the sun rises and the moon shines, the other in the specialized sphere of modern scientific discourse in which these phenomena are caused by the rotation of the Earth and the light of the sun. Of course, the scientific findings may seem to deny the evidence of ordinary experience. It may be said that the sun *only appears* to rise and that, *in reality*, this phenomenon is caused by the earth's movement and not by the sun's. This may be pragmatically appropriate language in the context of elementary science teaching; otherwise, its subordination of appearances to reality is only possible from the perspective of a Platonist. For non-Platonists, appearances are the immediate forms in which reality presents itself and in which we must engage with it. It is true that Earth revolves on its own axis and around the sun, but it is also true that the sun rises and sets. To ascribe motion exclusively to Earth in one context does not make it false to ascribe motion exclusively to the sun in another. These are two distinct truths, not a single truth accompanied by a necessary fiction or a higher truth accompanied by a lower one. The two truths are *incommensurable*, not because they have nothing in common and cannot be informed by one another, but because they belong within different domains of human activity, one general and universal and the other highly specialized. In spite of Copernicus, Galileo, Kepler, and Newton, and with no detriment to their achievements, the universe as humanly experienced remained stubbornly geocentric.

We return to Temple's claim that geology—or science more generally—"proves to us that we must not interpret the first chapters of Genesis literally." What does this familiar claim actually mean? As a thought experiment, we may apply the principle stated here to another biblical passage, Ecclesiastes 1:5 (as rendered in the King James Version familiar to the first readers of *Essays and Reviews*): "The sun also ariseth, and the sun goeth down, and hasteth to his place where he arose." Holy Scripture here ascribes to the sun a constant circular movement around an evidently stationary earth. Does science show that we must not interpret the Preacher's words literally? If so, in what sense? Science does indeed make available to us a radically different perspective on the earth's relation to the sun, one that for certain purposes is useful and obligatory to adopt. Yet science teaches that we must not interpret the Preacher's words literally *if and only if* "interpreting literally" means ascribing to a scriptural text a direct and exclusive relationship to its referent. In that case, a literal interpretation of the Ecclesiastes text would have to insist that the sun revolves around Earth independently of the perspective of any human observer and that the scientific claim that Earth revolves around the sun is absolutely false. But it is not clear that a "literal interpretation" of the Ecclesiastes text would commit us to any such conclusion. A literal interpretation would reflect on the author's perception of a never-ending cycle of days and its place within his pessimistic worldview. Literal interpretation takes seriously the wording of the text as it stands, within its literary and historical contexts, and it seeks to clarify the authorial perceptions and purposes underlying it. In no circumstances, however, is a literal interpretation obliged to demonstrate a direct and exclusive relationship between the text and the reality to which it refers.[14] One can interpret the text literally without having to claim that, according to the Bible, the sun revolves around the earth.

That does not make the modern scientific worldview irrelevant to the interpreter. A premodern reader of Ecclesiastes very well might find confirmation here that the sun revolves around Earth in an absolute sense. A post-Copernican reader would read the text differently, aware that it speaks from the distinctive perspective of the human observer. But the change of worldview does not undermine the text, destroying its credibility and damaging the reputation of the Bible as a whole. Rather, it shows that truth is plural and that the sphere in which the biblical text may be held to be true is different from the sphere of the Copernican revolution. The two truths do not compete with one another. It requires no mental effort to believe that Earth revolves around the sun while recognizing that the movement of the sun around a stable Earth is a fundamental fact of human experience of the world.[15]

---

14. The hermeneutical distinction between meaning and reference is forcefully asserted by Hans Frei, *The Eclipse of Biblical Narrative: A Study in Eighteenth and Nineteenth Century Hermeneutics* (New Haven, CT: Yale University Press, 1974).

15. In the background of these remarks is Heidegger's elusive yet compelling insistence on the priority of human being-in-the-world, characterized by "care" or "concern," over the theoretical knowledge, which is simply a mode of that being-in-the-world: "Only in some definite mode of its own being-in-the-world

Nineteenth-century readers of the Bible do not seem to have worried about its geocentrism and its anthropocentrism, that is, its assumption of the standpoint of human participants in the world, addressed as such by God. They do not discredit the Bible because it contains statements about the sun rising and setting even though modern science has shown such statements to be not true in an absolute and exclusive sense. Similar mental adjustments might have been made in response to the new scientific hypotheses about the age of the earth or the origin of species. These discoveries would naturally make a significant impact on the reading of the biblical text, but that impact need not have been negative. Genesis 1 gives a carefully ordered account of the preconditions for human life on earth. Light and darkness alternate, dry land emerges from the primal ocean, plants and animals come into being— and humans are created in the image of God to fill the earth and make it their home. All these events must have occurred for the world to be as it is. Science offers the nineteenth-century reader a radically different version of the story of the world's origins—one in which the human race enters the scene belatedly and contingently, as one species among others, surviving against the odds and achieving mastery over its competitors and environment.[16] Once again, scientific advances demonstrate that anthropocentric accounts of the world's existence can no longer claim absolute and exclusive truth. Yet such accounts might remain valid within their own frame of reference. Just as the sun continues to rise and set in a post-Copernican universe, so the world as imagined in Genesis 1 can still provide the context for human existence in a post-Darwinian one. Genesis 1 speaks of the coming into being of the humanly significant world, the world that matters to us. Its timeframe is that of a humanized time: the *time* of day and night gathered into a recurrent

---

can Dasein [being human] discover entities as Nature" (Martin Heidegger, *Being and Time*, trans. John Macquarrie and Edward Robinson [Oxford: Blackwell, 1962], 93). In the case of the sun, ontological priority belongs to its role in demarcating the time that Dasein has and takes for its projects: "When the sun rises, it is *time for* so and so. . . . The sun dates the time which is interpreted in concern" (465; italics original).

16. The key text here is Charles Darwin's *The Descent of Man, and Selection in Relation to Sex*, ed. James Moore and Adrian Desmond (London: John Murray, 1871; repr., London: Penguin, 2004). This work, hugely successful and influential in its own time, has more recently been totally overshadowed by *The Origin of Species*, in which currently objectionable doctrines of race and gender are less in evidence. As his modern editor's note, "A contextual understanding of Darwin's process of creation shows how issues of race, gender, and class were integral to his thought—indeed, one cannot explain the origins and development of the *Descent of Man* without them. Science is a messy, socially embedded business, Darwin's particularly so" (Moore and Desmond, "Introduction," vi).

seven-day week that closes with a day of rest and the *lifetime* of successive generations that stretches back into a remote past and lays the foundation for the present. To read Genesis this way is still to read it literally, but to do so within its specific domain—the world humanly experienced and thus given.

Narratives in Competition

In the debate between science and religion that took shape during the mid-nineteenth century, the possibility of plural truths occupying distinctive domains was inadequately recognized. The assumption established itself that Genesis and therefore the whole Bible had been discredited or "disproved" by modern science. Frederick Temple himself, future archbishop of Canterbury, seems to envisage a Bible, which if not discredited is at least significantly *diminished* by modern geology, history, and criticism. As science advances, the Bible recedes. The concept of a "debate" between science and religion presupposes a prior breach between science and religion, geology and Genesis, a conflict in which evidence-based science was perceived to have conquered and occupied territory previously held by irrational and ungrounded belief systems.

How and why did this breach come about? Why was geology supposed to have inflicted such fatal damage on Genesis and the Bible—Genesis and *therefore* the Bible? The conclusion might have been drawn that geology *clarified* the meaning of Genesis by assigning it to its proper domain. Why was that conclusion found unconvincing? A broad range of historical, political, and cultural factors converge to produce the event in which, at some point in the mid- to late-nineteenth century, Genesis is perceived to have been discredited. The event is at the same time a collective *decision*, not a unanimous decision, of course, but nevertheless a decision that must universally be considered and recognized as an enduring entity within our cultural landscape.

Like all accounts of origins, Genesis takes the form of a story. Like all stories, Genesis must compete with other stories for an audience's attention. The decision against Genesis is also a decision in favour of other stories that many modern hearers or readers find more engaging and more in keeping with their sense of self. One such story, increasingly popular during the nineteenth century, is alluded to in the title of Temple's essay: "The Education of the World." The essay opens the *Essays and Reviews* volume, and its title sums up the ethos of the whole collection. The world is imagined as a single individual;

world-history becomes biography, the story of a single educational process extending from childhood to adult maturity. The metaphor is indebted to Lessing, whose essay "On the Education of the Human Race" was widely read and imitated—not least, and on a grand scale, by Hegel.[17] Twentieth-century echoes of it are still perceptible in Freud's view of religion as representing an "infantile" stage of human development that must be "outgrown,"[18] and in Dietrich Bonhoeffer's concept of a world "come of age."[19]

In Temple's mid-Victorian rendering of this metaphor, we are invited to contemplate a three-stage process of development, that is,

> a childhood, a youth, and a manhood of the world. The men of the earliest ages were, in many respects, still children as compared with ourselves, with all the blessings and with all the disadvantages that belong to childhood . . . Our characters have grown out of their history, as the character of the man grows out of the history of the child.[20]

As in the Lessing essay, three stages of the world's education are sharply differentiated. "First come Rules, then Examples, then Principles. First comes the Law, then the Son of Man, then the Gift of the Spirit."[21] The law's commandments and prohibitions were appropriate to the world's childhood, and Christ's example was appropriate to the world's adolescence, but the world's adulthood requires us to move beyond the law and the gospel to the age of the Spirit. To reinforce this potentially controversial claim, Temple draws on Pauline language derived from Galatians 4:

> The world was once under tutors and governors until the time appointed by the Father. Then, when the fit season had arrived, the Example to

---

17. G. E. Lessing, "Die Erziehung des Menschengeschlechts" (1780), in *Gotthold Ephraim Lessing Werke*, vol. 8, *Theologiekritische Schriften III, Philosophische Schriften* (Munich: Hanser, 1979), 489–510. An English translation was published in 1858 (*The Education of the Human Race: From the German of Gotthold Ephraim Lessing*, trans. F. W. Robertson [London: Smith, Elder, and Co., 1858]). Robertson's translation was revised by Henry Chadwick, trans., *Lessing's Theological Writings* (London: Black, 1956), 82–98.

18. Sigmund Freud, "The Future of an Illusion," in *Sigmund Freud*, vol. 12, *Civilization, Society and Religion*, ed. Albert Dickson (London: Penguin, 1991), 183–241.

19. Dietrich Bonhoeffer, *Letters and Papers from Prison*, ed. Eberhart Bethge, trans. Reginald Fuller and John Bowden (London: SCM, 1971), 325–29, 341–47, 359–63, 380–83.

20. Temple, "Education of the World," 4.

21. Temple, "Education of the World," 5.

which all ages should turn was sent to teach men what they ought to be. Then the human race was left to itself to be guided by the teaching of the Spirit within.[22]

Here Temple tries in vain to insert a permanent backward glance into the educational process in order to preserve some kind of role for Christ, "the Example to which all ages should turn." But there is little opportunity for the backward glance amid the relentless forward movement required by the educational metaphor. The adulthood of the human race is marked by self-reliance on its own powers of thought, discovery, and invention. In contrast, Genesis would be the product of the world's childhood. If modernity is celebrated as the world's coming-of-age, it is inevitable that the Genesis account of the world's origins will be set aside. The educated adult has outgrown stories intended for children, preferring stories that reflect his or her adulthood. The retelling of the world's history as a painful learning process that comes to fruition in the present is guaranteed to appeal to the progressive adult who identifies with its hero.

In spite of twentieth-century disillusion, it is still possible to narrate human history as a story of progress or "ascent." Like most powerful and influential stories, this one is true, illuminating, and useful in some respects, but not in others. Like other such stories, it is open to ideological distortion as soon as it is given exclusive canonical status. No story provides a final and definitive account of the reality to which it relates; if this is true of the Genesis narrative of creation and fall, it is equally true of modern narratives of human ascent.

FitzRoy's Cliff

But perhaps truth *is* singular, not plural. Perhaps truths are all of the same kind, tightly interlocked like the pieces of a jigsaw puzzle. Perhaps truth is independent of the perspectives and interests of the communities concerned with it. Only a singular all-comprehending truth can produce a conflict between Genesis and natural science and then resolve it by acclaiming modern scientific progress and viewing Genesis as a product of the world's childhood. Genesis would then have no part in the human activity of truth telling,

---

22. Temple, "Education of the World," 5.

except as a document of the history of religion. Alternatively, commitment to a singular truth might result in an attempt to *harmonize* Genesis and science by showing that they can coexist peaceably and cooperate effectively within the same intellectual space. As science advances under its own momentum, it may seem to provide confirmatory evidence of the truth of the biblical account; evidence, indeed, of the truth of the Christian religion itself.

During the decades before the publication of *Essays and Reviews* and *The Origin of Species*, there is much concern with the issue of evidence. Older appeals to the evidence of fulfilled prophecy and biblical miracles are still in circulation, but they have been forced onto the defensive by Deist critiques dating back to the 1720s. Newer "evidences" of Christian truth are sought especially in the natural sciences.[23] Science discloses the intricate construction of living creatures and their perfect adaptation to their environments, and so—in a pre-Darwinian world—it confirms the existence, wisdom, power, and benevolence of a creator deity.[24] Yet the biblical deity is just, as well as benevolent, and the event that most clearly expresses both sides of the divine character is the biblical flood. As represented in Genesis, this flood was a universal event. So long as it lasted, water covered the entire surface of the globe. Such an event would surely have left its traces in the geological record. Scientific confirmation of the biblical flood would be a valuable addition to the arsenal of evidences needed to defend church and religion against the assaults of atheism and other undesirable ideologies.

This brings us, unexpectedly perhaps, to the celebrated "voyage of the *Beagle*"—the trip to South America and beyond that launched the career of the young Charles Darwin, providing him with a vast store of empirical data on which to draw as he refined his theories about life's origins in the years

---

23. The classic text in this genre is William Paley, *Natural Theology, or Evidence of the Existence and Attributes of the Deity, collected from the Appearances of Nature*, ed. Matthew D. Eddy and David Knight (1802; repr., Oxford: Oxford University Press, 2006). Paley's work was followed in the 1830s by a series of nine *Bridgewater Treatises on the Power, Wisdom and Goodness of God, as Manifested in the Creation*, a project funded by a bequest from the Earl of Bridgewater, who had died in 1829. On the Bridgewater Treatises see John Robson, "The Fiat and Finger of God: The Bridgewater Treatises," in *Victorian Faith in Crisis: Essays on Continuity and Change in Nineteenth-Century Religious Belief*, ed. Richard J. Helmstadter (Stanford: Stanford University Press, 1990), 71–125; Jonathan Topham, "Science and Popular Education in the 1830s: The Role of the Bridgewater Treatises," *British Journal for the History of Science* 25 (1992): 397–430; Topham, "Beyond the 'Common Context': the Production and Reading of the Bridgewater Treatises," *Isis* 89 (1998): 233–62.

24. Thus, the first of the Bridgewater Treatises, published at the time of Darwin's voyage on the *Beagle*, was Thomas Chalmers's *The Adaptation of External Nature to the Moral and Intellectual Constitution of Man*, 2 vols. (London: William Pickering, 1833).

that followed. Actually there were two voyages of the *Beagle*, and they are the subject of a three-volume work published in 1839 by the *Beagle's* captain, Robert FitzRoy, and entitled: *Narrative of the Surveying Voyages of his Majesty's Ships* Adventure *and* Beagle, *between the Years 1826 and 1836, describing their Examination of the Southern Shore of South America and the* Beagle's *Circumnavigation of the Globe.*[25] During the first voyage, which lasted four years, FitzRoy assumed command of the *Beagle* following his predecessor's suicide in 1828. In 1831, FitzRoy was instructed to undertake a second voyage, and it is at this point that Charles Darwin enters his account. Darwin was then aged 22 and had recently graduated from Cambridge; FitzRoy was 26. FitzRoy writes:

> Anxious that no opportunity of collecting useful information, during the voyage, should be lost; I proposed to the Hydrographer that some well-educated and scientific person should be sought for who would willingly share such accommodations as I had to offer, in order to profit by the opportunity of visiting distant countries yet little known. Captain Beaufort approved of the suggestion, and wrote to Professor Peacock, of Cambridge, who consulted with a friend, Professor Henslow, and he named Mr. Charles Darwin, grandson of Dr. Darwin the poet, as a young man of promising ability, extremely fond of geology, and indeed all branches of natural history. In consequence an offer was made to Mr. Darwin to be my guest on board, which he accepted conditionally; permission was obtained for his embarkation, and an order given by the Admiralty that he should be borne on the ship's books for provisions. The conditions asked by Mr. Darwin were, that he should be at liberty to leave the Beagle and retire from the Expedition when he thought proper, and that he should pay a fair share of the expenses of my table.[26]

And so the *Beagle* sailed off on the five-year voyage which prepared Darwin for the unique role assigned to him within modern intellectual history and popular culture.

---

25. FitzRoy, *Narrative of the Surveying Voyages of his Majesty's Ships* Adventure *and* Beagle (London: Henry Colburn, 1839). On FitzRoy, see H. E. L. Mellersh, *FitzRoy of the* Beagle (London: Mason & Lipscomb, 1968).

26. FitzRoy, *Narrative*, 2.18–19.

It is not clear that the book of Genesis was much on his mind at the time; his diary never refers to it.[27] He seems already to have absorbed the view that scientific questions should be pursued without reference to theology. FitzRoy came to hold a quite different view. In the concluding chapter of his account of the *Beagle*'s voyage, he claims to have found traces of the Genesis flood, which convinced him of the truth of the biblical narrative. Initially, he had been sceptical:

> I suffered much anxiety in former years from a disposition to doubt, if not disbelieve, the inspired History written by Moses. I knew so little of that record, or of the intimate manner in which the Old Testament is connected with the New, that I fancied some events there related might be mythological or fabulous, while I sincerely believed the truth of others; a wavering between opinions, which could only be productive of an unsettled, and therefore unhappy, state of mind. . . . Much of my own uneasiness was caused by reading works by men of Voltaire's school; and by those of geologists who contradict, by implication, if not in plain terms, the authenticity of the Scriptures.[28]

FitzRoy's account of his earlier scepticism indicates that he is now operating within the genre of the exemplary conversion narrative. The voyage of the *Beagle* is at the same time a journey from doubt to faith, a journey that FitzRoy's readers are supposed to reenact for themselves. Faith is produced by evidence, and credit for discovering this evidence goes to none other than Mr. Darwin himself:

> In crossing the Cordillera of the Andes Mr. Darwin found petrified trees, embedded in sandstone, six or seven thousand feet above the level of the sea: and at twelve or thirteen thousand feet above the sea-level he found fossil sea-shells, limestone, sandstone, and a conglomerate in which were pebbles of the "rock with shells." Above the sandstone in which the petrified trees were found, is "a great bed, apparently about one thousand feet thick, of black augitic lava; and over this there are at least five grand

---

27. R. D. Keynes, ed., *Charles Darwin's* Beagle *Diary* (Cambridge: Cambridge University Press, 1988).

28. FitzRoy, *Narrative*, 2.657.

alternations of such rocks, and aqueous sedimentary deposits, amounting in thickness to several thousand feet." These wonderful alternations of the consequences of fire and flood, are, to me, indubitable proofs of that tremendous catastrophe which alone could have caused them;—of that awful combination of water and volcanic agency which is shadowed forth to our minds by the expression "the fountains of the great deep were broken up, and the windows of heaven were opened."[29]

Marine fossils on mountains had been a long-standing topic of scientific debate. Did these fossils indicate that what was now a mountain had once been a seabed that was raised far above sea level by a long series of natural causes such as earthquakes and volcanic eruptions extending over not thousands but millions of years? Or were the remains of sea creatures deposited on already existing mountainsides in a single catastrophic event occurring in the relatively recent past? FitzRoy finds a place for volcanic activity as well as rainfall in the scriptural reference to "the fountains of the great deep." First there were the trees, then successive layers of lava and sedimentation from the raised sea level, and finally intact marine fossils. These are, "*to me*, indubitable proofs" of the Genesis flood narrative—"to me" though not necessarily to "Mr. Darwin." But FitzRoy's readers are tacitly invited to make his profession of faith their own.

Hearers or readers of conversion narratives are dependent on testimony, reports of another's experience—in this case Darwin's experience as interpreted by FitzRoy. Yet readers may be invited to make the reported experience their own wherever possible—to see for themselves. FitzRoy's readers are unlikely to follow Darwin high up into the Andes, but more accessible evidence of the Genesis flood is available at sea level, although admittedly still in a remote South American location. FitzRoy is particularly interested in the compressed remains of shells:

One remarkable place, easy of access, where any person can inspect these shelly remains, is Port San Julian. There, cliffs, from ten to a hundred feet high, are composed of nothing but such earth and fossils; and as those dug from the very tops of the cliffs are just as much compressed as those at any other part, it follows that they were acted upon by an immense

---

29. FitzRoy, *Narrative*, 2.667–68.

weight not now existing. From this one simple fact may be deduced the conclusions—that Patagonia was once under the sea; that the sea grew deeper over the land in a tumultuous manner, rushing to and fro, tearing up and heaping together shells which once grew regularly or in beds: that the depth of water afterwards became so great as to squeeze or mass the earth and shells together by its enormous pressure; and that after being so forced down, the cohesion of the mass became sufficient to resist the separating power of other waves, during the subsidence of that ocean which had overwhelmed the land.[30]

So sea creatures as well as land creatures perished in the Genesis flood. Rainwater cascading down from above uprooted them from their natural habitat, hurling them together with such force as to crush them and embed them permanently in the earth, so that what emerges as the flood waters recede is a new cliff. The consequences of this discovery at Port San Julian are momentous:

> If it be shewn that Patagonia was under a deep sea, not in consequence of the land having sunk, but because of the water having risen, it will follow as a necessary consequence that every other portion of the globe must have been flooded to a nearly equal height, at the same time; since the tendency to equilibrium in fluids would prevent any one part of an ocean from rising much above any other part, unless sustained at a greater elevation by external force; such as the attraction of the moon, or sun; or a strong wind; or momentum derived from their agency. Hence therefore, if Patagonia was covered to a great depth, all the world was covered to a great depth; and from those shells alone my own mind is convinced, (independent of the Scripture) that this earth has undergone an universal deluge.[31]

The conversion process is complete: "My own mind is convinced." The first-person singular again functions rhetorically as an invitation to the reader to assent to the speaker's conviction. We too are supposed to be convinced by this chain of scientific argumentation that Earth has undergone a universal

---

30. FitzRoy, *Narrative*, 2.666.
31. FitzRoy, *Narrative*, 2.666.

deluge, even if we never make the journey to Patagonia to examine FitzRoy's cliff for ourselves. The evidence for the universal flood could be read from the Patagonian cliff even if we did not also read of it in Genesis.

Or so it is claimed. In reality, it is the Genesis story that has led FitzRoy to his imaginative account of the inundation of Patagonia and his un-Darwinian interpretation of Darwin's findings in the Andes. FitzRoy's problem with the unimaginable extension of geological time is not that it is implausible in and of itself but that it contradicts the Bible. He seeks to embed the world of the natural sciences in the world of the Genesis narrative, with science producing "evidence" and Genesis being the framework within which that evidence is set. Thus Genesis and geology are supposed to coexist harmoniously within the same space—the space of a truth that is singular and uniform. If that is how truth is envisaged, then Genesis will be discredited as soon as geology refuses to cohabit with it and chooses to live on its own. Conversely, the Genesis that is supposedly discredited by natural science is not the text as such but the text as read through the distorting lens of a monopolistic scientific truth claim (of which the fundamentalist creationism represented by FitzRoy is simply the mirror image). For Christians and for Jews, the text finds its natural habitat within distinctive literary contexts and communal settings which enable it to communicate its own truth in its own ways.

Chapter SEVEN

Knowing Creation in the Light of Job and Astrobiology

WILLIAM P. BROWN

The so-called "conflict" between science and theology is a misnomer. While fundamentalists, both religious and scientific, continue to monopolize attention in the popular media as they cast caricatures at each other, those in the middle, while not making the national news, continue to engage science and theology in mutually constructive ways. As "faith seeking understanding," should not theology welcome the understandings of science?

Yes, and more so now than ever before. Once considered the "queen of the sciences," theology has consistently engaged the big questions of life, including humanity's place in creation. Today, a relatively new field of science dares to ask the same question from its own vantage point. That science is astrobiology—the study of life, including human life, from a cosmic perspective. So what can theology learn from astrobiology, given their shared interest? Much, I submit. Does astrobiology even have something to offer in the interpretation of Scripture? Indeed it does. My thesis is that astrobiology elucidates one of the most theologically enigmatic books of the Bible. But before exploring astrobiology's hermeneutical payoffs, I offer some background about its scientific mission.

This emerging field of multidisciplinary work builds on three scientific revolutions, spanning nearly four hundred years of research, that have significantly revised the way human beings have come to know the cosmos. Each one has overturned so-called "common sense" notions about the physical world. Briefly, they are the following:

1. *The Copernican Revolution* (1543) debunked the view that Earth is stationary and located at the center of the solar system. As a result, the earth became "Earth," a bona fide planet ("wanderer") among the other planets orbiting the sun.

2. *The Darwinian Revolution* (1859) demonstrated that life evolves through "descent with modification" made possible by natural selection. The result is a plethora of diverse species adapting to their respective environments—some successfully, others not. Evolution is not about the "survival of the fittest" (a phrase coined by Herbert Spencer) but about the "survival of the fit enough." In the light of biological evolution, *Homo sapiens* is shown to be an emergent species, one of 8.7 million species estimated to be on this planet, all traceable back to a so-called "last universal common ancestor" (LUCA). The resulting picture is not so much a towering tree of life as it is a sprawling bush filled with both dead and growing branches.

3. *The Shapley-Hubble Revolution* (1925) demonstrated the existence of galaxies beyond our own. Edwin Hubble's measurements of the Doppler-shift revealed, furthermore, that galaxies are traveling away from Earth at a speed relative to their distance from our planet, demonstrating observationally that the universe is expanding. Hubble's contemporary Harlow Shapley was the first to observe that the Milky Way is much more expansive than was commonly thought at the time. Ironically, Shapley opposed Hubble's contention that other galaxies existed beyond our own. But when he received a letter from Hubble himself containing critical observational data, he allegedly told a colleague, "Here is the letter that destroyed my universe."[1]

Of these three revolutions,[2] the first and the third have to do with reconceptualizing cosmic *space*, while the second has to do with reconceptualizing biological *life*. Each one, in its own way, counters the notion that the human species is independently unique in origin and physically central to the universe. We are one species among many, all surviving on a "pale blue dot" of a planet in an ordinary galaxy of at least 100 billion stars (possibly as high as 400

---

1. For the quote, see "Harlow Shapley," Wikipedia, https://en.wikipedia.org/wiki/Harlow_Shapley.
2. Minus, of course, Einstein's theories of special and general relativity.

billion) in a universe populated by about a trillion galaxies, according to the latest estimates.

Astrobiology

Is there a fourth revolution at hand, one that may demonstrate *life* in *space*? That remains to be seen, but many scientists are hoping, if not expecting, to discover exoplanetary life in the near future.[3] Regardless of whether that hope is fulfilled or not, it is safe to say that the emerging field of astrobiology proposes the *possibility* of a new layer of complexity regarding the universe as we know it, a biological complexity. Simply put, astrobiology is "the study of the origin, evolution, distribution, and future of life in the universe."[4] According to the "NASA Astrobiology Strategy 2015" roadmap, three basic questions drive astrobiological research: (1) How does life begin and evolve? (2) Does life exist elsewhere in the universe? (3) What is the future of life on Earth and beyond?[5] While the first question is a standard one for biology, it takes on a new twist with the follow-up questions: What makes Earth habitable and inhabited? What are the requisite environmental conditions for life to begin as well as evolve in complexity? Is life fundamentally a planetary phenomenon?

Drawing from a host of disciplines, astrobiology is the most far-reaching and multidisciplinary of the sciences. Indeed, it is not a single science but a growing coalition of sciences, including astronomy, planetary science, geology, chemistry, and biology, as well as their many subdisciplines. As such, astrobiology invites us to look at the "big picture," the cosmos, while also beckoning us to examine life down to its most fundamental constituents. This looking at both the macro and the micro testifies to astrobiology's comprehensive reach and integrative scope. Another marker of distinction among the sciences, which many understandably consider a liability, is that astrobiology is the only science that has yet to find its subject matter—its holy grail, exoplanetary life. Hence, at least for the time being, astrobiology remains one of the

---

3. In 2013 the World Economic Forum predicted that evidence of exoplanetary life will be discovered "in ten years' time," as quoted in Margaret S. Race, "Preparing for the Discovery of Extraterrestrial Life: Are We Ready?" in *The Impact of Discovery of Life Beyond Earth*, ed. Steven J. Dick (Cambridge: Cambridge University Press, 2015), 264.

4. "About NAI," NASA Astrobiology Institute, http://nai.nasa.gov/about/.

5. For the full document, see https://astrobiology.nasa.gov/uploads/filer_public/01/28/01283266 -e401–4dcb-8e05–3918b21edb79/nasa_astrobiology_strategy_2015_151008.pdf.

most speculative of the sciences. As of this writing, NASA has confirmed 3,268 exoplanets,[6] thirty-three of which are considered habitable. That is to say, they are likely to be rocky planets orbiting their parent star within the "habitable zone."[7] Kepler-452b is one such planet. Located 1,402 light-years away, the planet is 60 percent larger than Earth (thus a "superearth") but lies at a distance from its parent star that would preserve water in a liquid state.[8] Closer to home, flowing water has been detected on the Martian surface, as well as underneath the frozen surfaces of Enceladus (a moon of Saturn) and possibly Europa (a moon of Jupiter). Whether these planets actually host life, remains to be seen. Even with favorable planetary conditions, we still do not know whether life is probable or improbable, prevalent or rare, for the origin of life in the universe remains an "unsolved puzzle."[9] Indeed, astrobiology is itself a puzzle that welcomes the help and collaboration of various disciplines, including those outside the natural sciences.[10]

In light of its speculative and comprehensive nature, I tend to think of astrobiology as the new "queen of the sciences." As theology, or at least a certain stream thereof, is focused on the *deus absconditus* ("the hidden God"[11]), astrobiology is in search of the *vita abscondita,* the "hidden life." In fact, the search for life beyond Earth can easily have a (pseudo)religious impulse. One physicist goes so far as to say, "There's no scientific project more obviously religious than the search for extraterrestrial intelligence."[12] At the very least, the question "Are we alone in the universe?" is one that is open to theological inquiry as much as it is to scientific investigation.

As such, astrobiology has a strong hermeneutical component that raises questions about how to recognize life specifically "as we do *not* know it," about

---

6. NASA Exoplanet Archive, http://exoplanetarchive.ipac.caltech.edu/.

7. Planetary Habitability Laboratory, http://phl.upr.edu/projects/habitable-exoplanets-catalog.

8. See "Kepler-452b: Earth's Bigger, Older Cousin—Briefing Materials," NASA, http://www.nasa.gov/keplerbriefing0723/.

9. Dirk Schulze-Makuch, "Landscape of Life," in *The Impact of Discovery of Life Beyond Earth*, ed. Steven J. Dick (Cambridge: Cambridge University Press), 81.

10. One such collaborative setting was at the Center of Theological Inquiry in Princeton, New Jersey, where various scholars from the humanities and the sciences have been exploring "the societal implications of astrobiology." I was privileged to be a part of the research team in 2015–2016. See http://www.ctinquiry.org.

11. See, e.g., Samuel L. Terrien, *The Elusive Presence: Toward a New Biblical Theology*, Religious Perspectives 26 (San Francisco: Harper & Row, 1978).

12. Paul Wallace, *Stars Beneath Us: Finding God in the Evolving Cosmos* (Minneapolis: Fortress, 2015), 139.

how to recognize it and read it meaningfully.[13] To prepare for the discovery of life elsewhere in the universe, astrobiology considers alternative pathways to metabolic life. Call them "biological thought experiments." Can there be such a thing as silicon-based life, an alternative to the carbon-based life we know? Can liquid methane, in addition to liquid water, serve as a medium for life? What might life look like in such strange settings? How alien can life get and remain recognizable as life from our perspective? Are our means of detecting life on another planet too restrictive? What, in fact, is life? Astrobiologists have their own quite varied suspicions and hopes, but they all might agree with J. B. S. Haldane, the great evolutionary biologist of the early last century, who said, "Now my own suspicion is that the Universe is not only queerer than we suppose, but queerer than we can suppose."[14] Astrobiology, in short, is in search of the strange.

Bible and Theology

Then what about the "strange new world within the Bible," to quote Karl Barth?[15] If the astrobiologist asks what life might look like, life that we do not currently know, then I ask what might the biblical text look like, whose meanings we may have yet to grasp, through the lens of astrobiology? To be more specific, how does one read the biblical text knowing that Earth is *not* the center of the universe, that creation extends far beyond our sight and imagination, that the cosmos is as much a process as a place, that humankind may not be the only intelligent life in the cosmos, and that the universe is far "queerer than we can suppose"?

First and foremost, I can say that astrobiology directs my attention to biblical texts that stress the cosmic extent of creation and the cosmic scope of divine activity. God, the creator of all, is cosmic (Gen 1:1–31). Christ, in whom all things were made, is cosmic (Col 1:15–20). The Spirit, which hovered over "the face of the deep," is cosmic (Gen 1:2). With the help of the natural sciences, we can now talk of the God of deep time and deep space, the God

---

13. Lucas Mix appropriately raises the concern of bias, including anthropic bias, in the search for life in the universe (*Life in Space: Astrobiology for Everyone* [Cambridge, MA: Harvard University Press, 2009], 3, 65, 68).

14. J. B. S. Haldane, *Possible Worlds* (1927; repr., New Brunswick, NJ: Transaction, 2002), 286.

15. Karl Barth, "The Strange New World within the Bible," in *The Word of God and the Word of Man*, trans. Douglas Horton (Gloucester, MA: Peter Smith, 1978), 28–50.

of possibly multiple geneses, the God of the galactic gardens. Perhaps we can even talk of God's "preferential option" for life itself. And so, I ask, is there a text in the Bible that comes closest to matching such a cosmically expansive and sublime perspective?

Job

The book of Job is itself something of a thought experiment. It is filled with "What if?" questions about human integrity, divine intention, and the nature of the universe. *What if* the paragon of righteousness were to fall into unimaginable ruin? *What if* piety is something other than the basis for reward and blessing? *What if* God is no protector of the righteous? *What if* the universe is indifferent to human concern? *What if* God were active far beyond human purviews? *What if* humanity is only one of God's many "great acts"?

As the climax to this tale of trauma, God's speeches provide the most panoramic and poetic view of creation in all of the Hebrew Bible (Job 38–41). Not coincidentally, they offer the closest thing to an astrobiological perspective in Scripture. God's answer does more than simply put Job in his place. God unveils the wonders of the cosmos, revealing the unfathomable depth and diversity of creation. Through the power of poetry, God transports Job to a world far beyond his ken: the earth's foundations, the singing stars, the swaddled sea, the gates of deep darkness, the storehouses of hail, the dwelling place of light. There is, moreover, a peculiar direction to this sequence of presentation: God's answer begins with the earth's foundations and ends with the watery abyss, the Leviathan's abode. It is a journey from the familiar to the unfamiliar, a journey into sublime chaos without a single stop to consider humanity's place in the cosmos.

After describing the vastness of creation, God provides something of a taxonomy of zoological diversity. God shows Job a host of animals: lion and raven, mountain goat and deer, wild ass and ox, ostrich and war horse, hawk and vulture, Behemoth and Leviathan—six pairs total. Each animal, God proudly points out, exercises its own strength and embodies its own dignity. They are not scavengers warranting pity or contempt (see, e.g., Job 24:5–8; 30:3–8, 29), but creatures eliciting admiration, each one holding its rightful place in creation. In God's answer Job encounters life as he does *not* know it. God reveals to Job that life is larger than life as he knows it, as much as the universe is far vaster than the world Job knows. The cosmos is revealed as utterly strange and sublime; consequently, Job suffers displacement of the most unimaginable kind. He is already an outcast in his community; now he is a castaway in the cosmos.

In God's answer, Job is treated as an antitype of Adam. Unlike Adam, to whom God brought the animals to be known and named in the garden (Gen 2:19–20), Job is poetically taken out of his world and taken to where the wild things are to learn *their* names and *their* ways of life, their habits and habitats. God gives Job a lesson not in astrobiology per se, but in something comparable. Call it "Extreme Biology." God asks Job,

> Can you hunt the prey for the lion,
>> or satisfy the appetite of the young lions,
> when they crouch in their dens,
>> or lie in wait in their covert? (38:39–40)

God does not challenge Job to kill the lion, as if to test his physical prowess in the face of predatory danger. Rather, God challenges Job to imagine himself *providing for* the lion, as if to test the extent of his care and compassion.[16] Such a question overturns Job's familiar world. In God's wild kingdom, Job is asked not to be the lion hunter but the lion's provider. What was the source of mortal fear for Job is now the recipient of providential care.

Job's zoological tour begins with the lion and ends, climactically, with Leviathan, whose abode is none other than the abyss. Through the power of divine poetry, Job is plunged into the watery depths, bringing him into dangerous proximity to this magnificent chaos monster—close enough to examine how tight its scales are fastened together (41:15–17 [Hebrew vv. 7–9]). As the final entry in God's taxonomy of the wild, Leviathan is the crown of creation, bearing a certain regal demeanor:

> It surveys everything that is lofty;
>> it is king over all that are proud. (41:34 [26])

What Job had deemed chaos down under, God has elevated to the status of royalty—creation turned upside down. To use a literary analogy, it is as if

---

16. Cf. Job 10:16, where Job complains that God has hunted him down "as a lion."

God handed Job a letter, which Job then dutifully showed his wife, saying, "Here is the letter that destroyed my universe."

Remarkably, there is no talk of God having to exercise dominion over these animals (only the possibility of doing so in 40:19). Instead, there is much talk of freedom, vitality, strength, and fearlessness regarding these creatures. God proudly describes them, inviting Job to admire each of them, to be aghast and astonished by them, to be enthralled by them. Does God swell with pride in showing off these creatures? As God was eager to show off Job to Satan in the prologue, praising Job's pious integrity (1:8; 2:3), so now God praises these creatures before Job's eyes, showing off their sublime integrity. God the biophile admires them for what they are. The Creator delights in all these creatures, who live and move and have their being in God as God intended. As if in response to Irenaeus's claim that "the glory of God is a human person fully alive,"[17] the book of Job proclaims that the glory of God is *all* creation fully alive, everywhere and anywhere throughout its cosmic extent. Each creature is an alien endowed with inalienable dignity.[18]

With God describing each creature in loving detail, Job is afforded a point of view far beyond himself, a perspective that is God's perspective, yet one that the animals also share. Job is invited to see the looming battle through the lens of the fearless warhorse, to spy out corpses through the eyes of the hungry vulture, to roar for prey as the lion, to cry for food like the raven's brood, to roam free on the vast plains with the onager, to laugh at the horse and its rider like the ostrich, to play in the high mountains with the goats, and even to swim with the likes of Leviathan. I wonder whether, through this zoological tour, God is inviting Job to reimagine himself for one brief moment as Enkidu of the Gilgamesh epic, the wild man who once roamed with the wild herds before becoming civilized to serve as the counterpart to Gilgamesh, the famed king of Uruk (Tablet I). But that's another story. Regardless, Job is challenged to share not only God's perspective of creation, a distinctly cosmic perspective, but the perspectives of the wild in creation, the wisdom of the wild, where even folly is not disparaged, as in the case of the ostrich (Job 39:13–18). Welcome, Job, to *Terra sapiens*.

---

17. Irenaeus, *Against Heresies*, 4.20.7.

18. For a discussion of dignity, human and otherwise, in light of astrobiology, see Robin Lovin, "Astrobiology and Theology," in *The Impact of Discovery of Life Beyond Earth*, ed. Steven J. Dick (Cambridge: Cambridge University Press, 2015), 222–32.

Job and Astrobiology

All in all, God brings the periphery of Job's purview into the center, turning Job's world not so much inside out as outside in. One telling passage is Job 38:25–27:[19]

> Who has cut a channel for the downpours,
>> and a way for the thunderbolts
> to bring rain upon a no-man's land,
>> upon an uninhabitable desert,
> to satisfy the desolate wasteland,
>> and to bring forth grass growth?

For more astronomically oriented readers, God could have added these words:

> Who has made the comet's gaseous tail,
>> and cut a way for the watery plumes of Enceladus
>>> to provide an icy ring for Saturn?
> Who brings the rains of liquid methane
>> to fill Titan's lakes and deltas?
> Who keeps Europa's ocean warm and active,
>> swaddled under its icy surface,
>> preserving the threshold of life?

Or so one could imagine. God's answer turns the cosmos into something "wholly other" (*ganz Andere*, à la Rudolf Otto), a *mysterium* that verges on the monstrous, thanks particularly to Behemoth and Leviathan. God's answer to Job yields the Bible's most sublime presentation of "creation's self-revelation" (*die Selbstoffenbarung der Schöpfung*), as Gerhard von Rad described biblical wisdom.[20] Job responds with an overwhelming sense of wonder, as his penultimate words attest: "I spoke of things I did not understand, things too wonderful for me to know" (42:3b; cf. Prov 30:18). But there is more. Job's final words highlight another existential outcome of his cosmic tour: "Therefore, I relent and am comforted [*wenikhamti*] concerning dust and

---

19. Author's translation.
20. Gerhard von Rad, *Wisdom in Israel*, trans. James D. Martin (Nashville: Abingdon, 1988), 144–76.

ashes" (Job 42:6).[21] This translation differs significantly from most standard versions (e.g., NRSV, NIV, but cf. CEB), particularly regarding the second clause. The second verb (*nakham*) fundamentally denotes a change of heart and can exhibit a wide range of nuance. In the book of Job, however, this verb consistently conveys a more specialized meaning: it occurs six other times and consistently with the sense of "comfort."[22]

The Comforting Cosmos

How is it, then, that God's answer comforts Job in his anguish, succeeding where Job's friends have failed? Job's "repentance," as indicated in most translations of 42:6b, was an issue only for his friends, never for Job and not for God. Repentance, after all, is rendered irrelevant by God in the very next verse (v. 7). What *is* rendered relevant in Job's final testimony, however, is his comfort. Before the sublime sweep of the cosmos and life's alien diversity, in the throes of wonder and awe, Job has found solace in his desolation, in his state of displacement and decentered-ness, and on his heap of "dust and ashes."[23]

This, admittedly, is the crux of the book of Job, and the translation proposed here only deepens the enigma. It is commonly assumed that Job finds no comfort in God's answer, since his suffering is left entirely unaddressed. Lacking in God's response is any acknowledgment of Job's plight, much less any explanation for it. "Cold comfort" at best. But the translation stands exegetically; therefore, one must account for the fact that Job admits to finding genuine comfort in his encounter with God and creation. What, then, could be the connection between Job's professed state of comfort and the fierce landscapes and creatures he has encountered? God reveals to Job a cosmos that is far from cozy: one that is immense and fundamentally indifferent to his plight and that exists in bewildering otherness. Does the cosmos share the enchantment that Edward Abbey says about the desert, namely, that "it doesn't

---

21. Author's translation. For detailed argumentation, see Thomas Krüger, "Did Job Repent?" in *Das Buch Hiob und Seine Interpretationen. Beiträge zum Hiob-Symposium auf dem Monte Verità vom 14.–19. August 2005*, ed. T. Krüger, ATANT 88 (Zürich: TVZ, 2007), 217–29.

22. Job 2:11; 7:13; 15:11; 16:2; 21:34; 29:25; 42:11 (cf. the nominal form in 15:11).

23. The pairing of "dust and ashes" in 42:6b is also attested in Gen 18:27, in which Abraham abases himself while challenging God's justice over the fate of Sodom and Gomorrah. The phrase conveys diplomatic humility before the Deity. The pairing of "dust and ashes" finds its only other parallel in Job 30:19: "[God] has cast me into the mire, and I have become like dust and ashes." The reference to "dust and ashes" connotes the evanescence of Job's fragile life. Likewise in Job 42:6b.

give a shit"?[24] Is this what Job finds "comforting" about the universe, a vast cosmos that renders his anxious concerns, yes, comfortingly trivial? Such a universe might offer him the "gift of blessed indifference," to quote the Reformed theologian Belden Lane.[25] While the cosmos provides Job no answer and no response to his protest of pain, it does give him the opportunity to be drawn outside of himself. In short, Job's experience of the cosmos could be called an exercise in apophatic wonder, one that elicits a self-negation of sorts, a kenosis of the ego. Job's comfort comes from being decentered by the overwhelming magnitude of creation—a Copernican comfort, if you will. But is that all? Self-kenotic comfort might be all there is to assuage Job's anguish if the cosmos were characterized only by its sheer vastness. But the universe is far from empty. According to God's answer, there are these denizens that flourish far beyond Job's own world, in inaccessible mountains and desert wastelands, gracing creation with alien diversity.

Although ignored by the cosmos, decentered as he is, Job is not entirely ignored by God. In one place and in one place alone, Job is given the benefit of a direct reference. In the voluminous Book of Nature, as it were, Job finds a footnote reference to himself. When Job is introduced to the mighty, lumbering Behemoth, God has this to say about Job: "Behold Behemoth, which I made *with* you ['*immak*]. . . . It is the first of the great acts of God" (40:15a, 19a). For all the alien otherness of these wild creatures, God tells Job that he bears a connection with this one monster of creation. Behemoth is created by God "with" Job. The preposition is the key, as it is in Genesis 3. In the Garden, the man was "with" the woman (Gen 3:6); the woman was created "to be with" him (v. 12). Call it the preposition of connection, perhaps even companionship. In Job's case, God has given Job a truly strange bedfellow. As the woman and the man share common substance ("flesh" and "bone"), so Job shares a bond of some sort with this alien creature. In God's creation, Job discovers himself to be a monster's companion and by extension a companion to all things wild and alien.[26]

From an astrobiological perspective, it seems almost incidental that these wild creatures that populate the book of Job are all Earth-bound. From Job's

---

24. Quoted in Belden C. Lane, *The Solace of Fierce Landscapes: Exploring Desert and Mountain Spirituality* (Oxford: Oxford University Press, 1998), 117.

25. Lane, *The Solace of Fierce Landscapes*, 57.

26. Indeed, the word *behemot* resembles a plural form, suggesting that the figure of Behemoth serves as an exemplar of all nonhuman creatures (cf. Ps 73:22).

perspective, these creatures, particularly Behemoth and Leviathan, could easily pass as aliens from another planet. In popular media, particularly in the realm of popular science fiction, "alien" typically connotes two opposing positions, either as enemy intent on conquering or destroying the earth or as savior ready to provide solutions, whether technological or spiritual, to intractable human problems. In Job, however, such "alien" creatures break such a binary. They neither conquer nor save. They are simply there—worlds unto themselves as much as they are worlds apart from Job. If, according to E. O. Wilson, "Each species is a small universe in itself,"[27] then Earth is, figuratively speaking, its own multiverse! As both modern cosmology and the book of Job demonstrate, the cosmos seems a "rather outsized stage for the drama of human life and history."[28] In light of its vastness and the possibility, if not probability, of life elsewhere, one can easily imagine other dramas and developments of life taking place, or yet to take place. In Job, God presents the world as richly pluriform, replete with the parallel universes of life, species that either had remained hidden to Job, their dignity unrecognized, or had existed far beyond his sight and understanding until God revealed them. But they are all, Job discovers, connected to him in the common exercise of life, in the common bond of creaturehood.

The irony runs deep. At the nadir of his despair, Job complained of being a "brother of jackals, and a companion of ostriches" (30:29), ostracized by his friends and family. He saw such animals only with contempt. But God shows Job that he is actually in good company with these creatures, all of whom have their own dignity. To be a companion of jackals and ostriches, lions and Leviathans, Behemoths and onagers is no cause for lament but rather cause for wonder and ultimately cause for comfort. It is among these alien creatures, not among his friends or family, not in a culture shaped by honor and shame, that Job has found an alternative community, open and diverse, a community of freedom. Through the mighty figure of Behemoth, Job discovers himself to be inextricably connected to all life, grasping perhaps something of the biologist's dictum, "I link, therefore I am"[29] (with apologies to Descartes).

---

27. Edward O. Wilson, *The Creation: An Appeal to Save Life on Earth* (New York: Norton, 2006), 123.

28. Douglas F. Ottati, *Theology for Liberal Protestants: God the Creator* (Grand Rapids: Eerdmans, 2013), 224.

29. Attributed to S. J. Singer by Edward O. Wilson, *Consilience: The Unity of Knowledge* (New York: Vintage, 1998), 121.

Or to cast it more theologically, Job has discovered the "feeling of absolute *inter*dependence" (with apologies to Schleiermacher).

This, then, is the crux of the Joban "thought experiment." Job is compelled to imagine himself as kin to a monster, to Behemoth, the "first of the great acts of God" (40:19). Where one might expect reference to humanity's place in the order of creation as one of "the great acts of God," we find instead effusive descriptions of Behemoth and Leviathan—two monstrously magnificent beasts that have displaced humanity's position at the top of the created order. And so we might ask, in what world are these creatures deemed the greatest of God's creative acts? Certainly not in Job's world. They are, in effect, creatures of another genesis and creations of another world. Given its concluding description (41:34 [26]), the formidable figure of Leviathan parallels the distinctly royal setting of humanity's own creation in "the image of God" in Genesis 1:26–28 (cf. Ps 8:5–8 [6–9]). It seems, then, that Leviathan and Behemoth fall within the orbit of God's "images" as well (see also 40:19a); they are theriomorphic theophanies in their own right. Indeed it could be said that, from the perspective of God's answer to Job, creation itself—in all its depth and breadth, its diversity and sublimity—is made "in the image of God" in so far as it reflects God's might, magnitude, and wisdom.

The book of Job is the Bible's own Copernican revolution. God's answer decenters Job once and for all, and along with Job, all humanity. It serves as Job's "baptism" into raw, alien nature—nature apart from him, apart from his provincial culture, beyond his patriarchal gaze, life as he does not know it, yet life that is "with" him. Job's journey begins in trauma and terror, proceeds to awe and wonder, and arrives in comfort. Job is strengthened to begin his life anew. But the question remains: Where is the comfort in this? Perhaps it is in Job realizing his connection with these wild and fearless creatures, a connection that resonates with his own yearnings for freedom, his yearning to be fully "selved," fully alive and well. Yes, Job's journey of comfort began when his friends "sat *with* him on the ground" in silence (Job 2:13). But such a promising beginning was quickly derailed by words that committed epistemic violence: Job himself was turned into a monster by his friends, a monstrosity of sin and a repulsive alien. Ultimately, Job finds himself in good company with the aliens that thrive beyond his familiar purview.

God, admittedly, does not sit with Job in his travail. God does not even declare, "I am with you," which is the kind of divine pronouncement that one might find at the heart of a salvation oracle. The God of the whirlwind remains the God of the whirlwind. So, if Job does not find "comfort" from a solicitous God who meets his every need, then where does he find it? It can only be in the world that God has revealed to Job. It is a world that is cosmically queerer than he can suppose and yet is made *with* him. Job has found comfort in "knowing creation" more fully, a creation that takes him out of the comfort zone of his terrestrial cocoon, out of his mesophilic life, and into a world of extreme, sublime grandeur, a world of otherness with which he ultimately finds deep connection. Job is the alien whose alienation is overcome by a distinctly alien creation. "Welcome to my world," God seems to say, "and have a look around," to which Job could easily respond in the words of the psalmist,

> O Lord, how manifold are your works!
>   In wisdom you have made them all;
>   the earth is full of your creatures. (Ps 104:24)

The day may come when we can say that the cosmos, too, is full of God's creatures.

Chapter EIGHT

Knowing and Being Known

Interpersonal Cognition and the Knowledge of God
in Paul's Letters

SUSAN GROVE EASTMAN

The last few decades have witnessed a resurgence of interest in the notion of human beings as interpersonally constituted, made in and for relationships with other human beings. This is by no means a new idea, as any cursory reading of the history of Christian and Jewish thought will demonstrate. But for a few centuries the notion of the individual as a freestanding, self-determining, and bounded agent has dominated conceptions of the person in Western thought. Philosopher Timothy Chappell calls this "individualism about persons," traceable to Cartesianism if not precisely to Descartes.[1] The individual who says *cogito ergo sum* is presumed to be an autonomous, isolated subject; cognition is the disembodied and private activity of essentially discrete persons.

Such autonomous individualism is under attack in many quarters. From the claims of neuroscientists who posit a neurologically supported "we-centric space" that precedes individual cognition, to developmental psychologists who prioritize the parent-child relationship as the "cradle of thought," to philosophers of mind who describe a neurological feedback loop extending from the embodied self into the environment, persons are seen as foundationally constituted in relationship with others.[2] The interpersonal constitution of

---

1. Timothy Chappell, "Knowledge of Persons," *European Journal for Philosophy of Religion* 5, no. 4 (Winter 2013): 3–28.

2. The claim of a "we-centric" space comes from Vittorio Gallese, "'Being Like Me': Self-Other Identity, Mirror Neurons, and Empathy," in *Perspectives on Imitation: From Neuroscience to Social Science*, vol. 1, *Mechanisms of Imitation and Imitation in Animals*, ed. Susan Hurley and Nick Chater (Cambridge,

the self in turn has profound implications for human cognition as occurring "between ourselves" rather than simply "between our ears."[3] Philosophers and psychologists working from such an *a priori* interpersonal standpoint sometimes describe their work as based on a second person perspective in which the starting point for understanding persons is an interpersonally constituted self-in-relation. In Chappell's words, "Individuality presupposes relationality."[4]

In what follows, I want to explore how an interpersonal constitution of the self illuminates human knowledge of creation and its Creator. I begin with an earlier expression of such knowledge in socially embedded and irreducibly embodied terms. In the latter half of the eighteenth century, a Hasidic master named Levi Yitzhak of Berditchev composed a poem called "Song of You."[5] It goes like this:

> Lord of the world.
> Lord of the world.
> Lord of the world,
> I'll sing You a little song of You.

> *You-You-You*

> Where will I find You?
> And where won't I find You?

> So – here I go – You,
> And – there I go – You,
> always You, however You,
> only You, and ever You.

MA: MIT Press, 2005), 101–18; psychoanalyst Peter Hobson has written on the origins of thought and formative systems of "self-in-relation" in his book *The Cradle of Thought: Exploring the Origins of Thinking* (Oxford: Oxford University Press, 2002). For an overview of philosophical and scientific depictions of the self as extending beyond bodily boundaries into the environment, see particularly Shaun Gallagher, *How the Body Shapes the Mind* (Oxford: Oxford University Press, 2011).

3. See, e.g., Andy Clark, *Supersizing the Mind: Embodiment, Action, and Cognitive Extension* (Oxford: Oxford University Press, 2011).

4. Chappell, "Knowledge of Persons," 4.

5. Translation from Peter Cole, *The Poetry of Kabbalah: Mystical Verse from the Jewish Tradition* (New Haven: Yale University Press, 2012), 236–37.

You-You-You, You-You

East – You – West – You,
North – You – South – You.

You – You – You

The heavens – You. Earth – You.
On high – You, and below . . .
In every direction, and every inflection.
Still You. However You. Only You. Ever You.

You — You — You

Here is second-person knowledge of and engagement with God—not God as an object of third-person propositional statements (although those also have their place), nor God as the extension of first-person self-awareness, but God as an Other who is addressable and who addresses human beings. Such personal knowledge comes easily, lightly, to the poet whose life is lived in the constant recognition of this divine Other.

God's pervasive presence is a source of confidence and exuberant joy, but this joyful second-person encounter is neither private nor disembodied; rather, it is corporate and corporeal. The translator, Peter Cole, tells us that in 1781 Levi Yitzhak represented the Hasidic movement in an inner-Jewish debate at Warsaw:

He was asked why the Hasids jump and leap about while praying "as if the fear of heaven were not upon you. . . . Such conduct is not proper before even a human king." Levi Yitzhak replied, "Do not bring proofs from a human king . . . he fills only the place where he sits. . . . The King of Kings, the Holy One, blessed be He, whose glory fills the world . . . there is no place where He is not, and wherever we turn, there He is. Therefore it is proper to leap and jump after the Master of the World, always searching for Him. The Lord is everywhere!"[6]

---

6. Cole, *The Poetry of Kabbalah*, 425.

The poet joyfully acclaims what his senses perceive, and he uses all his senses, indeed his whole body, to express that joy alongside his fellow Hasids. Levi Yitzhak knows that God is everywhere, and for that very reason he searches personally for this same God with his whole being.

Levi's poem prompts additional questions about creation and knowledge of God: How is knowledge *that* God exists related to a personal knowledge *of* the presence of God, and in what would such knowledge consist?[7] And how is genuine personal knowledge of God, as distinct from human beings yet engaged with them, distinguished from mere self-projection?

One way to explore these questions is by putting very different and yet surprisingly compatible interlocutors into conversation with each other: second-person accounts of the development of human cognition in experimental psychology and the first-century writings of the apostle Paul. I believe the conversation will be mutually illuminating. I shall argue that in Paul's view knowledge of God is socially embedded and thereby involves the same capacities for personal knowledge as knowing other human beings as distinct from ourselves and yet in relationship with us. Specifically, I shall claim that God's self-revelation engages interpersonally constituted human cognitive capacities and takes place in the midst of human interaction. It is not an otherworldly, esoteric, and private affair.

As we shall see, in both second-person and Pauline accounts of human knowledge, the *experience of being known* precedes and grounds the capacity to know another. In both cases, relationality precedes individuality and constitutes the person as a knowing subject. Thus relationality is a gift more than an achievement. Given regardless of individual abilities, the gift of relational identity generates and sustains human capacities for further relationship and for cognition of self and other. My argument thus takes a thoroughly participatory approach to questions of human personhood and experience, which I believe will be illuminating for Paul's understanding of the knowledge of God—or, to put it more precisely, of the ways God engages humanity.

I will begin with some comments about the second-person character of human knowing, then make some observations based on Paul's letters, and finally bring these two worlds of discourse into mutual conversation.

---

7. Implicit here are philosophical debates concerning the relationship between propositional and personal forms of knowledge. For helpful discussion of this, see Eleonore Stump, *Wandering in Darkness: Narrative and the Problem of Suffering* (Oxford: Oxford University Press, 2012), 43–63.

The Second-Person Character of Human Thought

One of the pioneers of new approaches to human identity and cognition is Andrew Meltzoff, who conducted infant imitation studies in the 1970s.[8] Meltzoff and others have conclusively demonstrated that within an hour of birth, newborns imitate others' facial expressions, even though they cannot, of course, see their own faces. These studies have been conducted around the globe in a variety of cultures. They imply an innate propensity for interpersonal connection manifested by mimetic activity in human neonates long before the development of language or the capacity for abstract thought. We might say that parent and child act in concert with one another in an interpersonal dance at the very beginning of human development.[9]

The implications of these findings are immense and have contributed to an extensive body of literature in philosophy of mind, neuroscience, and psychology. Scientists and philosophers differ within their respective fields, however, on how to interpret this data. In order to sharpen our understanding of a second-person interpretation of the data, I will contrast it with first-personal simulation theory, here represented by Meltzoff's theory of how infants know minds.

First-Person Simulation Theory

Meltzoff calls his theory the "'Like me' hypothesis." He articulates it in explicitly first-personal, self-referential terms, proposing a three-step sequence from the experience of imitation to understanding other minds.[10] According to Meltzoff, first the infant imitates other faces and experiences what such motor simulation feels like. Secondly, a proprioceptive feedback loop linking perception and sensory experience *within* the infant provides repeated information about what it is like to smile, for example. This feedback loop

---

8. Andrew Meltzoff and M. Keith Moore, "Imitation of Facial and Manual Gestures by Human Neonates," *Science* 198, no. 4312 (1977): 75–78.

9. See, e.g., Daniel Stern, *The Interpersonal World of the Infant* (New York: Basic, 1985); Colwyn Trevarthen, "The Self Born in Intersubjectivity: The Psychology of an Infant Communicating," in *The Perceived Self: Ecological and Interpersonal Sources of Self-Knowledge*, ed. Ulric Neisser (New York: Cambridge University Press, 1993), 121–73; Beatrice Beebe et al., "Forms of Intersubjectivity in Infant Research: A Comparison of Meltzoff, Trevarthen, and Stern," in *Forms of Intersubjectivity in Infant Research and Adult Treatment* (New York: Other, 2005), 29–53.

10. Andrew N. Meltzoff, "Understanding Other Minds: The 'Like Me' Hypothesis," in *Perspectives on Imitation: From Neuroscience to Social Science*, vol. 2, *Imitation, Human Development, and Culture*, ed. Susan Hurley and Nick Chater (Cambridge, MA: MIT Press, 2005), 55–77 (56).

between the infant's "bodily state and mental experience"—all interior to the self—generates a detailed inner map linking mind and behavior, which in turn becomes the basis for understanding others. In Meltzoff's words, "Infants imbue the acts of others with felt meaning, not through a process of step-by-step formal reasons, but because the other is processed as 'like me.'"[11] This is a version of simulation theory, in which awareness of others' mental states begins with an interior mapping of our own physical, emotional sensations, which we then project onto others. Similarly, the neuroscientist Vittorio Gallese suggests that an *intrasubjective* "mind-body brain system" links first-person experience of self with third-person experience of others.[12]

It is important to note what this theory assumes. First, it assumes that infants already know what "me" is "like" in order to recognize when others are "like me." Neonates must be able to know and identify their own feelings and experience in a first-personal, discrete, and self-contained way. Furthermore, such self-knowledge requires the existence of a private language implicit in the infant's articulation of her experience to herself.[13] For example, through repeated experiences of the feeling of a smile, when baby sees mommy smile, she somehow communicates within herself, even if at a subconscious level, "That makes me feel happy; mommy must be happy too! Mommy is like me!"

But how does the baby know what happy is? How indeed does she know that she herself exists as a "me"—a feeling and thinking subject? How does the infant have a sense of self to use as a basis for knowing others, and how does the projection of such a private experience onto others constitute a real knowledge of others' mental states? Implicit here is a view of the self as essentially inward and hidden and thus in some way disconnected from the visible, public body.

---

11. Meltzoff, "Understanding Other Minds," 57. Meltzoff recognizes that infants also are aware when others imitate them, so that "infants map from the other to the self" as well as mapping "from the self to the other," but he takes the latter as primary (60).

12. Vittorio Gallese, Christian Keysers, and Giacomo Rizzolatti, "A Unifying View of the Basis of Social Cognition," *Trends in Cognitive Science* 8 (2004). doi:10.1016/j.tics.2004.07.002.

13. Joshua Johnson, "The Private Language Argument and a Second-Person Approach to Mindreading," *European Journal for Philosophy of Religion* 5, no. 4 (Winter 2013): 75–86. Both Peter Hobson and Vasudevi Reddy also criticize simulation theory as requiring an impossible private language. See Reddy, *How Infants Know Minds* (Cambridge, MA: Harvard University Press, 2008), 19–21; Hobson, "Wittgenstein and the Developmental Psychopathology of Autism," *New Ideas in Psychology* 27 (2009): 243–57. See also the discussion by Shaun Gallagher, "The Practice of Mind," in *Between Ourselves: Second-Person Issues in the Study of Consciousness*, ed. Evan Thompson (Exeter: Imprint Academic, 2001), 83–108; and Eleonore Stump, *Wandering in Darkness*, 70, 509n35.

Hence, the only way to access another's thoughts and intentions is by a process of inference from one's own bodily experience and the projection of that experience onto others.[14] This is a first-person interpretation of data derived from studies of infant imitation.

Second-Person Theories

Second-person theorists diverge from Meltzoff's simulation theory in their understanding of the *starting point* of human capacities for personal knowledge. From the first-person perspective, mutual engagement begins with the infant's innate capacities and motivation to connect with others. Relationality presupposes individuality. It is difficult to see how an infant could develop as a knowing subject without such capacities and initiative.

In theories of cognitive development grounded in a second-person perspective, however, relationship with another is the starting point for the knowledge of self and others. The infant sees himself in the gaze of another and arrives at a limited knowledge of himself through the sensory feedback of his adult partners. In other words, the infant begins to have the idea of an "I" or a "me" *through* engagement with others, not prior to such engagement. Vasudevi Reddy puts this claim very strongly: "It is the other's attention at grips with the infant that makes attention exist for the infant."[15] "You have to be addressed as a subject to become one."[16] When Reddy describes stages of the parent-child interaction through which children begin to attend to other people and eventually to share perception of objects, each stage begins with the child's *response* to the parent's attending activity, followed by the child's *initiative* in directing that attention.[17] The child is not passive, but neither is she autonomous or primarily self-referential. She is a relationally constituted acting subject. This is not to say that there is no individual self or that the infant begins as a blank slate. With significant exceptions, infants are active participants in the interplay between parent and child, and they arrive on the

---

14. Meltzoff's theory has been challenged precisely on these grounds. See, e.g., Wolfgang Prinz, "Construing Selves from Others," in in *Perspectives on Imitation: From Neuroscience to Social Science*, vol. 2, *Imitation, Human Development, and Culture*, ed. Susan Hurley and Nick Chater (Cambridge, MA: MIT Press, 2005), 181.

15. Vasudevi Reddy, "A Gaze at Grips with Me," in *Joint Attention: New Developments in Psychology, Philosophy of Mind, and Social Neuroscience*, ed. A. Seemann (Cambridge: MIT Press, 2011), 137–57 (138).

16. Vasudevi Reddy, *How Infants Know Minds* (Cambridge, MA: Harvard University Press, 2008), 32.

17. Vasudevi Reddy, "Before the 'Third Element': Understanding Attention to Self," in *Joint Attention: Communication and Other Minds*, ed. N. Eilan et al. (Oxford: Clarendon, 2005), 85–109 (96).

scene with their own distinct genetic makeup. But they develop a sense of self as well as recognition of other persons *through and in* the interplay with their parents, not as a *prerequisite for* such interplay. To the contrary, the interaction itself is the prerequisite for awareness of self and a capacity for thought. This view is irreducibly intersubjective, and it assumes and requires the initiative of the adult partner. Individuality presupposes relationality. It would be difficult if not impossible to imagine the development of human capacities for personal knowledge without the presence of an attending partner who is motivated to connect with the child.

In fact, Peter Hobson argues that primary social engagement is necessary for the development of language and along with that, of all human cognition. In Hobson's view,

> Central to mental development is a psychological system that is greater and more powerful than the sum of its parts. The parts are the caregiver and her infant; the system is what happens when they act and feel in concert. The combined operation of infant-in-relation-to-caregiver is a motive force in development, and it achieves wonderful things. When it does not exist, and the motive force is lacking, the whole of mental development is terribly compromised.[18]

Note here the primacy of the system of self-in-relation-to-other for the development of thinking and the role of such connection as a motive force for mental development.

Paul and the Knowledge of God in Second-Person Perspective

Keeping these images and ideas in mind, we turn to the writings of Paul, asking what such interpersonally grounded modes of knowledge have to do with Paul's understanding of human knowledge and the knowledge of God. First, two brief passages reveal the priority of divine knowledge over human knowledge. Then two key texts in Romans introduce Paul's views of how the Spirit of God mediates knowledge of God's presence and action.

---

18. Hobson, *The Cradle of Thought*, 183.

Knowing God and Being Known by God

Writing to churches in Galatia that are turning away from his gospel, Paul asks how they can go back to their former way of life "now that you have come to know God—or rather, to be known by God" (Gal 4:9).[19] It is an illuminating self-correction, replacing any confidence about knowing God with the experience of being known by God. Similarly, in his famous chapter on love in 1 Corinthians 13, Paul concludes:

> For we know only in part, and we prophesy only in part, but when the perfect comes, the partial will come to an end. When I was a child, I spoke like a child, I thought like a child, I reasoned like a child; when I became an adult, I put an end to childish ways. For now we see in a mirror, dimly, but then we will see face to face. Now I know only in part; then I will know fully, even as I have been fully known. (1 Cor 13:9–12)

Here is a profound cognitive humility; divine knowledge of human beings far exceeds and precedes any human cognitive abilities.

These two passages highlight three aspects of Paul's views about human knowledge: it is imperfect and analogous to children's ways of knowing, it is thoroughly interpersonal, and it is initiated and sustained by the assurance of *being* known and loved by God. God's knowledge of human beings grounds any truthful knowledge by human beings.

The Spirit and Interpersonal Knowledge of God

Keeping these three points in mind, we turn to Paul's understanding of the Spirit of God as the one who mediates knowledge of God. In the first appearance of the Spirit in Romans, it bestows the experience of being loved. Paul puts it this way:

> The love of God has been poured into our hearts through the Holy Spirit who has been given to us. For while we were still weak, at the right time Christ died for the ungodly. Indeed, rarely will anyone die for a righteous person—though perhaps for a good person someone might actually dare to die. But God proves his love for us in that while we were sinners

---

19. Unless otherwise indicated, all scriptural quotations are my translation.

Christ died for us. . . . For if while we were enemies, we were reconciled
to God through the death of his Son, much more surely, having been
reconciled, will we be saved by his life. (Rom 5:5–8, 10)

Here Paul claims a particular kind of relational bond between God and those
whom he addresses as "we."

First, the bond is grounded in the gift of the divine presence and proceeds
from the desire of the giver, not the capacities or "fittingness" of the receivers.[20]
Paul highlights how shocking this is when he says, "someone might dare
even to die for a good person," but Christ died for the weak, the ungodly,
sinners, God's enemies—all of whom are embraced in the plural "we" that
includes Paul and his readers. This "we" refers not just to some particularly
incapacitated individuals but to the entire human race, all of whom, in Paul's
view, suffer from cognitive impairment because they have been subjected to
a disordered mind and have turned their backs on God (Rom 1:28). Thus
Christ's death on behalf of the cognitively impaired is a gift of relationship
extended to recipients who are not initially capable of reciprocating at all. The
absence of any prerequisites is striking. This is a distinctively second-person
understanding of redemption. Human cognition of God rises from an already
given divine-human interaction.

Second, the gift is experienced as love from God to humanity, demonstrated and enacted through Christ's self-giving death for human beings
in the midst of their weakness, sinfulness, and even hostility toward God.
From Paul's perspective, this divine self-giving is the christological basis for a
second-person understanding of God's action in the world, including human
knowledge of that action. It is a divine, bodily sharing of humanity's condition
under judgment for sin, which in turn opens the door to a mutual engagement
between God and human beings under the banner of "no condemnation"
(Rom 8:1).[21]

Third, Paul speaks in the *plural* first-person. He does not say, "The love
of God has been poured into *my* heart through the Spirit given to *me*," but

---

20. For an extensive exploration of this theme, see now John Barclay, *Paul and the Gift* (Grand
Rapids: Eerdmans, 2015).

21. For another analysis of the significance of the incarnation for interpersonal indwelling, as well
as the role of the Spirit in that interpersonal union with God, see Eleonore Stump, "Omnipresence,
Indwelling, and the Second-Personal," in *The European Journal for the Philosophy of Religion* 5, no. 4
(Winter 2013): 29–53 (43–45).

rather, "The love of God has been poured into *our* hearts through the Spirit given to *us*." The point is obvious but often ignored in discussions of spiritual experience, which tends to be depicted in individualistic terms. For Paul, experiential knowledge of God is bound up in our relationships with other people.

This interpersonal quality becomes clear when Paul returns to the topic of the Spirit in Romans 8, where he depicts "life in Christ Jesus" as a participatory relational bond between God and believers that is free of condemnation, governed by gift, and mediated by the Spirit of God. Two aspects of this relational bond need emphasis here. First, as in Romans 5:5–10, Paul again uses plural pronouns to depict those among whom the Spirit dwells. To get at Paul's meaning, it is necessary to translate his deceptively simple prepositional phrase, "in you," in a variety of ways:

> But you all are not *in* the flesh, together you are *in* the Spirit, since in fact the Spirit of God dwells *in* you all—that is, *in your midst*. If anyone does not have the Spirit of Christ, such a one does not belong to him. But if Christ is *in your midst*, on the one hand the body is dead through sin, but on the other hand, the Spirit is life through righteousness. Now if the Spirit of the one who raised Jesus from the dead dwells *among you*, the one who raised Christ from the dead also will give life to your mortal bodies through his Spirit dwelling *in your midst*. (Rom 8:9–11)

Here the life-giving Spirit dwells "between ourselves"—that is, in the midst of human interaction. This personal experience of God is interpersonal at the foundation of human life, in the cradle of thought generated between people who together share the Spirit's presence.

Therefore, such a relational constitution of believers has further implications for human thought and speech. In Romans 8:5–6, Paul writes: "Those who are according to the flesh think [*phronousin*] the things of the flesh, but those who are according to the Spirit [think] the things of the Spirit. For the mindset [*phronēma*] of the flesh is death, but the mindset of the Spirit is life and peace." Apparently, the Spirit has "thoughts and intentions" and those who are in sync with the Spirit share the same thoughts and intentions. There is, so to speak, a shared semantic content between the Spirit and the Spirit's adherents. Similarly, the Spirit cries out in public worship through the lips of believers, and human beings indwelt by the Spirit themselves simultaneously speak: "When we cry 'Abba! Father!' it is the Spirit *testifying together with* our spirit that we are children of God" (8:15–16). Paul is describing the community gathered in worship and collectively crying out to God in prayer, as its members experience a shared awareness and joint recognition of their new status and inheritance as children of God. This is concretely, explicitly, a shared speech-act and joint attention in which a new knowledge of God and others arises. Through this communal action, Paul's addressees know themselves together as coheirs with Christ and each other, *suffering together* so as to be *glorified together with* Christ and with each other. Every facet of this depiction of Christian existence is "with" others in a shared "family life."

Again, Paul says, "We know that in everything the Spirit *works together* [*synergei*] for good *with* those who love him, who are called according to his purpose. For those whom he foreknew he also predestined to be formed together with one another into the image of his Son, that he might be the first-born of *many brothers and sisters*" (8:28–29). Divine agency awakens human agency in the interplay between persons, issuing in a new network of saving relations that surpasses other relational systems, including one's family of origin. When Paul indicates the shocking intimacy and immediacy of this reconstitution of persons-in-relationship by adducing the familial cry, "Abba! Father!" he evokes the crucial interaction between parent and child that human beings internalize and carry through adulthood. Now that internalized relationship is transformed through a new set of interpersonal interactions, experienced within the community constituted by God's prior and sustaining action in Christ, and mediated by the indwelling of God through the Holy Spirit.

Cumulatively, Paul emphasizes the mutual life of believers "in Christ" and "with" each other, which conveys human knowledge and interaction that operates in an interchange of giving and receiving, free of condemnation, judgment, despair, and death. Paul seeks visible, embodied, social manifestations of that gifted interchange between persons, which in contemporary scientific terms may be enacted through neurologically supported mimetic interactions. He envisions transformed cognitive capacities arising from such mutually responsive interaction, which renews body and mind together in the service of God (Rom 12:1–2).

In the shared experience of the love of God poured into human hearts through the gift of the Spirit (Rom 5:5), in a relational context free of condemnation (Rom 8:1) and inhabited by the Spirit as the shared source of thought and speech, and in the accompanying reconstitution of a shared mindset, might we see Paul limning a new divine-human, intersubjective "cradle of thought"? Knowledge of creation and God born out of such a relational matrix stands over against "the mindset of the flesh," suggesting that it also is possible for cognition to be shaped in distorted, misleading, and potentially lethal ways through destructive interpersonal matrices.

To be sure, there are no neurological "traces" of the indwelling Spirit. The Spirit cannot be detected by an fMRI test or recorded in a video of infant-parent interaction. There is no neurobiological "proof" of the presence of the Spirit or of the knowledge and experience of God mediated by the Spirit. Neurobiological explanations of ecstatic visions will not get at Paul's interpersonal understanding of the knowledge of God's presence and action in the world. Private, esoteric experience is not his concern.[22] Rather, insofar as the knowledge of God's presence and action takes place in the tangible bonds between persons, this is where any neurological mirroring or second-person identity formation occurs. This is Paul's second-person perspective.

Thus the language of mutual indwelling between the Spirit and the community suggests that knowledge of God is deeply second-personal for Paul. Its second-person quality derives, not least, from its origin in human response to the divine knowledge of humanity. Believers come to know God—or rather, come to be known by God; they are addressed as subjects and thereby become knowing subjects. All human knowledge, whether of ourselves, of the created order, or of God the creator, exists as response; it is called into being.

Conclusion

Reflecting on Paul's picture of the Spirit-indwelt relational network of believers discloses an intriguing set of characteristics. Paul assumes that human beings are participatory creatures, permeable and intensely vulnerable to the relational matrices in which they live. For Paul, human beings never perceive, intend, emote, or act purely on their own initiative; they are always constituted in

---

22. Contra Colleen Shantz, *Paul in Ecstasy: The Neurobiology of Paul's Life and Thought* (Cambridge: Cambridge University Press, 2009). Shantz bases her analysis on neurobiological explanations of experiences such as trances and visions, using such explanations as a way to understand Paul's own account of a heavenly ascent, in 2 Cor 12:1–4. But notably, Paul does not refer to the Spirit in that account, and indeed, downplays the value of elitist esoteric experience in favor of concrete, embodied service and love.

interpersonal interchanges that are also internalized—for good or for ill. His interconnected view of human beings intersects with contemporary notions of persons as selves-in-relationship, summoned into self- and other-awareness by intersubjective engagement as the ground of their existence.

I have called this intersubjective engagement "second-personal," but, as indicated by Paul's use of the plural second-person address, it is far more complex than a simple dyadic interaction between two entities such as God and the individual. Human persons are always constituted in relationship to others in complex ways, and the knowledge of God takes place within and among those interpersonal engagements.[23] Appropriating Hobson's phrase, I have called this relational system a "cradle of thought," in Christ and indwelt by the Spirit, that reworks personal identity and social cognition from the ground up. This takes place in the context of divine gift given to the cognitively impaired—according to Paul, the entire human race—through Christ's incarnation, death, and resurrection.

Putting Paul in conversation with second-person theories about the development of human cognition thus yields intriguing connections:

From a second-person perspective, human identity and thought are irreducibly intersubjective. Such primary intersubjectivity highlights the initiative of the human interlocutor who in a sense calls the person of the infant into awareness and being. Cognition is primarily relational, taking place between persons before it can happen within individuals.

From a Pauline theological perspective, it is the divine interlocutor who calls persons into being and who forms and reforms them through an irreducibly intersubjective relationship that is experienced in relations with other persons. The initiative lies with God. Recalling Levi Yitzhak's "Song of You," we remember that Levi says, "It is proper to leap and jump after the Master of the World, always searching for Him. The Lord is everywhere!" Paul would agree, but then he would add a caveat: "The Lord is everywhere, always searching after human beings!"

In both second-personal and Pauline perspectives, an emphasis on the initiative of the other locates personhood and cognition in the realm of interpersonal gift rather than individual achievement. Such giftedness has profound

---

23. For that matter, the indwelling Spirit is always known in relationship to God as the Spirit of God who raised Christ Jesus from the dead, and as the Spirit of Christ. Within Paul's proto-Trinitarian language, the Spirit is a relational entity as well.

implications for issues of inclusion in human personhood. If personhood is a gift that originates outside oneself, then no one can be excluded from the category "person" based on any cognitive or emotional impairment in the self. Paul's theology of radical grace sharpens the point. In Paul's view, all human beings are impaired, turned away from the divine-human relationship that constitutes their good, and unable to take the initiative to change that situation themselves. From a first-person perspective, the situation is hopeless because you begin with self-knowledge. Paul's perspective, however, is second-personal and grounded in divine grace: God in Christ has taken the initiative to assimilate to the human condition, becoming "like" human beings and sharing human experience and language to generate and carry the weight of intersubjective personhood. For Paul, this divine movement generates the capacity in human beings for I-Thou mutual engagement. Paul calls this special divine action "grace" and characterizes it as a gifted relationship that occurs without prerequisites on the part of human beings. However, humans are not simply passive recipients. Divine action in turn awakens and sustains human agency and interaction.

Finally, Paul's emphasis on the limitations of human knowledge inculcates a certain humility regarding human capacities to know God, or even to know oneself and others fully. For Paul, such partial knowledge is simply an aspect of life on the way to eschatological redemption: "Now I know in part, then I shall know fully, even as I have been fully known" (1 Cor 13:12b). The irreducibly intersubjective knowledge of God, and even of self and others, is *ipso facto* likewise irreducibly mysterious and exceeds explanation. In this sense, then, knowledge of God in creation is a matter of deepening engagement with the mystery of God's presence, awaiting the promised "face-to-face": "Now we see in a mirror dimly, but then we shall see face-to-face" (1 Cor 13:12a). In the present time, "The mystery, by the necessity of its subject matter, remains."[24]

---

24. Thomas G. Weinandy, *Does God Suffer?* (South Bend, IN: University of Notre Dame Press, 2000), 31.

Chapter NINE

Sanctifying Matter

MARILYN McCORD ADAMS

Introduction

Focal Lenses

There is a great difference between knowing creation and knowing creation *as* creation. Much depends on the conceptual lens through which knowledge of the world is acquired and the methods by which such knowledge is sought. The physical sciences know a lot about creation, but they do not know or seek to know the world *as* creation. They abstract from issues about metaphysical source to focus instead on matter and motion, mass-energy conversions, chemical elements and compounds and their constituents, space-time curvature, and the speed of light. The conceptualities of the physical sciences (their mathematical models, their experimental methods, and theoretical posits) have represented the material world as a site of both intelligibility and mystery—constructive mystery that provokes awe and wonder, the better to stimulate further inquiry and discovery. How can we not be impressed by and grateful for such results?

"Knowing" Creation as Uncreated

Many second-half-of-the-twentieth-century analytic philosophers went further. They proposed, if not insisted, that we take the physical sciences to be a theory of everything. Their posit carried with it the eschatological hope that sooner or later the physical sciences will be able to explain everything in the world as we know it, at least everything that is really real.[1]

---

1. Early proponents of this position included Professor John Anderson, an influential teacher of David M. Armstrong (see his *A Materialist Theory of Mind* [New York: Routledge, Kegan & Paul, 1968]).

Theories are supposed to fit the facts that they purport to explain. To be sure, all theories focus on some data while marginalizing or explaining away others. Abstraction can be theoretically advisable and legitimate insofar as different conceptualities and methods may be fruitful for investigating different aspects of the world. But the conceptuality of the physical sciences fails to capture some of the most prominent features of our experience—not only secondary qualities (e.g., the color purple, the sound of a trumpet, and the taste of chocolate) but also mind, meaning, and value. Philosophers who demanded that the physical sciences provide a theory of everything were forced to hold either that secondary qualities, such as mind, meaning, and value, are not real (eliminative materialism)[2] or that these recalcitrant phenomena really are reducible to or constituted by what the physical sciences study directly (reductive or constitutive materialism).

The attempt to make good on such philosophical claims spawned energetic research programs to develop mostly reductive and constitutive theories of how secondary qualities and mental states can be seen to be material at bottom.[3] Not only have materialist theories of the mind been the majority report in late-twentieth-century analytic philosophy, materialist theories easily became the default position among philosophers of biology, who maintain that vital functions are fundamentally to be explained in terms of physics and biochemistry.

Knowing Creation as Minded

More recently, prominent philosophers have urged us to think again.[4] When assessing theoretical proposals, explanatory power and fruitfulness are not the only desiderata. There is also saving the phenomena. Mind, meaning,

---

Another early player was J. J. C. Smart (see his "Sensations and Brain Processes," *The Philosophical Review* 68 [1959]: 141–56; "Materialism," *The Journal of Philosophy* 60 [1963]: 651–62; and "Colours," *Philosophy* 36 [1961]: 126–42).

2.   Eliminative materialism was argued for by the Churchlands. See P. M. Churchland, "Eliminative Materialism and Propositional Attitudes," *The Journal of Philosophy* 78, no. 2 (February 1981): 67–90, and *Matter and Consciousness* (Cambridge, MA: MIT Press, 1988). See also P. S. Churchland, *Neurophilosophy: Towards a Unified Science of Mind/Brain* (Cambridge, MA: MIT Press, 1986).

3.   For a recent and sympathetic assessment of the various moves to develop the materialist research program, see Derk Pereboom, *Consciousness and the Prospects of Physicalism* (Oxford: Oxford University Press, 2011).

4.   For a particularly cogent articulation of this critique, see Thomas Nagel, *Mind & Cosmos: Why the Materialist Neo-Darwinian Conception of Nature Is Almost Certainly False* (Oxford: Oxford University Press, 2012). Much earlier, Saul Kripke gave proponents of mind-body dualism a boost in his *Naming and Necessity* (Cambridge, MA: Harvard University Press, 1980). Mind-body dualism has been championed by Richard Swinburne (see his books *The Evolution of the Soul* [Oxford: The Clarendon Press, 1986] and *Mind, Brain, & Free Will* [Oxford: Oxford University Press, 2012]), and is now the majority report in the Society of Christian Philosophers.

and value—and, more broadly, life itself—are the most important phenomena, and we should not be prepared to credit theories that marginalize or explain away the most important *explananda*. The conceptualities of physics and chemistry do not include mind, meaning, and value. That is why—if they are supposed to be theories of everything—the mental must be treated as unreal or as reducible to or constituted by what the physical sciences do traffic in. However much psychology may try to map correlations between mental states and brain activity, and no matter to what extent biochemists analyze the chemistry underlying vital functions, the physical sciences themselves cannot explain why any physical and chemical configurations should be correlated with any vital or mental states, and why with these rather than those—once again, because mental and vital properties do not fall within their conceptual scope. Observers who think the physical sciences are our only source of explanation must regard such correlations as brute facts and accidental side-effects of base-line material states and processes. The eschatology of Bolzano-thermodynamics is more pessimistic still: life and the mental are temporary and fleeting because the physical universe is headed for a state of equilibrium. Bertrand Russell sums up the human predicament this way in "A Free Man's Worship" and counsels stoic resignation that enjoys life while it lasts.[5]

As privileged as he was, Russell was evidently abstracting from the worst aspects of the human condition, from the experiences of millions who lead lives of unrelieved misery. Evolutionary psychology adds to the grimness by explaining our cognitive capacities and motivations in terms of their contributions to individual or species survival (in terms of their prospects for increasing the probabilities of reproduction and gene pool transmission). Survival and reproductive success are the explanatory valuables. The resulting motivational structure breeds tribalism and in-group altruism, perhaps with a fragile overlay of outgroup altruism due to generalized instincts toward parental care.[6] Put otherwise, morality is reduced to strategies for solving coordination problems in social groups that we depend on for survival.[7]

---

5. Bertrand Russell, "A Free Man's Worship," *Mysticism and Logic* (Garden City, NY: Doubleday-Anchor, 1957), 44–54.

6. For the latter thesis, see C. Daniel Batson, *Altruism in Humans* (Oxford: Oxford University Press, 2011).

7. See Benjamin Fraser and Kim Sterelny, "Evolution and Moral Realism," *British Journal of the Philosophy of Science* (2016), https://doi.org/10.1093/bjps/axv060, which stakes out a reductive position while providing very helpful methodological remarks.

The Physical Sciences, Recontextualized

Protesting philosophers find this picture of human beings and our place in the cosmos altogether unacceptable. In reassessing, they locate the mistake not in the enterprise of the physical sciences but in the *philosophical* attempt to turn the physical sciences into a theory of everything. If mind, meaning, and value are reasserted as priorities, then the metaphysics of the world as we know it must be reworked to include teleology so that mind, meaning, and value emerge not as accidental side-effects but as preeminent values aimed at the processes of creation. The physical sciences and their discoveries will have to be recontextualized within that wider metaphysical frame. Just as the attempt to domesticate the mental and the vital into the physical required adjustments to our estimates of what the mental really is and which mental phenomena are really real, so the reverse process of domesticating the physical sciences may involve correcting, adjusting, and supplementing their results, while leaving most of their impressive achievements in place.

Knowing Creation as Personified and Purposeful

The Material as Purposed and Purposeful

Christian theology knows creation *as* creation. Knowing creation *as* creation requires a conceptual lens that prioritizes persons and purposive action. The Bible features personality as the heart of the universe because God is personal. God's existence cannot help being permanent and requires no explanation. Divine agency cannot help being personal because God essentially acts through intellect and will. God acts personally to make the material world *on purpose* and *for a purpose*. We are all caught up in God's purpose in creation. We enter into divine purposes by stages through a process of initiation.

Most obviously, God makes this material world because God loves it. Theologically, this is trivially true: out of all possible choices, this material world (with the possible addition of immaterial angels) is the world that God has made. God is Spirit. But like good parents and their offspring, God wants material creation to be as godlike as possible while still being itself. Because God is active, God makes matter dynamic. Because God is life, God *nudges* matter to evolve the structures that can host life. Because God is personal, God *nudges* matter again to evolve structures that can host personal life. Divine purpose for material creation finds focus in material persons because in material persons matter becomes as godlike as possible while still being itself.

Moreover, God makes material creation because God wants to inhabit it. Metaphysically, this is also trivial, for God is present to whatever God produces. As creator and conserver of everything else, God is present to anything and everything, wherever and whenever it is. What is more, created causal power cannot be exercised apart from God's general concurrence. Necessarily, God must act together with creatures, whenever and wherever and if ever they do anything. Where creatures are concerned, God is really present to their being and really present in their action.

Concurrence as Perichoresis

Concurrence takes a special form with material persons because personhood is essentially perichoretic. It is impossible to be personal alone. The Godhead is not an isolated ego but three persons, each of whom indwells the others by reaching out in love and appreciation, by knowing even as they are known. Trinitarian friendship, their reciprocal identity-conferring relationships of self-giving love, proceeds in such harmony of outlook and valuation that the Trinity express themselves in one action, one will *ad extra*.

Because human beings are material persons, the human psyche is tied to an animal life cycle. Developmental psychologists agree that personhood is essentially perichoretic. They explain that human beings are born full of personal potential but that such capacities have to be evoked and developed in a personal surrounding. Many take a page from Kantian ethics to suggest that autonomy is the goal of human development, something we grow into if all goes well.[8] Various scales are offered to map and norm the individual's progress. According to psychoanalytic versions, the human infant begins as a booming, buzzing confusion of inputs and impulses, but by the age of three months or earlier has the cognitive capacity to differentiate and center its psychic field on a human face. A few months later, its cognitive skills progress enough to recognize that the face goes away, and this realization launches the long process of ego development over the course of which the ego deploys a variety of self-management strategies that organize, structure, and restructure the personality. Therapy assists the ego in consciously identifying, sorting,

8. E.g., Lawrence Kohlberg, *The Philosophy of Moral Development: Essays on Moral Development* 2 vols. (San Francisco: Harper & Row, 1981, 1984).

and discarding dysfunctional defenses and—when successful—brings the individual to the goal of rational self-government.[9]

Once again, theology recontextualizes. From the beginning, whether recognized or unnoticed, the omnipresent Godhead is really present to all levels of human personality, interacting constantly in many and various ways to enable normal human development, working to foster creativity, nudging the human psyche with "aha" insights, and precipitating seismic shifts towards "out of the box" thinking (say, to invent Riemannian geometry or to put two and two together to get sixteen)! Material persons are no more made for solo action than the divine persons essentially are. Autonomous ego management is not the ultimate goal of human development. A further stage builds on its achievements and capacities but moves beyond them into conscious recognition and intentional cooperation with indwelling Godhead, into a restructuring of personality that puts friendship with God at its functional center so that more and more everything that the human person says and does flows from that lived partnership.[10] John's Gospel speaks of this as being "born again" "from above." John's Jesus declares that all that he says and does comes out of his relationship with the Father. John's Gospel presents Jesus in his human nature as the paradigm of mature perichoretic human personality.

Knowing Creation as Holy

Holiness as Core

Fully to know creation *as* creation requires cultic categories. The creation narrative of Genesis 1 gives us the clue with its liturgical rhythms and punctuating refrain: "and God saw that it was good," "and there was evening, and there was morning, the *nth* day." In the Bible and in Christian theology, cultic categories presuppose personal agency and purposive action, while recontextualizing them. For cult is about trafficking with the holy. In the Bible and in Christian theology, holiness is rooted in a personal God. Cultically conceived, God's purpose in making us in a material world such as this is

---

9. For an explanation and critique, see James E. Loder, *The Transforming Moment: Understanding Convictional Experiences* (San Francisco: Harper & Row, 1981).

10. Once again, see James E. Loder, *The Transforming Moment*. James W. Fowler draws on work by Piaget, Kohlberg, and others to chart stages of faith in *Stages of Faith: The Psychology of Human Development and the Quest for Meaning* (New York: Harper Collins, 1981).

nothing less than the sanctification of matter. God is out to make the whole of material creation holy and to do so in ways that enlist us.

As the holiness code (Leviticus 17–27) insists, sacred and profane do not mix. A holy God cannot dwell with an unholy people or inhabit an unclean place.[11] This seems to be an obstacle to divine-human life together in a material world such as this. The Synoptic Gospels proclaim the revolutionary solution to this problem: it is not defilement but holiness that is "catching."[12] Metaphysically, it is trivially true then that God cannot help but take the sanctifying initiative when creating. Divine omnipresence and general concurrence already make the whole material world God's temple, whatever state it is in. The fact that all material creatures are essentially godlike to some degree makes them reflections of the glory of God. In fact, the cosmos that God creates is "a moving likeness."[13] God sets up a cosmic frame ripe for development. Once again, because the probabilities would otherwise be so low, it seems reasonable to suppose that God nudges cosmic evolution to produce apt environments and material structures to host life and that God nudges biological evolution to produce bodies with brains to host personal life.

Manifest Holiness

God is holy and the source of all holiness. Material creation cannot help being holy because of divine omnipresence and general concurrence. But where creatures are concerned, *manifest* holiness comes in degrees. Of all the sites in the material world, the possibilities for transparency to divine presence and purposes reach their peak in material persons. Cultically conceived, God appoints human beings, material persons, as a royal priesthood.[14] Through the stages of human development, God works with us to grow our personal capacities through the various stages of ego development to structure and restructure human personality and eventually to ordain us into mature perichoresis. Material persons "catch" and "carry" holiness, not by magic, not merely by metaphysical necessity and unwittingly, but by the increasingly conscious intention of making lived partnership with God the functional center of our

---

11. See, e.g., Lev 11:44–45; 19:2.

12. Jesus heals ritually unclean lepers (Mk 1:40–46; Lk 17:11–19) and bleeding women (Mk 5:25–34) by touch.

13. Plato, *Timaeus* 37d, as trans. by F. M. Cornford, *Plato's Cosmology* (New York: Humanities, 1952), 99.

14. See 1 Pet 2:9.

personalities—by allowing our relationship with the indwelling Godhead to be the relationship from which our thoughts, words, and deeds flow.

As chosen priests, our cultic work is to cooperate with God to make the holiness of material creation ever more manifest. We do this by growing into the knowledge and love of God and one another, by coming more and more to experience the Creator *as* Creator, by owning God's purposes as our purposes, by exercising camaraderie toward our fellow priests, and by showing courtesy toward God's nonpersonal creatures. Unsurprisingly, the human vocation to cooperate with God in the sanctification of matter "begins at home," with the material persons that we are. It is foundational to our calling that we slog through the stages of human development culminating in perichoretic restructuring. Because growing up is a messy process and because with us perichoresis will remain unstable this side of the grave, we work with God toward the sanctification of matter when we acknowledge our mistakes and brokenness and ask God's help.

We work with God to manifest the holiness of material creation by showing courtesy to God's nonhuman creatures. This task requires discernment to strike the right balance between permission and restraint. For material creation is by nature cannibalistic. Lions eat lambs. Swallows eat bugs. Even larger molecules gobble up smaller ones. Material creatures "run interference" with one another so that the flourishing of one is bought at the expense of others. Courtesy honors the godlikeness of creatures by allowing them room to "do their thing," while restraint quarantines and infringes the better to make room for other creatures to be themselves. We need food and shelter. We have to eat something. (Even vegans do violence to carrots.) Freud was right: eating is a hostile act because we destroy what we eat. Tricky decisions get made about whose lives and flourishing are more important. Isn't courtesy to the Ebola virus trumped by the sacred worth of human beings? A royal priesthood working for the sanctification of matter will repeatedly turn to God for wisdom and for insight into the subtleties of divine purposes. At the very least courtesy calls on us not to waste food or to rape the environment!

In the Bible, God's aims are social. God wants to showcase the holiness of material creation by forming a holy nation,[15] by building a holy city.[16] The eschatological goal is not Bolzano-equilibrium that does away with all

---

15. Exod 19:6; Deut 14:2; 24:19; 1 Pet 2:9.
16. Heb 11:10; Rev 21:2–27.

complex macrostructures, but the "more than subtle" organization of a just society, a utopia in which individuals need not compete to flourish because the good of each is harmonized with the common good. Certainly, human beings are political animals, and yet human beings are socially challenged. The competitive, cannibalistic dynamics of material creation run right through us. Limited imagination combines with the fear of death and resource shortages to guarantee that human societies and institutions spawn systemic evils, which are structures of cruelty that privilege some while degrading others. Perichoretic restructuring of human personality is what holds out hope that a society of material persons could ever be otherwise. To the extent that we are reborn into living partnership with indwelling Godhead, the fear of death and shortages will fade because we will know and feel God as our life source. We will come to believe that life is a gift God will keep giving forever. Not all at once but eventually we will become thoroughly convinced that we have nothing to gain by denying the necessities of life to others, and so we will find it increasingly easier to embrace and advocate for the root and branch social reforms needed to make God's dream of a holy society come true. In the meantime, our cultic work is to take out our brooms and cleanse the temple, to take out our shovels and uproot systemic evils. Everywhere, we can bear witness to society's need for restructuring in order to honor the sacred worth of every human being.

Chapter TEN

The Vision of the Hazelnut

PETER VAN INWAGEN

> And in this [vision] he [also] showed me a little thing the size of a hazelnut, which seemed to be lying in the palm of my hand. And it was as round as any ball. In my mind's eye I looked at it and thought, "What can this be?" And the answer came, "It is all that is made." I wondered how it could continue to be, for I thought it was so small that it might suddenly fall into nothingness. And I was answered in my mind, "It endures, and ever shall endure, because God loves it. And so do all things partake of being: by the love of God." In this little thing I saw a threefold nature: that God made it, that God loves it, and that God keeps it.
>
> THE SHEWINGS OF JULIAN OF NORWICH,
> OR REVELATIONS OF DIVINE LOVE, CH. 5[1]

A great treatise on the theology of creation might be written as a commentary on these words. I am incapable of writing a great treatise on the theology of creation, but I will undertake a brief reflection on the implications of Lady Julian's vision of the "hazelnut" for the theology of creation. I will

---

1. This is my paraphrase in modern English of the text of the Westminster Manuscript. Here are Julian's actual words (with modernized spelling and punctuation): "And in this he shewed me a little thing, the quantity of a hazelnut, lying in the palm of my hand as it had seemed. And it was as round as any ball. I looked thereupon with the eye of my understanding, and I thought, what may this be? And it was answered generally thus: 'It is all that is made.' I marveled how it might last. For methought it might suddenly have fall to nought for littlehead. And I was answered in my understanding: 'It lasteth and ever shall for God loveth it. And so hath all thing its beginning by the love of God.' In this little thing I saw three properties. The first is that God made it. The second is that God loveth it. And the third is that God keepeth it." *The Shewings* (1375).

attempt to articulate the profound insight into the relation between Creator and creatures that is presented in this brief passage.

(1) It has been remarked that stained glass is meant to be seen from inside, not from outside—a way of saying that non-Christians often do not see things pertaining to the church from the right angle to understand them. A nice illustration of this fact is provided by the contrast between Julian's description of her vision and a remark of Richard Feynman's (Feynman was perhaps the greatest physicist of the twentieth century after Einstein):

> It doesn't seem to me that this fantastically marvelous universe, this tremendous range of time and space and different kinds of animals, and all the different planets, and all these atoms with all their motions, and so on, all this complicated thing can merely be a stage so that God can watch human beings struggle for good and evil—which is the view that religion has. The stage is too big for the drama.[2]

There are two red herrings that I must dispose of before comparing Julian's words with Feynman's.

The first is Feynman's idea that Jews and Christians and Muslims[3] believe that God has made the physical universe in order to have a stage on which he "can watch human beings struggle for good and evil." This idea has no place in any theology I have ever encountered.[4] It is no doubt true that most of the universe has no more to do with human beings than the waters of the tidally warmed subsurface oceans of the Jovian moon Europa have to do with beavers. No doubt a distant galaxy that is wholly devoid of life has nothing to do with us. And yet the Christian will say of it (as Julian would have said of it if she had known of such things as galaxies) that God loves it and keeps it. I think that the proper Christian attitude toward the parts of the cosmos

---

2. A remark made in conversation. It is reported in James Gleick, *Genius: The Life and Science of Richard Feynman* (New York: Pantheon, 1992), 372.

3. I have to suppose that when Feynman speaks as if there were something called "religion" (and speaks of it as the kind of thing that can have a "view"), he is speaking of what is common to the Abrahamic religions.

4. It is true that Christianity, at least, teaches that human beings were created to have a central place in the economy of the universe. ("Do you not know that we are to judge angels" [1 Cor 6:3].) But a keystone has (literally) a central place in the "economy" of an arch—and yet arches are not built for the sake of giving keystones something to do.

that have no connection with or relevance to the lives and activities of human beings is well expressed in a speech by the angelic guardian of the planet Venus in C. S. Lewis's theological fantasy *Perelandra* (or *Voyage to Venus*). Her speech is addressed to the unfallen Venerean counterparts or analogues of Adam and Eve:

> Though men or angels rule them, the worlds are for themselves. The waters you have not floated on, the fruit you have not plucked, the caves into which you have not descended and the fire through which your bodies cannot pass, do not await your coming to put on perfection, though they will obey you when you come. Times without number I have circled [the sun] while you were not alive, and those times were not desert. Their own voice was in them, not merely a dreaming of the day when you should awake. They also were at the centre.

A distant lifeless galaxy is not desert (a *desert* is not desert), and its own voice is in it. It too is at the center. And God keeps it and loves it, although not in the same way he loves a human being or a beaver or a blade of grass. The love he has for a galaxy (or a grain of desert sand or an electron) is an ordinate love, a love of a kind appropriate to its object. As one of us can love a certain tree or a certain house or a certain landscape, so God can, and does, love every thing, every being, he has made. And he loves each of them for itself, for what *it* is. He loves each of the component stones of an arch for what *it* is and not for its relation to the keystone.

This is the first red herring: human beings are not the only actors on the stage. If the universe is a stage, it is a stage on which many, many dramas are being performed.[5] The human drama occupies only one tiny corner of the stage—although the many dramas are no doubt parts of a great and harmonious whole, the drama of creation, the "Divine Comedy." The human drama is only one of the vastly many subdramas that make up the great drama. If ours were the only play being performed on the universal stage, there might be some point in saying that the stage was too big for the drama. But this brings us to the second red herring to be disposed of.

Christians believe that the story they call salvation history, while it is

---

5. This is true even if human beings are the only rational biological beings. Every bacterium is a greater drama than *King Lear*.

indeed in one way only a tiny part the whole drama of Creation, is an extremely *important* tiny part of the whole:

> For the creation waits with eager longing for the revealing of the children of God; for the creation was subjected to futility, not of its own will but by the will of the one who subjected it, in hope that the creation itself will be set free from its bondage to decay and will obtain the freedom of the glory of the children of God. We know that the whole creation has been groaning in labor pains until now. (Rom 8:19–22)

Given this alleged central role played by human beings and their story within the great drama (they are the keystone), is there not after all some point to Feynman's complaint that "the stage is too big for the drama"? The simple answer is no, for when Feynman was speaking those words, in another part of his mind he knew perfectly well that if a cosmos was to contain rational animals like ourselves, it would have to be as vast as the actual cosmos. As the physicist Stephen Barr has said (in a review of a book by the paleontologist Stephen Jay Gould):

> Gould is overawed by . . . large numbers. The vast age and size of the universe in comparison to human scales are . . . evidence to him of human insignificance in the cosmic scheme. But [the] universe must be as old as it is for life to have had time to evolve, and as large as it is for such huge times to be possible. (General Relativity relates the size and longevity of the universe.) . . . There are basic physical reasons why living things must be small compared to the universe.[6]

So much for the red herrings. The most important theological misunderstanding in Feynman's statement has to do not with the relation between the cosmos and human beings but rather with the relation between God and the cosmos—the physical universe considered as a whole, as a single object. What Feynman doesn't see is the very thing that led Julian to say, "I thought

---

6. Stephen Barr, "Mismeasure of Man," in *The Believing Scientist: Essays on Science and Religion* (Grand Rapids: Eerdmans, 2016), 42–45, quote on p. 44. "Mismeasure of Man" is a review of Stephen Jay Gould, *Full House: The Spread of Excellence from Plato to Darwin*, and was originally published in *Public Interest* (Spring 1997). The title "Mismeasure of Man" is an allusion to the title of Gould's earlier book *The Mismeasure of Man*.

it was so small that it might suddenly fall into nothingness."[7] In her report of her vision, Julian represents herself as seeing "all that is made" from God's perspective—although of course her description of the cosmos as God sees it necessarily involves various kinds of license (e.g., God does not see physical things like hazelnuts by being affected by the light reflected from them). One license is this: it would have been metaphysically more accurate—and altogether useless from either a literary or a devotional point of view—if Julian had represented all that is made as having not the apparent size of a hazelnut but as having the size of a point in space, as occupying a region of zero volume, as being *infinitely* small. To say that the universe is, from God's point of view, a little thing the size of a hazelnut is to do it altogether too much honor. Anything God creates—the *totality* of what he creates, the totality of any intrinsically possible creation—must be infinitely less than himself. And this *must* is the "must" of absolute unqualified necessity. To ask God to create something whose being stood to his being like the being of a hazelnut stands to your or my or Julian's being would be to ask him to do the intrinsically impossible; it would be like asking him to make a cubical ball—or a stone so heavy he was unable to move it.[8]

Because he is infinitely greater than any other possible being, God is infinitely greater than the gods of classical antiquity would have been if they had existed. Zeus is an instructive example of the kind of "greatness" supposedly possessed by the pagan gods. We learn from Homer (*Iliad*, VIII, 19–30) that King Zeus once found it necessary to issue a warning to the other gods in case any of them should contemplate disobeying his order not to aid one or the other side in the Trojan war:

> Test my power and discover it. Hang a golden chain from the sky to the earth and take hold of it, all of you, gods and goddesses together. Tug as you will, but you shall not drag Zeus the King, supreme in wisdom, to earth. But if I were to pull at it, I should draw you all up—and the earth

---

7. Or "methought it might suddenly fall to nought for littlehead."

8. But does not Scripture tell us that "with God all things are possible" (Matt 19:26 NIV)? Does Scripture not tell us that "nothing will be impossible with God" (Luke 1:37)? It is generally agreed by Christian theologians and philosophers that there are many things that these texts, taken in context, do not imply that God is able to do: to make a cubical ball, for example, or to end his own existence, or to change the past. There is indeed one thing that Scripture explicitly tells us that God is unable to do—to break a promise he has made. "If we are faithless, he remains faithful—for he cannot deny himself" (2 Tim 2:13).

and sea with you. And then I would fasten the chain to some pinnacle of Olympus and leave you all suspended between sky and earth. That is how much greater I am than gods and men.

Homer's Zeus is more powerful than all the other Olympian gods combined. (Throw in the earth and sea if you like—let the other gods add the weight of the earth and the sea to their end of the chain.) His individual power and their collective power are, nevertheless, *commensurable*. If the other gods did earnestly engage in a celestial tug-of-war with Zeus, they would exert a force of some magnitude (some number of newtons) earthward, and Zeus would exert some force of greater magnitude heavenward. There would be some number greater than 1 (7, perhaps, or 23.16 or 42.91) that was the ratio of the heavenward force to the earthward force: Zeus stands to Poseidon and Apollo as a stronger man stands to weaker men.

And what is more, the power of Zeus and the power of Poseidon and Apollo are in a certain sense *independent* of one another. The Homeric gods are no more than some of the more important of the inhabitants of the world. They are inhabitants of a world that they did not bring into existence. They are inhabitants of a world that brought *them* into existence. Zeus began to be at a certain point in space and time owing to the causal interaction of entities whose existence preceded his. (Some *mountains* are older than Zeus.) Like any comic-book superhero, he has an "origin story." The causes that brought Zeus into existence conferred a certain degree of native power on him. And the same is true of his brother Poseidon and his son Apollo, but their causes gifted them with power inferior to Zeus's.

God, however, not only has unlimited power, but (a) his existence and his unlimited power are eternal and uncaused (as the truth of a mathematical theorem is eternal and uncaused), and (b) the existence and the limited power of any other being have been *given* to that being by God—and the same is true of every being there ever could be or could have been. It is senseless to speak of any being as engaged in a contest of power with God,[9] as senseless as it would be to speak of a financial struggle between a son and a father if the son's financial resources consisted entirely of an allowance voluntarily provided him by his father.

---

9. "And war broke out in heaven" (Rev 12:7). But the war was between the angelic forces commanded by Michael and the angelic forces commanded by Satan.

(2) Someone might reply, "That's all very well, and no doubt it would be regarded as good theology by those who take theology seriously, but the plain fact is, we now know that the universe is vastly older and larger than anything Julian and her contemporaries could have imagined. They would have been unable to conceive of anything approaching the vast abyss of time and space that cosmology has revealed to us. No one who is aware of the real size and age of the universe—as some of us are today—can imagine even for a moment that it makes any sense to suppose that there is a perspective from which 'this tremendous range of time and space' would appear to be 'a little thing, the size of a hazelnut.'"

I do not know how much Julian knew of what her more learned contemporaries thought about the age and the size of the cosmos, about what they called the *mundus*, the world. But let us consider what those learned men (I suppose they were all men) knew and thought they knew.

As to the age of the cosmos, they had no opinion. They did indeed think that the creation of humanity had taken place only a few thousand years before Christ—for they believed that God had revealed in Holy Scripture the number of human generations that had lived and died between Adam and Jesus of Nazareth. But they would have affirmed that, for all human reason and observation could discover, the universe might have existed for *thousands* of thousands (or, for that matter, for thousands of thousands of thousands—that is, for billions) of years, while Adam still slept in his causes. (Few if any of them thought that Genesis 1:1–25 was what we should today call a literally true narrative of the events between "Let there be light" and the creation of Adam and Eve.) The Dominicans, indeed, maintained (following Thomas Aquinas) that, although it was God's good pleasure to create a world that had a beginning in time, if he had so chosen, he was perfectly capable of creating a world that had no beginning.

But what did they think about the *size* of the cosmos? That is a more important question than the question of what they thought about its age—for the suggestion we are considering is that no one who was aware of the vastness of the universe revealed to us by scientific cosmology could take seriously the idea that there was a perspective from which it could be seen as "a little thing."

The Greeks (who were the source of what Julian's learned contemporaries believed about astronomy) had the diameter of Earth about right, and they knew that the result of measuring the angle between two fixed stars did not vary at different latitudes or longitudes. That is to say, they knew that in comparison with the hypothetical sphere of the fixed stars,[10] the *stellatum*, Earth could be treated as a dimensionless point.

The Greek and medieval astronomers were, of course, unable to calculate the dimensions of the stellar sphere since they could detect no stellar parallax, but that did not stop poets from speculating about its size. *The South English Legendary*[11] gave the *stellatum* a minimum radius that was (in present-day terms) a bit greater than 10 light-minutes (i.e., somewhat larger than the radius of the orbit of Earth and somewhat smaller than the radius of the orbit of Mars). How does this compare with the size of the physical universe that modern cosmology reveals to us? That question cannot be answered, for no one knows how large the physical universe is. But what *is* known pretty accurately is the size of the "Hubble universe," the *observable* universe. The oldest light—or, to be pedantic, the oldest radiation—that reaches us was produced by an event that occurred about 378,000 years after the Big Bang. (It is coming to us from every direction, for that event filled all space.) The Big Bang occurred 13.824 billion years ago (the accepted figure at the moment at which I write), and the number 378,000 is smaller than the uncertainty in the number 13.824 billion, so we may say that the oldest light that reaches us has been traveling for 13.824 billion years and has therefore traveled 13.824 billion light-years. Now choose any direction. The matter that emitted the bit of "oldest light" now reaching us from that direction and the matter that now constitutes us and our environment have been moving apart throughout all that time, owing to the continuing expansion of space. The two clusters of matter are now about 46 billion light-years apart. We may therefore say that the *observable* universe has a diameter of 92 billion light-years.[12]

---

10. The sphere of the fixed stars was generally supposed to be the second largest thing that God had made—the largest having been the theoretically necessary but empirically undetectable sphere called the *primum mobile* (the first movable) that enclosed it. Every physical or material (as we should say today) thing besides the *primum mobile* and the *stellatum* and the stars was inside the *stellatum*. I have to wonder whether Julian described the little thing in the palm of her hand as being "round as any ball" because the *stellatum* was a sphere.

11. A Middle English hagiographical poem of the late thirteenth century. ("Legendary" means "collection of stories.") See C. S. Lewis, *The Discarded Image: An Introduction to Medieval and Renaissance Literature* (Cambridge: Cambridge University Press, 1964), 96–99.

12. Although, of course, when we look at any part of the universe that is now 46 billion light-years from us, we see it as it was 13.824 billion years ago when it was only 13.824 billion light-years away and was in a very primitive—more or less homogenous—state. The fog of radiating matter we seem to be observing at that distance has presumably by now developed into mature galaxies that are 46 billion light-years distant from us and whose light will never reach us—that is, will never reach the matter of which

The ratio of 46 billion years to 10 minutes is a largish number—about 2.42 × 10^{15}—but a universe with a radius of 10 light-minutes is no more imaginable by human beings than is a universe with a radius of 46 billion light-years. (If you dispute that statement, that is because you have mistaken your mastery of an algorithm for manipulating exponents for your powers of imagination.) I have put *The South English Legendary*'s determination of a lower bound of the distance to the fixed stars in terms of light-minutes for the purpose of comparing it with the radius of the Hubble universe. What the poem said was this: if one could travel straight up at a rate of 40 miles per day,[13] one would not have reached the *stellatum* after 8,000 years of travel. (If one lit a celestial bonfire to signal to the inhabitants of Earth one's completion of 8,000 years of travel on that formidable journey, its light would reach them in 10 minutes and 27 seconds.) Try to imagine a ball whose radius equals the distance that would be traversed by an immortal equestrian who traveled in a straight line at a rate of forty miles per day for 8,000 years.[14] Here is an aid to your imagination: its surface area is about 625 million times the surface area of the earth.

Whether Earth is a ball about 13,000 kilometers in diameter at the center of the medieval *mundus* or a ball of that same size at the center[15] of the present-day Hubble universe, it is a tiny island lost in unimaginable vastness. Knowing what we now know about the size of the universe is therefore no barrier—either cognitive or emotional—to supposing that there is a perspective from which that universe can be viewed as a tiny, tiny thing. At any rate, it is no more a barrier to that supposition than a belief that the universe was of "medieval" dimensions would be.

---

we are now composed—because those galaxies and that matter are moving apart at an ever-increasing speed, far greater than the speed of light.

13. I imagine that 40 miles is an estimate (rather an optimistic one) of the distance a rider on a good level road could travel on a fast horse in a day. (And the writer was really even more optimistic than that: his actual words were "forty mile and yet some del [deal] more.")

14. Our equestrian would travel a distance equal to the diameter of Earth in about 200 days. Hence, the diameter of *The South English Legendary*'s *stellatum* was, at a minimum, something like 15,000 times the diameter of Earth.

15. Earth was at the center of the *mundus*—at the center of the universe—because it was made primarily of stuff that could fall (it contained *all* the stuff that could fall), and, so the medievals supposed, there was a single, unchanging point in space, equally removed from the *stellatum* in every direction, to which all the stuff that could fall was trying to fall *to*; the geometrical center of the *mundus* was a *special* place. The Hubble universe, however, is not the universe but is simply the part of it we can observe. That we should be at the center of the part of the universe we can observe does not imply that we are in a special place—it no more implies that than the fact that the lookout in the crow's nest of an old sailing ship is at the center of the part of the sea he can observe implies that he is at a special place in the sea.

(3) Let us return to Julian's vision. The power and the charm of her description of the vision make it difficult to take her words literally and to subject their literal sense to logical analysis, and perhaps no one ever has. I think, however, that it is instructive to do so. If one does take her words literally, one finds that they resist logical analysis. Why should the fact that a thing is very small lead someone observing that thing to "marvel that it might last"? Why should the observer have the impression that "it might suddenly fall into nothingness"? It simply makes no sense to suppose that the size of a thing has any connection with its power to continue to exist. Having a size is one of the common properties of "dwellers all in time and space." And every spatially finite thing, everything that has a finite size, is "a little thing" compared with some other thing. (Even if there happens to be a largest thing, as the medievals believed, it is not—unless it is infinite in extent—the largest *possible* thing: there *could* be something in comparison with which it was a little thing.) Nothing is great or small but comparing makes it so. If someone were to say that a thing's smallness was an obstacle to its continuing to exist, this statement would invite the reply, "Smallness relative to what?" If, moreover, you were to encounter a woman who was gazing at a hazelnut, and she looked up and said, "This nut is so small, I can't see how it can continue to exist," I suspect you would regard that as a puzzling, perhaps even an unintelligible, statement. You would do so because experience has shown you that things the size of hazelnuts do not normally find it difficult to continue to exist, and they exhibit no tendency to fall suddenly into nothingness.

Well, a vision is a vision. And a description of a vision is a description of a vision.[16] If the content of Julian's vision was, to borrow William James's word, ineffable, then it is hardly surprising that anyone who takes her description literally and logically analyzes it finds it to be logically incoherent. Any attempt to describe an ineffable experience must be metaphorical. Metaphor is the only resource that language provides to describe the ineffable, and metaphors are notoriously resistant to logical analysis.

Suppose we take it upon ourselves to try to describe in discursive metaphysical terms what Julian describes in metaphorical terms. We might reasonably

---

16. I assume throughout this essay that *The Shewings* is not a work of fiction like *The Divine Comedy*. I assume that its text comprises attempts to describe experiences Julian really had. Whether these experiences were true divine revelations or simply products of her illness—she was very seriously ill and perhaps delirious when she had them—is, of course, another question.

say that her metaphor is this: apparent size represents significance or importance. (If a writer wants to represent significance and insignificance in terms of a visual metaphor, what shall he or she choose to represent these things if not size?) For God, everything else is insignificant—insignificant not in itself (whatever that might mean) but in comparison with himself. And that is not because he is vain or narcissistic but simply because he is, of absolute necessity, right about everything, and everything else is and must be insignificant in comparison with him. Why all other things are insignificant in comparison with God has already been stated: First, his goodness and power and knowledge are, of absolute necessity, infinitely greater than theirs. And second, the goodness, power, and knowledge they have, they have only as a gift from him. (Milton's Satan, who reluctantly accepts the first, tries to deny the second: "Who saw / When this [alleged] creation was? rememberest thou / Thy making . . . ? / We [angels] know no time when we were not as now; / Know none before us, self-begot, self-rais'd / By our own quick'ning power . . . / Our puissance is our own."[17] If Milton has quoted him correctly—I have been unable to verify the quotation—the Father of Lies lies even to his closest associates, perhaps even to himself.) It is for this reason that size is associated in the vision with capacity to continue to exist: smallness represents insignificance, and in the great scheme of things, the only truly significant being is the One who alone exists of his own nature. The *small* things, the insignificant things—that is, all things other than God—are things that exist only because a being that has existence of itself lends existence to them. (Remember that I do not offer these words as interpretation of Julian's words, much less as a replacement for them or an improvement on them.)

But if we are so insignificant, if we are down there in the minuscule hazelnut, why does God pay any attention to us? Why indeed does he notice us at all? Most readers of this essay will have heard at least one atheist say something along these lines: "Oh, sure, the creator of a universe billions of years old containing trillions of galaxies each of which contains billions of stars is going to take an interest in a few animals who have spent a few millennia inhabiting a planet orbiting one star. It is just as absurd as me taking interest in a single cell in my body. In fact, do the math; it's billions of times *more* absurd."[18]

---

17. Milton, *Paradise Lost*, 5.856–64.

18. If this argument is not quite the same as Feynman's, it certainly belongs to the same family of arguments. And, like his argument, it contains red herrings. This universe that contains "trillions of

Julian answers the question "Why does God pay attention to us?" and her answer is a simple one and not metaphorical at all. He pays attention to us because he loves us. And he loves us because he loves everything. And he loves everything because he *is* Love (1 John 4:8). That is not to say that God is an abstraction. The noun "love" in the sentence "God is love" does not function as it functions in "Love is patient; love is kind; love is not envious or boastful or arrogant or rude" or even as it functions in "The love that moves the sun and the other stars."[19] God is Love as he is Goodness and Knowledge and Power: all these things are *perfectly* realized in him. And insofar as they are present in a rational created being, their presence in that being is a sort of imperfect (which is not to say flawed) copy of his goodness and knowledge and power. We may equally well say that God is Goodness or that God is Knowledge or that God is Power. And in a way that is difficult and perhaps impossible for us to grasp in this present life, all these "God is" statements are really the same statement. In a human being the various virtues are separable and distinguishable because a human being is composed of parts, and a human being's knowledge and goodness (for example) are differently "seated" in his or her parts. But "there is but one living and true God, everlasting, without body, parts, or passions."[20] Human beings speaking of God speak (wrongly but inevitably) of God's love and God's power as two things, for love and power are two things in us human beings, and human beings are the only model of God that human beings have (and given their cognitive limitations, it's a good model for them to have, for they are made in his image and likeness).

Nevertheless, "God is love" is—God teaches us through John—the one among the many "God is" statements that gives us human beings the best insight into his nature that we are capable of receiving. And God, being love, of necessity loves everything that he has made.[21] It is not for nothing that *The*

---

galaxies each of which contains billions of stars," this "tremendous range of time and space," and the human race are *equally* insignificant compared with God; by that standard each person has no significance whatever. I expect that people like Feynman, people looking at the stained glass from the outside, would suppose that if there *were* a being who had made the universe, the Local Group and all its content would be more significant in relation to that Creator than would a grain of sand. And, of course, although a human being cannot at any given moment be individually aware of very many things, including the cells that make up his or her body, God is aware of every aspect of every being.

19. "The love that moves the sun and the other stars" does not refer to God or to his love for the sun and the stars; it refers rather to the love of the most excellent part of the *mundus*—the *primum mobile*—for God.

20. Articles of Religion: Article I, in *The Book of Common Prayer* (London: Collins, 1968), 38.

21. To say that God loves everything he has made is not to imply that he loves sin or suffering

Shewings of Julian of Norwich is also called *Revelations of Divine Love*, for it is divine love that is principally shown in her visions.

If human beings and their universe are insignificant in comparison with God, if they are *ontologically* insignificant, what is the significance of that insignificance? The answer is "none." Ontological insignificance is without significance for Love. Human beings are insignificant beings. But they are nevertheless *beings*; they are nevertheless *there*; they are nevertheless *real*. Unlike sin and death and suffering, they are substance not shadow. And Love loves all that is.

(4) In conclusion, I offer some (highly speculative) thoughts on the final statement of our selection from Julian's description of her vision: "In this little thing I saw a threefold nature: that God made it, that God loves it, and that God keeps it."

These words are, I believe, a description of what theologians call the economic Trinity. Although all three persons play an equal and undivided role in their relations to the created world, it is natural for human beings to "appropriate to" each triune person a certain relation to the world. The creation of the world is appropriated to the Father (the *fons et origo* of being),[22] love of its inhabitants to the Son (who, in an appalling act of love, became the atoning sacrifice for our sins—and not for ours only but also for the sins of the whole world), and its providential governance to the Spirit (our *parakletos*

---

or death, for sin and suffering and death are not things he has made. They are not things he has made because they are not things at all. Sin and suffering and death are, as Saint Augustine was perhaps the first to see clearly, *defects* in things. And a defect in a thing is not a smaller thing that is a part of it. The phrase "the crack in the Liberty Bell" does not denote a thing (or object or entity). When the Liberty Bell cracked, no new thing came into existence—although the bell did really then become cracked. Nevertheless, sin and death and suffering are not illusions. Saint Augustine was not Mary Baker Eddy. Sin is not a made thing, but human beings are made things, and they really do sin. Suffering is not a made thing, but human beings are made things, and they really do suffer. Death is not a made thing, but human beings are made things, and they really do die. If Buddhism says, "Suffering is real, but the self that—so the unenlightened suppose—suffers is not real," Christianity says, "The self that suffers is real, but suffering is not real."

22. But appropriation is only appropriation; the Nicene Creed says of the Son *per quem omnia facta sunt*—through (or "by") whom all things were made. The term that is opposed to "the economic Trinity" is "the ontological Trinity"—the three Persons as they really are, as they are apart from the limitations inherent in the human experience of God that lead us to appropriate the various relations of the undivided God to the created world to one or another of the Persons. Julian's next statement after our quoted passage is, "But what is to me sothly the maker, the keper, and the lover I canot tell"—which I would paraphrase as "But what he truly is who is to me the Maker, the Keeper, and the Lover, I cannot tell." A created being, she is able to know the Triune God only through his operations in creation.

and guide). In Julian's vision, creation ("all that is made") displays, in its very nature, the signature of its Trinitarian Creator. For I do not think that when Julian said, "In this little thing I saw three properties," she meant by "property" exactly what we today mean by "property"—that is "feature" or "attribute" or "characteristic." I think that her meaning was closer to what we should express by the word "nature."[23] But "in this little thing I saw three natures" does not sound right, for we think of a thing as having only one nature (unless that "thing" is Christ—but "How can someone have two natures?" is a question whose answer is beyond human understanding), and that is why I have paraphrased "In this little thing I saw three properties" as "In this little thing I saw a threefold nature."

---

23. Consider these words from the Prayer of Humble Access: "But thou art the same Lord, whose property is always to have mercy." Here, pretty clearly, "property" means "nature": it is God's nature always to have mercy: always to have mercy is *proper* to God.

Chapter ELEVEN

Are We Hardwired to Believe in God?

Natural Signs for God, Evolution,
and the *Sensus Divinitatis*

C. STEPHEN EVANS

The attempt to show that there is a "natural" knowledge of God's existence—that is, a knowledge of God that does not presuppose any special religious authority or revelation—is usually termed "natural theology." Natural theology has often been pursued through arguments or "proofs." Since the time of the ancient Greeks, philosophers have given arguments for and against the existence of God, and such arguments continue to be presented.[1]

Natural theology understood in this way, as an attempt to develop arguments for God's existence, poses a puzzle. Arguments for God's existence are frequently criticized and declared to be conclusively refuted, yet the arguments continue to be presented. Some people, including well-trained, well-educated philosophers, find the arguments convincing. Many others, equally well-trained and well-educated, find them to be without merit. The arguments never seem to convince the critics. However, the refutations never seem to silence the proponents, who continue to refine and develop the arguments.

There are of course many possible ways to explain this impasse. I shall defend the claim that the reason the debate continues has to do with the nature of the

---

1. This essay grew out of various lectures delivered at various places when I was writing my book *Natural Signs and Knowledge of God: A New Look at Theistic Arguments* (Oxford: Oxford University Press, 2010), as well as lectures given subsequent to the publication of the book. It is thus partly a condensation of some of the main points of the book, and parts of the essay overlap with material contained in different chapters of the book. This material is reused by permission of Oxford University Press.

arguments themselves. Many of the classical arguments for God's existence, such as the cosmological, teleological, and moral arguments, are grounded in what I shall call "natural signs" that point to God's reality. These theistic arguments derive their force and enjoy whatever plausibility they possess from the signs that lie at their core. The nature of a sign, as I shall develop the notion, is to be a "pointer," something that directs our attention to some reality or fact and makes knowledge of that reality or fact possible. It is the fact that the arguments focus our attention on signs that explains the continuing appeal of the arguments. These signs for God are "natural signs" because the awareness of them and tendency to see them as pointing to God are hardwired into human nature.

However, these signs, like signs in general, do not necessarily point in a conclusive or compelling fashion. Signs must be read, and some are harder to read than others or, one might say, easier to interpret in alternative ways, even if the possible interpretations are not all equally plausible. The natural signs that point to God's reality are like those signs that can be interpreted in more than one way and are thus sometimes misread. They point to God but do not do so in a coercive manner. To function properly as pointers, they must be interpreted properly. For this reason, the theistic arguments, which attempt to articulate these signs and develop them into inferential arguments, fail to be conclusive proofs that compel assent from everyone. However, I shall try to show that the arguments' weaknesses do not necessarily undermine the value of the signs the arguments embody. Even if an argument developed from a sign fails as an argument, the sign may still point to God's reality and make knowledge of God possible for those who have the will and ability to read the sign properly. Seeing the theistic arguments as articulations of natural signs therefore helps us understand both the appeal of the arguments as well as their lack of conclusiveness.

It also helps us resolve a lively current dispute in the philosophy of religion: the argument between the evidentialists and so-called Reformed epistemologists. Evidentialists, as the name implies, maintain that any knowledge we have about God must be based on evidence, a view that until recently was taken for granted by most defenders and critics of religious belief.[2] Reformed epistemologists, such as Alvin Plantinga and Nicholas Wolterstorff, maintain that belief in God may be "properly basic," not the result of any kind of

---

2. The most eminent evidentialist in contemporary philosophy of religion is Richard Swinburne. For his views on the justification of beliefs, see his *Epistemic Justification* (Oxford: Clarendon, 2001).

inference.[3] Seeing the theistic arguments as articulations of natural signs helps to show how both camps may be correct in some of their main contentions.

The Reformed epistemologists are right to argue that the knowledge of God does not have to be based on formal arguments, since a natural sign is something that can direct an individual to the reality of which it is a sign without any process of inference. However, the evidentialists are right to insist that the knowledge of God, at least in standard cases, is based on what may be called evidence. For one thing, it is possible to become aware of the mediating role of the sign and to use the sign as the basis for an inferential argument. On the view I shall defend, the main theistic arguments are arguments of just this kind. However, even when the sign is not functioning as the basis for an inferential argument, it may still be regarded as evidence in the sense that it is something that makes a certain truth more evident to someone.

This claim is not as contrary to Reformed epistemology as it might seem, since the Reformed epistemologists, while denying that belief in God is based on *evidence*, do claim that there is a *ground* for the belief. I hope to adjudicate the dispute between evidentialists and Reformed epistemologists by paying careful attention to the notion of evidence. This will help us understand in what senses a "ground" may be regarded as evidence and that such "grounds" may legitimately be understood as natural signs.

After developing my case for natural signs as the basis for reasonable belief in God, I shall then try to look at the issues from the viewpoint of contemporary cognitive science and evolutionary psychology, which increasingly support the claim that a tendency towards religious belief is something that has been hardwired into human nature by evolution. This raises an important question: Does this kind of scientific explanation for natural religious beliefs undermine the idea of natural signs for God or support it?

Why Should God Employ Natural Signs to Make His Reality Known?

Suppose that it is true that God exists, and that God is the kind of being that Christians, Jews, and Muslims have traditionally believed in. Roughly, we can take this as meaning that there is an all-powerful, all-knowing, and completely

---

3. See Alvin Plantinga, "Reason and Belief in God," in *Faith and Rationality*, ed. Alvin Plantinga and Nicholas Wolterstorff (Notre Dame, IN: University of Notre Dame Press, 1983), 16–91.

good personal being who is responsible for the existence of everything in the universe. Furthermore, let us assume, as do these great religions, that God created humans for a purpose involving a special relation to himself and that God cares about humans and wants them to fulfill this purpose, a fulfillment that would involve eternal happiness for humans.

If all this were the case, what kind of knowledge of God would we expect God to make possible for humans? One thing we might expect is that the knowledge of God would be widely available. If we assume that God cares about all humans and that all of them are intended by God to enjoy a relation with God, then it would seem reasonable to believe that God would make it possible at least for many humans to come to know his existence, since one can hardly enjoy a special relation with a being that one does not know exists. I shall call this the "Wide Accessibility Principle."[4]

The Wide Accessibility Principle can plausibly be combined with a certain egalitarian picture of how God relates to human beings. If there is a God who loves all humans and desires a relation with them, we would not expect, for example, God to restrict the knowledge of God to philosophers capable of understanding extremely abstract and complicated arguments, just as we would not expect God to limit the knowledge of himself to one sex, or one race, or one nation. Similarly, if there is knowledge of God at all, we would not expect that knowledge to be limited to highly intelligent or highly educated people.

If God exists, what else besides the Wide Accessibility Principle would we expect to be true of knowledge of God? It is plausible to think that the knowledge of God would not only be widely available but also easily resistible. I shall call this the "Easy Resistibility Principle." According to this principle, though the knowledge of God is widely available, it is not forced on humans. Those who do not wish to love and serve God find it is possible to reject the idea that there is a God. The plausibility of this principle stems from the assumption that God wants the relation humans are to enjoy with him to be one in which they love and serve him freely and joyfully. Since God is all-powerful and all-knowing, one can easily imagine that people who do not love God would nevertheless, if his reality were too obvious, come to the conclusion that it would be foolish and irrational to oppose God and God's purposes, however grudgingly the conclusion might be held.

---

4. See my *Natural Signs and Knowledge of God*, 12–17, for a fuller account of this principle, as well as the "Easy Resistibility Principle" discussed in the next paragraph.

One might think that the Wide Accessibility Principle and the Easy Resistibility Principle are in contradiction, but this is not so. They do embody different divine purposes, and we can imagine that there might be tension between them in some cases, such that God cannot fully realize one purpose without compromising the other. However, we have no *a priori* reason to think that it would be impossible for God to make it possible for many (or even all) humans to know about him, and yet simultaneously make it possible for those who do not wish to serve him lovingly and freely not to know about his reality.

The two principles I have here explained are memorably described by Pascal:

> If He had willed to overcome the obstinacy of the most hardened, He could have done so by revealing Himself to them so manifestly that they could not have doubted of the truth of His essence . . . It was not then right that He should appear in a manner manifestly divine, and completely capable of convincing all men; but it was also not right that He should come in so hidden a manner that He could not be known by those who should sincerely seek Him. He has willed to make Himself quite recognizable by those; and thus, willing to appear openly to those who seek Him with all their heart and hidden from those who flee from Him with all their heart, He so regulates the knowledge of Himself that he has given signs of Himself, visible to those who seek Him and not to those who seek Him not. There is enough light for those who only desire to see and enough obscurity for those who have a contrary disposition.[5]

If Pascal is right, then we would expect both the Wide Accessibility Principle and the Easy Resistibility to hold, and thus that God would make knowledge of himself widely available for those who wish to have it, but that God would not force such knowledge on those who do not wish to know God. Those who wish not to know God should be able to explain away or discount any evidence God presents for his reality. I believe that the notion of a natural sign will meet these Pascalian constraints on the knowledge of God. Such signs are widely available pointers, or clues that point to God's reality, but they point in such a way that allows those who do not wish to believe in God to reinterpret or dismiss the sign.

---

5. Blaise Pascal, *Pensees* (New York: E. P. Dutton, 1958), 118 (§430).

The Concept of a Natural Sign

To develop my thesis that there are natural signs that point to God's reality and that these signs lie at the core of many of the classical theistic arguments, I must first try to explain in some detail what I mean by a natural sign. My inspiration for the term comes from Thomas Reid; my concept is in several respects inspired by Reid's work and overlaps significantly with his concept.[6]

Reid's notion of a natural sign is developed and used mainly as part of his account of perception.[7] He defended a direct realist account of perception and refuted the representational theories of perception characteristic of many of the early modern philosophers who were his predecessors. This representational account of perception holds that humans are not directly aware of mind-independent physical objects but only of mental entities, commonly called "ideas" in the eighteenth century, that (for some of these philosophers) represent physical objects or allow us to infer their existence. This type of representational account of perception, which Reid characteristically calls "the Way of Ideas" or "the Ideal philosophy," inevitably leads, on Reid's view, either to idealism or skepticism. Reid thinks that the philosophies of George Berkeley and David Hume make this clear. That result is unsurprising, since it is hard to see how humans can gain knowledge of extramental realities if we are only directly aware of mental realities. Neither reason nor experience allows us to bridge the chasm between our minds and the external world that looms if representationalism is true.

Much of the dispute between Reid and the defenders of the "Way of Ideas" turns on the nature and function of sensations.[8] Philosophers such as John Locke, who think of perception as rooted in sensations, typically see those special sensory ideas as immediate objects of awareness that give us an indirect connection to extramental entities. In the case of ideas of primary

---

6.   Reid himself probably took the term "sign" from George Berkeley, who employed it in his *New Theory of Vision* (New York: E. P. Dutton, 1910) to explain the perception of distance by sight. There Berkeley develops a distinction between types of signs that seems close to Reid's distinction between natural and artificial signs. See, e.g., 144.79–80. What follows in this section of this essay is taken with some modifications from *Natural Signs and Knowledge of God*, 28–34.

7.   For good accounts of Reid's account of perception, see James van Cleve, "Reid's Theory of Perception," in *The Cambridge Companion to Thomas Reid*, ed. Terence Cuneo and Rene van Woudenberg (Cambridge: Cambridge University Press), 101–33.

8.   For a clear account of Reid's view of sensations and perception, see Todd Buras, "The Function of Sensations in Reid," *Journal of the History of Philosophy* 47, no. 3 (2009): 329–53. Much of what I have to say about Reid on sensations and their role in perception is taken from Buras's work.

qualities, for example, Locke sees these ideas as resembling or mirroring external entities. Such a relation between ideas and physical things allows the ideas to represent them to us or else serves as the basis for an inference to such extramental entities.

Reid's account of sensations is entirely different. Reid learned from Berkeley that sensations (and mental ideas in general) do not resemble the physical objects they are supposed to represent. For Reid, sensations are not the primary objects of perceptual awareness but are "natural signs" that make perceptual awareness possible. Sensations are not (usually) the objects of perception but the means whereby we perceive real objects. Sensations are not linked to perceptions conceptually, and thus it is not a necessary truth that we perceive the world by way of sensations. Nevertheless, our actual constitutions are such that it is causally necessary for us to have sensations to perceive the world.

How is it that we perceive objects by way of sensations? Reid says it is not by way of inference; the transition from sensation to perception is immediate, at least in a psychological sense. Nor is it by any relation of "resemblance" or "mirroring" between the sensation and the object perceived. Rather the sensation is a *sign* of what is perceived, either a natural sign or an artificial sign. The key idea is that sensations are not normally themselves the objects of perception but the *means* whereby we perceive other things. We do not normally perceive sensations but perceive by way of sensations. Of course, it is possible to make sensations themselves the objects of conscious awareness, and for some special purposes we do this. For example, suppose one is being examined by an ophthalmologist who wants to determine whether a person's eyesight is working properly. In such a case, one peers at a chart and is asked about one's sensations. In this situation one might focus on the visual sensations themselves (are they clear and sharp, or fuzzy?) rather than what one normally sees by way of the sensation.

Two things are required for the sensation to be a natural sign. First, there must be a real causal connection between the thing and the sensation.[9] Second, the sensation must play a key role in producing the conception and belief, which are the constituents of perception. Sensations give rise to perceptions in

---

9. A qualification is required here. Reid has a technical and idiosyncratic view of causation. In his technical sense the object perceived is not the cause of the sensation. However, in the loose and "ordinary" sense of causation employed by people generally there is a causal connection.

two different ways, corresponding to a distinction Reid draws between original and acquired perceptions. In original perception, we are hardwired to take a particular type of sensation as a sign of a particular type of object that is perceived. With respect to original perceptions, "Nature hath established a real connection between the signs and the things signified; and nature hath also taught us the interpretation of the signs."[10] One of Reid's favorite examples is the way that the sensation of touching a solid object produces the perception of a body having the quality of hardness.[11] Reid believes that we would never gain perceptual knowledge of the external world without such original perceptions, and he argues that the process that moves us from sensation as a sign to the perception of an object in original perception is irresistible. Even philosophers like Hume who profess to doubt the connections (as Reid interprets Hume) confess that in daily life they are unable to do so.

In acquired perceptions, sensations also serve as natural signs of the objects perceived, but in this case the principles that govern the link between sensation and object perceived are more general in nature; there is no hardwired link between a particular type of sensation and a particular type of perception.[12] Rather, the links are grounded in more general principles of our constitution, involving experience and reflection. For example, since cloves of garlic regularly are conjoined with a distinctive smell, the one we call "garlicky," after experiencing garlic cloves on several occasions (especially while cutting them up), I learn to recognize a garlicky smell as the smell of garlic. Once I learn this connection, however, the movement from sensation to perception is just as immediate as it is in the case of an original perception; no inference is necessary to perceive a clove of garlic is present by way of its smell.

It is clear that acquired perceptions presuppose original perceptions, since I can only learn by experience that a particular sensation is conjoined with a particular object if I am able to know that the object is present.[13] Acquired perceptions remain natural in the sense that they are the product of principles of our constitution. But their partial dependence on experience and learning

---

10. Thomas Reid, *An Inquiry into the Human Mind on the Principles of Common Sense*, ed. Derek R. Brookes (Edinburgh: Edinburgh University Press, 1997), 190.

11. Reid, *An Inquiry into the Human Mind*, 54–58.

12. This paragraph and the one that follows are indebted to an email received from Todd Buras, which contained a particularly clear explanation of the distinction between original and acquired perception.

13. Reid makes this explicit in *Inquiry*, 191.

means they are subject to improvement, correction, and variability in a way that our original perceptions are not. For instance, when certain auditory sensations suggest the direction of an object, this is an acquired perception. Such acquired perceptions, unlike original perceptions, are resistible. As I gain more experience and reflect on that experience, I may come to believe that the perception of direction by sound is unreliable in certain circumstances (e.g., an echo chamber). For Reid, perception in general is not infallible; the justification provided to our perceptions by the sensations that "suggest" them is always *prima facie*. However, acquired perceptions are subject to defeat in ways that are not the case for original perceptions.[14]

Sensations are far from the only natural signs in Reid. Perceived objects can themselves serve as natural signs for other perceptions, both original and acquired perceptions. Our ability to recognize other persons as conscious beings and to communicate with them depends on natural signs. Perceptual recognition of "the thoughts, purposes, and dispositions of the mind" are made possible originally by way of perceptions of "the features of the face, the modulation of the voice, and the motion and attitude of the body."[15] These natural signs of human mental states constitute a "natural language of mankind," without which communication in general, including the use of artificial signs such as those employed in human language, would be impossible. The signs in these cases are not the perceptions but the actual physical states perceived. Although these perceived facial and bodily characteristics give rise to original perceptions, they do not seem to be irresistible, since we learn by experience that people can simulate these signs to deceive others. Our disposition to rely on them in general is very strong, but that disposition, like our disposition to believe in the testimony of others, is one that can be strengthened, modified, and even blocked on some occasions by experience.[16]

To summarize, a natural sign for Reid is something, either mental (such as a sensation) or physical (such as a perceived facial gesture), that has a causal connection (in the "loose" sense of causality) "upstream" with what the sign signifies and also plays a causal role (again in the loose sense) "downstream" in

---

14. For Reid's discussion of the way experience and reflection give rise to acquired perceptions, see *Essays on the Intellectual Powers of Man*, ed. Derek R. Brookes (Edinburgh: Edinburgh University Press, 2002), 234–41. For Reid's explanation of how it is that we make mistakes in perception, see 241–52.

15. Reid, *Inquiry*, 59.

16. For Reid's view of testimony, see C. A. J. Coady, "Reid on Testimony," in *The Cambridge Companion to Thomas Reid*, 180–203.

generating a characteristic judgment. According to Reid, some of the natural signs that produce original perceptions are irresistible because we are hardwired to move from the particular sign to a particular type of perceptual judgment. In other cases, the natural signs, both for original perceptions and especially for acquired perceptions, are resistible because the resulting judgments can be strengthened, modified, or overridden by experience. When a sign is functioning as a sign, one's conscious attention is not focused on the sign but on what it signifies (even though it is possible, and occasionally appropriate, to turn one's attention to the sign itself).

Natural Signs for God

So how does the concept of natural signs, which I employ to examine theistic arguments, compare to Reid's concept? There are many fundamental similarities between theistic natural signs—namely, natural signs that point to God—and Reidian natural signs. The most important similarity is that both understand a sign as something that brings an object to our awareness and produces a belief in that object's reality. Natural signs of God are the means whereby a person becomes aware of God. As is the case for Reidian natural signs, theistic natural signs should be linked upstream to what the sign signifies and downstream to a conception of what is signified as well as a belief in the reality of what is signified. In other words, a natural sign for God ought to be connected both to God and to a human disposition to conceive of God and believe in God's reality.

Let us look first at the link between the sign and God. If God exists, then God is the creator and sustainer of every finite reality, so the idea of a causal link between God and the sign is unproblematic. However, just because God is the creator of everything finite does not mean that such a causal connection is sufficient. Presumably, natural signs for God will be distinctive in some way; if everything is a natural sign for God, then there will be no natural signs in any distinctive sense. What is needed, I think, is the idea that God not only causes the sign's existence but also that God creates the sign to be a sign. The function of the sign needs to be part of the reason why the sign exists, and this function must be anchored in God's creative intentions.

What about the other link, the connection "downstream" to the belief or judgment about God? Here, theistic signs, much like Reidian signs, must empower us to form judgments that what the sign signifies, in this case God, really exists. Again, this must be understood not merely as a casual relation but as a functional one. For Reid, our tendency to form certain judgments because of signs is part of our "design plan," so to speak. If there are theistic signs, they also must not only characteristically give rise to beliefs about God; doing so must be part of their intended function.

What are the natural signs for God? In *Natural Signs and Knowledge of God*, I focus on the signs embedded in some of the classical arguments for God's existence: our sense of wonder that there is a universe in the cosmological argument, our sense that nature and human life are purposeful and not meaningless in the argument from design, and our sense that we are morally accountable beings bound by obligations that are not of human making, as well as our sense that human beings have a special kind of value or dignity as persons made in the image of God in the argument from morality. (The last case is a particularly clear example of a "natural sign" since it points to real likenesses between God and humans.) Besides these, there are other important natural signs, particularly a global sense of gratitude that we often feel for our lives as a whole. In this essay, I do not have space to develop any of these at length. Instead I want to focus on the question as to whether such claims fit or do not fit with contemporary scientific accounts of the origins of religious beliefs.

Contemporary Scientific Accounts of the Origins of Religious Belief

Interestingly, the claim that there is a causal link between certain characteristic human experiences and belief in God is now strongly supported by contemporary cognitive scientists. Contrary to earlier social scientific theories about religious belief, contemporary scientists are prone to think that humans are hardwired to be religious; belief in God or gods is the result of the operation of a cognitive faculty. For example, Pascal Boyer, the Henry Luce Professor of Individual and Collective Memory at Washington University in St. Louis, affirms that "the content and organization of religious ideas depend, in important ways, on noncultural properties of the human mind-brain."[17] Many

---

17. Pascal Boyer, *The Naturalness of Religious Ideas: A Cognitive Theory of Religion* (Berkeley: University of California Press, 1994), 3.

scientists agree with Boyer.[18] Of course most of these scientists are atheists, and they believe this hardwired link is an evolutionary accident; the tendency to believe in God is a byproduct of a cognitive mechanism evolved for other purposes. I will shortly discuss whether our tendency to believe in God being the result of evolution invalidates the belief. Regardless of how its evolutionary status is interpreted, contemporary scientists agree with theologians that there is a natural tendency to believe in God, the kind of disposition theologians such as John Calvin traditionally called the *Sensus Divinitatis,* or sense of divinity.

How strong must the connection be between a theistic natural sign and the belief that the sign gives rise to? We have seen that for Reid some natural signs are irresistible in their operations, while others may be strengthened or inhibited by other experiences and beliefs. Theistic natural signs are more like the second type of Reidian natural signs. On the one hand, to be a natural sign at all there must be some inbuilt propensity, when the sign is encountered, to form the relevant judgment. If such theistic natural signs exist, then we would expect belief in God to be widespread, found in reasonably young children and across many cultures, and we would expect those beliefs to be typically occasioned by similar experiences. This is exactly what contemporary cognitive scientists affirm. This expectation is consistent with the "Wide Accessibility Principle."

However, the propensity to believe in God, though strong, is far from irresistible. There is every reason to think that the beliefs originating from theistic natural signs are subject to modification (strengthening, weakening, or even being blocked) by experience and other beliefs like Reidian natural signs. However, theistic natural signs may be even more subject to disturbances in their operations than Reidian natural signs. The reason has to do with the "Easy Resistibility Principle." Since God wishes humans to relate to him freely and lovingly, and since an irresistible awareness of God's reality would make this difficult, there is good reason to think that those who might be motivated to disbelieve in God would be able to inhibit the operation of the natural disposition to form a belief in God when one encounters a theistic natural sign.

---

18. See, e.g., Scott Atran, *In Gods We Trust: The Evolutionary Landscape of Religion* (Oxford: Oxford University Press, 2002); Justin L. Barrett, *Why Would Anyone Believe in God?* (Walnut Creek, CA: Altamira, 2004); S. E. Guthrie, *Faces in the Clouds: A New Theory of Religion* (New York: Oxford University Press, 1993); Dean Hamer, *The God Gene: How Faith is Hardwired into Our Genes* (New York: Doubleday, 2004). This is just a fraction of the new books that have appeared in this area, and does not include the large number of articles that have appeared in scholarly journals.

Besides this kind of motivated disbelief, there is also the possibility that the disposition will fail to produce belief in God in some people simply because the individuals have been taught (by parents or teachers or other figures) that there is no God; thus they will ignore or override the disposition. Clearly, the existence of many atheists in the contemporary world supports the claim that the natural tendency to believe in God is resistible.

Does Evolution Undermine the Reliability of Natural Signs for God's Reality?

As I noted above, the cognitive scientists who believe that we humans are hardwired to believe in God think this hardwiring came about through an evolutionary process. Most of these scientists are atheists who think that evolution itself is an unguided process, and they certainly don't believe that God designed the process to make humans believe in him. Rather, they think the tendency to believe in God is an unintended byproduct of other factors in our nature that had survival value. Is their view of the matter correct? Does the fact that the tendency to believe in God came about through a Darwinian process imply that these beliefs are unreliable? To consider this question, I shall first take a particular natural sign as my example: our sense that the universe is purposive. This example should be particularly favorable to the atheist since it is often claimed that evolutionary theory shows us that the apparent design we see in nature is merely apparent.

Is the apparent purposeful order we see in nature an illusion? Nothing in the scientific theory of evolution requires one to think so. The evolutionary process itself depends on the laws of nature; the mechanisms that make the evolutionary process work depend, for example, on the existence of stable reproductive mechanisms, which in turn depend on the laws of physics and chemistry. Far from showing that the order in nature is illusory, evolution actually shows that the order we experience on the surface of things, so to speak, depends on a still deeper, hidden order.

Atheists, rather than taking the laws of nature for granted as a brute fact, ought to reflect more on the fact that the natural world seems "fine-tuned" to produce a world with beauty and value. It seems to us that many of the laws of nature and the values of the constants that are part of those laws could have been very different, yet they have values precisely within the narrow range that make living organisms and their complex systems possible. This fine-tuning is itself a powerful argument for God's existence.[19] It may not be a natural sign according to my definition because the evidence is not widely available to those without a scientific education. Nevertheless, it suggests that it is a mistake to consider evolutionary theory a defeater for the claim that the natural world contains purposive order. If anything, it shows that the order we experience in nature is part of the deep structure of nature.

If our experience of the world as purposive is a natural sign for God, it does not depend on an argument or inference to function any more than our sensations of green grass require an argument to generate a reasonable belief in green grass. For the experience to function as a natural sign, the only thing required is that the order and purposiveness we perceive truly be present and that it be something God created to introduce us to his reality. That can surely be the case even if God chose to actualize that order through an evolutionary process.

Atheists often seem to think that evolution and God are rival, mutually exclusive hypotheses about the origins of the natural world. Sometimes it is because they think theistic and natural explanations are rivals. What can be explained scientifically, they say, needs no religious explanation. However, this fails to grasp the relationship between God and the natural world by conceiving of God as one additional cause within that natural world. If God exists at all, God is not an entity within the natural world but the creator of that natural world, with all of its causal processes. If God exists, God is the reason for the natural world and for the causal processes of the natural world. In principle, therefore, a natural explanation can never preclude a theistic explanation.

The atheist might respond by claiming to identify characteristics of an evolutionary explanation that are incompatible with divine causation. A number of features of evolution could be cited to justify this claim. One is simply that evolution requires the death and suffering of vast numbers of sentient creatures. Surely, the atheist might claim, a loving God would not employ such a process to create a world. Such an objection seems initially plausible, but on reflection that plausibility vanishes. First, that the natural world includes a great quantity of suffering on the part of sentient creatures has always been

---

19. For a good presentation of the fine-tuning argument for God, see Robin Collins, "A Scientific Argument for the Existence of God: The Fine-Tuning Design Argument," in *Reason for the Hope Within*, ed. Michael J. Murray (Grand Rapids: Eerdmans, 1999), 47–75.

evident. This is not something that Darwinian evolution brought to our attention. This is of course one of the features of the world that gives rise to the problem of evil, an issue discussed from ancient philosophy onwards. I grant that this is a problem that a theistic view of the world must confront, but dealing with the problem of evil adequately would require another paper (or book perhaps), and I will not try to answer the problem in a paragraph or footnote. All I wish to say at this point is that the theory of evolution does not really make the problem any worse. There are many responses to the problem of evil. If those responses are adequate, then nothing in the theory of evolution is going to change the situation. If the responses are not adequate, then the theists' cause is lost without bringing evolution into the picture. Either way, the theory of evolution does not appreciably change the plausibility of theism.

It is worth noting that any speculations as to what process God would use to create the world are just that: speculations. We have no reliable way of testing our intuitions about such matters, since we have no experience with world creation. It is also worth noting that there are possible reasons why a good God might prefer a long and slow process of creation, even one that involves pain and suffering.[20]

There are of course other reasons an atheist or agnostic might give to support the claim that theism and evolution are incompatible. For example, it is sometimes claimed that because evolutionary theory posits that the process by which plants and animals have evolved is one that involves random genetic mutations, the process cannot be one that is designed. Surely, they might say, a process that depends on random mutations cannot be guided, and so God cannot have used an evolutionary means to achieve his ends.

However, this argument fails because it depends on an equivocation in what is meant by "random." When scientists claim that genetic mutations are random, they do not mean that they are uncaused, or even that they are unpredictable from the point of view of biochemistry, but only that the mutations do not happen in response to the adaptational needs of the organism.[21] It is entirely possible for a natural process to include randomness in that sense, even though the whole natural order is itself created and sustained by God.

20. For a number of thoughtful suggestions as to why this might be the case, see Michael J. Murray, *Nature Red in Tooth and Claw: Theism and the Problem of Animal Suffering* (Oxford: Oxford University Press, 2008).

21. For a good discussion of this point see Alvin Plantinga, *Where the Conflict Really Lies: Science, Religion, and Naturalism* (Oxford: Oxford University Press, 2011), esp. 11–12.

Thus the sense of "randomness" required for evolutionary theory does not imply that the evolutionary process must be unguided.

Moral Obligation as a Natural Sign for God

My argument that it is entirely possible for a natural sign for God to have come about through an evolutionary process can be made still sharper by considering one additional natural sign for God: our sense of moral obligation. Most humans agree that we are morally obligated to act in certain ways. Other things being equal, people ought to tell the truth to each other, keep their promises, and be grateful to those who have shown great kindness. Practically everyone agrees that it is wrong for one person to inflict pain on another simply because the person inflicting pain enjoys it, and I have never met anyone who agreed with the claim that it would be morally permissible to breed human children as a food source. Decent people know such things through conscience. Many people, religious and otherwise, feel morally accountable for their actions, but religious people have a natural explanation of this: we feel accountable because we *are* accountable to God. Moral obligations are God's laws, and that is why they apply to all people and why they take precedence over humanly generated obligations.

Of course, many atheists agree that there are objective moral obligations but reject the idea that they point to God. However, a problem emerges at this point for the atheist who wants to view the products of evolution as totally unguided. Our tendency to believe in moral obligations seems, like the tendency to believe in God, something that is hardwired into us by evolution. However, in a much-discussed and cited article, Sharon Street has argued that a Darwinian account of the origins of our moral beliefs undermines the credibility of those beliefs themselves as objectively true claims.[22] We have no reason to think that the beliefs about moral obligations the unguided evolutionary process has instilled in us are objectively true, for an unguided evolutionary process cares only about survival and sexual reproduction. There is no good reason to think that those characteristics that make survival and reproduction more likely will correlate with true beliefs about moral goodness.

This situation puts pressure on the atheist to give up belief in objective

---

22. Sharon Street, "A Darwinian Dilemma for Realist Theories of Value," *Philosophical Studies* 127 (2006), 109–66.

morality altogether, undermining the claim that we can have such a morality without God. So an atheist who wants to hold on to the objective truth of morality should reject the claim that an evolutionary account of our cognitive abilities necessarily undermines faith in the ability of those faculties to give us true beliefs. The parallel with hardwired religious beliefs is clear. If the atheist holds that the moral beliefs that evolution provides track with moral realities, then it is not clear why the fact that some religious beliefs have an evolutionary basis gives us a reason to doubt them. The fact that our tendency to believe in God has an evolutionary explanation by itself gives us no reason to think this tendency produces an illusion. For that matter, from an evolutionary perspective, *all* our cognitive faculties must have a biological explanation. However, unless someone wants to embrace total skepticism regarding the reliability of our cognitive faculties, the mere fact that a cognitive mechanism has an evolutionary explanation gives no reason to doubt that this mechanism is conducive to truth.

The parallel between moral beliefs and religious beliefs is especially interesting because it reveals a possible connection between the two types of beliefs. Why do philosophers like Sharon Street think that evolution "debunks" moral knowledge and gives us a reason to doubt that there is genuine moral knowledge? I submit it is not simply because our capacity to develop moral beliefs is thought to be the result of an evolutionary process. Rather, it is because those moral convictions are believed to have resulted from an evolutionary process that is *unguided*. Nature is seen as essentially "matter in motion" (as physicists in the past might have described things) without final causes. When nature is seen as lacking purpose in this way, it is hard to see why evolution should have produced true moral beliefs in us since it seems unlikely such beliefs would have much in the way of survival value (or so Street argues). It is not Darwinian evolution per se that creates the problem but the combination of Darwinian evolution and a naturalistic view of the universe. It is not Darwinian evolution that creates the problem with objective morality but Darwinian evolution that assumes a naturalistic universe.

If, however, we think of evolution as the process by which God created humans and gave them the qualities they need to know God and relate to him, then the situation is entirely different. As the creator of the entire natural order, God controls the entire process, including the process of evolution. There is no unguided evolution and thus no reason to think that the moral and religious beliefs we are hardwired to hold are unreliable. One implication of this is that evolutionary theory as a scientific account of how humans came to be provides no evidence for the unreliability of our "natural" moral and religious beliefs. It is only when evolutionary theory is incorporated into a naturalistic metaphysical view that it seems to rule out God. But to appeal to evolutionary theory *interpreted naturalistically* to rule out theism is a classic instance of begging the question. Of course, if we start by assuming that God does not exist and that evolution is unguided, we will have reason to doubt our natural religious beliefs. However, doing so says no more than that it is possible to give evolutionary theory a naturalistic interpretation. The fact that it is possible to give a naturalistic interpretation of evolutionary theory in no way shows that evolutionary theory provides any *evidence* for naturalism. For as the example of religious scientists clearly shows, it is equally possible to give evolutionary theory a theistic interpretation.

Conclusion: Trusting Natural Signs

We began by arguing that there are natural signs that give human beings a tendency to believe in God. The particular example that I explored is purposiveness. Our experience indicates an orderly world in which that order produces value. Humans have a natural tendency to see an orderly process with a good outcome as "no accident." Should we trust that tendency?

If either the order or the value were an illusion, then the trust might be misplaced. However, the order in the natural world is certainly not an illusion. Rather, as science has progressed, we have discovered that the "surface order" we observe in nature is the result of a deeper, more profound order.

What about the value produced by that order? I see no reason to assume that the value we seem to observe in nature is illusory. Of course, someone who is an atheist *might* accept moral nihilism or some antirealist account of value. If there are no objective values, then any apparent objective value we see in nature will be illusory. However, the atheist who rejects moral nihilism and continues to believe in objective value cannot take this route. Such a person will affirm that there is value in nature and that our beliefs about value have some degree of reliability. It is hard to see how such a person would know that we have misplaced the value produced by orderly processes. Yet this person continues to trust that our natural response to value is in order. Such a trust seems to presuppose that it is not an accident that our moral beliefs track with moral truths. But that seems to imply that there is indeed purposiveness in the natural order, for our moral faculties themselves are evidence of purposiveness. Morality may itself be a natural sign for God; many people naturally see the moral law as one that rests on a transcendent lawgiver. However, besides being a natural sign in its own right, morality also supports our belief that the purposiveness we experience in nature is not illusory.

Of course, none of this "proves" the existence of God. I have already admitted that natural signs for God can be reinterpreted, explained away, and denied. Even Thomas Reid's perceptual natural signs can be doubted by skeptics or idealists who deny we have any knowledge of an external world. It is easier still to be a skeptic about theistic natural signs. However, this is what we should expect if the "Easy Resistibility Principle" is true. The natural signs that point to God are still there, and for many their force can be felt. They are indeed "widely available." No proof of their validity can be given, but I have argued that Darwinian evolutionary theory, shorn of naturalistic metaphysics, provides no reason to doubt the validity of the signs either. Those who know how to read them and are willing to do so may find they point to a reality that transcends the natural world.

Chapter TWELVE

Knowing Nature

Aristotle, God, and the Quantum

ROBERT C. KOONS

Aristotle's theory of nature offered several advantages from a Christian point of view.[1] It allowed for a profound difference between human beings and other material entities based on a distinction between rationality and subrationality, which fit nicely with the biblical conception of humans as the unique bearers of the divine image in the physical world. At the same time, Aristotelianism conceived of human desires and aspirations as continuous with the striving of all natural entities to their essence-determined ends, providing an objective and scientific basis for objective norms in ethics, aesthetics, and politics. The scientific revolution of the last three hundred years, while clearly enabling an amazing degree of progress in our understanding of the physical basis of the world (both at the very small and very large ends of the scale), occasioned the unnecessary loss of many metaphysical insights of Aristotle and the Aristotelian tradition, insights which remain essential to the understanding of middle-sized objects—like human beings. The quantum revolution of the last one hundred years has gradually transformed the imaginative landscape of natural science, creating new opportunities for the recovery of those same Aristotelian themes.

1. Introduction

In Aristotle's philosophy of nature, the metaphysical relationship between material wholes and their parts is a complex and varied one. In some cases,

1. I would like to acknowledge the support I received during the 2014–15 academic year from the James Madison Program in American Ideals and Institutions at Princeton University (for a visiting fellowship) and the University of Texas at Austin (for a faculty research grant).

the parts are wholly prior to the whole, namely, when the whole is merely an unorganized *heap* of parts. In other cases, however, the whole is ontologically prior to its parts in the sense that the parts derive their reality and causal agency from participation in the life of the whole. This is true most centrally of organisms (including human beings) and their functional parts.

Consequently, in the Aristotelian image of nature, there are metaphysically fundamental entities at multiple levels of scale. Some metaphysically fundamental things are composed of smaller things, possessing a nature that is irreducible to the natures and spatial relationships of their parts. In contrast, the "modern" image of nature—dominant from the time of Galileo and Bacon until the quantum revolution and most fully developed in the theories of Newton and Maxwell—is one in which all fundamental material entities are simple and microscopic in scale. On the quintessentially modern view, every composite thing is a mere *heap* (in Aristotelian terms), wholly reducible to the autonomous natures and interactions of their ultimate constituents.

In this modern revolution, the ascendancy of the microscopic was combined with a rejection of two of the four *causes*, or modes of explanation, in Aristotle's philosophy: namely, *formal* and *final* causes. The Aristotelian scheme of understanding action or causation in terms of the exercise of causal powers and dispositions of things, anchored in the enduring natures of those things, was replaced by exclusive reliance on mathematical *laws* of motion, which paid very careful attention to the spatial arrangements and relative motions of the microscopic parts of things.

The quantum revolution of the last century has transformed the image of physical and chemical nature in profound ways that are not yet fully understood by philosophers or physical scientists. The new image of nature has in fact revived Aristotelian modes of understanding across a wide swath of scientific disciplines, a transformation that has occurred spontaneously, gradually, and almost without being noticed. As the neo-Aristotelian framework takes shape and rises to the level of common knowledge, thereby influencing our metaphysical imagination, our understanding of our shared human nature and our place in the cosmos will improve in ways concordant with classical Christian humanism.

In section 2, I will lay out the principal elements of Aristotle's image of nature, with its multileveled world that included real agency at the biological and personal levels.

I will then briefly describe in section 3 the anti-Aristotelian revolution of the seventeenth century and its metaphysical consequences, including the immediate movement toward some form of mind-matter dualism and the subsequent shrinking of the domain of the soul to a vanishing point. The ultimate result of this revolution is the dominance within philosophy of *microphysicalism*, the thesis that all material reality is exhausted by the autonomous natures of fundamental particles (or waves) and their spatial and temporal interrelations.

In section 4, I point out the ways the quantum revolution has reversed the advantages enjoyed by microphysicalism under the Newton-Maxwell regime. Quantum theory reveals a world in which wholes are typically prior to their parts—that is, either the causal powers or the spatial locations (or both) of microparticles depend upon the irreducibly holistic features of their respective systems. This is the well-known fact of the *nonseparability* of quantum properties.

The so-called *measurement problem* in quantum mechanics has now made it quite unclear how the familiar "classical" properties (like spatial position) of macroscopic objects relate to the quantum states of their ultimate constituents. Quantum mechanics is thus open to multiple, empirically equivalent *interpretations*, some of which simply deny that macroscopic objects are wholly derivative, obtaining their macroscopic properties by a mere summation of the properties of their parts. I will describe a neo-Aristotelian interpretation of quantum mechanics: Nancy Cartwright's *dappled world* model.

Finally, in section 5, I will call for philosophers, theologians, and scientists to collaborate in a new philosophy of nature.

2. Aristotle's Image of Nature

In Aristotle's philosophy of nature, as developed in his *Physics* and *Metaphysics*, all material things have two metaphysical factors or grounds: their *matter* and their *form*. The matter of a thing consists of its parts or components—the matter of a mixture is the elements that compose it, and the matter of an organism is made up of its discrete parts. There is really no such thing as *matter* as such (except as a kind of useful fiction or limiting-case idealization, so-called "prime" matter). Instead, *matter* is a relative term. The many parts and components are (collectively) *the matter of* the whole they compose.

Correspondingly, there are two new kinds of causal explanation in addition to the familiar idea of causal production (efficient causation): formal and material. Material explanation is bottom-up, that is, we explain the characteristics of a whole in terms of how the characteristics of its parts and their interrelations constrain and define the whole. We can explain the flammability of a book in terms of the flammability of its pages, and we can explain the shape of one of the Great Pyramids in terms of the spatial relations among its constituent blocks of stone.[2]

Formal causation, in contrast, is top-down. To give the formal cause of a thing is to elucidate its essence, the what-it-is-to-be a thing of its kind. The essence of a composite thing constrains and partially determines the natures and mutual relations of its parts. The essence of each part depends (to some degree, at least) on the essence of the whole in which it participates. For example, to be a heart is to be an organ that plays a certain role in an organism's circulatory system. To be *flesh* is to be organic material that participates actively in the organic functions of an animal. To be *a gene* is to be part of a DNA molecule that codes for the production of certain proteins in the natural cellular activity of the cell. And so on.

This combination of formal and material causation in Aristotle's work is usually given the label of *hylomorphism*, from the Greek *hyle* for "matter" and *morphe* for "form." A hylomorphic model of nature dominates much of natural philosophy in the period of late antiquity (the so-called "Neo-Platonists" actually relied heavily on Aristotle's philosophy) and the High Middle Ages.

Once we have the formal and material causes of complete material things (which Aristotle called ουσιαι or *substances*), we can predict and explain how they will interact. That is, we will have an account of the active and passive causal powers of things: what changes they can cause in others and what changes they can undergo themselves. This way of accounting for change— namely, change as the result of the exercise of causal powers, rooted in the forms or essences of the agent and patient involved—is called *efficient* or *moving* causation. The Aristotelian model of efficient causation does not simply seek to describe the changes as conforming to some abstract laws of nature or of motion (as is the case in much modern philosophy) but rather attempts to understand the changes as expressions of the formal and material causes

---

2. In addition to these three, Aristotle posited a fourth mode of causal explanation: final or teleological. See sec. 4.1, "The Revenge of Teleology."

of the entities involved in the interaction. In part, this is because Aristotle conceives of time as the product of change, and not vice versa. It is essences (the formal causes) of things that propel time forward by inducing change and initiating activities. Unlike early modern philosophers, Aristotle did not think of change as the byproduct of the inexorable forward movement of time and the guidance of abstract and global laws of nature.[3]

The Aristotelian conception of efficient causation through causal powers allows for the existence of exceptional situations in which the causal power of one substance is frustrated or distorted by the action of another substance or by the absence of one of its natural preconditions. In an Aristotelian framework, it is natural to speak of the *malfunctioning* of a substance when its causal powers are blocked or disabled. Additionally, a complex substance can become denatured, losing (perhaps permanently) some of the causal powers that define its natural kind. This loss of characteristic powers can be identified with the phenomenon of being *damaged*. We can further distinguish between a substance's normal and abnormal environment by identifying which external conditions do or do not damage or disable it.

Final causation or teleology—the universal directedness of things to their natural ends—readily follows from this Aristotelian foundation. Active and passive causal powers make inherent and ineliminable reference to an ideal future, to how things *would* proceed if those powers could express themselves fully and without interference. As Thomas Aquinas puts it in the *Summa Theologiae*, "Every agent acts for an end: otherwise one thing would not follow more than another from the action of the agent, unless it were by chance."[4] This applies even to inanimate agents. David Armstrong referred to this as the "proto-intentionality" of causal powers, and George Molnar spoke in such cases of "physical intentionality."[5] Thus, the intentionality of human desires and aspirations (their being about some possible, ideal future) is perfectly continuous with the proto-intentionality of all Aristotelian substances, whether animate or inanimate, conscious or nonconscious, rational or subrational.

In particular, as Aristotle notes, the heterogeneous parts of animals require

---

3. For a defense of the Aristotelian model of efficient causation, in light of modern experimental science, see: Nancy Cartwright, *How the Laws of Physics Lie* (Oxford: Clarendon, 1983); Cartwright, *Nature's Capacities and Their Measurement* (Oxford: Clarendon, 1994).

4. Thomas Aquinas, *Summa Theologiae*, 1.44.4.

5. David M. Armstrong, *The Mind-Body Problem* (Boulder, CO: Westview, 1999), 138–40; George Molnar, *Powers: A Study in Metaphysics* (Oxford: Oxford University Press, 2003), 60–66.

explanation in terms of their end (τέλος).[6] Teleology in biology is simply the application to living things of Aristotle's general scheme of explanation. If organisms truly exist as genuine substances (ουσιαι), then they must have forms that supply them and their parts with genuine, irreducibly biological causal powers. As we have seen, to bear causal powers is *ipso facto* to be ordered to certain kinds of ideal futures. Thus, there is an unbreakable connection between the substantial reality of organisms and the genuineness of biological teleology.

As Georg Toepfer has put it in a recent essay:

> Teleology is closely connected to the concept of the organism and therefore has its most fundamental role in the very definition of biology as a particular science of natural objects. . . . The identity conditions of biological systems are given by functional analysis, not by chemical or physical descriptions. . . . This means that, beyond the functional perspective, which consists in specifying the system by fixing the roles of its parts, the organism does not even exist as a definite entity.[7]

Consequently, in the Aristotelian image of nature, *substances* (metaphysically fundamental things) exist at many levels of scale and composition. For this reason, we cannot give a complete description of the material world by simply aggregating a large number of microscopic descriptions. Exclusive attention to the microscopic scale necessarily omits crucial facts about the natures of macroscopic substances and the causal powers derived from them.

Aristotelians can thus acknowledge real and irreducible agency at many different levels of scale: chemical, thermodynamic, biological, and sociopolitical, as well as microphysical. In particular, the rational agency of human beings is not threatened by their complete materiality. The macroscopic behavior of the whole human being is not merely a byproduct or *epiphenomenon* of the interactions of his microscopic parts and those of his environment. The human being as such makes a real contribution to the flow of events in the material world without requiring any interaction between the body and some separate wholly immaterial soul. For Aristotelians, the human soul is the form of the living human body.

---

6. Aristotle, *Parts of Animals*, 1.1.640b–641b.

7. Georg Toepfer, "Teleology and its constitutive role for biology as the science of organized systems in nature," *Studies in History and Philosophy of Science Part C: Studies in History and Philosophy of Biological and Biomedical Sciences* 43 (2012): 113, 115, 118.

This does not mean that human beings cannot survive death. Thomas Aquinas argued convincingly that the human form (as conceived by Aristotle) could survive the death of the body, since the life of human beings includes a purely intellectual set of activities (namely, understanding and contemplating universal truths) that do not depend on any corporeal organ (not even the brain). Thus the human form or soul can exist by enabling and sustaining these purely intellectual activities even after it has ceased to inform and structure the organic processes of the body. With God's help at the moment of resurrection, the human soul can resume its natural function as the form of a living human body.[8] While we are embodied, our souls are *not* separate entities that interact causally with the microscopic parts of our body. Instead, the embodied soul is the form that inherently structures the powers and interrelations of those parts, grounding all their causal powers (from the "inside," so to speak).

As Edward Feser and many others have pointed out, Aristotle's scheme of universal natural teleology fits beautifully with one form of the argument from design, as exemplified by Thomas Aquinas's Fifth Way.[9] Since God is the uncaused First Cause of all of nature, he must be the ultimate source of all of nature's inherent teleology. Thus, the prototeleology of the inanimate and subrational world is wholly grounded in the wisdom and foresight of God.

3. The Anti-Aristotelian Revolution

From the late Middle Ages (after the death of Thomas Aquinas), through the scientific revolution and the birth of modern philosophy in the seventeenth century, Western Europeans abandoned three key elements of the Aristotelian system. First, beginning with John Duns Scotus (1266–1308), they replaced Aristotle's matter-form relation with the early modern conception of *matter as such*, as something with an inherent nature of its own. Second, they replaced Aristotle's model of interlocking causal powers (active and passive) and time as the measure of change with a model of abstract laws of motion and a fixed and independent temporal dimension. Third, and consequent to the first

---

8. See Brian Leftow's clear exposition of the Thomistic understanding of the soul in "Souls Dipped in Dust: Aquinas on Soul and Body," in *Body, Soul and Survival*, ed. Kevin Corcoran (Ithaca, NY: Cornell University Press, 2001), 120–38; and "Soul, Mind, and Brain," in *The Waning of Materialism*, ed. George Bealer and Robert Koons (Oxford: Oxford University Press, 2010), 395–416.

9. Edward Feser, *Neo-Scholastic Essays* (South Bend, IN: St. Augustine's, 2015), 49–58; Aquinas, *Summa Theologiae*, 1.2.3.

two, they abandoned Aristotle's formal and final causation, limiting teleology to the relation between conscious agents and their felt desires and impulses.

3.1 The Introduction of Matter as Such

As described by Richard Cross, the scholastic philosopher Duns Scotus replaced Aristotle's *relational* conception of matter (*x* is the matter of *y*, or the *x*'s are collectively the matter of *y*) with a *substantive* conception of "matter," in which matter *as such* has its own determinate nature and causal dispositions.[10] For Aristotle, the relation of matter to form was a relation of potentiality to its actualization, that is, to say that the *x*'s are collectively the matter of *y* is to say that the *x*'s have the joint potential to compose something of *y*'s nature. Thus, if there were such a thing as pure or prime matter (matter as such), it would be a thing of pure potentiality with no positive nature of its own.

In contrast, Scotus and the scholastic philosophers who followed him, including William of Ockham (1287–1347), thought of matter as stuff with its own intelligible nature.

3.2 Abstract Laws of Motion

Early modern science and philosophy in the sixteenth century inherited this late-medieval conception of matter as a kind of stuff. The essence of matter was quantitative: all matter takes up definite volume (by filling a region of space). By accounting for the relative density of matter in its various locations, we can assign to each chunk of matter a certain absolute quantity, which corresponds to something like weight and, eventually, mass.

What about the inherent causal dispositions of matter? In this simplest picture, the one embraced by the French philosopher and mathematician René Descartes (1596–1650), matter has the disposition to move in a constant velocity (by inertia, or conservation of momentum) unless it is deflected from this movement by a collision with other material bodies. The discovery of gravity (Isaac Newton in the late seventeenth century) and eventually of electromagnetic forces (James Clerk Maxwell in the nineteenth century) spoiled the simplicity of this late-scholastic/early-modern model and in effect reintroduced at the microphysical level instances of something very much like Aristotelian forms (e.g., the form of the electron as negatively charged).

10. Richard Cross, *The Physics of Duns Scotus: The Scientific Context of a Theological Vision* (Oxford: Clarendon, 1998), 74–77.

This partial recovery of Aristotelian metaphysics was obscured by the simultaneous replacement of causal powers by laws of motion in thinkers like the French philosopher Nicolas Malebranche (1638–1715) and the Scottish philosopher David Hume (1711–1776). Instead of thinking about bodies as having the *power* of moving and moving other bodies (by gravitational mass or electric charge), scientists and philosophers were content to use abstract laws of motion to describe the regular relationships between inputs and outputs. These laws of motion were conceived of as "laws of nature" (with Newton's Three Laws as a paradigm).

There was a shift *from* using hypothesizing natures and their powers to describe possible motions *to* using mathematical equations and functions, which was reflected in the earlier pragmatism of René Descartes and the English essayist and statesman Francis Bacon (1561–1626), who was the inspiration for the founding of the Royal Society in 1660. Descartes and Bacon expressed their lack of interest in a deep understanding of why things acted the way they did. They argued that modern science should instead focus simply on predicting and controlling the behavior of things.

> It is possible to attain knowledge which is very useful in life, and, instead of that speculative philosophy which is taught in the schools, we may find a practical philosophy by means of which, knowing the force and action of fire, water, air, the stars, heavens and all other bodies that environ us . . . [we can] employ them all in uses to which they are adapted, and thus render ourselves the masters and possessors of nature.[11]

3.3 Rejection of Formal and Final Causation

Once modern philosophers and scientists had replaced talk of causal powers and interactions with abstract laws of motion, quite naturally the concepts of formal and final causation fell into disuse. Laws of motion were supposed to be universal and exceptionless, leaving no room for malfunction or damage.

The pragmatism of philosophers like Descartes and Bacon contributed to the removal of teleology from natural science. Understanding the natural end of something contributed nothing to our control over it. Control required

---

11. René Descartes, *Discourse on the Method of Rightly Conducting the Reason*, trans. Elizabeth Haldane and G. R. T. Ross, *The Philosophical Works of Descartes* (Cambridge: Cambridge University Press, 1973), 1:119; see also Francis Bacon, *The Advancement of Learning* (London: Dent, 1915), 96.

merely a detailed knowledge of the internal disposition of its matter, in such a way that laws of motion could be used to predict and control its behavior. Attention to natures, causal powers, and inherent directedness were merely distractions from this urgently needed project:

> But this misplacing hath caused a deficience, or at least a great impro-ficience in the sciences themselves. For the handling of final causes, mixed with the rest in physical inquiries, hath intercepted the severe and diligent inquiry of all real and physical causes, and given men the occasion to stay upon these satisfactory and specious causes, to the great arrest and prejudice of farther discovery.[12]

The French biologist Claude Bernard (1813–1878) clearly expressed the modern attitude in saying, "The final cause does not intervene as an actual and effica-cious law of nature."[13] Bernard cannot conceive of any causation except that expressed by abstract laws. He drew the logical consequence: "Vital properties are in reality only the physicochemical properties of organized matter."[14]

3.4 The Dualism of Modernity: A Fractured World

If the natural world consists entirely of uniform "matter," and if this matter simply obeys universal and exceptionless "laws," what place is left for human thought and agency? Beginning with scholastic philosophers like Duns Scotus, European thinkers began moving away from the Aristotelian hylomorphism of Thomas Aquinas (1225–1274) toward some form of mind-body dualism. Scotus and Ockham, followed by Bacon and Descartes, explicitly limited the scope of teleology and purpose to the conscious desires of human egos, egos that are now radically divorced from the world of matter.

3.5 The Soul of the Gaps: The Abolition of Human Agency and Teleology

However, this dualism of the late scholastic and early modern world did not constitute a stable position but quickly collapsed into an austere form of

---

12. Francis Bacon, *The Advancement of Learning*, 987.

13. Claude Bernard, *Lecons sur les phenomenes de la vie commune aux animaux et aux vegetaux* (Paris: Libraire Philosophique J. Vrin, 1966), 336.

14. Claude Bernard, *Lecons sur les phenomenes de la vie commune aux animaux et aux vegetaux*, 22–2; cited in Etienne Gilson, *From Aristotle to Darwin and Back Again: A Journey in Final Causation, Species, and Evolution*, trans. John Lyon (Notre Dame, IN: University of Notre Dame Press, 1984), 35–36.

materialism. Dualism introduced a kind of "soul of the gaps": mental entities are an extraneous, adventitious addition to the scientific worldview, introduced simply to explain those features of human life and experience that science has not yet explained in terms of the motions of matter. As we gained a more and more complete understanding of the operations of the brain, the nerve cells that make up the brain, and the organic molecules that make up those cells, there seemed to be less and less room for the intervention of immaterial souls of the Cartesian kind. Eventually, a more austere and monistic form of materialism took hold, pioneered by the English philosopher Thomas Hobbes (1588–1679), French thinkers like Baron d'Holbach (1723–1789), and the German materialists of the nineteenth century.

This materialism ultimately takes the form of *microphysicalism*, the thesis that every truth (causal and otherwise) about any macroscopic substance is wholly grounded in and explained by the microphysical facts, which includes both the intrinsic properties of the microparticles *and* binary spatial relations among their positions and velocities in the uniform background of absolute space. Moreover, this grounding of macroscopic truths in microscopic facts licenses an ontological *reduction* of macroscopic things to their microphysical parts and their spatial relations: the former are *nothing over and above* the latter.

This microphysicalism, common to both ancient materialists like Democritus (c. 460 BC–c. 370 BC) and Lucretius (99 BC–55 BC) and to modern physicalists like the American philosophers W. V. O. Quine (1908–2000) or David K. Lewis (1941–2001), has always stood in tension with a commonsense understanding of ourselves as *rational agents*. For example, in the *Phaedo*, Plato puts an argument against metaphysical microphysicalism into Socrates's mouth:

> And it seemed to me it was very much as if one should say that Socrates does with intelligence whatever he does, and then, in trying to give the causes of the particular thing I do, should say first that I am now sitting here because my body is composed of bones and sinews, and the bones are hard and have joints which divide them and the sinews can be contracted and relaxed and, with the flesh and the skin which contains them all, are laid about the bones; and so, as the bones are hung loose in their ligaments, the sinews, by relaxing and contracting, make me able

to bend my limbs now, and that is the cause of my sitting here with my legs bent . . . and should fail to mention the *real causes*, which are, that the Athenians decided that it was best to condemn me, and therefore I have decided that it was best for me to sit here and that it is right for me to stay and undergo whatever penalty they order.[15]

Microphysicalists have essentially three options in response to this argument: (1) they can deny the existence of real or objective values altogether (the goodness of Socrates's remaining in Athens), (2) they can assert that our intentions or decisions are never really sensitive to these objective values (Socrates's rational appreciation of this value), or (3) they can claim that objective values and our sensitivity to them are somehow wholly grounded in the microphysical facts. None of these three seems promising. Jonathan Dancy, Christine Korsgaard, and many others in recent years have created powerful objections to a Humean subjectivism about value.[16] And, in any case, it seems that subjective values must ultimately be grounded in objective value if reason is to have any normative force at all. Even if one supposes that particular things are good for an agent only because he or she desires them, one must still suppose that desires (other things being equal) *ought to be satisfied*—that there is something objectively worthy about seeking to satisfy them. Finally, as J. L. Mackie and others have recognized, it is hard to believe that the objective value or to-be-sought-ness of certain states or actions could be wholly grounded in the sort of facts described by microphysics.[17] Microphysics provides no room for the rational teleology of human values.

3.6 The Triumph of Microphysicalism

Why do so many philosophers find physicalism—the thesis that the only fundamental facts are physical facts—so attractive? The inherent plausibility of physicalism comes from our attraction to *microscopism*: the thesis that only the ultimately microscopic facts are fundamental. Without the microscopist presumption, there is no reason to privilege physics over other sciences. There

---

15. *Phaedo*, 98c–99b.
16. Jonathan Dancy, *Practical Reality* (Oxford: Oxford University Press, 2003); C. M. Korsgaard, "Scepticism about Practical Reason," *Journal of Philosophy* 83 (1986): 5–25.
17. Mackie, *Ethics: Inventing Right and Wrong* (Harmondsworth, UK: Penguin, 1977).

are many nonphysical sciences—chemistry, thermodynamics, biology, even cognitive psychology—that have been successful in identifying real causal mechanisms in our world, and there has been absolutely no sense that these other sciences have been progressively replaced by pure physics as science advances. What gives physics its privileged position is the microscopist presumption together with the fact that it studies the smallest things, the things of which the objects of other sciences are composed.

But what accounts for the attractiveness of microscopism? One motivation has been maintaining a unified picture of nature and our scientific knowledge of nature: the unity-of-nature ideal or the unity-of-science ideal. This gives us some reason to minimize the number of fundamental forces that we posit and to resist accepting any violations of the fundamental conservation laws. In turn, these reasons justify to some extent a reluctance to embrace mind-body dualism, with its need for mind-body interaction.

However, the unity-of-nature ideal does not give us reason to embrace anything as extreme as microscopism, much less microphysicalism. There are no obvious reasons why large, composite objects, fully located within the one world of nature, could not possess and exercise fundamental causal powers, even in the absence of new fundamental forces or violations of energy conservation.

The real core of the appeal of microscopism has to do with a sense that modern science has vindicated a kind of Democritean ontological reductionism. The thought is that we simply don't *need* to posit any fundamental agency except at the level of the smallest particles or units of matter. We could, in principle, explain everything in terms of the powers and interactions of the microparticles, in the sense that everything at higher or larger scales is wholly grounded in the goings-on at the microphysical level.

Modern science provides a framework for a kind of bottom-up reductionist narrative: political and social phenomena reduce to individual psychology, individual psychology to biology (including neuroscience), biology to thermodynamics, thermodynamics to chemistry, chemistry to atomic physics, and atomic physics to particle physics. As progress in science increases the strength of every link of this chain, antireductionists seem to be always on "the wrong side of history," forced into an increasingly extreme form of obscurantism.

Microphysicalism, therefore, depends on a Democritean starting point, meaning:

1. Facts about microscopic atoms and the void are, metaphysically speaking, *fundamental* or ungrounded facts.
2. This ungrounded foundation consists of microscopic entities with certain intrinsic characteristics (the characteristics were shape and size for Democritus, but this can be extended to include things like charge, mass, spin, and so on) and certain instantaneous spatial relations.
3. All spatial relations can be ultimately grounded in a large number of simple relations among the microscopic entities such as distance.

As Democritus put it, "atoms and the void" constitute the uniquely fundamental level of reality, and everything else completely *depends on* and *is determined by* them—everything is *wholly grounded* by them.

Aristotle's hylomorphic model denied the fundamentality or ungroundedness of the microscopic realm. For Aristotelians, the intrinsic characters and mutual relations (including spatial relations) of the microscopic entities are often grounded in the natures of the macroscopic entities of which they are parts.

4. The Quantum Counter-Revolution

Quantum mechanics is a branch of fundamental physics, which dealt initially with very small entities like atoms and photons and eventually illuminated macroscopic phenomena like supercooled fluids and superconductors. Quantum theory started with Max Planck's theory of black-body radiation in 1900 and Albert Einstein's 1905 paper on the photoelectric effect. Planck and Einstein proposed that energy comes in discrete packets called "quanta." A full-fledged theory of quantum phenomenon was developed in the 1920s by Niels Bohr, Werner Heisenberg, Erwin Schrödinger, Max Born, and others. By 1930, David Hilbert, Paul Dirac, and John von Neumann formalized the theory as governing the probabilities of certain macroscopic observations of a quantum world, which in itself lacks any determinate values for such familiar properties as particle position, momentum, and trajectory. Quantum theory is now the basis for our modern understanding of chemistry, optics, electronics, and thermodynamics.

4.1 The Revenge of Teleology

Classical mechanics can be formulated in two ways: in terms of differential equations based on Newton's laws of motion or in terms of integral equations based on the conservation of energy (i.e., the analytic or Hamiltonian method). In the latter case, the model's structure imposes certain constraints on the possible evolution of the system, and the dynamical laws pick out the actual evolution on the basis of some minimization or maximization principle like the principle of *least action*.[18]

The Newtonian model is Democritean, but the Hamiltonian is Aristotelian in being both essentially holistic and teleological. The total energy of a closed system is an irreducibly holistic or nonseparable property of the system: it cannot be reduced to the intrinsic properties of the system's constituents taken individually. More important, *variational* principles like the least action principle treat the holistic character of an entire trajectory as fundamental, rather than as the set of instantaneous facts about the composition of forces that constitutes the fundamental facts for the Newtonian model. The least-action principle is a form of teleological explanation, as Leibniz already recognized.[19]

In classical mechanics, either model can be used, and they are provably equivalent. Hence, classical mechanics leaves the metaphysical question of microphysicalism versus hylomorphism unresolved. However, with the quantum revolution, the Hamiltonian picture becomes mandatory, since fundamental entities can no longer be imagined to be moving in response to the composition of forces exerted at each moment from determinate distances. Teleology reigns supreme over mechanical forces, as Max Planck noted.[20] In addition, *the total energy and action of a closed system are essentially holistic or*

---

18. Wolfgang Yourgrau and Stanley Mandelstam, *Variational Principles in Dynamics and Quantum Theory* (New York: Dover, 1979), 19–23, 164–67; Robert Bruce Lindsay and Henry Morgenaw, *Foundations of Physics* (New York: Dover, 1957), 133–36; Cornelius Lanczos, *The Variational Principles of Mechanics*, 4th ed. (New York: Dover, 1986), xxvii, 345–46.

19. Jeffrey K. McDonough, "Leibniz's Two Realms Revisited," *Noûs* 42 (2008): 673–96; Jeffrey K. McDonough, "Leibniz on Natural Teleology and the Laws of Optics," *Philosophy and Phenomenological Research* 78 (2009): 505–44.

20. See Max Planck, "The Principle of Least Action," in *A Survey of Physical Theory*, trans. R. Jones and D. H. Williams (New York: Dover, 1960), 69–81; Val Dusek, "Aristotle's Four Causes and Contemporary 'Newtonian' Dynamics," in *Aristotle and Contemporary Science*, vol. 2, ed. Demetra Sfendoni-Mentzou, Jagdish Harriangadi, and David M. Johnson (New York: Peter Lang, 2001), 81–93; Mariam Thalos, *Without Hierarchy: The Scale Freedom of the Universe* (Oxford: Oxford University Press, 2013), 84–86.

nonseparable properties of that composite system, which stands in contradiction to the demands of microphysicalism.

Furthermore, by forcing reliance on the Hamiltonian model, quantum mechanics brings the holistic character of causal interaction into sharper relief. As noted by Justin Tiehen and Frederick Kronz, the Hamiltonian model for complex quantum systems is nonseparable: "In that case, the time evolution of the density operator that is associated with a part of a composite system cannot in general be characterized in a way that is independent of the time evolution of the whole."[21] The causal power responsible for the evolution of the system is an irreducibly joint power, not supervening on the binary causal powers of the component particles.

Aristotelian philosophy of nature requires processes as the natural results of the exercise of causal powers. These Aristotelian processes (κινησες) have intrinsic direction and pacing.[22] Aristotle did not, as his late medieval and early modern critics supposed, anthropomorphize nature by attributing vague urges or drives to it; rather, he developed a framework within which animal and human drives could be seen as special cases of the intrinsic directedness of holistic processes. The system as a whole consequently acquires its own intrinsic teleology (or, better, *entelechy*).

4.2 Nonseparable States

The most obvious blow that quantum mechanics strikes to microphysicalism comes from the undeniable *nonseparability* of the quantum properties of entangled systems. As noted by Paul Teller, Richard Healey, Michael Silberstein and John McGeever, and Frederick Kronz and Justin Tiehen, among many others, the quantum state of a pair of entangled particles (i.e., particles in the singlet state, as in the Einstein-Podolsky-Rosen thought experiment) is irreducibly a state of the pair as such: it is not even determined by the intrinsic properties of the individual particles or the spatial distance or relative velocity

---

21. Frederick Kronz and Justin Tiehen, "Emergence and Quantum Mechanics," *Philosophy of Science* 69 (2002): 343–44.

22. Adam Schulman draws out a fascinating parallel between Aristotle's account of motion as "potential" and "indeterminate" in *Physics* III and *Metaphysics* III and Richard Feynman's sum-over-possible-histories approach to quantum mechanics. Aristotle denies that the location of a moving body is fully *actual* except at the beginning and end of a continuous process of locomotion. Feynman's sum-over-histories approach is a way of fleshing this out: the moving body takes every possible trajectory between the two points, with mutual interference explaining why the paths with least action predominate. Schulman, "Quantum and Aristotelian Physics" (PhD diss., Harvard University, 1989).

between them.[23] In these cases, the whole is literally more than the sum of its parts.

For a long time, philosophers assumed that this sort of quantum weirdness could be limited somehow to the microscopic domain, being swamped at the phenomenological level by phenomena that conform to the requirements of microphysicalism. However, this kind of quantum holism is very much the rule rather than the exception, producing measurable results at the phenomenological level nearly all the time.[24]

4.3 The Measurement Problem

The so-called "Copenhagen" interpretation of Niels Bohr and Werner Heisenberg's quantum theory gives us reason to doubt all three of the premises of Democritean microphysicalism, which are (1) the fundamentality of individual particles, (2) the intrinsicality of the fundamental properties of these properties, and (3) the fundamentality and definiteness of the spatial location and relative distance of these particles. In the Copenhagen interpretation, the microphysical facts consist merely in the attribution to microscopic entities of certain potentialities, and these potentialities essentially include causal relations to macroscopic systems. A quantum doesn't typically have any position or momentum at all, not even a vague or fuzzy one; it merely has the potential to interact with macroscopic systems as if it had some definite position, momentum, or other observable feature at the moment of the interaction. Thus the quantum world, so understood, can be neither metaphysically fundamental nor a complete basis for the macroscopic world.

Of course, this situation gives rise immediately to a puzzle: What is the relationship between the macroscopic and quantum worlds? Presumably, macroscopic physical objects are wholly composed of quanta. Our ingrained habit of thought, anchored in the seventeenth-century scientific revolution, leads us to expect that we can always analyze the nature and behavior of macroscopic wholes in terms of their microscopic parts. How then can the

---

23. Paul Teller, "Relational Holism and Quantum Mechanics," *British Journal for the Philosophy of Science* 37, no. 1 (1986): 71–81; Richard Healey, "Holism and Nonseparability," *Journal of Philosophy* 88 (1991): 393–421; Michael Silberstein and John McGeever, "The Search for Ontological Emergence," *Philosophical Quarterly* 49 (1999): 186–90; Frederick Kronz and Justin Tiehen, "Emergence and Quantum Mechanics," 325–30.

24. Hans Primas, "Foundations of Theoretical Chemistry," in *Quantum Dynamics for Molecules: The New Experimental Challenge to Theorists*, ed. R.G. Woolley (New York: Plenum, 1980), 41.

microscopic quanta *fail* to be metaphysically fundamental and the complete basis for the macroscopic world?

Hylomorphism offers a ready answer to this puzzle. The microscopic constituents of macroscopic objects have (at the level of actuality) only an indirect relation to space and time: they are located (roughly) somewhere at a time only *qua* constituents of some fundamental, macro- or mesoscopic substance (in the Aristotelian sense). Such microscopic objects are not metaphysically fundamental in their entirety, and their metaphysically fundamental features do not provide a complete basis for the features of the substantial wholes they compose. This is a welcome result, since it makes physical theory compatible with the *Phaedo* argument.

The Copenhagen interpretation is not the only way to make sense of quantum mechanics. Recent years have seen the emergence of the many-worlds (Everett) interpretation, Bohm's mechanics, and various objective collapse theories. The very fact that we now face a plethora of competing interpretations of quantum mechanics puts the relationship between physics and metaphysics on a very different footing from the one under the classical paradigm. Microphysicalism was the only plausible interpretation of classical physics. In contrast, some interpretations of quantum mechanics are extremely friendly to hylomorphism. I will sketch one of these, which I will call "Pluralistic Quantum Hylomorphism."

Pluralistic Quantum Hylomorphism is an interpretation inspired by some remarks of Heisenberg, and similar interpretations have been defended by Wolfgang Smith, Nancy Cartwright, and Stanley Grove.[25] On this view, the world consists of a variety of domains, each at a different level of scale. Most of these domains are fully classical, consisting of entities with mutually compatible or commutative properties. At most one domain is accurately described by quantum mechanics. Since for quantum objects location does not "commute" with other observables like momentum, the quantum objects are only intermittently located in ordinary, three-dimensional space, although they always retain a probability of interacting with classical objects at a definite location. Interaction between quantum properties and classical properties,

---

25. Werner Heisenberg, *Physics and Philosophy: The Revolution in Modern Science* (London: George Allen and Unwin, 1958); Wolfgang Smith, *The Quantum Enigma: Finding the Hidden Key*, 3rd ed. (San Rafael, CA: Angelico, 2005); Nancy Cartwright, *The Dappled World: A Study of the Boundaries of Science* (Cambridge: Cambridge University Press, 1999); Stanley F. Grove, *Quantum Theory and Aquinas's Doctrine on Matter* (PhD diss., Catholic University of America, 2008).

including those of experimenters and their instruments, precipitates an objective collapse of the quantum object's wavefunction because of the joint exercise of the relevant causal powers of the object and the instruments and not because of the involvement of human consciousness and choice.

Paul Feyerabend offered a helpful tripartite distinction of philosophies of science: the positivist, the realist, and the structural.[26] The positivist is the antirealist, who denies that reality has any structure that is independent of our interests and assumptions. The realist believes that there is a single, unified structure of reality, realized at a single scale. And the structuralist understands reality to comprise a plurality of relatively autonomous structures. The realist or monist perspective contributed to the rise and development of modern science, but the quantum revolution has seen a return to the pluralism of Aristotle:

> Einstein and especially Bohr introduced the idea that [scientific] theories may be context-dependent, different theories being valid in different domains. Combining these ideas with abstract mathematics such as various algebras, lattice theory, and logics then led to a powerful revival of the structural approach. Thus the search for a generalized quantum theory is exactly in Aristotle's spirit: we do not take it for granted that the quantum theories we have are the best way of dealing with everything, looking either for new interpretations or suitable approximation methods to solve hairy cases; we rather try to identify domains and theories suited for them and then look for ways of relating these theories to each other.[27]

Here is how Nancy Cartwright describes this pluralist view:

> Quantum realists should take the quantum state seriously as a genuine feature of reality and not take it as an instrumentalist would, as a convenient way of summarising information about other kinds of properties. Nor should they insist that other descriptions cannot be assigned besides quantum descriptions. For that is to suppose not only that the theory is true but that it provides a complete description of everything of interest in reality.[28]

---

26. Paul Feyerabend, "Foreword," in Hans Primas, *Chemistry, Quantum Mechanics, and Reductionism: Perspectives in Theoretical Chemistry* (Berlin: Springer, 1983), i–xii.

27. Paul Feyerabend, "Foreword," vii.

28. Nancy Cartwright, *The Dappled World*, 232.

Thus, the hylomorphic interpretation combines features of both the old Copenhagen and newer objective collapse interpretations. It is a fully realist view about the microscopic, unlike Bohr's version of the Copenhagen interpretation, and it is ontologically pluralistic, in contrast to other objective collapse theories. It admits a plurality of objective domains, and it does not treat wave collapse as a phenomenon explainable within the pure quantum domain, by some as-yet-unknown microphysical interaction.

Unlike the Copenhagen view, the Pluralistic Quantum Hylomorphism interpretation fully embraces the reality of quantum objects and quantum states. In addition, the Copenhagen view suffers from being too narrowly dualistic, distinguishing the classical world from the quantum world. In contrast, the hylomorphic interpretation embraces a salutary kind of ontological pluralism, recognizing that the nonquantum or supraquantum world is a "dappled" world (as Nancy Cartwright puts it) divided naturally into multiple domains at multiple scales.

Pluralistic Quantum Hylomorphism shares two crucial advantages with the Copenhagen view. First, it embraces realism about classical objects and classical states, and so it can make sense of our experimental practices in a straightforward way. Second, it fits the actual practice of scientists well, who are ontological pluralists in practice (as Nancy Cartwright has documented).

5. Conclusion: Back to the Aristotelian Future

The quantum revolution has had philosophical effects that can be organized into three levels: new conclusions that are logically *entailed* by the new model, new directions that are *suggested or encouraged* by the revolution, and old, heretofore abandoned positions that are once again logically *consistent* with our most mature science.

At the level of entailment, we can put the rejection of the Democritean, microphysicalist empire of the nineteenth century. It is no longer possible to maintain that the properties of physical wholes are completely determined by the intrinsic properties and spatial relations of their microscopic parts. A more pluralistic approach to the ontology of the material world is now necessary. Finally, teleology (in the form of least action principles) has been fully vindicated as an essential part of our account of the natural world.

At the level of suggestion and encouragement, the quantum revolution provides strong support to a more thoroughgoing form of scientific pluralism, one that takes such sciences as solid-state physics, thermodynamics, chemistry, biology, and social psychology to be every bit as fundamental as particle physics. The holistic and teleological character of quantum mechanics does not by itself entail the reality of teleology and agency at the biological or personal levels, but it does dramatically change the imaginative landscape of modern science, making the supposition of top-down, formal causation in the realms of biology, and psychology more plausible. In fact, the trend of science in the last fifty years has been toward greater differentiation, not unity. Taking these scientific results at their face value means accepting causal agency (understood in Aristotelian terms) at many levels, including the macroscopic level of complete organisms. The idea that there could be a natural and fundamental teleology governing human choices is once again fully credible, and God as the ultimate source and ground of teleology is once again an attractive path for natural theology.

Finally, the quantum revolution gives us a form of physics that is fully consistent with more humane social and psychological sciences, including new emphases on personhood, free will, meaning, and the science of happiness. Indeterministic conceptions of human free will, of the sort championed by Robert Kane,[29] are consistent with many interpretations of quantum physics, including Pluralistic Quantum Hylomorphism. At the same time, given its commitment to the full embodiment of that mind, the neo-Aristotelian model of the will is not challenged by advancements in neuroscience.

The quantum world should also affect our understanding of God's role as creator, especially as creator and sustainer of the material and subpersonal dimensions of the world. In the model of classical mechanics, God was the Great Engineer, who organized matter in space for extrinsic purposes, as a hydraulic engineer might organize a system of pipes, valves, and pumps. Human freedom, then, must be shoehorned into the picture, as an anomalous exception to the natural order. On the alternative Aristotelian model, God infuses substances with a variety of intrinsic causal powers and propensities, powers that depend on but are not reducible to the intrinsic features of their parts at the microscopic level. These created powers are inherently ordered to specific ends or destinations, making the purposiveness and freedom of human agents more continuous with the rest of creation.

---

29. Robert Kane, *The Significance of Free Will* (Oxford: Oxford University Press, 1998).

At both the rational and subrational levels, an Aristotelian conception of nature is open to the subtle influences of divine influence and persuasion, allowing for the recognition of robust miracles without the violent metaphor of "violations" of the "laws of nature." We can then take more seriously the idea of an ordered and meaningful economy of miracles, as described by C. S. Lewis and N. T. Wright.[30] In addition, the inherent purposiveness of nature at all levels points to the conclusion that the world's First Cause is purposeful and intelligent. On this basis, we can build an inference to divine design that is independent of the details of the world's prehistory.

---

30. C. S. Lewis, *Miracles: A Preliminary Study* (London, Macmillan, 1969); N. T. Wright, *The Resurrection of the Son of God*, Christian Origins and the Question of God 3 (London: SPCK, 2003).

Chapter THIRTEEN

Knowing Nature

Beyond the False Dilemma of Reduction
or Emergence

WILLIAM M. R. SIMPSON

1. Preliminary Remarks

Although the philosophy of the Middle Ages was far from monolithic, medieval metaphysics from the thirteenth century can be broadly characterised within the Latin tradition by its dual commitment to the Aristotelian principles of *matter* (*hyle*) and *form* (*morphe*).[1] Together, these concepts were employed to explain how nature could be carved into unified substances that exercise causal powers. Among some scholastic philosophers, the matter of a substance was conceived as a determinable substrate underlying the various processes of change, and form was conceived as a determination of matter specifying the powers of a substance. Among others, the roles of matter and form were understood differently.

However, whilst Aristotle's *hylomorphic* approach to the metaphysical analysis of substance came to be interpreted in various ways, a few of which I explore in this paper, it continued to frame philosophical debate and shape natural theology until the rise of *corpuscularianism* in the seventeenth century. Strict demarcations between medieval and early modern philosophy are increasingly discouraged. Nonetheless, the widespread rejection of form as the

---

1. These concepts have also been construed as pragmatic explanatory notions, e.g., B. C. Van Fraassen, *The Scientific Image* (New York: Oxford University Press, 1980). For arguments in favour of a realist interpretation, see C. A. Freeland, "Accidental Causes and Real Explanations," in *Aristotle's Physics: A Collection of Essays*, ed. L. Judson (Oxford: Oxford University Press, 1995), 49–72.

determining principle of matter, initiated by the early mechanistic philosophers and led by René Descartes, constitutes a conspicuous discontinuity between medieval and modern notions of the natural order. For modern corpuscularists, like Robert Boyle, matter was reconceived as an arrangement of determinate constituents governed by physical laws that requires no additional principle. Cartesian science soon came under criticism and was replaced by Newtonian physics, which in turn was superseded in the twentieth century by quantum mechanics. However, the demise of the Aristotelian concept of form is often presented as one of the lasting and inevitable triumphs of modern science, in which an opaque medieval philosophy and its hylomorphic account of substance were forced into retreat by a more perspicuous account of the nature of matter.

In this paper I take some first steps toward a different philosophical evaluation of the demise of form in the light of recent scholarship.[2] My comments are "broad brush" and preliminary in character; they are intended to encourage further discussion. In assessing the merits of hylomorphism, I believe we must distinguish between two general approaches that I shall call *classical Aristotelian* and *late scholastic*.[3] I claim that, in doing so, it is plausible that the widespread rejection of form, which continues to this day, is a historical contingency: it results in part from the early corpuscularists' conflation of classical Aristotelian and late scholastic metaphysics, combined with a type of *simplistic reductionism* fostered by the early mechanists, which contemporary science does not support.

I begin by offering a characterisation of the evolving way in which hylomorphism was interpreted in medieval philosophy. I consider the classical role played by forms in carving nature into substances with causal powers (sec. 2), the "reification" of form in scholasticism (sec. 3), and the concept of matter that emerged with corpuscularianism, which led to the rejection of hylomorphism (sec. 4). I then formulate three contemporary models of the metaphysical relations between microscopic and macroscopic levels, based on corpuscularist, scholastic, and classical Aristotelian positions (sec. 5). All three models, I claim, may be subject to empirical objections but in *different* ways

---

2. I draw in particular from the contemporary metaphysical scholarship of Theodore Scaltsas and Anna Marmodoro in sec. 2, and historical studies by Robert Pasnau in sec. 3–4.

3. I am not using the labels "classical Aristotelian" and "late scholastic" as strictly historical categories, but as my own terms of art, to serve the dialectical purpose of this discussion.

(sec. 6). The charge of scientific obstruction levied against Aristotelian hylomorphism in general finds its proper target in late scholasticism. Nonetheless, if simplistic reduction is empirically successful, the postulation of Aristotelian or late scholastic conceptions of form is vulnerable to the charge of being superfluous in many cases. However, simplistic reductionism is incompatible with emergence, and the concepts of matter and form adopted by late scholastics are jointly incompatible with quantum physics. I conclude with the provocative suggestion that the classical doctrine of hylomorphism, however neglected, is ripe for rehabilitation (sec. 7).

2. Matter and Form in Aristotelian Hylomorphism

2.1 Being and Change

Aristotle distinguished *two ways of being* in his account of change: being-in-*potency* (or potentiality) and being-in-*act* (or actuality).[4] A substance is a unit of being with the potential to change in various ways. For example, animals are substances with powers of growth and nutrition. Following Anna Marmodoro, I shall consider a power to comprise these two ways of being with respect to some activity: in the first instance, it is a state in which something stands in potential to engage in this activity; in the second, a state in which this activity is manifested (or in act).[5] For a power to manifest, it must be exercised. When an animal feeds and develops, for example, it exercises its powers of growth and nutrition and undergoes change.

Aristotle also introduced the concepts of *matter* (*hyle*) and *form* (*morphe*) in his account of how material things are constituted: matter is that which changes and gets determined, and form is a determination that specifies certain powers.[6] Both principles complete each other in the analysis of a *material substance*. For instance, when an animal consumes a plant, it transforms the matter of the plant into its own flesh by exercising its powers of growth and nutrition. In so doing, the substance of the animal is a subject of change. By gathering flesh where there was previously a privation, the matter of the

---

4. See Aristotle, *Physics*, in *Complete Works of Aristotle*, vol. 1, *The Revised Oxford Translation*, ed. J. Barnes (Prinçeton: Princeton University Press, 2014), 1.7.

5. Interpretations of Aristotle vary widely. In this section, I take myself to be broadly in accordance with Marmodoro's exegesis and adaptation of Aristotle's account of powers. See A. Marmodoro, *Aristotle on Perceiving Objects* (New York: Oxford University Press, 2014).

6. See, e.g., Aristotle, *Physics*, 2.3.

substance is now determined by a different form. In exercising its power to nourish by being consumed, the matter of the plant is also a subject of change. By being transformed into the flesh of the animal, it is stripped of powers that were essential to the substance of the plant. In this case, the matter is now said to be determined by the *substantial form* of the animal instead, since the animal exists where its form was previously in privation.

For Aristotle, the natural order is comprised of both substances and nonsubstantial entities whose causal powers are specified by forms that determine their matter.[7] A causal relation between two substances can be analysed in terms of the actualisation of their different powers: in our example, when the animal consumes the plant, certain powers belonging to both substances must manifest together. Since the powers of one substance depend upon the powers of other substances for their actualisation, however, it is only within this *communion of being* that the powers of everything can be completely defined.[8]

2.2 Substantial Form and Actual Parts

In order to understand Aristotle's account of the unity of a substance, as interpreted by Aquinas, we must distinguish a material substance, such as a living animal, from a composite entity, like a Lego-brick house. On this view, a composite is composed of *actual parts*, which exist independently of the whole and retain their distinct identities whilst comprising a composite. A substance, by contrast, is a unified whole; it is not comprised of Lego-like constituents. Whilst an animal has organs and limbs that are integral parts of its body, they are not *actual* parts from which the substance derives its being but depend ontologically upon the whole. According to Aristotle's *Homonymy Principle*, a hand that is severed from a living body is a hand in name only.[9] Whilst a living substance like an animal can decompose into different chemicals that do not depend upon the substance for their existence, they are not numerically identical to *actual* parts that existed prior to the decomposition of the substance. The separate things into which a substance can decompose are said to exist only in *potential*, just so long as they remain united within a single

---

7. Regarding nonsubstantial entities, such as primary elements (or quantum fields), see sec. 5.3.

8. Concerning this nexus of powers and their ontological dependencies, see, e.g., A. Marmodoro, "Causation without Glue: Aristotle on Causal Powers," *Aitia I. Les Quatre Causes d'Aristote. Origins et interpretations*, ed. C. Viano, C. Natali, and M. Zingano (Louvain: Peeters, 2013).

9. Aristotle, *Metaphysics*, 1035b24–25.

substance.[10] Theodore Scaltsas suggests this *metaphysical unity* is achieved by transforming the material elements that generate a substance, stripping them of their distinctness and reidentifying them in terms of the causal role specified by the form.[11] Conceived in this way, matter and form should not be regarded as actual parts, which somehow attach to create a composite, but may be considered the *constituent metaphysical principles* of a unified substance.

2.3 Classical Hylomorphism

From this exposition, though brief and contentious, I can derive a few propositions characterising classical hylomorphism (CH) that were subsequently challenged during the rise of corpuscularianism. Most significantly,

(CH1) Substantial form carves nature at the joints.[12]

It "carves nature at the joints" by identifying a substance as an element within a fundamental ontology and specifying its causal powers. For Aristotle, animals have powers of perception that plants do not, and humans have rational powers that other animals do not; they must therefore have different forms. For Aquinas, these forms carve the natural world into created beings and determine the ends to which they are ordered. In classical hylomorphism, the concepts of *formal* and *efficient* causation can each be assigned a definite content. First,

(CH2) Substances are *efficient* causes.

A substance is a being that effects change by exercising causal powers that comanifest with the powers of other substances (sec. 2.1). Second,

(CH3) Substantial forms are *formal* causes.

---

10. See, e.g., Aristotle, *On Generation and Corruption*, 1.10, esp. 327b23–b33. Also, Aristotle, *Metaphysics*, 1040b5–15 and 1040b5–15. This "Thomistic" construal is controversial. It is defended in A. Marmodoro, "Aristotle's Hylomorphism without Reconditioning," *Philosophical Inquiry* 36, nos. 1–2 (2013): 5–22. See also D. Oderberg, *Real Essentialism* (New York: Routledge, 2007).

11. See T. Scaltsas, *Substances and Universals in Aristotle's Metaphysics* (New York: Cornell University Press, 1994), 6.6.

12. The metaphor derives from Plato's *Phaedrus*. By "carving nature," I mean constructing a natural ontology.

Substantial forms are the *sine qua non* of causal activity in virtue of the role they play in determining the matter of a substance and specifying its causal powers. However, formal causation can be robustly divided from efficient causation if we accept the following proposition:

> (CH4) Substantial forms do not have the same ontological standing as a substance or the elements from which it is generated.[13]

In classical hylomorphism, substantial forms do not need to be actual parts in order to characterise the natural order and be causally efficacious (sec. 2.2). Rather, they are constituent principles that underpin one of the primary motivations of Aristotelian metaphysics: to secure the status of living things— like plants, animals, and people—as basic substances within a fundamental ontology of what exists.

3. Matter and Form in Scholasticism

Whilst the concepts of matter and form were widely deployed in scholastic metaphysics, both in accounting for substantial change and the unity of generated substances, these doctrines were clearly developed by certain scholastics in ways that were incompatible with classical hylomorphism. No single systematic view characterises the late scholastic period; nonetheless, it is possible to pick out some suggestive tendencies within scholastic metaphysics that serve as a prelude to corpuscularianism. They include the "reification" of matter and form (sec. 3.1) and a confounding of the distinction between formal and efficient causation (sec. 3.2).

3.1 Reifying Matter and Form

I shall use the term *reification* to refer to the tendency to treat matter and form as having the same ontological standing as a substance or actual parts. The necessity of *some* substrate underlying all forms of change was widely accepted within the Latin tradition. As Franco Burgersdijk observed, "All seem

---

13. For Marmodoro, forms are "metaphysical operations" rather than items in the ontology (see *Hylomorphism without Reconditioning*). However, one might allow that forms exist *in a different way* to a substance, or are items of a different ontological type, just so long as they reidentify the material elements of the originative matter (see Scaltsas, *Substances and Universals*).

to have granted to Aristotle that the generation and corruption of natural things requires . . . a common subject."[14] In this way, Aristotle sought to affirm the continuity of natural processes and avert the conclusion that change must involve creation from nothing. However, the classical construal of the substrate of substantial change as a determinable potentiality, which was defended by Thomas Aquinas,[15] was widely criticised by other scholastics for failing to "bottom out" in anything concrete or determinate and was never widely accepted, even in the thirteenth century. Duns Scotus, for example, insisted against Aquinas that this underlying matter should have actual parts.[16] William of Ockham, writing in the early fourteenth century, echoed Averroes in requiring that prime matter have extension.[17] The metaphysical misgivings concerning a merely determinable substrate were starkly expressed by the seventeenth-century Ockhamist, André Dabillon, who insisted that either "the things that compose an actual being actually exist," or a "substantial whole would be composed of *nothing*."[18] Since this position is untenable, he claimed that it must be the case that both "matter and form are real substantial beings that exist actually in nature."

In addition to reifying the substrate of change, increasing its independence from form, many scholastics seem to attribute a quasi-substantial status to form, suggesting its actual independence from substance. A significant example of this tendency lies in the widespread rejection of the so-called "unitarian doctrine" of substantial form.[19] In classical hylomorphism, a substance has a *single* substantial form. For Aquinas, "A substantial form does not have being in itself, independent of that to which it is united, so neither does the matter to which it is joined. From their union results that being in which the reality

14. F. Burgersdijk, *Collegium physicum, disputationibus XXXII absolutum*, 3rd ed. (Cambridge, 1650), as translated in R. Pasnau, *Metaphysical Themes 1274–1671* (Oxford: Oxford University Press, 2011).

15. See Aquinas, *On the Principles of Nature.*

16. For discussions of Scotus's view on matter, see R. Cross, "Prime Matter," in *The Physics of Duns Scotus: The Scientific Context of a Theological Vision* (New York: Oxford University Press, 1998), and R. Pasnau, "Form and Matter," in *The Cambridge History of Medieval Philosophy* (Cambridge: Cambridge University Press, 2009).

17. For a discussion of Ockham's view, see Pasnau, "Matter and Extension," *Metaphysical Themes.* For further discussion of changes in the way material substance was understood that "ploughed the way for corpuscularianism as well as atomism," see H. Lagerlund, "Material Substance," in *The Oxford Handbook of Medieval Philosophy*, ed. J. Marenbon (New York: Oxford University Press, 2012).

18. A. Dabillon, *La physique des bons esprits* (Paris: Sebastien Piquet, 1643), as quoted in Pasnau, *Metaphysical Themes.*

19. William de la Mare targeted Aquinas's affirmation of unicity in *Correctorium Fratris Thomae* in 1279. See W. de la Mare, *Correctivum fratris Thomae*, in *Les premières polémiques Thomistes: le Correctorium Corruptorii "Quare"*, ed. P. Glorieux (Kain: Le Saulchoir, 1927).

subsists in itself, and from them is produced something essentially one."[20] For many scholastics, however, a *plurality* of substantial forms existed within the same entity. For example, the form of corporeity (by which an animal is embodied) and the form of the soul (by which an animal is living) were commonly held to be present simultaneously within a human substance.

If multiple substantial forms can exist in a composite together, they must be regarded instead as actual parts, or something like them. Yet if substances have actual parts, wherein lies the *unity* of the substance? For certain scholastics, it seems the temptation was to preserve their commitment to the unifying and joint-carving character of form by portraying certain forms as special elements *within* a composite with the power to pull its different parts together. Francisco Suárez, a philosopher of the late sixteenth and early seventeenth centuries, seems to be considering such a position when he writes, "The aggregation of multiple faculties or accidental forms in a simple substantial subject is not enough for the constitution of a natural thing. . . . A form is required that, as it were, *rules over all those faculties and accidents*, and is *the source of all actions* and natural motions of such a being."[21] In this way, form becomes reified as something with the power to organise other parts within some kind of causal structure. This marks a departure from the *classical* hylomorphism of Aristotle, in which matter and form play the role of constituent principles (sec. 2.3), toward a kind of *mereological* hylomorphism instead, in which they function as actual parts.[22]

3.2 Confounding Formal and Efficient Causation

Once matter and form have been reified, formal and efficient causes become difficult to distinguish from one another (CH2–4). For the classical hylomorphist, substances share a common source of determinable potentiality that is informed one way and then another. For certain scholastics, however, forms appear to carry a separate substantiality of their own, imposing their

---

20. Aquinas, *Aquinas on Being and Essence*, trans. A. A. Maurer, 2nd ed. (Toronto: Pontifical Institute of Medieval Studies, 1968), ch. 6.

21. F. Suárez, *Disputationes metaphysicae* (Paris: Vivès, 1866; repr., Hildesheim: Olms, 1965), as quoted in Pasnau, *Metaphysical Themes*. The text is somewhat ambiguous: Suárez goes on to claim that "the whole variety of accidents and powers has its root and unity" in the form. His tendency to treat form as actual parts is considered in D. M. Knight, "Suarez's Approach to Substantial Form," *Modern Schoolman* 39 (1962): 219–39.

22. Aquinas sometimes refers to forms as "parts," but without supposing they are *actual* parts or obey the axioms of mereology. See Aquinas's *On Being and Essence* and *On the Principles of Nature*. I do not explore the notion of "subsistent forms" here. See Aquinas, *Summa Theologiae* (Lander, WY: The Aquinas Institute, 2012), 75–76.

effects upon different kinds of determinate matter. In this way, forms became more like efficient causes.[23]

It is enough for my purposes to note that the meanings of matter and form were modified in certain variants of scholastic hylomorphism. Whilst the metaphysical role of form, both in joint-carving and the generation of substance, remained the same in intention, the ways in which these tasks were implemented rapidly shifted from their classical moorings. Among some of the late scholastics, matter and form had been reified and formal causation had been conflated with efficient causation—placing the concept of form in direct competition with scientific mechanisms.

4. The Rise of Corpuscularianism

The mechanical philosophy of the seventeenth century represents a development in these tendencies (sec. 3.1–2) that culminated in the complete reification of the substrate of change as material corpuscles with fully determinate properties, combined with a rejection of the doctrine of substantial forms as ontologically redundant. Abandoning the hylomorphic principles underlying classical Aristotelianism and late scholastic variants, the corpuscularists proposed an alternative ontology consisting of material bodies and their constituent parts.

One of its earliest instantiations was the mechanical philosophy of Descartes, who famously conjectured that reality could be neatly divided between *thinking things* and *extended things*. For Descartes, the extended things were wholly characterised by the geometric properties (shape, size, and position) and the mechanical property of the motion of particles of matter, which is governed by general laws of nature. A thorough-going reductionist in his approach to the material world, Descartes believed that "there is nothing in all of nature whose character (*ratio*) cannot be deduced through these same principles,"[24] and generally dismissed substantial form as "a philosophical entity which is unknown to me."[25]

It would be difficult to overstate the enduring impact of Descartes's

---

23. See Pasnau, *Metaphysical Themes*, sec. 24.4.

24. From C. Adam and P. Tannery, eds., *Oeuvres de Descartes*, rev. ed., 12 vols. (Paris: Vrin/CNRS, 1964–76), 4.187, as quoted and translated in Pasnau, *Metaphysical Themes*.

25. See René Descartes to Morin, 12 September 1638, in *The Philosophical Writings of Descartes*, vol. 3, ed. J. Cottingham et al. (Cambridge: Cambridge University Press, 1984). Descartes does make use of this term elsewhere, but this is likely a verbal concession.

metaphysics, although Cartesian science was a short-lived affair by contrast. Isaac Newton rejected Descartes's identification of matter with extension and developed an alternative account of motion that would rapidly secure Newtonian mechanics as an archetype of modern physics. The common commitment to corpuscles, however, continued to set the agenda for natural philosophers from the seventeenth century. Buoyed by swift advances in the experimental sciences, corpuscularianism swiftly supplanted scholasticism in many parts of Europe, as scientists like Boyle contrived plausible mechanical explanations for natural phenomena, specifically targeting cases in physics where scholastics had attributed certain phenomena to the activities of forms.[26] Henry Oldenburg, who served as the first secretary for the Royal Society, memorably complimented Boyle for having "driven out that drivel of substantial forms" which "has stopped the progress of true philosophy [science], and made the best of scholars not more knowing as to the nature of particular bodies than the meanest ploughmen."[27]

Whilst corpuscularists maintained a commitment to the notion of a substrate underlying all change—in Boyle's view, a "substance extended, divisible, and impenetrable"[28]—the doctrine of substantial forms was swiftly abandoned during the course of the seventeenth century. It had disappeared from mainstream philosophy by the end of the eighteenth century, when the French mechanist Pierre Simon de Laplace gave voice to a vision of a universal mechanism that would dominate the metaphysical imagination of philosophers until the turn of the twentieth century—a cosmos whose state at any future time is entirely fixed by the present locations and momenta of small particles and the laws of Newtonian mechanics;[29] a world built upon a wholly determinate substrate in which formal causation could have no role to play (CH3).

5. Redrawing the Battle Lines

My purpose in what follows is to draw the battle lines between corpuscularianism, late scholastic hylomorphism, and classical Aristotelian hylomorphism in a way

---

26. See R. Boyle, "The Origin of Forms and Qualities," in *The Works of Robert Boyle*, ed. M. Hunter and E. Davis (London: Pickering & Chatto, 1999–2000). This part of the text is also available online at earlymoderntexts.com.

27. H. Oldenburg, *Correspondence*, ed. and trans. A. R. Hall and M. B. Hall (Madison: University of Wisconsin Press, 1965), III:67.

28. See *Works of Robert Boyle*, V:305.

29. See P.-S. Marquis de Laplace, *A Philosophical Essay on Probabilities*, trans. F. W. Truscott and F. L. Emory (New York: John Wiley & Sons, 1902).

that is relevant to current metaphysical discussions concerning causal powers and modern science.[30] To this end, it is helpful to simplify and recast these approaches in a more contemporary format and to connect them with different explanatory targets. All three metaphysical positions share a common commitment to some underlying substrate of change. However, whilst each view is concerned with explaining how nature is carved at the joints, they differ with respect to the goals of predicting specific phenomena and the isolation of basic causes supposed to produce certain effects. I shall refer to these explanatory targets as (T1) *joint-carving*, (T2) *prediction*, and (T3) *isolation* respectively. They also differ with regard to the ontological status they assign to the concept of *structure*.

5.1 Simplistic Reduction

The shift toward corpuscularianism in the seventeenth century was advanced by the early mechanists who sought to distance themselves from the apparently fruitless complications of scholasticism (sec. 4). On their view, the substrate underlying all change could be carved into simple mechanisms comprising an arrangement of actual parts whose motions are governed by physical laws (T1). This metaphysic incorporated the explanatory target of predictability (T2) and excited the possibility of bringing nature entirely under control. The engine of change within the natural world was deemed to comprise powerful mechanisms that could be empirically isolated and studied (T3). For corpuscularists following Laplace, the world could be divided into microscopic and macroscopic bodies. The relations between these two different "levels" might be characterised as follows:

(Mic) The microlevel powers of basic microbodies can be defined in isolation from any of the macrobodies they constitute.

(Mac) The macrolevel powers of macrobodies are nothing over and above the sum of their microlevel powers.

I shall call this view *simplistic reduction*. On this account, the composition of any macrolevel entities and their activities, such as the "middle-sized dry goods" of ordinary experience, can be analysed without remainder in terms

---

30. For recent anthologies on the subject of causal powers, see A. Marmodoro, *The Metaphysics of Powers: Their Grounding and Their Manifestations* (New York: Routledge, 2010); J. Greco and R. Groff, eds., *Powers and Capacities in Philosophy: The New Aristotelianism* (New York: Routledge, 2013); and D. D. Novotný and L. Novák, eds., *Neo-Aristotelian Perspectives in Metaphysics* (New York: Routledge, 2014).

of microlevel constituents and their causal powers, such as an arrangement of different microparticles, thus comprising a structure of physical properties and governing laws that are determined at the microphysical level.[31]

There are few philosophers of science today who would be willing to defend microphysical reduction without many qualifications. For example, among Humean microphysicalists the explanatory goal is typically restricted to prediction by the deduction of macroscopic descriptions offered by "higher-level" macroscopic theories from the descriptions of "lower-level" microphysical theories instead (T2).[32] On this view, it would make no odds whether change is ultimately wrought through the collision of marbles or the shenanigans of a faerie ring since causal powers have no role to play in such explanations. However, among analytic philosophers in general, some form of simplistic reduction remains a perennial temptation.[33]

5.2 Structured Emergence

In contrast with the early mechanists, the scholastics were not simplistic reductionists and causal powers were not supposed to be confined to any particular length scale. For those rejecting the unitarian doctrine of substance, as defended by Aquinas, the notion of form might be conceived instead as an organising power that is present within the natural world. Such powers impose a structure upon certain materials at different levels of complexity. I shall characterise this approach as *structured emergence*; whilst microphysical entities may exist with their own causal powers, such as subatomic particles, complex macroscopic entities can also emerge with novel capacities due to the organising activities of macrolevel forms, such as biological entities. In this case, we might retain (Mic) but must reformulate (Mac) as follows:[34]

(Mac*) The macrolevel powers of any macrolevel body are a
combination of powers due to their basic microlevel parts and
powers due to their macrolevel forms.

---

31. For Descartes, the exception was the human soul.

32. Such explanations appeal to (nongoverning) bridging laws, rather than mechanisms or anything in nature with the causal power to produce change. See, e.g., J. Butterfield, "Emergence, Reduction, and Supervenience: A Varied Landscape," *Foundations of Physics* 41, no. 6 (2011): 920–59.

33. E.g., Mumford favours a vector-sum approach to how physical powers combine. See S. Mumford and R. L. Anjum, *Getting Causes from Powers* (Oxford: Oxford University Press, 2011).

34. (Mic) should be restricted to the essential powers microelements possess independently of any composite.

Structured emergence differs from other kinds of emergence in appealing to forms that are supposed to carve out composite entities and account for their novel powers. It has a number of contemporary advocates.[35] Yet it is not obvious how positing such elements is meant to *explain* how macrolevel composites obtain novel powers, since it is also unclear how the addition of an element is supposed to unify a collection of elements as a single substance. Simply positing the existence of a special element with the power to unify microlevel elements into a macrolevel substance is an *ad hoc* manoeuvre. Such an approach can be found among recent accounts of hylomorphism but was rejected by Aristotle as regressive.[36]

An alternative approach reconceives the notion of a substance as a *functional unity* instead: if certain elements behave differently when they are organised within a certain structure, we might characterise this emergent behaviour as a function of the elements comprising this structure. This function can then be used to reidentify the basic parts that comprise the composite at a higher level of description. For William Jaworski, such structures are believed to be objectively isolated by the sciences (T3) insofar as scientists are supposedly constrained by the natural order to adopt certain explanatory schema in order to predict different kinds of behaviour (T2).[37] On this view, causal structures are fundamental constituents of composite entities that should be characterised as causal powers (T1). Because they are powers, the existence of structures is supposed to explain emergent behaviours at higher ontological levels. Since they are structures, these powers are thought to explain how the various elements that comprise the composite are compelled to behave differently when they are parts of the whole.[38]

Such a move, however, supplants the *classical* conception of a unified substance, which was defended by Aquinas, with a *mereological* conception of composition, which was rejected by Aristotle.[39] In addition to reifying the

35. I think Rea's "reconditioned hylomorphism" and Jaworski's "structure realism" can be viewed as examples of structured emergence. See M. C. Rea, "Hylomorphism Reconditioned," *Philosophical Perspectives* 25, no. 1 (2011): 341–58, and W. Jaworski, *Structure and the Metaphysics of Mind: How Hylomorphism Solves the Mind-Body Problem* (New York: Oxford University Press, 2016).

36. See Aristotle's discussion of the syllable regress in Aristotle, *Metaphysics*, 7.17.

37. Historians of science are increasingly inclined toward more critical views of the strictly objective character of the sciences. For an introduction to constructivist approaches, see J. Golinski, *Making Natural Knowledge: Constructivism and the History of Science* (Chicago: University of Chicago Press, 2005).

38. For a book-length exposition of Jaworski's adaptation of hylomorphism, see *Structure and the Metaphysics of Mind*.

39. See Aristotle, *Metaphysics*, 7.17.

concept of form as a constituent property, it requires a substrate of permanent constituents united within a structure as actual parts. For Jaworski, this substrate is fundamentally physical, but gets to be structured in different ways, resulting in different composites with both physical and nonphysical powers. For these reasons, I suggest that structured emergence finds more affinity with late scholasticism (sec. 3) than classical hylomorphism (sec. 2).

5.3 Transformative Hylomorphism

The classical Aristotelian conception of hylomorphism does not readily fit into *any* contemporary categories. Nonetheless, I think it is a distinct and coherent option and that certain scholastics—like Scotus, Ockham, and Dabillon—were mistaken to dismiss it on metaphysical grounds. Like these scholastics, classical hylomorphists designate living beings as substances that exercise causal powers. Unlike these scholastics, however, classical hylomorphists resist the tendency to conceive of substance as a composite arrangement of parts glued together by reified forms. I suggest that form should be conceived instead as a constituent principle of substance (sec. 2.2), whilst any change in the world must be accounted for in terms of their causal powers.

I shall characterise this position as *transformative hylomorphism*, but can only briefly sketch its contours here. Unlike structured emergence, this account requires a substance to be a *metaphysical unity* in order for it to feature in any fundamental ontology. The elements from which a substance is generated must therefore be transformed through the exercise of various powers (sec. 2.1–2).[40] By contrast, *functional unities* are cheaply constructed; any vortex in the vicinity of a plughole might be conceived as a functional arrangement of parts.[41] For the transformative hylomorphist, however, new substances are not created and destroyed every time someone empties their bathtub.

For Aristotle, the paradigmatic examples of substances are living things, whose activities are characterised by certain goals, aims, or intentions that cannot be accounted for simply by taking different combinations of the powers of nonliving things; the powers of living things must be specified by substantial

---

40. The claim that the parts need to be transformed in order to be unified has notably been advanced by Scaltsas, in *Substances and Universals*; Marmodoro, in *Hylomorphism without Reconditioning*; and R. Koons in "Staunch vs. Faint-hearted Hylomorphism," *Res Philosophica* 91, no. 2 (2014): 151–77.

41. Its molecular constituents might be thought to acquire additional powers within the vortex.

forms.[42] Yet plants, animals, and people decompose into nonliving things when they die. For Aristotle, the four elements of antiquity are nonliving entities that do *not* decompose into other entities, possessing one of each of the two pairs of tangible contrarieties, which are their basic powers.[43] They comprise the primary building blocks of all nonliving things.

However, the primary elements are transmutable, and the manifestations of their powers are defined by Aristotle in terms of tangible qualities that are experienced by living things, rather than simply in terms of their effects upon each other. For these reasons, I suggest that Aristotle's primary elements do not require substantial forms. For Marmodoro, they are built out of "primary powers."[44] In fact, I suspect that many things in nature to which various scholastics and contemporary hylomorphists have assigned forms are not substances *in their own right*. Rather, the natural order is manifested by complex activities arising within a communion of being that comprises certain primary elements (perhaps particles or fields) and living things (plants, animals, and people) (cf. sec. 2.1). Moreover, the powers that manifest these various activities are only defined within this communion, which comprises every entity in nature and its ontological dependencies.[45] It follows that the powers of nonliving things also depend upon living things for their complete definition.

My object is not to establish the privileged status that Aristotle assigns to the lifeworld to the satisfaction of determined physicalists. Rather, the onus is on simplistic reductionists to show that all phenomena, both living and nonliving, are comprehensively explicable in terms of the same fundamental physics. I am encouraged by the fact that fewer philosophers and historians of science today are prepared to endorse this promissory claim or consider fundamentalism the best way to characterise the relationship between physics and the life sciences.[46] In a fully developed and self-consistent account of transformative hylomorphism, I suggest, *the natural order should*

---

42. I do not mean to exclude the possibility of some kind of continuum between living and nonliving things: microbes might technically be classified as living without being admitted as *fundamental* substances.

43. The four elements are known as earth, air, fire, and water; the tangible contrarieties are paired as the hot or the cold, and the wet or the dry. See Aristotle, *On Generation and Corruption*.

44. Marmodoro argues that powers are the building blocks of the primary elements, and that "it follows that all there is in nature is built out of powers." See in A. Marmodoro, *Aristotle on Perceiving Objects*, 1.1.

45. Cf. A. Marmodoro, "Potentiality in Aristotle's Metaphysics" (unpublished, 2013), intended for *The Handbook of Potentiality*, ed. K. Engelhard and M. Quante (Springer, forthcoming).

46. As notable examples of contemporary philosophers of science rejecting fundamentalism and embracing scientific pluralism, see N. Cartwright, *The Dappled World: A Study of the Boundaries of Science*

not be conceived fundamentally as a "physical" world, nor a physical world that gets to be structured in different ways to form various composites with "nonphysical" powers, but must be metaphysically understood to comprise a variety of different substances and entities, both living and nonliving, which are continually engaged in exercising and comanifesting their causal powers.

From this standpoint, the division of reality into microscopic and macroscopic levels should not be regarded as metaphysically fundamental but a logical abstraction useful for some scientific models but not others. I think the transformative hylomorphist should agree with the simplistic reductionist in this respect: there are no *ontological levels* with emergent powers (sec. 5.1). Rather, emergent behaviours must ultimately be explained by the basic powers defined within the communion of being and the complex ways in which they comanifest. If we are to retain (Mac), however, we must modify (Mic):

(Mic*) The microlevel powers of any macrobody are wholly specified by its form.

On this view, we may not *presume* that the "microlevel" powers of a macroscopic body can be regarded simply as combinations of the powers of microscopic parts determined in isolation. For instance, a living thing may be said to possess atoms among its potential constituents (sec. 2.2), but there is little reason to suppose that the behaviour of a localised electron abstracted from the tip of the horn of a rampaging rhinoceros could be adequately described by the Schrödinger equation.[47] For one thing, contemporary physics has reconceived particles as the excitations (or "quanta") of infinitely extended quantum fields.[48] For another, the behaviours of living things are shaped by the goal of self-preservation, and the ephemeral quanta of particle physics are not. For the transformative hylomorphist, *abstraction* does not lead to a determinate substrate of unchanging constituents underlying all change, whose powers can be characterised independently of any context, but only

---

(Cambridge: Cambridge University Press, 1999); and H. Chang, *Is Water H$_2$O? Evidence, Realism and Pluralism* (Dordtrecht: Springer, 2012).

47. I owe this graphic illustration to Andrew Pinsent.

48. In contemporary particle physics, the fundamental forces are mediated by distinct quantum fields that package energy in their own peculiar quanta, in place of the pellet-like portions of matter conserved within classical physics. For example, the electromagnetic force is mediated by photons, and the weak force by vector bosons.

a determinable potentiality that is determined by different forms. For these reasons, the metaphysical principles of both matter *and* form are required to explain the existence of any substance in nature that exercises causal powers.

6. Reduction, Emergence, and Mechanisms

I have outlined three metaphysical models descending from the medieval Latin tradition that I believe to be relevant to contemporary discussions about causal powers in metaphysics and the philosophy of science: simplistic reductionism, structured emergence, and transformative hylomorphism. The first derives from the corpuscularianism of the seventeenth century and corresponds to certain kinds of reductive physicalism, the second distils some of the implications of late scholastic conceptions of matter and form developed during the long Middle Ages and has resurfaced among recent mereological interpretations of hylomorphism, and the third is a little-known neo-Aristotelian implementation of the classical hylomorphism appropriated by Thomas Aquinas.

6.1 Supervenience and Causal Redundancy

Many analytic philosophers today would prefer to describe themselves as *nonreductive* physicalists, suspicious of any form of simplistic reduction (sec. 5.1) or strong emergence (sec. 5.2) and believing we might be spared any fuss with the physical sciences by making macroscopic properties *supervene* upon some corpuscularian arrangement of physical constituents instead. In this way, they seek to preserve a taxonomy of higher-level entities without requiring them to put in an appearance in any fundamental theory of what exists. However, I have not included nonreductive physicalism for good reason: I do not think supervenience affords a robust model of the relations between different levels. My reasons for this misgiving are advanced in detail by Elliot Sober and Jeremy Butterfield.[49] I shall simply note two points here.

First, the closely related notion of multiple realisability requires that instances of some macrolevel set of properties are varied as regards their representation on the microlevel, such that any extensionally correct definition of this set will be highly disjunctive. For example, a clock can be implemented in the electrical components of a computer, *or* the system of cogs and gears in

---

49. See E. Sober, "The Multiple Realizability Argument against Reductionism," *Philosophy of Science* 66 (1999): 542–64, and J. Butterfield, "Emergence, Reduction, and Supervenience."

a pocket watch, *or* the regulated flow of liquid in a clepsydra. Concerning the widely supposed failure of reduction in such cases, Sober asks: "Are we really prepared to say that the truth and lawfulness of the higher level generalisation is inexplicable, just because the . . . derivation is peppered with the word 'or'?"[50] Corpuscularians will most certainly say *no*: multiple realisability offers no ontological barrier to reduction in a world that rests upon a concrete floor of ungrounded microphysical facts.

Secondly, supervenience can be conceived as a special case of multiple realisability, in which the microlevel definitional extensions become infinitely long. Although this distinction may seem to frustrate reduction, there may be no principled way of knowing when (and if) this special case *actually* applies. As Butterfield observes, "Our inability to complete, or even begin, such a definition is no more evidence that a satisfactory definition would be infinite than that it would be incomprehensibly long. In other words, we have no reason to deny that the example supports a definitional extension."[51]

Whilst we may be unable to complete many microreductions in practice, if the causal powers of a composite are supposed to be grounded *in principle* on certain fundamental facts about its microconstituents, then the philosopher who hypostatises composite entities over and above their actual parts could be implicated in an illicit kind of double-counting since their existence and nature are wholly accounted for by their actual parts. This is the corpuscularian position maintained by simplistic reductionists (sec. 5.1), with which nonreductive physicalists have sought to compromise.[52] Attempts to establish the nonreductive character of supervenience or multiple-realisability are often made by appealing to mental properties like pain, which are widely held to be irreducible, and expected to trickle down to other properties that are thought to be multiply realised. The conviction that certain entities and their powers are not reducible to a combination of microphysical constituents is better served either by denying that the structures in which such powers are realised *are* microphysical alongside structured emergentists or by rejecting the fundamentality of microphysical constituents in the first place (sec. 5.2) like transformative hylomorphists (sec. 5.3). However, nonreductive physicalism, with its reliance on supervenience, fails to clarify the relations between the

---

50. See E. Sober, "The Multiple Realizability Argument," 552.
51. J. Butterfield, "Emergence, Reduction, and Supervenience."
52. T. Merricks, *Objects and Persons* (New York: Oxford University Press, 2003).

macroscopic and microscopic levels; it merely blurs them. In so doing, it fails to offer a cogent alternative to simplistic reduction (sec. 5.1).

6.2 Causal Mechanisms and Emergence

Classical and late scholastic conceptions of substantial forms are not well-served by nonreductive physicalism. Both conceptualisations are supposed to be joint-carving (CH1) insofar as they are meant to underscore the unity and characterise the causal powers of different entities that comprise the natural order. For this reason, however, both positions are also vulnerable to attack by simplistic reductionists, but in *different* ways.

Since certain scholastics effectively conceived forms as constituent parts of a composite that interact with other entities, and multiplied their presence throughout the natural world, they were directly vulnerable to replacement by the discovery of mechanisms in nature that were productive of the same effects, filling out the operation of a form in terms of more basic parts and their activities in a way that admits generalisations. For example, water's power as "the universal solvent" can be modelled in terms of the particular polar arrangement of its oxygen and hydrogen atoms, along with many of its other distinctive properties. To postulate a form that *directly* causes these phenomena, by contrast, is merely to offer a black box. As Boyle protested, "I leave substantial forms to those who think they understand them, and try instead to explain phenomena in terms of things that I do understand."[53] (I take his point to mean if we are seeking to isolate causes and predict effects [T2 and 3], causal mechanisms are more explanatory.)

By contrast, the classical doctrine of hylomorphism did not reify substantial forms (CH4) and was not directly threatened by—nor, indeed, in competition with—mechanical explanations *per se*. It is one thing to account for the changes of a whole in terms of various activities of its parts, that is, by appealing to some *internal* mechanism. It is another thing to claim to have reduced these changes solely to the activities of mechanisms defined in isolation from the whole, that is, by appealing to *extrinsic* mechanisms. If this kind of reduction is universally successful, both Aristotelian and scholastic notions of form are causally redundant and should be abandoned.

The early mechanists, like Laplace, were optimistic about the possibility of

---

53. See Boyle, "The Origin of Forms and Qualities," at earlymoderntexts.com, 41.

explaining every change in the world in terms of microphysical mechanisms. In evaluating corpuscularianism and its offspring, however, we should ask whether history has vindicated their expectations. I think we have reason to be skeptical. There are many cases in the natural sciences of novel and robust behaviours emerging in complex systems that cannot be accounted for in terms of microphysical mechanisms determined in isolation and simplistically combined,[54] and many of the scientific claims that the early mechanists advanced against their scholastic brethren now seem risibly antiquated.

With the fall of the deductive-nomological model in the philosophy of science and the rise of causal explanation, "new mechanists" have emerged. They explicitly reject the monolithic project of explaining nature in terms of abstract and idealised physical systems, refocussing their efforts on the special sciences of biology, psychology, and neuroscience, and seeking to understand them on their own terms instead.[55] Both transformative hylomorphists and structured emergentists may draw encouragement from such developments in resisting simplistic reduction. Ironically, the modern conception of form as a structure that confers causal powers, as advanced by some contemporary proponents of structured emergence (sec. 5.2), resonates with the claims of some of the new mechanists concerning the "ontic structures" believed to be brought to light by the special sciences.[56]

6.3 Quantum Holism and the Collapse of Structure

In the present climate of scientific pluralism, the empirical challenge posed by simplistic reduction to an ontology that posits irreducible entities above the microphysical scale may seem to have abated, and one might therefore suppose structured emergence and transformative hylomorphism to be on a similar footing. Nonetheless, the threat of ontological reduction is being advanced today from the opposite direction. It is one thing to mark the

---

54. See, e.g., A. A. Corradini and T. O'Connor, eds., *Emergence in Science and Philosophy* (New York: Routledge, 2010).

55. For a helpful introduction to the New Mechanists, see *The Stanford Encyclopedia of Philosophy*, plato.stanford.edu/archives/win2016/entries/science-mechanisms.

56. Concerning "ontic structures," see C. F. Craver, "The Ontic Account of Scientific Explanation," in *Explanation in the Special Sciences: The Case of Biology and History*, ed. M. I. Kaiser et al. (Dordrecht: Springer Netherlands, 2014), 27–52. For a comparison of new mechanist philosophy with certain types of hylomorphism, see D. De Haan, "Hylomorphism, New Mechanistic Philosophy, and Explanations in Biology, Neuroscience, and Psychology," in *Neo-Aristotelian Perspectives on Contemporary Science*, ed. W. M. R. Simpson, R. Koons, and N. Teh (New York: Routledge, 2017).

historic failure of the early mechanists to explain change in a complex living world as combinations of the causal powers of simpler, nonliving parts. It is another thing to resist the pressure from contemporary forms of holism, which suggest that any physical parts in nature must ultimately be grounded either within an all-encompassing whole or a set of overlapping quantum fields. Cosmic holism is increasingly in vogue among philosophers acquainted with quantum physics.[57] Taken at face value, the phenomenon of entanglement, for instance, suggests that physical reality is interwoven in a way that prevents complex systems from being fundamentally analysed as products of simpler states associated with separate microphysical parts. According to some philosophers of physics, quantum entanglement entails the failure of part-whole relations.[58] If this is the case, there may not *be* any physical constituents that can be "structured" as a plurality of complex entities in the way structured emergentists seem to suppose (sec. 5.2).[59]

I have considered this issue in further detail elsewhere.[60] For the purpose of this discussion, I wish simply to register these observations: it does not follow that *every* kind of metaphysical joint-carving is prohibited in an entangled cosmos, nor does it follow that a world that fails to "bottom out" into Lego-like constituents must be devoid of causal powers. For transformative hylomorphists, causal powers are neither derived from nor identical to structures with physical parts; rather, physical structures and their constituents are explicable in terms of causal powers (sec. 5.3). I have suggested that an entangled world might be understood in terms of a plurality of entities comanifesting their powers to form a single process.[61] However, in *addition* to the powerful elements comprising quantum phenomena, there are living substances in which these elements are *transformed*, thus comprising a larger communion of being from which quantum physics prescinds.[62] Moreover, it is only within this causal nexus that the powers of everything in nature are completely defined (sec. 2.1).

---

57. See, e.g., Schaffer, "Spacetime the One Substance," *Philosophical Studies* 145 (2009): 131–48; and Schaffer, "Monism: The Priority of the Whole," *Philosophical Review* 119 (2010): 31–76.

58. Elise Crull, for example, has claimed that "nature is impervious to how we choose to slice it." See E. M. Crull, "Why We Can't Have Nice Things," academia.edu (draft), 2015.

59. I am aware of Humean ontologies of (nonrelativistic) quantum mechanics in which corpuscularianism can be restored. However, I argue that such ontologies must (implausibly) exclude causal powers.

60. Simpson, "Half-Baked Humeanism," in *Neo-Aristotelian Perspectives on Contemporary Science*, ed. W. M. R. Simpson, R. Koons, and N. Teh (New York: Routledge, 2017).

61. Simpson, work in progress.

62. I hope to develop this account further in future work.

For these reasons, transformative hylomorphists can agree with structured emergentists concerning the vanity of trying to reduce everything in biology, neuroscience, and psychology to fundamental physics but should reject both the reification of matter in terms of physical constituents and the identification of forms as structures with physical parts (cf. sec. 3.1). Since Aristotelian causal powers are not ultimately defined through the clinical isolation of mechanisms and causes, transformative hylomorphism must also part ways with the *scientism* of structured emergence and simplistic reduction. Scientific modelling should not be confused with metaphysics, and the goals of prediction and control (T2 and T3) that shaped early corpuscularianism must be disentangled from the task of understanding "how things in the broadest possible sense . . . hang together in the broadest possible sense" (T1).[63] For the transformative hylomorphist, carving nature at the joints is part of the abstract and all-encompassing work of philosophy; it cannot simply be outsourced to our "best sciences."

7. Reconsidering Classical Hylomorphism

The seventeenth century is often portrayed as a watershed between medieval Aristotelianism and modern science, the one side clinging to arcane metaphysical principles, and the other advancing comprehensively mechanistic explanations. However, things are not so simple. I have demonstrated significant disparity between the classical conception of form adopted by Aquinas and certain scholastic notions targeted by early corpuscularists, and shown significant continuity between late scholastic notions of matter and the corpuscularian conception that carried the day (sec. 2–4).

Two standard objections to hylomorphism are that substantial forms obstruct scientific progress and that they are causally redundant. In considering the metaphysical relations between higher and lower levels in scientific explanation, however, I distinguished between two different ways of implementing the role of form. I introduced *transformative hylomorphism* (sec. 5.3) and *structured emergence* (sec. 5.2), based on classical Aristotelian and late scholastic notions of forms respectively. I also defined *simplistic reductionism*, based on

---

63. As Wilfrid Sellars aptly expressed it. See W. Sellars, "Philosophy and the Scientific Image of Man," in *Frontiers of Science and Philosophy*, ed. R. Colodny (Pittsburgh: University of Pittsburgh Press, 1962), 35–78.

the mechanical explanations of the early corpuscularists, which rejects them both (sec. 5.1). I argued that naïve varieties of structured emergence have rendered themselves vulnerable to accusations of obscurantism and scientific obstruction by effectively competing with mechanistic explanations (sec. 6.2). The charge of ontological redundancy in general, however, involves a metaphysical commitment to simplistic reduction. Given the reality of emergent phenomena in contemporary science and the inadequacy of supervenience as a metaphysical compromise between reduction and emergence, I think we should give up simplistic reduction (sec. 1–2). In doing so, a primary objection is removed both to transformative hylomorphism and more sophisticated varieties of structured emergence. However, by identifying forms with structures that have physical parts, structured emergence is vulnerable to dismissal by quantum theorists who deny the existence of basic physical constituents that can be glued together to comprise separate entities (sec. 6.3). I suggest that transformative hylomorphism, which does not posit a determinate substrate of physical constituents, offers a viable alternative that deserves further development. The metaphysical principles of classical hylomorphism upon which this model is based were championed within the medieval Latin tradition by Aquinas, yet they were subsequently confused with scholastic innovations and have been overshadowed by a Laplacian corpuscularianism that can no longer be maintained. However, with these historical contingencies set aside, I believe classical hylomorphism may be restored to contemporary consideration.[64]

64. I would like to thank, in particular, Hasok Chang, John Marenbon, Anna Marmodoro, and Daniel De Haan for helpful discussions of this paper. I would also like to acknowledge my college, Peterhouse, for financial support and the support of the Institute for the Study of Philosophy, Politics, and Religion, Cambridge.

Chapter FOURTEEN

Creation, Providence, and Evolution

DENIS R. ALEXANDER

Here is the road map for this chapter. Following some brief historical reflections, we will present a robust view of a Trinitarian Christian theism that provides a matrix within which the natural sciences in general, and biology in particular, can happily flourish. We will then consider how this relates to the Christian doctrine of providence and assess how readily (or not) the supposedly "chance" processes of evolution can be baptized into this Christian understanding of creation whereby God's providential purposes for the created order are fulfilled.

Biology in Its Historical Context

Historically, the Christian doctrine of creation has done much to shape the biological sciences that we study today. This is ironic because for many people biology, at least at first look, can often appear threatening to faith, replete with words like "chance," "random," "stochastic," "purposeless," and so forth.

The situation today seems very different from that of John Ray (1627–1705), a key Christian founder of the discipline of natural history that later came to be called biology. Ray complained that far too many scholars were taken up with the humanities and that natural history was being neglected. The heritage of Renaissance humanism was indeed one which often tended to look down upon biology. As the Italian scholar and poet Francesco Petrarch (1304–74) put the question in the fourteenth century: "What is the use—I beseech you—of knowing the nature of quadrupeds, fowls, fishes and serpents and not knowing or even neglecting man's nature, the purpose for which we are born, and whence and whereto we travel?"[1] But it was largely due to John Ray and other passionately Christian natural historians of the seventeenth century that the tide began to turn, especially as the study of natural history became closely linked with the argument from design and as animal behaviour became employed in moral teaching.

John Ray came to study at Trinity College, Cambridge, in 1643 at the tender age of sixteen (not atypical for that era), later becoming a fellow of Trinity and writing one of the foundational works in the history of biology, *The Wisdom of God Manifested in the Works of Creation.* Ray taught some of the materials that later became his book not in a lecture hall but in Trinity College chapel because he saw teaching science as an act of worship. John Ray declared that he had published his *Ornithology* for "the illustration of Gods glory, by exciting men to take notice of, and admire his infinite power and wisdom."[2]

Meanwhile Robert Hooke, first curator of the Royal Society, made good use of the newly constructed microscopes to popularize the world of the flea to a fascinated reading public, declaring that the more objects are magnified with the microscope, "the more we discover the imperfections of our senses, and the Omnipotency and Infinite perfections of the great Creatour."[3] The new world revealed by the microscope made quite an impact. The French priest Nicolas Malebranche exclaimed, in a glorious example of seventeenth-century hyperbole, "One insect is more in touch with Divine wisdom than the whole of Greek and Roman history."[4] In Bishop Thomas Sprat's *History of the Royal Society,* Sprat went so far as to claim that the formal study of nature had been part of the original religion of Adam in Paradise.[5]

By deploying such theological resources, the Christian natural philosophers of the seventeenth century and beyond provide social validation for

---

1. F. Petrarch, "On His Own Ignorance and That of Many Others," trans. Hans Nachod, in *The Renaissance Philosophy of Man*, ed. E. Cassirer, P. O. Kristeller, and J. H. Randall (Chicago: University of Chicago Press, 1948).

2. J. Ray and F. Willughby, *The Ornithology of Francis Willughby of Middleton* (London: By A. C. for John Martyn, 1678).

3. R. Hooke, J. Martyn, and J. Allestry, *Micrographia: Or Some Physiological Descriptions of Minute Bodies Made by Magnifying Glasses: With Observations and Inquiries Thereupon* (London: J. Martyn and J. Allestry, 1665), 8.

4. Nicolas Malebranche, "Eloge du P. Malebranche," in *Oeuvres Complètes*, ed. G. Rodis-Lewis (Paris: J. Vrin, 1958–70), 5:461.

5. T. Sprat and A. Cowley, *The History of the Royal-Society of London for the Improving of Natural Knowledge* (London: J. Martyn and J. Allestry, 1667), 394.

investigations that were undervalued by Renaissance humanism.[6] The allegorical interpretations of the natural world that had remained such a dominant feature of commentators up to 1600 gradually gave way to a focus on the properties of nature "in itself," properties perceived in more functional terms. God had created living things for particular reasons, mainly for human benefit. As the theologian and philosopher Henry More pointed out, "Those *Herbs* that the rude and ignorant would call *Weeds* are the Materials of very sovereign Medicines."[7] Opium was previously looked upon as a poison, wrote the chemist Robert Boyle, but was "now imploy'd as a noble remedy."[8] Everything had its purpose in God's good creation. The study of biology became incorporated into a natural theology in which the natural world was created for the good of humankind and demonstrated the wisdom and power of God.

In Britain, biology remained incorporated within the tenets of natural theology well into the nineteenth century. The logic and rational structure of Charles Darwin's theory of evolution had its roots in the natural theology that Darwin imbibed during his student days at Cambridge (1828–31). This was an era when the teaching of science was carried out by ordained Anglican clergy, and more than 50 percent of the students at that time were destined for the Anglican ministry. Darwin's exams covered two texts by Archdeacon William Paley, the great proponent of natural theology, and after his final exams were over Darwin proceeded to read for his own enjoyment Paley's *Natural Theology or Evidences of the Existence and Attributes of the Deity* (1802). In his autobiography, Darwin later reflected that

> I am convinced that I could have written out the whole of the Evidences with perfect correctness, but not of course in the clear language of Paley. The logic of this book, and, as I may add, of his Natural Theology, gave me as much delight as did Euclid. The careful study of these works . . . was the only part of the academical course which, as I then felt, and as I still believe, was of the least use to me in the education of my mind.[9]

---

6. Peter Harrison, *The Bible, Protestantism, and the Rise of Natural Science* (Cambridge: Cambridge University Press, 1998); and Harrison, "The Cultural Authority of Natural History in Early Modern Europe," in *Biology and Ideology from Descartes to Dawkins*, ed. D. R. Alexander and R. L. Numbers (Chicago: University of Chicago Press, 2010), 11–35.

7. H. More, *An Antidote against Atheisme, or, an Appeal to the Natural Faculties of the Minde of Man, Whether There Be Not a God* (London: J. Flesher, 1655).

8. R. Boyle, *A Disquisition About the Final Causes of Natural Things* (London: H. C., 1688).

9. Charles Darwin, *The Autobiography of Charles Darwin*, ed. Nora Barlow (London: Collins, 1958), 59.

Darwin's *On the Origin of Species* (1859) has even been dubbed "the last great work of Victorian natural theology."[10] Darwin's own faith, as he wrote *Origin*, was far from the committed Christianity of the seventeenth-century natural philosophers such as John Ray and was later to drift into agnosticism, but the rational structure of natural theology provided a framework within which evolution could readily be incorporated. It is partly for this reason that evolution was embraced by all mainstream Christian denominations within a few decades of the publication of *Origin*. The Scottish evangelical Henry Drummond (1851–1897) maintained that natural selection was "a real and beautiful acquisition to natural theology" and that *Origin* was "perhaps the most important contribution to the literature of apologetics" to have appeared during the nineteenth century.[11] Whilst Drummond's enthusiasm for Darwin's new theory was not shared by all his contemporaries, his comments highlight the fact that for many Christians a traditional creation theology has provided a natural home for the theory of evolution ever since Darwin.

A Trinitarian Christian Creation Theology

Our aim here is to capture some of that robust theism displayed by those early Christian natural philosophers who laid the groundwork for the scientific disciplines we practice today. The proposal is that a traditional Trinitarian creation theology as introduced for us in the biblical texts, expounded by the early church fathers, then by Thomas Aquinas in the thirteenth century, and by the Reformers a few centuries later provides the matrix within which biology can flourish and provide a coherent and providential story of life. So the emphasis here is not on natural theology per se but on a theology of nature that can help us interrogate topics such as providence in the light of chance and randomness.

The biblical creation narrative is composed of a myriad of different insights, scattered liberally throughout the Old and New Testaments, and the overall discussion between science and faith is pretty much set by the degree to which we allow that range of insights to impact upon our thinking.

---

10. J. Durant, *Darwinism and Divinity: Essays on Evolution and Religious Belief* (Oxford: Blackwell, 1985), 16.

11. G. A. Smith and Stirling Tract Enterprise (Firm), *The Life of Henry Drummond (1851–1897)* (Stirling: Drummond Trust, 1997).

A picture emerges of God as creator, the source and ground of all that exists. Everything that exists apart from God only exists because God brought it into existence. So God is the ground of all existence, and in this view "existence" refers to anything that exists, be they material or immaterial—the laws of nature, quantum vacuums, Higgs bosons, trees, rabbits, mathematical principles, and the elements of the periodic table. If it exists and is not God, then it must by definition be part of the created order within this theistic matrix.

One challenge comes from the way in which we use the word "create" in the English language and then apply it to God. When human beings make things, they work with already existing material to produce something new. The human act of creating is not the complete cause of what is produced, but God's creative act *is* the complete cause of what is produced. As the theologian Bill Carroll puts it, "God's causality is so different from the causality of creatures that there is no competition between the two, that is, we do not need to limit, as it were, God's causality to make room for the causality of creatures. God causes creatures to be causes."[12] Carroll adds, "Creation is not essentially some distant event; rather, it is the on-going complete causing of the existence of all that is. At this very moment, were God not causing all that is to exist, there would be nothing at all. Creation concerns first of all the origin of the universe, not its temporal beginning."[13] Here Carroll is drawing from the thirteenth-century theologian Thomas Aquinas, who writes, "Over and above the mode of becoming by which something comes to be through change or motion, there must be a mode of becoming or origin of things without any mutation or motion, through the influx of being."[14] So creation is about ontology, the existence of things and the meanings of their existence.

Since our great creator God is not encompassed or constrained in any way by the present created order, we as human creatures are in no position to guess how God might wish to create or to tell him how he ought to. As God says, speaking through the prophet Isaiah,

> For my thoughts are not your thoughts,
>   neither are your ways my ways. . . .

---

12. W. E. Carroll, "Aquinas and Contemporary Cosmology: Creation and Beginnings," in *Science and Christian Belief* 24 (2012): 5.

13. Carroll, "Aquinas and Contemporary Cosmology," 18.

14. Aquinas, *De substantiis ceparatis*, 9.49.

> As the heavens are higher than the earth,
> so are my ways higher than your ways
> and my thoughts than your thoughts. (Isa 55:8–9)[15]

The context of that passage is the way in which God works out salvation for his people in ways that are certainly past human understanding, but the same point can be made of God in relation to the created order. "Our God is in heaven" says the psalmist, "he does whatever pleases him" (Ps 115:3). Historians of science have often pointed to this sense of the transcendence of God and the consequent radical contingency of the created order as one of the great motivations for empiricism, for the experimental method. For no one could simply guess how the created order might work starting from commonsense or simple human logic. Quantum mechanics, for example, is rather weird, and mental pictorial representations should not be attempted, otherwise one ends up with a headache. As a very different example, if we had visited this planet 4 billion years ago when it was a desolate inchoate mass of disorganized materials undergoing frequent asteroid bombardment, no one would have predicted that after a 3.8 billion years evolutionary history it would become the home of saints and sinners.

God's free unconstrained acts of creation were emphasised by Roger Cotes in his preface to the second edition of Isaac Newton's great work the *Principia Mathematica*. In words clearly approved by Newton himself: "Without all doubt this world . . . could arise from nothing but the perfectly free will of God. . . . These [laws of nature] therefore we must not seek from uncertain conjectures, but learn them from observations and experiments."[16] René Descartes makes a similar point in these words:

> Since there are countless different configurations which God might have instituted here, experience alone must teach us which configurations he actually selected in preference to the rest. We are thus free to make any assumption on these matters with the sole proviso that all the consequences of our assumption must agree with experience.[17]

---

15. Unless otherwise noted, Scripture quotations in this essay come from the NIV.
16. Isaac Newton, represented by Hooykaas, after Cotes's preface to 2nd edition of *Principia*, in R. Hooykaas, *Religion and the Rise of Modern Science* (Edinburgh: Scottish Academic, 1972), 49.
17. René Descartes, *Principles of Philosophy*, trans. R. P. Miller and V. R. Miller (London: Reidel, 1983), 100.

Along with the transcendent otherness of God in the biblical literature comes an insistence on the simultaneous immanence of God in the created order, that moment-by-moment involvement in upholding and sustaining creation. God's faithfulness is displayed in the nomic regularity, the law-like behaviour of energy and matter, which renders the world coherent and makes the scientific enterprise possible. This is a Trinitarian immanence. Right at the beginning of the Bible in Genesis 1:3, the Spirit of God hovers over the waters ready to bring order out of the formless and empty earth. Or in Hiebert's memorable translation, far from being the hovering of a bird, the *ruach* becomes the wind sweeping in on a storm from the Mediterranean: "God's *ruach* swept over the surface of the water."[18] As the theologian Jürgen Moltmann expresses the point, "The divine Spirit (*ruach*) is the creative power and the presence of God in his creation. The whole creation is a fabric woven by the Spirit, and is therefore a reality to which the Spirit gives form."[19] Calvin put it this way in his *Institutes*: "For it is the Spirit who, everywhere diffused, sustains all things, causes them to grow, and quickens them in heaven and on earth. . . . In transfusing into all things his energy, and breathing into them essence, life and movement, he is indeed plainly divine."[20]

The New Testament insists that we live in a christological creation. Using one of the most powerful metaphors in the whole of the New Testament, John tells us in the prologue to his gospel, "Through the Logos all things were made; without him nothing was made that has been made." In Colossians 1, Paul writes that by the Son of God "all things were created: things in heaven and on earth, visible and invisible, whether thrones or powers or rulers or authorities; all things were created through him and for him. He is before all things, *and in him all things hold together*" (vv. 16–17, emphasis added). In other words, the complete created order, in all its breadth and diversity, goes on consisting by the same divine Word, the Lord Jesus, who brought everything into being in the first place.

The point is further underlined by the author of Hebrews: "The Son is the radiance of God's glory and the exact representation of his being, *sustaining all things by his powerful word*" (Heb 1:3, emphasis added). God is the one "for

---

18. T. Hiebert, "Air, the First Sacred Thing: The Conception of Ruach in the Hebrew Scriptures," in *Exploring Ecological Hermeneutics*, ed. N. C. Habel and P. L. Trudinger (Leiden: Brill, 2008), 15.

19. Jürgen Moltmann, *God in Creation: An Ecological Doctrine of Creation* (London: SCM, 1985), 99.

20. John Calvin, *The Institutes of Christian Religion*, ed. A. N. S. Lane and H. Osborne (London: Hodder and Stoughton, 1986), 1.13.14–15.

whom and through whom everything exists" (Heb 2:10). Here is no absentee landlord but the key to existence. As Jesus said of his heavenly Father, "He *causes* his sun to rise on the evil and the good, and *sends* rain on the righteous and the unrighteous" (Matt 5:45, emphasis added). Trinitarian creation entails an active "holding in existence" of the complete created order. No wonder that the twenty-four elders of John's vision in the book of Revelation worship before the throne, saying,

> You are worthy, our Lord and God,
>> to receive glory and honour and power,
> for you created all things,
>> and by your will they were created
>> and *have their being* [present tense]." (Rev 4:11, my italics)

It is this Spirit-energised, christological created order that the Old Testament insists is a biologically fruitful created order. In Psalm 104, God "makes grass grow for the cattle, and plants for people to cultivate" (v. 14), and it is God who supplies food for lions who "roar for their prey and seek their food from God" (v. 21). "How many are your works, LORD!" cries the psalmist. "In wisdom you made them all; the earth is full of your creatures" (v. 24). And then, we have the remarkable observation that God's creative work is involved in the very processes of animal life and death that would have been so familiar to the rural communities of that time:

> When you hide your face,
>> they (the animals) are terrified;
> when you take away their breath,
>> they die and return to the dust.
> When you send your Spirit,
>> they are created,[21]
>> and you renew the face of the earth. (vv. 29–30)

Job reflects these realities perfectly when he says of God, "In his hand is the life of every creature and the breath of all mankind" (Job 12:10). Job's theme

---

21. Here "created" is *bara'*, the strong word used for *create* in Hebrew that is only used when God is the author.

is picked up by Paul in Acts 17 when he reminds his listeners in Athens that "in [God] we live and move and have our being" (Acts 17:28). "O LORD, you preserve both man and beast," writes the psalmist (Ps 36:6 NASB). And the book of Job, of course, has further wonderful descriptions of God as the author of the biological world who provides "food for the raven when its young cry out to God and wander about for lack of food" (Job 38:41). The eagle soars at God's command and builds his nest on high, and "Its young ones feast on blood, and where the slain are, there it is" (Job 39:30). Here, there is no shrinking back from the biological realities of the created order.

As we consider both the transcendence and immanence of God in creation, a further striking observation emerges from the biblical narratives, that is, the three tenses of creation. Creation in the Bible, like salvation, has three tenses: past, present, and future. There is a definite biblical sense of looking back at creation—at all that God has done in the past to bring this world of rich biological diversity into being. We also read of a God who is actively involved in the created order in the present, as we have just outlined. God the Father, God the Son, and God the Holy Spirit are all intimately involved in the ongoing sustaining of the created order. As Jesus remarked in John 5 after he healed the man on the Sabbath, "My Father is always at his work to this very day, and I too am working" (John 5:17). And as far as future creation is concerned, God tells us through the prophet Isaiah, "See, I will create [*bara'*] new heavens and a new earth" (Isa 65:17). So the biblical doctrine of creation tells us about a dynamic process in which God is the author of the narrative, and Jesus is "the Alpha and the Omega, the First and the Last, the Beginning and the End" (Rev 22:13). God's creation encompasses past, present, and future. That's the matrix.

All analogies are limited, but God's continuing creative activity has been likened to the continual flow of digital signals that enable pictures on our TV screens. Our favourite TV drama is a self-contained world, and talk of digitally encoded signals adds nothing to it. Yet without the continuous signals, the drama would cease to be conveyed to your living room. God is the continuing author of creation.

To use a different analogy, God is both the musical composer and conductor in relation to the symphony of creation—the one who is immanent in the whole creative process as the beautiful harmony emerges from the coordinated output of the many different musical components.

So what do biologists do in their research? Well, clearly what they do is to describe, as best they can, both the created order that God continually undergirds and sustains and the "secondary causes" whereby God brings about his aims and purposes. And biologists do this not by invoking the actions of God, the Primary Cause, to explain those parts of the process that seem particularly difficult to understand but rather by seeing the authorship of the Creator expressed in the whole biological process from beginning to end. So when my atheistic biologist colleagues pose the question, "Well, what difference does it make to your biology whether God exists or not?" three points immediately come to mind. The first is that if there were no God, nothing would exist, so we certainly wouldn't be doing science. Second, without God, nomic regularity would be unexpected and certainly not guaranteed. The faithfulness of God in guaranteeing the reproducibility of the properties of matter is critical for the success of science. And third, the fact of common grace and the fact that all human beings are made in the image of God, irrespective of our belief in God, entails that we as a scientific community can share the same scientific methods and approaches to understanding the biological world. In creating all humankind in his image, God has delegated authority to the whole of humankind to subdue and care for the earth, and science represents one way of fulfilling that responsibility. Where the theistic matrix becomes most relevant is not in seeking to bring God into our scientific papers on occasion, as if God were merely some further component within our repertoire of scientific explanations—a theologically problematic stance that reduces God to the status of one explanatory component amongst many—but rather in the interpretation of our discoveries within the light of that theistic matrix. Putting it simplistically, science is about empirical explanations for the being and becoming of material things, and theology is about their overall interpretation.

This also helps to explain why Christians, of all people, should not use the term "methodological naturalism"[22] when referring to their scientific research. Naturalism is the philosophical belief that everything arises from natural causes and explanations, excluding any reference to God, so Christians cannot commit to naturalism in any form without contradiction, even if "naturalism" is qualified by "methodological." Biologists study the very works of God in

---

22. It should be noted that there are other definitions of "naturalism"; e.g., see M. C. Rea, *World Without Design: The Ontological Consequences of Naturalism* (Oxford: Clarendon, 2004).

their daily research, which is a holy enterprise, so labeling such investigations as "naturalistic" is wholly inappropriate for Christians.

Biology and Providence

How are we to understand the term "providence" in relation to God's creation? Bruce Ware provides us with a definition of the term:

> God exhaustively plans and meticulously carries out his perfect will as he alone knows best, regarding all that is in heaven and on earth, and he does so without failure or defeat, accomplishing his purposes in all of creation from the smallest details to the grand purposes of his plan for the whole of the created order.[23]

Searching for the word "providence" in the NIV translation reveals only Job 10:

> Your hands shaped me and made me.
>   Will you now turn and destroy me?
> Remember that you molded me like clay.
>   Will you now turn me to dust again?
> Did you not pour me out like milk
>   and curdle me like cheese,
> clothe me with skin and flesh
>   and knit me together with bones and sinews?
> You gave me life and showed me kindness,
>   and in your providence watched over my spirit. (Job 10:8–12)

This passage provides yet another example of the immanence of God in the created order, in this context in the creation of the human individual. We are reminded of the psalmist's declaration of faith in God:

> For you created my inmost being;
>   you knit me together in my mother's womb. (Ps 139:13)

---

23. Bruce A. Ware, "Prayer and the Sovereignty of God," in *For the Fame of God's Name*, ed. Sam Storms and Justin Taylor (Westchester, IL: Crossway, 2010), 128.

God's providence is seen in the Bible as being worked out through the biographies of believers and nonbelievers alike. The Old Testament envisages God moving "the heart of Cyrus king of Persia to make a proclamation throughout his realm" (Ezra 1:1) just as much as he then moved the hearts of God's people to return to Jerusalem to "build the house of the LORD" (Ezra 1:5). But at the same time God's providence is seen as being worked out in every other aspect of the created order, including the world of animals and plants, as we have already noted when considering the immanence of God in his creation. Ware's definition of providence, robust as it is, does seem to be well supported by Scripture. God will bring about his purposes through the created order, come what may.

At this stage of the discussion, misconceptions can easily arise, so we need to head them off before they become a distraction. They can be addressed by flagging what God's providential working in biology does *not* entail.

God's Providence Does Not Entail the Intentionality of Micromanagement

There are implications to envisaging God as Primary Cause and all the components of the universe as representing the secondary causes whereby God brings about his creation, namely, that genuine causation exists amongst the secondary causes. God causes creatures to be causes. The creation has its own integrity, not because it is "free" in an autonomous way but because God faithfully guarantees the properties of the material world by undergirding and sustaining its consistency. Matter does what matter does, and it is up to science to describe the God-dependent consistency of the properties of matter, which is of course what renders feasible the reproducibility of experiments.

Charles Darwin struggled with the question of God's providence in creation, writing to his good friend Asa Gray, a Professor of Botany at Harvard and a Christian, in a letter dated July 3, 1860. "Do you believe," wrote Darwin "that when a swallow snaps up a gnat that God designed that that particular swallow should snap up that particular gnat at that particular instant?" Gray's reply is not available, but it was a question clearly on Darwin's mind, who repeats his question in a letter to his brother-in-law Hensleigh Wedgwood and then reports Hensleigh's wise answer to Asa Gray in a letter written on September 10, 1860: "Hensleigh Wedgwood. . . . is a very strong Theist, & I put it to him, whether he thought that each time a fly was snapped up by a swallow, its death was designed; & he admitted he did not believe so, only that God ordered general laws & left the result to what may be so far called chance, that there was no design in the death of each individual Fly."

Wedgwood correctly draws attention to the question of God's intentionality ("no design in the death"). Of course the fly is as much part of the created order as anything else, but God's intention is to uphold the properties of the whole created order so that the system as a whole providentially fulfills his purposes, not to micromanage every event within the created order; otherwise creation's functional integrity would indeed be subverted. Many biblical passages (beyond the scope of this chapter to discuss) suggest that God works in the created order by top-down causation of the system, with the main metaphor being that of God "speaking to" or "commanding" the created order.

The idea of the functional integrity of the created order should not be confused with deism. Deism refers to the idea that God creates the "laws of nature" and then removes himself from any further active involvement in creation. Indeed, this appears to have been Darwin's theological perspective when he was writing *The Origin of Species*, which is consistent with the comments in his letter to Asa Gray. By contrast, as will already be apparent, the perspective presented here is one of Christian theism, the active moment-by-moment involvement of God in the created order, without which nothing would exist and no secondary causes could be considered. Indeed, without that constant sustaining, the concept of the "laws of nature" would not exist either.[24] The "laws of nature" are simply a useful way to describe God's faithfulness in the created order.

God's Providence Does Not Entail Occasionalism

There is an extreme version of micromanagement known as "occasionalism." This is the view that God is the only true cause of events and therefore, in its strongest version, that God's creation is a series of trillions of individual acts of creation joined together. The view was widespread in the Islamic theology of the tenth and eleventh centuries, popularized by al-Ghazālī (c. 1055–1111) in his influential work *The Incoherence of the Philosophers*. The best-known occasionalist in the Western philosophical tradition is Nicolas Malebranche (1638–1715), who claimed, "There is only one true cause because there is only

---

24. L. Jaeger, "The Idea of Law in Science and Religion," *Science and Christian Belief* 20 (2008): 133–46.

one true God. . . . The nature or power of each thing is nothing but the will of God. . . . All natural causes are not *true* causes but only *occasional* causes."[25] For Malebranche, since God is the true cause, all natural causes are merely "occasions" of Divine will.[26]

But the view being presented in this essay is not like that; it represents a seamless cloth of God's authorship and yet maintains the cloth's functional and causal integrity. God causes creatures to be causes that are truly "true causes." That's what functional integrity entails.

God's Providence Does Not Entail Determinism

How can God providentially move human hearts and ensure that the created order fulfills his intentions and purposes without subverting genuine human freedom? The short answer, of course, is that we don't know, although a voluminous amount of literature addresses precisely that point. Unfortunately, some of it has a strong emphasis on providence and sovereignty at the expense of human free will, whereas other offerings downgrade providence in an attempt to defend free will. Such dichotomous extremes are quite unnecessary, and Scripture happily illustrates the realities of both genuine human free will and God's providence on virtually every page, seeing no necessary tension between these two essential aspects of the created order. Clearly, what is a problem to our very limited minds is no problem for God.

"Determinism" in this context may be defined by the thesis that our lives are not really up to us and are constrained to follow one particular future. Conversely, note that it is precisely the nomic regularity of the created order, guaranteed by God's say-so, that renders genuine free will possible. Biologists see free will as a Darwinian trait that all adult humans in good health display in the same way they typically have two arms and two legs. A free will worth having can be defined as "the ability to intentionally choose between courses of action in ways that make us responsible for what we do." A properly working brain enables this ability to prosper, so nomic regularity is crucial. A suitable discussion of free will lies well beyond the scope of this chapter,[27] but free

---

25. "Occasionalism," *Stanford Encyclopedia of Philosophy*, Oct 20. 2008, http://plato.stanford.edu/entries/occasionalism/#NicMal.

26. Jonathan Edwards provides another well-known example of an occasionalist; e.g., see O. D. Crisp, "Jonathan Edwards and Occasionalism," in *Abraham's Dice: Chance and Providence in the Monotheistic Traditions*, ed. K. W. Giberson (Oxford: Oxford University Press, 2016).

27. There is a huge literature on the topic of free will. Books that are in general supportive of the

will is mentioned here simply to reiterate that a created order constantly sustained by the creator God is needed for genuine free will. Free will is one of God's great gifts to humanity. Without it genuine love and morality would be equally impossible. It is a consequence, not a casualty, of the nomic regularity guaranteed in God's created order.

Providence and Evolution

For some the theory of evolution is incompatible with the idea of God's providential working in the created order. That view is mistaken, although it is much easier to demonstrate now than it was at the time of Darwin since our understanding of evolutionary history is so much greater.

Darwin had to cope with the accusation that his theory was dependent on chance, and indeed the word "chance" does crop up a lot in *On the Origin of Species*. As Darwin wrote, "Variation is a very slow process, and natural selection can do nothing until favourable variations *chance to occur*" (emphasis added). John Herschel (1792–1871), a mathematician, astronomer, and polymath, was one of the most famous natural philosophers (scientists) of his era and referred to by Darwin in the *Origin* as "one of our greatest philosophers." This helps explain why Darwin was so upset when Herschel, having read the *Origin*, referred to Darwin's new theory as the "law of higgledy-piggledy."[28] In Darwin's mind, however, natural selection was like a law imposed by God upon the properties of matter. This is clear from his "sketch" of 1842 in which Darwin outlined his ideas that later became *On the Origin of Species*. In the sketch Darwin wrote, "We must look at every complicated mechanism and instinct, as the summary of a long history of useful contrivances, much like a work of art. . . . It accords with what we know of the law impressed on matter by the Creator, that the creation and extinction of forms, like the birth and death of individuals should be the effect of secondary [laws] means."[29]

Despite Darwin's view that natural selection reflected a law-like orderly

assertions made all too briefly here, albeit written from contrasting perspectives, include: D. R. Alexander, *Genes, Determinism and God* (Cambridge: Cambridge University Press, 2017); P. G. H. Clarke, *All in the Mind? Challenges of Neuroscience to Faith and Ethics* (Oxford: Lion, 2015); J. Baggini, *Freedom Regained: The Possibility of Free Will* (London: Granta, 2015); Alfred R. Mele, *Surrounding Free Will: Philosophy, Psychology, Neuroscience* (Oxford: Oxford University Press, 2015).

28. T. V. Carey, "John Herschel," *Philosophy Now* 48 (October/November 2004), 32–35.

29. Darwin, *The Foundations of the Origins of Species, a Sketch Written in 1842* (Cambridge: Cambridge University Press, 1909), 51. Darwin's ideas about chance changed through his lifetime and

process, evolution was frequently presented as a "theory of chance" in the years that followed the publication of the *Origin*. How this perspective changed has much to do with the so-called neo-Darwinian synthesis, the process whereby natural selection was baptised into population genetics in the 1920s and 1930s. Today we find Richard Dawkins explaining in the preface of *The Blind Watchmaker* that one of the reasons for writing the book was to combat the "myth" that evolution is a theory of chance:

> Take, for instance, the issue of "chance," often dramatized as *blind* chance. The great majority of people that attack Darwinism leap with almost unseemly eagerness to the mistaken idea that there is nothing other than random chance in it. Since living complexity embodies the very antithesis of chance, if you think that Darwinism is tantamount to chance you'll obviously find it easy to refute Darwinism! One of my tasks will be to destroy this eagerly believed myth that Darwinism is a theory of "chance."[30] .

How can Dawkins be so sure that Darwinism is not a theory of "chance"? There are many different aspects of the evolutionary process that illustrate Dawkins's point. Here we will mention just four.

First, and most important, is the process of natural selection itself. The genome of an organism, the sum of the information contained in its DNA, is subject to continual change. Changes can happen through a wide range of mechanisms, including point mutations, deletions, insertions, duplications, and many of these changes occur during DNA replication. As DNA is replicated, proofreading enzymes check the sequence and correct any errors, but occasionally, like any proofreader, they miss some errors, so the daughter cells contain new DNA that is slightly different from the parental DNA. A major cause of variation also results from sexual reproduction. During the formation of the germ cells (in the process known as meiosis), the paired diploid chromosomes are reduced to just one of each pair in each germ cell, randomly distributing any single chromosome from either the mother or the father to the germ cell in the process. Before separation occurs, the pair of chromosomes

a thorough analysis of his views can be found in C. N. Johnson, *Darwin's Dice: The Idea of Chance in the Thought of Charles Darwin* (New York: Oxford University Press, 2014).

30. R. Dawkins, *The Blind Watchmaker* (London: Penguin, 1991), xv, emphasis original.

snuggle up to each other and exchange ("recombine") little stretches of DNA nucleotide sequences. So there are two different kinds of variation arising from this process: from the random assortment of chromosomes to the germ cells and from the exchange of genetic material between chromosomes. Therefore, the set of single chromosomes (one to twenty-three for the human) in each germ cell is not quite like either parent.

The slightly different DNA in the progeny will then lead to offspring that may be more "fit" from an evolutionary perspective, meaning more likely to pass their particular sets of gene variants on to more progeny in the future. That's the process known as natural selection—the testing out of variant genomes in the workshop of life to see which are most successful at generating organisms that are evolutionarily fit in a particular ecological niche.

Changes come into the genome randomly in the sense that the changes come about without respect to the well-being or otherwise of the organism— the main meaning of the word "random" in the context of evolutionary biology. As it happens, mutations are not random in the strictly mathematical sense; they occur with equal probability throughout the genome,[31] although that makes little difference here. If we knew enough about the molecular details of the system in principle if not in practice, then we might be able to predict where the next replication error might occur in the genome in a given cell. But other mutations occur due to the decay of a radioisotope somewhere in the solar system. And radioactive decay is described by quantum theory, meaning that it is impossible in principle, not just in practice, to know when a particular radioactive particle might cause a change in the genetic letter sequence in a particular genome. But note that, as far as the overall process of evolution is concerned, it really doesn't matter how variation comes into the genome, whether by predictable or unpredictable processes, because in every case natural selection will exert its stringent winnowing effect, acting like a sieve to allow the propagation of variant genomes for the development of the fittest organisms. In evolutionary biology, in the balance between chance and necessity, it is necessity that wins in the end.

A *second* important observation subverts the notion that evolutionary history is a process dependent on chance. As we consider the 3.8 billion years

31. L. C. Francioli, P. P. Polak, A. Koren, et al., "Genome-Wide Patterns and Properties of De Novo Mutations in Humans," in *Nat Genet* 47 (2015): 822–26; K. Chan and D. A. Gordenin, "Clusters of Multiple Mutations: Incidence and Molecular Mechanisms," *Annu Rev Genet* 49 (2015): 243–67.

of evolution, the striking increase in biological complexity is obvious. For the first 2.5 billion years of life on earth, things only rarely got bigger than one millimetre across, about the size of a pin-head. There were no birds, no flowers, no animals wandering around, no fish in the sea, but at the genetic level there was a lot going on, namely, the generation of many of the genes and biochemical systems later used to build the bigger, more interesting living things we see around us today. As a biochemist, I would be fascinated to travel in a time-machine back to when living things were only one millimetre across, although I think most people would find the planet pretty boring at that time. But then gradually the oxygen levels in the atmosphere increased by photo-synthesis to the point at which more complex life-forms could be sustained.

Once multicellularity got going in evolutionary history, then living things started getting bigger, but initially not by much. With the flourishing of the late Ediacaran fauna (named after the Australian hills where their fossils were first found) 575–543 million years ago, we move into the centimetre scale. Only in the so-called "Cambrian explosion" 525–505 million years ago did the size of animals begin to increase dramatically. In the Cambrian explosion, there was an "explosion" of new animal life forms and body plans that began to appear, and from these derived virtually all the animals we are now familiar with. Today we have creatures like ourselves with brains with 10^{11} neurons with their 10^{14} synaptic connections or more, the most complex known entities in the universe.

As the evolutionary biologist Sean Carroll from the University of Wisconsin-Madison remarks in a *Nature* review:

Life's contingent history could be viewed as an argument against any direction or pattern in the course of evolution or the shape of life. But it is obvious that larger and more complex life forms have evolved from simple unicellular ancestors and that various innovations were necessary for the evolution of new means of living. This raises the possibility that there are trends within evolutionary history that might reflect the existence of general principles governing the evolution of increasingly larger and more complex forms.[32]

32. S. B. Carroll, "Chance and Necessity: The Evolution of Morphological Complexity and Diversity," in *Nature* 409 (2001): 1102–9.

It is hard to envisage how a genuinely chance process could have led to this marked increase in complexity over the 3.8-billion-year history of evolution. Of course, individual events in this long history might always have been different. But our interest in the present context is not in individual events but in the process taken as a whole. Even mass extinctions, such as the Permian extinction that took place about 251 million years ago in which as many as 80 percent of marine species went extinct,[33] eventually led to increased speciation and diversity soon afterwards as new marine forms of life filled up the ecological niches left by their ancestors. Taken overall, from the origin of life to the present day, the evolutionary narrative is one characterized by increased complexity.

A *third* factor underlining the fact that evolution is far from being a random process comes from physics. In the midst of all the biological diversification and specialization just mentioned, there are certain physical constraints that generate some remarkable morphological and scaling rules, generating allometric laws. To pick just one example, consider Kleiber's Law, which states that the metabolic rate scales in proportion to the three-quarter power as first proposed by the Swiss biologist Max Kleiber in 1932. Since that time there have been literally hundreds of papers disputing, qualifying, and in fact mostly confirming this value, at least for many taxa of animals and plants. For our present purposes, the precise scaling value doesn't really matter; everyone agrees that such a scaling law does indeed exist. Remarkably, Kleiber's Law fits with both the plant and animal species that have evolved over a huge range of geographically and climactically different environments. Furthermore, it is possible to derive the Law mathematically by making various assumptions that impinge on the energetic efficiencies of these organisms. Even though animals can move, whereas plants cannot, the stringent constraints of energy control in both cases have ensured that the size and shapes of both plants and animals have evolved in response to the same mathematical and physical principles.[34]

Other allometric scaling values for biological structures are no less impressive. Body mass in relation to the cross-sectional areas of both mammalian

---

33. S. M. Stanley, "Estimates of the Magnitudes of Major Marine Mass Extinctions in Earth History," in *Proc Natl Aca Sci USA* 113 (2016): E6325–34.

34. J. R. Banavar et al., "Form, Function, and Evolution of Living Organisms," *Proc Natl Acad Sci USA* 111 (2014): 3332–37.

aorta and tree trunks, scales at three-quarters, as in Kleiber's Law. Sophisticated models have attempted to explain such relationships—for example, models based on the fact that living things are sustained by the transport of materials through linear networks that branch to supply all parts of the organism and that, in turn, constrain the basic parameters of being alive, such as body mass and metabolic rate.[35]

So, as we stand back and look at the whole sweep of evolutionary history, we see huge creativity in life and immense diversity, but in a highly organized way in which the morphology of animals and plants is constrained by the physical necessities of living on a planet with light and darkness, this particular gravity, these particular atmospheric conditions at particular times, and particular temperature ranges. So, given carbon-based life, there seem to be only so many ways of living on planet earth.

A *fourth* point that subverts the idea that overall evolution is a process of chance is the ubiquitous nature of convergent evolution. Much has been written on this topic, partly by Richard Dawkins in his book *The Ancestor's Tale*,[36] but most of all by Simon Conway Morris, Professor of Evolutionary Palaeobiology at Cambridge.[37] This point refers to the repeated but independent development of the same biochemical pathway, organ, or structure in distinct evolutionary lineages. In other words, as animals or plants face the challenges of adapting to particular environments at independent times and in independent circumstances, the evolutionary process has converged on the same adaptive solution, generating remarkably similar ways of meeting the challenge in hundreds of cases. Some of these adaptations are so spookily similar that it's difficult to believe that one species did not evolve from the other, but such is not the case.

Hundreds of examples could be given of convergence. Probably the best-known example of all is the evolution of the eye, which has evolved independently multiple times in quite different evolutionary lineages, perhaps

---

35. G. B. West, J. H. Brown, and B. J. Enquist, "A General Model for the Origin of Allometric Scaling Laws in Biology," *Science* 276 (1997): 1222–26.

36. R. Dawkins, *The Ancestor's Tale: A Pilgrimage to the Dawn of Life*, 2nd ed. (London: Weidenfeld & Nicolson, 2016).

37. Simon Conway Morris, *Life's Solution: Inevitable Humans in a Lonely Universe* (Cambridge: Cambridge University Press, 2003); Morris, *The Runes of Evolution: How the Universe Became Self-Aware* (West Conshohocken, PA: Templeton, 2015). Morris's research group has also developed the remarkable Map-of-Life website that highlights many examples of convergence. See www.mapoflife.org.

more than forty times.[38] The camera eyes of cephalopods like squid and octopus and the eyes of vertebrates are remarkably similar in their structural features. If you live on a planet of light and darkness, then you are very likely to get eyes at some stage of evolution. The adaptive advantages are huge and obvious. This even led Dawkins to suggest that evolution is "progressive," a notion that Darwin himself found problematic. Dawkins writes, "The cumulative build-up of complex adaptations like eyes, strongly suggests a version of progress—especially when coupled in imagination with some of the wonderful products of convergent evolution."[39]

Taken overall, evolution is a tightly constrained process. The late Harvard evolutionary biologist Stephen Jay Gould famously likened evolution to a drunk on a pavement, staggering around in a random manner. But the point about a pavement is that it's a very constrained space. In a commentary on Gould's idea of ultimate randomness in evolutionary history, Conway Morris writes that it is

> now widely thought that the history of life is little more than a contingent muddle punctuated by disastrous mass extinctions that in spelling the doom of one group so open the doors of opportunity to some other mob of lucky-chancers. . . . Rerun the tape of the history of life . . . and the end result will be an utterly different biosphere. Most notably there will be nothing remotely like a human. . . . Yet, what we know of evolution suggests the exact reverse: convergence is ubiquitous and the constraints of life make the emergence of the various biological properties (e.g. intelligence) very probable, if not inevitable.[40]

There is what Conway Morris calls a "hyperspace" of possibilities of being alive on planet earth, and the "task" of evolution is to find those spaces.[41] "Convergence offers a metaphor as to how evolution navigates the combinatorial immensities of biological 'hyperspace.'"[42]

---

38. L. Salvini-Plawen and E. Mayr, "On the Evolution of Photoreceptors and Eyes," *Evolutionary Biology* 10 (1977): 207–63.

39. Dawkins, *The Ancestor's Tale*, 568.

40. Conway Morris, *Life's Solution*, 127.

41. "Hyperspace" in this context refers to all those ecological niches and their accompanying set of living things which are well-adapted to living in a particular niche.

42. Conway Morris, *Life's Solution*, 127.

The rolling of the genetic dice is a wonderful way of generating both novelty and diversity, but at the same time it appears to be restrained by necessity to a relatively limited number of living entities that can flourish in particular ecological niches. If you live in a universe with this kind of physics and chemistry and on a planet with these particular properties, then this is what you are likely to get. Biological diversity is definitely not a case of "anything can happen." Only some things can happen, not in a deterministic way but in a highly constrained way.

There are many other examples illustrating the highly ordered process that we know as evolutionary history, but space limitations prevent listing them. In the light of the robustly theistic Trinitarian doctrine of creation that we have already outlined, a highly constrained and organized, albeit not deterministic, evolutionary process seems consistent with a God who has intentions and purposes for the world, a providential God who, as the hymn-writer Arthur Ainger wrote in 1894, "is working his purposes out as year succeeds to year."

Chance, Randomness, and Providence

As already mentioned, the word "random" in the context of evolutionary biology generally refers to the genetic variation that occurs without the good or ill of a living organism in mind. This is very different from the definition of "random" in other fields of enquiry like statistics or probability theory. A good indication of randomness is when events occur that provide no basis for the predictability of future events by a judicious observer examining the same system. Quantum technologies are generating new ways of ensuring genuine randomness in fields such as cryptography.[43] But new variation that enters the genome never even approaches randomness in that sense. The human genome contains 3.2 billion base pairs. If mutations were truly random in this mathematical sense, then they would be expected to occur with equal probability throughout the genome prior to any process of selection. But in reality they are clustered in areas of the genome that are more prone to mutations than other regions for a variety of reasons.[44] And if an organism such as yeast is

43. A. Acin, and L. Masanes, "Certified Randomness in Quantum Physics," in *Nature* 540 (2016): 213–19.

44. Francioli et al., "Genome-Wide Patterns."

exposed to a mutagen, then once again there is a striking degree of mutational clustering.[45] So it is hard to find any sense in which the evolutionary process is random, except in the trivial sense that genomic variation occurs without the organism in mind—which is not unexpected!

Then what about "chance"? Here we need to distinguish between *epistemological chance* and *ontological chance*. Many examples of epistemological chance have already been provided. Genetic variations in the genome happen in an unpredictable way, at least as far as their specific locations in the genome are concerned, although general predictions about the regions where they happen with higher frequency can be made based on previous data sets. In any event, there are perfectly good reasons why mutations happen when and where they do happen (e.g., during cell replication). But due to the complexity of the system, it is impossible for human observers to know where the mutation will occur. The chance is associated with the incapability of humans to make predictions; hence, it is "epistemological" chance.

Ontological chance refers to chance arising from the properties of elementary particles, properties that are best described by the theory of quantum mechanics. Most (but not all) physicists believe that quantum events are unpredictable in principle and not just in practice. We have already cited the example of radiation which causes mutations and where the timing of the emission of radioactive particles is unknowable in principle and not just in practice. But also, as already noted, it makes no difference whether variation comes into the genome via what we call epistemological or ontological chance as far as evolution is concerned. In both cases natural selection still exerts its powerful winnowing effects.

It is not at all unusual to find processes that depend on chance with determined outcomes. Consider, for example, the national lottery. All those little balls with numbers on bouncing around in the machine are fulfilling their purpose, designed by the government, to take money from the poor,[46] make a few people rich, give out money to lots of good causes (which often benefit the rich), and in the process (in the UK context) generate a handy 12 percent tax for the government. A chance process is used to generate outcomes that

---

45. Chan and Gordenin, "Clusters of Multiple Mutations."

46. John Wihbey, "Who Plays the Lottery, and Why: Updated Collection of Research," Journalist's Resource, http://journalistsresource.org/studies/economics/personal-finance/research-review-lotteries-demographics; Paul Bickley, "The National Lottery: Is It Progressive?" *Theos* (2009), http://www.theosthinktank.co.uk/files/files/Reports/NationalLotteryreport.pdf.

are absolutely certain. If someone does not win the jackpot this week, then they certainly will next week or the week after. Many charities will definitely benefit, and the government will definitely receive its 12 percent. Chance processes are by no means incompatible with determined outcomes.

It is also interesting to see what Scripture says about chance or randomness. The answer is "not much." But when such concepts are mentioned, there is no doubt that God is providentially involved in the outcome. When the prophet Micaiah predicted that King Ahab would be killed in battle at Ramoth Gilead (1 Kgs 22:15–28), this indeed came to pass, but it happened by someone who "drew his bow *at random* and hit the king of Israel between the sections of his armour" (1 Kgs 22:34, emphasis added). As Proverbs 16:33 so vividly puts the point,

> The lot is cast into the lap,
>> but its every decision is from the Lord.

The Bible sees God's works occurring equally in all the various manifestations of his activity, whether in the more "law-like" workings of the natural world (Ps 33:6–11), in chance events (Prov 16:33), or in his control of the weather (Ps 148:8), which we describe today using chaos theory. There is never a hint in the Bible that certain types of events in the natural world are any more or any less the activity of God than other events.

So does it make any difference to our understanding of the providence of God in creation whether the evolutionary process involves the orderly and constrained history that we have been highlighting in contrast to genuine randomness in the more mathematical sense? The short answer is that if the process were genuinely random in the sense that any event was equally probable, then we certainly wouldn't be here and there would be no life on planet earth. But, in reality, we live in a highly ordered universe and the evolutionary process reflects that order. Reading Genesis 1 reminds us that order comes out of disorder through God's creative work. Studying evolutionary processes is helpful in bringing home that message.

Evolution raises plenty of theological questions concerning our understanding of Adam and Eve, the fall, the nature of sin, and especially the question of how the God of love could use a process involving so much pain and suffering to bring about his providential plan in this world. Fortunately, there are plenty of books that tackle these kinds of question as well as websites with useful materials.[47]

Historians have often observed that it was precisely those who were in the Reformed tradition with a strong belief in God's providential working in history and in the world who most readily embraced Darwinian evolution in the late nineteenth century.[48] More than a century later, there seems no reason why this should not still be the case.

47. For example: Michael Murray, *Nature Red in Tooth and Claw: Theism and the Problem of Animal Suffering* (Oxford: Oxford University Press, 2008); C. Southgate, *The Groaning of Creation: God, Evolution, and the Problem of Evil* (Louisville: Westminster John Knox, 2008); D. R. Alexander, *Creation or Evolution: Do We Have to Choose?*, 2nd ed. (Oxford: Monarch, 2014). See also http://biologos. org; http://www.cis.org.uk; and http://network.asa3.org.

48. J. Moore, *The Post-Darwinian Controversies: A Study of the Protestant Struggle to Come to Terms with Darwin in Great Britain and America, 1870–1900* (Cambridge: Cambridge University Press, 1981); D. N. Livingstone, *Darwin's Forgotten Defenders: The Encounter between Evangelical Theology and Evolutionary Thought* (Edinburgh: Scottish Academic, 1987).

Chapter FIFTEEN

"The Trees of the Field Shall Clap Their Hands" (Isaiah 55:12)

What Does It Mean to Say That a Tree Praises God?

MARK HARRIS

The question in my title raises a basic question for the theology of creation—about "nature" as a theological reality in its own right. The question is whether such a reality is entitled to respond to its Creator in the way that humans do, by means of praise.[1]

Humans are as much a part of creation as any other creature.[2] One might expect this to be so obvious as to hardly need saying. But our habit (in the Western world at least) of assuming a marked separation from the nonhuman world of "nature," a habit fed by centuries of scientific and technological achievement, suggests that we do not see creation as a level playing field. Any appraisal of creation as a theological theme should pay careful attention to the relationship between humans and nature, for better or worse. The

---

1. Answering this question in the affirmative leads to an even more intriguing question, namely whether nonhuman creatures are entitled to choose (like humans) whether they praise their Creator. Since this question engages with complex philosophical discussions concerning human free will, it is unfortunately beyond the scope of this chapter.

2. A note on terminology: by "creation" I mean everything that has been created by the Creator, i.e., the entire universe (and anything that lies beyond which is not the Creator), including the entire human world. I use the term "creature" to refer to all created entities, whether animate or inanimate, animal, vegetable, or mineral (including humans). "Nature" is a notoriously imprecise term, but throughout this chapter I use it to refer to all physical entities in the created universe *except for humans* and their social, cultural, and intellectual worlds.

contemporary environmental crisis has brought an added degree of urgency to this appraisal; our scientific and technological achievements have too often been played out irreversibly in destructive and exploitative behaviour of the natural world. In this, anthropocentrism has been singled out for particular blame. In his celebrated encyclical of 2015, *Laudato si'*, Pope Francis addresses the question of an appropriate Christian response to the prospect of ecological catastrophe. Highlighting the dangers of our "excessive anthropocentrism," which prizes "technical thought over reality," Francis urges us to pay a "renewed attention to reality and the limits it imposes."[3] Francis's point seems to be that we have lost sight of "reality." Seduced by the onwards march of science and technology, we have come to assume that we have attained a legitimate mastery over nature. I leave it to Francis and others to assess the ethical rights and wrongs of this situation; my own concern is to dig deeper, to examine the "reality" of nature assumed by modern theologies of creation. I will do this by paying special attention to a woefully neglected set of biblical texts found largely in the Psalms and Isaiah (such as the text in my title), which provide a potentially different perspective on this "reality" by including all creatures (not just humans) into the worshipping life of God.[4] I will argue that these texts of nature's praise indicate the need for a distinct theology *of nature*, rather than just more creation thought or more theological anthropology; consequently, I will use them to set out some of the key building blocks for such a theology of nature.

The title of Pope Francis's encyclical is highly apposite, since, in echoing the refrain of Saint Francis of Assisi's *Canticle of the Sun*, it evokes the very same possibility of a universal worshipping "reality" as do the biblical texts: "Praise be to you (*Laudato si'*), my Lord, through all your creatures." Saint Francis is famous for his deep affinity with nature, and the *Canticle* demonstrates

---

3. Pope Francis, *Laudato si'*, §115–16. (Text available at https://laudatosi.com/watch.)

4. Note that most of the British authors writing in this area have tended to refer to this motif of all creatures praising God as "creation's praise": Richard Bauckham, "Joining Nature's Praise of God," *Ecotheology* 7 (2002): 45–59; Bauckham, "Creation's Praise of God in the Book of Revelation," *Biblical Theology Bulletin* 38 (2008): 55–63; Dominic Coad, "Creation's Praise of God: A Proposal for a Theology of the Non-Human Creation," *Theology* 112 (2009): 181–89; David G. Horrell, *The Bible and the Environment: Towards a Critical Ecological Biblical Theology* (London: Equinox, 2010); David G. Horrell and Dominic Coad, "'The stones would cry out' (Luke 19:40): A Lukan Contribution to a Hermeneutics of Creation's Praise," *Scottish Journal of Theology* 64 (2011): 29–44. For myself, I prefer to call this "nature's praise," because of my concern to formulate a distinct theology of nature apart from special human issues. Indeed, "nature's praise" was the term used by Fretheim in the title of his pioneering paper of 1987, "Nature's Praise of God in the Psalms," *Ex Auditu* 3 (1987): 16–30.

that this affinity arose not simply from love of the wildlife with which he is so often pictured, but from a unified theological vision. Inanimate creatures (including the four elements) feature prominently in Saint Francis's *Canticle*, and he tells us that God is to be praised through Brother Sun and Sister Moon, through Brothers Wind and Air, Sister Water, Brother Fire, Mother Earth, and even through our sister bodily Death. These striking images are presumably Saint Francis's very own, but they are reminiscent of the venerable biblical tradition found especially in the Psalms and Second Isaiah, where all of God's creatures—even those without consciousness such as hills, valleys, snows, frost, and trees—express joyful praise of their Creator.[5] For instance, Isaiah encourages created entities that are not normally associated with deliberate and conscious actions to praise God the Creator in the most jubilant of terms:

> Sing for joy, you heavens, for the LORD has done this;
>> shout aloud, you earth beneath.
> Burst into song, you mountains,
>> you forests and all your trees. (Isa 44:23)[6]

Mindful of Pope Francis's injunction to renew our attention to "reality" in the face of our "excessive anthropocentrism," how should we interpret such a text? Its literary form (Hebrew poetry) raises difficult reality questions to begin with, but at least two options present themselves. First, we could interpret the text as a metaphorical account of *human* praise upon perceiving the created wonders of the mountains and trees. Or, second, we could suppose that the biblical author had a more literal sense in mind, and try to imagine how creatures such as mountains and trees might be said to praise God in and of themselves. The first option is clearly the easiest to adopt. And in support of this option, it is inescapable that this text, and the others like it, make heavy use of anthropomorphic metaphors: creatures are exhorted to praise God through *human* actions such as shouting and singing and to experience the preeminent human emotion associated with praise, namely *joy*.[7] A text that predicts that the mountains and hills shall "burst into song," and the trees of

---

5. E.g., Ps 98:8; 148.

6. Unless otherwise indicated, Scripture quotations in this chapter come from the NIV.

7. E.g., "The desert and the parched land will be glad . . . it will rejoice greatly and shout for joy" (Isa 35:1–2).

the field "clap their hands" (Isa 55:12), for example, is clearly metaphorical to some degree. This point alone might tempt us to conclude that all we have here is a series of imaginative metaphors expressing *human* praise, and not actually that of the meadows, valleys,[8] and other nonhuman creatures.[9] But in favour of the second option, it is important to remember the immense historical and cultural gulf between our time and that of the formation of the Hebrew Bible. It is possible that the ancient authors had a view of nature very different from us and that they had good theological reasons for it, which we have lost sight of due to the "excessive anthropocentrism" of our times. This point alone might suggest that we should avoid making a snap decision on how to interpret these texts. However, there is more at stake.

These questions cannot be addressed without registering a sea change in biblical scholarly thinking over recent decades, brought about by a growing ecological awareness. Anthropocentric readings of biblical texts are being increasingly questioned for this reason if no other, and commentators have brought a more inclusive, interconnected, and equitable view of creation to bear, a view that is unquestionably borne out by the content of some of the biblical texts of nature's praise themselves (e.g., Ps 148). But this interpretative sea change has by no means solved the problem of whether or how the nonhuman (and especially inanimate) world could be said to praise God, for we still find that our entire understanding of praise is based on it being a *conscious* expression, as is its emotive corollary, joy. In that sense, an inclusive view of creation makes the problem all the more acute, and it becomes all the more tempting to resort to the anthropocentric solution of earlier scholarship whereby the biblical motif of nature's joyful praise is merely a "poetic fancy," that is, it is a metaphor for human praise.[10] It is no doubt the acuteness of this problem that has prompted several British theologians recently to acknowledge the differences between our cultural view of nature and that of the Hebrew Bible, while also warning that any plausible solution must be

---

8. E.g., "The grasslands of the desert overflow; the hills are clothed with gladness. The meadows are covered with flocks and the valleys are mantled with grain; they shout for joy and sing" (Ps 65:12–13).

9. This kind of literary device (a form of personification), where elements from nature are used to express human emotions, is sometimes referred to disparagingly as the "pathetic fallacy." G. B. Caird, *The Language and Imagery of the Bible* (London: Duckworth, 1980), 173.

10. Bauckham, "Joining Nature's Praise," 47; Bauckham, *Bible and Ecology: Rediscovering the Community of Creation* (London: Darton, Longman & Todd, 2010), 79; Elizabeth A. Johnson, *Ask the Beasts: Darwin and the God of Love* (New York: Bloomsbury, 2014), 276.

"non-laughable."[11] Quite. But as a British scientist-theologian myself, I am aware that our infamous British reserve on the one hand, coupled with our famously eccentric sense of humour on the other, do not necessarily gift us with an accurate ability for judging what might count as "non-laughable" on any universal scale. And it is by no means unknown for natural scientists— who are professionally bound to maintain strictly "non-laughable" views of nature—to feel the need to articulate a deep sense of the numinous and the spiritual in nature as they go about their work, quite apart from any concerns for traditional theistic beliefs. Ursula Goodenough's "religious naturalism" is a case in point,[12] as is Jane Goodall's intense awareness of "the being-ness of trees."[13] As a result of all this, I find that I myself am not especially concerned to prioritise "non-laughable" solutions over "laughable" solutions (whatever they may be) but rather to examine the full scope of options open to us.

Although this chapter does not claim to solve the problem of how to interpret the texts of nature's praise definitively, it will make use of them to suggest a way forward towards a theology of nature. Indeed, there is an important sense in which the problem is insoluble within an inclusive view of creation. Nevertheless, I will argue that by resisting anthropocentric solutions an important benefit accrues, namely that a robust theology of nature (independent of humans and their special concerns) begins to take shape, and one that is not just another theological anthropology.

The Form of the Biblical Texts of Nature's Praise

As I have said, the relevant biblical texts are mostly couched in Hebrew poetry, which means that it is tempting to jump immediately to the conclusion that, in facing these texts, we are dealing with "poetic fancy."[14] A less cynical assessment might notice that many of these texts are liturgical at heart.[15] This means that, "poetic fancy" or not, they do not represent rational attempts to explore the motif of nature's praise because *they are already expressions of praise*

---

11. Horrell and Coad, "The stones would cry out," 43; Rachel Muers, "The Holy Spirit, The Voices of Nature and Environmental Prophecy," *Scottish Journal of Theology* 67 (2014): 331–32.

12. Ursula Goodenough, *The Sacred Depths of Nature* (New York: Oxford University Press, 1998).

13. Jane Goodall with Phillip Berman, *Reason for Hope: A Spiritual Journey* (New York: Grand Central, 2000), 73.

14. Fretheim, "Nature's Praise of God in the Psalms," 21.

15. E.g., those texts that fall within the so-called Enthronement Psalms, such as 96:11–12 and 98:7–8.

themselves. This point leads to an initial watertight conclusion before we even examine the texts themselves. Since the praise of nonhuman creatures is already articulated in the Bible in terms of praise, the reader is assumed thereby to be a participant in nature's act of praise, not a neutral observer. This means that any conclusions we make outside this inclusive world of praise—from the distanced and disinterested perspective of historical biblical scholarship, for instance—are deliberate acts of misreading not unlike those anachronisms of which biblical scholars so often warn modern Bible readers. My point is that these texts not only invite but *require* a confessional perspective which takes a theology of nature seriously.

Terence Fretheim is one such commentator who is open to the confessional perspective and who provides a correspondingly theological analysis that I will describe in the next section. For now, he has helpfully provided a comprehensive tabulation of passages that affirm nature's praise from across the whole Bible, classifying them into the categories of theophany, hymn, thanksgiving, lament, and oracle.[16] (Note that hymn is by far the most common category.) David Horrell, on the other hand, classifies the texts more according to their theological function rather than their form.[17] Many of the texts of nature's praise, he points out, are invocations: they exhort the nonhuman creation to praise God joyfully, and while some give the reason as God's transcendent glory,[18] many others have a more eschatological orientation, citing salvation or coming judgement as the reason for praise.[19] Other texts are less encouragements to the nonhuman creation to praise God and more testimonies that it already does so.[20]

We should also note that the literary devices used by the texts of nature's praise vary. Some texts describe nonhuman creation praising God in ways that conjure up a particular natural phenomenon,[21] but most use blatantly anthropomorphic language (the literary device known as personification),[22]

---

16. Fretheim, *God and World in the Old Testament: A Relational Theology of Creation* (Nashville: Abingdon, 2005), 267–68.

17. Horrell, *The Bible and the Environment*, 55.

18. E.g., Ps 148.

19. E.g., Pss 96; 98; Isa 44:23.

20. E.g., Ps 65:11–13 (Hebrew vv. 12–14).

21. E.g., the earth quaking (Ps 99:1) or the sea roaring (Ps 98:7).

22. Hilary Marlow, "'The Hills Are Alive!' The Personification of Nature in the Psalter," in *Leshon Limmudim: Essays on the Language and Literature of the Hebrew Bible in Honour of A. A. Macintosh*, ed. David A. Baer and Robert P. Gordon (New York: Bloomsbury, 2013), 189–203.

especially based on singing, shouting, or proclaiming.[23] This anthropomorphism/personification is an inescapable feature of the texts, somewhat overlooked by those interpreters who claim that creation praises God by "simply being itself," as we shall see.

Psalm 19 is a particularly revealing example of the use of anthropomorphisms in these texts, since the psalmist appears to recognise the reality-problem they raise. The psalm begins by testifying that the heavens "declare the glory of God" (v.1 [Hebrew v. 2]). The focus then settles upon the day and the night, and upon the sun, and its reliable rising and setting (vv. 4–6 [Hebrew vv. 5–7]). This in turn is connected immediately with *torah*, the "law of Yahweh" (v. 7 [Hebrew v. 8]). Clearly, this text is evidence of early belief in the idea we now refer to as the "laws of nature," and here the theological roots of the idea are made explicit, since *torah* is given by the divine lawgiver and connected with the *torah* that also governs humans. From that point of view, this psalm may be seen as an ancient example of the venerable argument from design, that the order and regularity of the natural world is evidence of its Creator. Of greater interest, though, is that this psalm explicitly recognises the problem of anthropomorphic language in expressing nature's praise:

> Day to day pours forth speech
>> and night to night declares knowledge.
> There is no speech, nor are there words;
>> their voice is not heard;
> yet their voice goes out through all the earth,
>> and their words to the end of the world.
>> (Ps 19:2–4 NRSV [Hebrew vv. 3–5])

The psalmist appears to have understood exactly the reality problem that troubles modern commentators concerning these texts: nature has no literal human words to express the glory of God, and its "voice" cannot be heard by us ("there is no speech, nor are there words; their voice is not heard"), and yet, the psalmist insists, natural elements such as the day and the night are active in communicating the glory and the knowledge of God ("yet their voice goes out . . . their words . . ."). In other words, the psalmist admits openly that

---

23. E.g., Isa 42:11; Jer 51:48.

nature's praise cannot be articulated literally (from a human standpoint), but maintains that it is no less real for that, and so we must resort to metaphor and specifically to anthropomorphism. Therefore, I suggest that this psalm should be seen less as an early example of the argument from design and more as an early recognition of the reality problem raised by nature's praise. Moreover, we should note that, while recognising the problem, *the psalm continues to insist that nature praises God* and thus that nature testifies of divine *torah* to humankind. And I further suggest that this point undermines our human temptation to seek a quick answer to the reality question by reading the texts of nature's praise simply as a form of "poetic fancy" referring to human praise alone. This highly anthropocentric solution was no doubt open to the psalmist, but, at least in this case of Psalm 19, the psalmist appears to have rejected it.

Having outlined the form of the texts, and the important role of the anthropomorphisms, I will now describe three contemporary approaches to the reality problem in order to then set out the main scope of interpretation.

Three Contrasting Approaches

In order to demonstrate the latitude of interpretation, I will concentrate on three commentators in particular (Fretheim, Bauckham, and Horrell). While each of these operates within the historical-critical paradigm of biblical scholarship (and thus attempts to determine what the original authors meant to say), it is notable that they nevertheless find very different interpretations of the "reality" at stake in the texts of nature's praise.

Terence Fretheim (1987)

I see Fretheim as representative of what I will later refer to as the "relational" interpretation.[24]

Fretheim has done much to set the whole agenda for study of the texts of nature's praise. When his ground-breaking 1987 paper was published, he could honestly say, "I know of no scholarly article written on just this topic; in fact, consideration of a biblical theology of nature as distinct from creation is quite uncommon."[25] Even now this is still a somewhat neglected topic. And

---

24. Note that chapter 8 of Fretheim's 2005 book is almost identical to his 1987 paper, and I will follow his original 1987 paper here.

25. Fretheim, "Nature's Praise of God," 16.

yet commentators have never been entirely silent, and Fretheim was able to list five distinct categories in his history of the interpretation of these texts:[26]

1. Outright praise inspired by (or parallel to) the biblical texts. Saint Francis's aforementioned *Canticle of the Sun* provides just such an example.
2. Allegorical interpretations. Frequented by medieval commentators, the nonhuman creatures who praise God stand for various types of *human* character.
3. Eschatological interpretations. The texts are taken to describe characteristics of the new heaven and earth of the eschatological future, when all creatures will be able to praise as humans do now.
4. Polemical interpretations. The biblical writers were deliberately opposing the astral cults and idolatry of other ancient Near Eastern religions by giving nonhuman creatures (the sun, moon, stars, wood, stone) a place in the natural order as givers (not objects) of praise.
5. Panpsychism. The biblical writers are assumed to have seen human and nonhuman creatures alike in terms of "a 'psychic whole' in which all of nature is permeated by a diffused awareness."[27] Thus the texts of nature's praise relate a kind of prescientific or primitive animism, whereby all created things, even the sticks and stones, possess an innate consciousness or spirit of their own.

Fretheim's own solution borrows elements from all five, while also pointing to a new way forward. Steering close to the wind of a panpsychic reading, he suggests that the texts indicate an "inwardness or interiority" in the relationship between God and natural phenomena, such that there is "a greater continuity between the animate and the inanimate than we have commonly been willing to claim."[28] Fretheim develops this in a number of ways.[29] First, he points to the numerous nature metaphors used for God in the Bible. If it is in some sense true to say that God is a rock (or light, water, wind, etc.), then it is equally true to say that a rock reflects the reality of God in its very existence. The biblical

---

26. Fretheim, "Nature's Praise of God," 17–21.
27. Fretheim, "Nature's Praise of God," 20.
28. Fretheim, "Nature's Praise of God," 21.
29. Fretheim, "Nature's Praise of God," 22–25.

motif of nature's praise uses nature metaphors to make essentially this point. Second, the fact that so many of the texts are calls to praise indicates that a response is required. God calls nonhuman creatures to fulfil their divine potential and thereby to witness to others. Third, the tradition of theophany in the Hebrew Bible shares many common features with the texts of nature's praise. When God's epiphany is told, the earth quakes, the heavens rain down, and the mountains and hills skip, in much the same way that these nonhuman creatures are said to rejoice in praise of God. Fretheim thus suggests that nature is bound closely to God by a mutual interaction, of which nature's praise is but one manifestation.

Having made these points, Fretheim's conclusions are tentative. He speaks of the "symbiosis" between human and nonhuman praise and of the many ways in which nature provides inspiration for human praise.[30] But having asserted numerous times that nature praises God in and of itself, he is reluctant to explore just *how* this might be in terms that our scientifically informed conception of nature might understand. It is possible that Fretheim has in mind the explanation that I turn to next, whereby nonhuman creatures are said to praise God simply by "being themselves,"[31] but viewing creatures' praise as evidence of their *relationship* with God—a relationship which is facilitated by "a certain inwardness" of every creature—is highly suggestive of a more panpsychist solution.[32] Fretheim is (in *my* final analysis, at least) difficult to pin down on the important reality question of just *how* the creatures praise God, while enriching the reality question's theological consequences.

Richard Bauckham (2002)

Richard Bauckham stands for the "simply being itself" interpretation (after Bauckham's own words).

Like Fretheim, Bauckham advocates the idea that nature's praise should act as a corrective to our anthropocentrism and should inspire our own praise. Also like Fretheim, Bauckham cites Saint Francis as a prominent example. But unlike Fretheim, Bauckham clarifies how the nonhuman creatures express their praise of God:

---

30. Fretheim, "Nature's Praise of God," 28.
31. E.g., "In this interaction with God the creatures become more of what they are or have the potential of becoming" (Fretheim, "Nature's Praise of God," 23).
32. Fretheim, "Nature's Praise of God," 27.

The passages about nature's praise are, of course, metaphorical: they attribute to non-human creatures the human practice of praising God in human language. But the reality to which they point is that all creatures bring glory to God simply by being themselves and fulfilling their God-given roles in God's creation. A lily does not need to do anything specific in order to praise God; still less need it be conscious of anything. Simply by being and growing it praises God.[33]

Bauckham appears to have no sympathies for Fretheim's more panpsychist solution. Instead, Bauckham is clear that the texts of nature's praise speak of the essential capacity of nonhuman creatures to praise God *simply by doing what comes naturally*. If it is "distinctively human" (i.e., natural) for us to praise God through conscious vocal expression, it is equally as natural for a frog to praise God by its jumping, feeding, mating, and croaking.[34] If we are unable to see this, Bauckham suggests, it is because we have isolated ourselves from nature by instrumentalising it:

> To recognize nature's praise is to abandon an instrumental view of nature. All creatures exist for God's glory, and we learn to see the non-human creatures in that way, to glimpse their value for God that has nothing to do with their usefulness to us, as we learn to join them in their own glorification of God.[35]

In Bauckham's view, nature's praise provides a valuable lesson in humility for humankind, particularly in the face of the ecological crisis. Accordingly, Bauckham goes on to develop a view of creation that eliminates hierarchy (e.g., the idea that humans are the special "priests of creation") and that sees the praise of creation in fully inclusive terms. Nonhuman creatures are fellow worshippers of God, and they do not need humans to voice their praise for them.

This is all well said, but I find difficulties in Bauckham's suggestion that creation praises God by "simply being itself." According to his logic, humans (like frogs) must join in the praise of God through what comes

---

33. Bauckham, "Joining Nature's Praise," 47.
34. Bauckham, "Joining Nature's Praise," 48.
35. Bauckham, "Joining Nature's Praise," 49.

naturally, whether or not they do it consciously or vocally. After all, vocal expression is only one component of what it means to be myself as a natural human being. Therefore, I am praising God by sipping this cup of coffee. I am praising God at this keyboard, wondering with an increasing sense of uncertainty whether those who uphold the "non-laughable" criterion might not have a point after all. I am praising God by my "human nature"—that which evolution has equipped me for naturally—including acts of selfishness and aggression to protect my own, perhaps even including those regarded as "sinful" in the Christian tradition (and therefore which would be regarded as going against my created nature). But all of these are literal acts of praise according to the logic of Bauckham's system, but they hardly ring true (to me at least). Hence, in spite of Bauckham's insistence upon a level playing field between humans and nonhumans, a gulf begins to open up again once we apply his model evenhandedly to humans. I, for one, find myself suspecting that this definition of praise, whereby creatures praise God simply by being themselves, is too platitudinous to hold up to scrutiny, at least where humans are concerned.

David Horrell (2010)

David Horrell represents the "eschatological" interpretation of the texts of nature's praise.

Horrell criticizes Bauckham's understanding of nature's praise like I did, asking what it means in our scientifically informed world "to say that a dog or cat praises God in its barking or miaowing?"[36] Moreover, Horrell points out that the texts of nature's praise never quite say that creatures worship God just by being themselves. There is too much exuberance and extravagance in these texts instead, not to mention the almost ubiquitous anthropomorphisms; such elements hardly qualify for saying that the creatures are just "being themselves."

Horrell does not reject outright Bauckham's suggestion that the creatures praise God by "being themselves," but he believes that any ecotheological assessment of nature's praise should also account for biblical texts where creation is represented as groaning in travail and waiting for eschatological redemption (Rom 8:19–23).[37] In other words, the praising texts must be balanced by "groaning"

---

36. Horrell, *The Bible and the Environment*, 55.
37. Horrell, *The Bible and the Environment*, 134.

texts,[38] raising the problem of suffering in creation—suffering caused by the ecological crisis but also (and more generally) by the process of evolution.[39] If there is any sense in which creatures might experience joy in God the Creator, then they also experience pain on account of God's work of creation. Therefore, we find that the difficulty of understanding how the nonhuman creation might be said to praise God is matched by the equivalent difficulty of understanding how this God may be said to preside over a natural world of suffering, pain, and death, some of which, it must be said, is caused by human sin, carelessness, and exploitation. For Horrell, the overall solution must be to take an eschatological view (which is, indeed, the view of Romans 8), where "both human and non-human praise strain forwards, anticipating an eschatological consummation in which the ambiguities of suffering will be no more."[40]

I see advantages and disadvantages to Horrell's approach. For on the one hand, his solution reflects the eschatological flavour of a number of the relevant texts, which speak of God's coming judgement (e.g., Pss 96; 98). But on the other hand, Horrell's approach pushes the reality question into the unknown temporal future where it is automatically less troubling. There is also the question of whether we are right to suppose that the biblical authors were exercised over the question of suffering in nature in the way that recent discussions in the science-and-religion field have been, motivated by the impact of evolutionary science. And it is unclear whether it is hermeneutically appropriate to read the praising and groaning texts alongside each other, almost as though they are part of the same literary and theological phenomenon. For myself, I believe that a robust biblical theology of nature needs to be established first (which is partly the aim of this chapter), in order to push the interpretation of these texts forward.

Clearly, the texts of nature's praise raise multivalent theological questions, for which no single response has yet found comprehensive answers. Accordingly, in the next section I suggest that a theology of nature built on these studies must employ this ambiguity positively.

---

38. And there is a substantial number of such texts, especially if we include the motif of nature mourning (e.g., Isa 24:4; 33:9; Jer 4:23–28; 12:4, 11; 23:10; Hos 4:3; Joel 1:10), as discussed by Bauckham (*Bible and Ecology*, 92) and Marlow ("The Hills Are Alive!" 189–90). Muers also adds to this list some texts which describe nonhuman creatures taking a stand for justice, such as Hab 2:11–12 (Muers, "The Holy Spirit," 330).

39. Horrell and Coad, "The stones would cry out," 41.

40. Horrell, *The Bible and the Environment*, 135.

The Scope of Interpretation

As I have said, in his ground-breaking 1987 paper, Fretheim listed five categories for the interpretation of the texts of nature's praise. Fretheim was not, however, concerned to address the reality question that has become so crucial. I therefore suggest a different set of interpretative solutions related to the scientific/naturalistic and theological issues that come to the fore in attempting to discern the reality underneath the texts. Four such solutions are immediately apparent:

A. *Personificational.* The texts are exuberant and metaphorical expressions of human praise or of human joy at the wonder of creation. The nonhuman creatures that express praise in the text are therefore "personifications," rhetorical representations of human persons expressing praise. This option has the advantage that it offers a straightforward solution to the reality question, but its anthropocentrism is extreme. Moreover, my discussion of Psalm 19 suggests that it is not always a persuasive option.

B. *Relational.* This represents Fretheim's conviction that the texts of nature's praise speak of a hidden relationship between the Creator and every creature. Fretheim's own view steers between panpsychism/animism and immanence, but I suggest that his panpsychism/animism should be replaced by "pansacramentalism."[41] In favour of "pansacramentalism" over panpsychism/animism, there is little evidence (beyond these texts) that the biblical authors themselves possessed a panpsychist or animist view of nature, and the persistent biblical polemic against idolatry implies that the authors rejected panpsychism/animism outright anyway. On the other hand, there is certainly positive scriptural evidence of belief in the fundamental sanctity of the natural order.[42]

---

41. "Pansacramentalism" is a term developed by Christopher Knight to describe his (Orthodox-influenced) view that all created things are orientated naturalistically towards the intentions of their Creator (Knight, *The God of Nature: Incarnation and Contemporary Science* [Minneapolis: Fortress, 2007], 31–33). Virginia Stem Owens's conclusion that "the world is one great sacramental loaf" is a similar kind of idea (Owens, *And the Trees Clap Their Hands: Faith, Perception, and the New Physics* [Eugene, OR: Wipf & Stock, 1983], 141).

42. A good example, extensively discussed in recent biblical scholarship, is the "cosmic temple" model of Genesis 1. See Mark Harris, *The Nature of Creation: Examining the Bible and Science* (Durham: Acumen, 2013), 47–48.

C. *"Simply being itself."* The insistence that the texts should be interpreted in terms of each creature praising God through what itself does
naturally as a creature and no more, as represented by Bauckham.[43]

D. *Eschatological.* The suggestion that the praising texts should be
combined with the groaning/mourning texts to point to a future
eschatological answer to the reality question, as represented by Horrell.

All of these solutions have their strengths and weaknesses, as I have
highlighted either here or in the previous section. I do not intend to favour
one option over another, since it is unclear to me that there is anything to be
gained by narrowing down our options. On the contrary, I want to suggest
that there is something to be said for holding all four solutions open as
complements to each other. Solution A reminds us that, rightly or wrongly,
we cannot avoid bringing a human-centred bias to bear. We should therefore
take special caution to make this bias conscious rather than unconscious.
Solution B tells us that the texts of nature's praise do not simply describe
nature *in vacuo*, but they describe creation in a complex web of relational
dependence upon its Creator; in other words, the reality question only has
meaning in a world that is created, sustained, and nurtured by the living
and intimate presence of God in the first place. Solution C reminds us
that the natural order of things *qua* creatures is divinely ordained and, as
such, reflects glory to God. And Solution D reminds us that the theological
relationship between creatures and Creator is not static, and neither has
it reached its *telos*. It must continue to evolve, one day reaching a point of
decisive fulfilment through the Creator's own initiative. Not only can each
of these options be found in the texts of nature's praise, but I believe that
they offer important and complementary elements for a theology of nature,
if we keep them all open.

Conclusions: Towards a Theology of Nature

I now conclude by discussing how we might construct a theology of nature
in light of the reality question underlying the texts of nature's praise. Short

---

43. Another discussion of praise which adopts this "simply being itself" interpretation is the
well-known book of David F. Ford and Daniel W. Hardy, *Living in Praise: Worshipping and Knowing
God* (London: Darton, Longman & Todd, 2005), 104.

of formulating a complete theology, this exercise is best begun by identifying the relevant building blocks. I present them here as ten theses.

1. A theology of nature must find a way to negotiate the difficult middle ground between the four interpretative solutions (A to D) defined in the previous section. This middle ground is a kind of no-man's-land since it represents a reality that is not immediately apparent to humans, who are only able to see our own spiritual depth but not that which might pertain to nature. I defined "nature" early on as all physical entities except the human world, but in the course of discussion it has become clear that if we humans are to respect this no-man's-land, we must recognise that we are even-handedly a praising part of nature too.

2. The fact that the texts of nature's praise force us into an uncertain no-man's-land leads us to consider the role of the natural sciences in pulling us back towards the boundaries. It is hard to avoid the fact that our view of nature is inescapably "naturalistic," informed by the method and scope of the natural sciences. The natural sciences aim to study nature objectively; they can only take a third-person perspective and not the first- and second-person perspectives that entry into the praise of the Creator requires. Hence, the sciences can clarify the necessary limits skirting around a theology of nature but not the solutions. Moreover, the natural sciences are human activities, and ones that cannot apprehend of themselves the need for praise in the first place. We must therefore admit that the no-man's-land possesses a mystery of its own, but this indeed seems to be necessary for any robust theology of nature that does not effectively become a theological anthropology.

3. Moreover, our inability to discern a spiritual depth to nature on naturalistic grounds is not a good reason to deny such a depth. In order to avoid anthropocentrism, it is desirable to affirm that nature's praise occurs independently of humans, even if we have no clear scientific basis for articulating how that praise occurs.

4. In fact, the call upon science raises an equally difficult challenge for understanding the human as a spiritual being. The natural sciences, by definition, must take a naturalistic view, so they are unable to

recognise spiritual dimensions to reality: prayer, praise, and all forms of human encounter with spiritual realities must be articulated in naturalistic terms. In this view, the spiritual life of humans reduces to their own cognitive activity and brain neurochemistry and is therefore no more spiritually enlightened or aware than the equivalent processes in other animals. But if we object that this naturalistic account of humans is too "flat" to account for the depth (or perhaps verticality) of human spirituality we experience, while at the same time refusing to allow such a spirituality to nature on naturalistic grounds, then we are clearly guilty of a massive inconsistency. Logically, we cannot impose a naturalistic view on nature's praise without also imposing such a view on human spirituality. In other words, the spiritual reality that humans claim to engage with is totally mysterious, as is the mechanism by which such engagements occur; perhaps the same is also true of the spirituality of nature. Whatever the case, the sciences help to clarify the problem but cannot solve it.

5. While we could maintain that panpsychism offers a possible (nonscientific) mechanism to solve this latter problem by saying that spiritually conscious mind-stuff permeates all matter, humans as well as trees, a preferable and more biblically supportable solution would be to emphasise divine immanence and pansacramentalism instead.

6. Hence, the relationship between nonhuman creatures and the Creator is pivotal in a theology of nature. In this, it is helpful to affirm a fully theistic model of God, which holds the Creator's immanence and transcendence equally in tension. The texts of nature's praise are important explorations of this theistic relationship between the Creator and every creature.[44]

7. Since it contains a relational component, a theology of nature is as much about God as it is about nature. We find that there is no clear distinction between divine immanence (God's movement towards nature) and the reality question of how inanimate creatures can be said to praise God themselves (nature's movement towards God).[45]

---

44. Harris, *The Nature of Creation*, 114.

45. Note that I have said nothing about the Trinitarian God of Christianity in this chapter, since my focus has been principally on *Old Testament* texts. However, I believe that a Christian Trinitarian response which developed this thesis in terms of the work of the Holy Spirit and Son in the divine economy of creation and salvation would be consistent with what I have said.

8. Such a theology of nature should describe the relationship between nonhuman creatures and the Creator *independently of humans*.

9. A theology of nature should hold creation as a basic tenet, but it must also integrate motifs of salvation and judgement, as reflected in the eschatological nature of some of the biblical texts of nature's praise. In other words, eschatology, soteriology, and divine judgement do not merely concern the world of humans.

10. Praise is not the only theological response of the creatures. Our theology of nature must also be a theology of nature's groaning, of nature's suffering, and of its praise and joy for creation.

In conclusion, the question in my title, "What does it mean to say that a tree praises God?" does not admit of an easy answer. I have suggested four possible solutions (A to D), but I have resisted favouring any one of them. If we are tempted to assume that this is all just personification (A), then, as I have argued above (3 and 4), we are guilty not only of hasty anthropocentrism but also of the massive inconsistency of treating nature naturalistically but not humans. We are forced towards other solutions, but none of them is satisfactory on its own. Hence, I have suggested (1) that we should suspend judgement on any particular solution for now and instead see what emerges if we hold all of the solutions in tension. In this way, I have suggested that an answer to my question indeed emerges. The answer points to the mystery of the being of God as much as to the mysteries of nature (6 and 7). For what we find is that there is no longer a clear distinction between God's immanence and the reality question underlying nature's praise. We might speak of this reality in terms of "pansacramentalism," or of the sanctity of nature, or even (rather vaguely) of the mysterious relationship between Creator and creation. In any case, it seems to me that we cannot enter this debate without encountering the being of God in glorious and immanent majesty. But that encounter is, of course, the entire reason and explanation for praise in the first place.

Chapter SIXTEEN

The Science-and-Religion Delusion

Towards a Theology of Science

TOM McLEISH

This chapter suggests that the categories in which we are accustomed to discuss relationships between science and theology need to be reappraised in terms of the natural universal discourse of both. In particular it asks how a "theology of science" might address the purpose that science fulfils within a Christian worldview in a way that goes beyond the instrumental to the human and covenantal. We suggest relationship in which science and theology are "of each other," and that frames science as the reconciliatory healing of a broken relationship between humans and nature—a humble aspect of the wider Pauline "ministry of reconciliation."

I am not alone in experiencing increasing discomfort with the current public articulation of the "science and religion" debate. Three of the four celebrated categories proposed by Ian Barbour seem to have been ignored or marginalised in the public forum in favour of a univocal assumption of conflict.[1] Attempts to reinstate them, when they are voiced, are couched in the frame of apologetics—they tend to assume a defensive stance. Yet until almost a century ago, the question, "How do you reconcile science with religious belief?" would have been met with incomprehension. Until the mid-nineteenth century (*not* the mid-seventeenth century), "conflict" was not a category

---

1. The four categories that Barbour used to describe the field of science and religion were: conflict, independence, dialogue, and integration. Ian G. Barbour, *Issues in Science and Religion* (London: SCM, 1966).

for understanding the relationship between science and religion. The prior understanding of close and natural relation is traceable, not to any theory of comfortable coexistence, far less to one of "nonoverlapping magisteria," but to an explicit theological framing of the experimental scientific project, as launched by Francis Bacon in the early modern era but drawing on much older scholarship.[2] It is not my task here to write history but, rather, given the excellent historical clarifications of Brooke,[3] Harrison,[4] and others, to take the now unveiled theological narrative active in history as encouragement to rearticulate a "theology *of* science" that resonates with current language and searches for meaning.[5] Such reframing of the new needs, as usual, to draw on the old, and I will suggest the critical connection of the Old Testament wisdom tradition to the narratives that underlie public talk about troublesome science and troublesome technology (different things) today.[6]

In summary, I want to suggest that:

1. the tense altercation around biblical interpretation of creation narratives is precisely the *wrong* public conversation to look for the important problems in science and religion (they are just the noisy ones). We ought to focus instead on the troubled public discourse around science-based technologies, and its evident lack of a narrative understanding of what science is (theologically and anthropologically).

2. the right place to begin to *read* biblically in theological thinking about science is not, initially, in contemplation of the ornamental, liturgical, and geometrical structure of Genesis 1 but in listening to and arguing with the present pain of the book of Job.

3. the right task before us is not reconciliation of theology *and* science but to work through a theology *of* science that is consistent with the long narrative of creation, fall, and resurrection.

---

2. Francis Bacon, *Novum Organum or True Suggestions for the Interpretation of Nature* (New York: Routledge, 1898).

3. John Hedley Brooke, *Science and Religion: Some Historical Perspectives* (Cambridge: Cambridge University Press, 1991).

4. Peter Harrison, *The Territories of Science and Religion* (Chicago: University of Chicago Press, 2015).

5. For a fuller account of some of this material, see Tom McLeish, *Faith and Wisdom in Science* (Oxford: Oxford University Press, 2014).

6. Such a connection of a need for flourishing of current narratives and the Wisdom Tradition has simultaneously been identified in the humanities, see Paul Fiddes, *Seeing the World and Knowing God* (Oxford: Oxford University Press, 2014).

4. to carry this task through suggests a radical reappraisal of science culturally, historically, and politically, as well as reframing the "interaction of science and religion."

In the following we discuss each of these claims before concluding what tasks await.

Narratives of Nature

A helpful example for exploring how we narrate science is given by nanotechnology—the application of physics, chemistry, and engineering to matter at length-scales 10 to 100 times the atomic. Nanotechnology is especially interested in the remarkable property of "self-assembly," by which specific structures form spontaneously from molecular building blocks (an example is the formation of membranes from lipid, or soap-like, molecules). In 2009, a major three-year European research project reported on a narrative analysis behind the ostensibly technical public debate evaluating risks and acceptability of nanotechnology. Their project report, *Reconfiguring Responsibility*, tells a very different story to that of the claims and counterclaims of official public consultations.[7] Its powerful application of qualitative social science unearthed underlying "narratives of despair"—stories that permeate the debate without necessarily surfacing within its superficial technical discussion. Identified by philosopher Jean-Pierre Dupuy,[8] these narratives draw on both ancient and modern myths and create an undertow to discussion of "troubled technologies" that, if unrecognised, renders effective public consultation impossible. The research team labelled the narratives:

1. Be careful what you wish for—the narrative of desire
2. Pandora's Box—the narrative of evil and hope
3. Messing with nature—the narrative of the sacred
4. Kept in the dark—the narrative of alienation
5. The rich get richer and the poor get poorer—the narrative of exploitation

---

7. Sarah Davies, Phil Macnaghten, and Matthew Kearnes, eds., *Reconfiguring Responsibility: Deepening Debate on Nanotechnology* (Durham: Durham University, 2009).
8. J.-P. Dupuy, *The Narratology of Lay Ethics*, in *Nanoethics* 4 (2010): 153–70.

To reiterate, these stories are not explicitly referred to in the group consultations, social media texts, interviews, or articles accessed by the research into public discussions on nanotechnology. One reason for this is that they would not be permitted in any official consultation for the UK government. But they do operate in the worldviews of the participants and, although unstated as such, are strong opinion-forming forces. The very existence of background narratives such as these goes a long way towards explaining why *technical* defences of new technology does little to assuage concerns that stem from the personal depths at which these narratives operate—such a conversation would simply consist of people talking past each other.

Dupuy sees the first three as ancient and the last two as modern metastories or "narratives of despair." It is, at first, rather astonishing to find such a superficially modern set of ideas as nanotechnology awakening such a powerful set of ancient stories, but it will become less so in what follows, for we will claim that the problematic engagement of the human with nonhuman material nature is actually very ancient. Let us briefly survey how the five narratives play out within the example of nanotechnology.

Any new technologies, especially those whose functions are hidden away at the invisible molecular scale, have made exaggerated claims of benefits: longer and healthier lives at low cost, self-repairing materials, and so on. But such hubris elicits memories of overpromising—so, the first metastory, "*be careful what you wish for.*" Overpromising and overdesiring the results of new technology tends to reduce our caution towards them and their possible undesired consequences.

The story of *Pandora's Box* enters at this point. In Hesiod's tale, a daughter of Zeus unwittingly releases all the troubles into the world by taking the lid from a box and trapping hope inside. It acts as a metaphor for the unwitting and irreversible release of damaging side effects of new technologies. Nanotechnology implies such irreversibility, in both knowledge gained and in the environmental release of its products. Pandora eventually released hope (usually read as a glimmer of good). However, as Dupuy points out, hope can be dangerous; it can drive a course of action onwards beyond the point at which a dispassionate risk analysis would have recommended a halt.

The third "ancient narrative" is a fascinating and perplexing one. Why would a secular age develop a storyline that warns us away from *messing with nature* because of its sacred qualities? The surge of secularisation has been charted in the last century in social theory from Emil Durkheim, in political philosophy from Hannah Arendt,[9] and little modified by Habermas (who recognises the signs of permanence in religious traditions).[10] But "the sacred" persists both within and without official religious communities.

The fourth narrative of being *kept in the dark* is at first sight a more modern one, speaking of asymmetries in political power between the governing and the governed.

The fifth narrative of *the rich get richer and the poor get poorer* extends the fourth. With exclusion comes lack of access to the benefits of knowledge and, worse, unequal exposure to their harmful consequences. This fifth narrative has, for example, been especially prevalent in the resistance to GM crops in India.[11]

The aforementioned European nanotechnology study is interesting, not only because it begins to make progress in perceiving why our newest technologies are so troubled but also through its unearthing of the fundamental importance of underlying narrative. Here are (at least) five ancient narratives in modern guise, coiling around a resistance to new science and new technology. They highlight, in the most lurid possible contrast, that science itself lacks any positive or affirming source at a similar depth—*there is a narrative vacuum where the story of science, as it emerges in the human relationship with nature, needs to be told.* What might happen to public debate on contentious science and technology if there were an active ancient narrative, more positive in its story of science, that persisted in contemporary debate?

A candidate for such a narrative appears in George Steiner's deeply felt discussion of meaning and language, *Real Presences*. He writes strikingly about the purpose of art: "Only art can go some way towards making accessible, towards waking into some measure of communicability, the sheer inhuman otherness of matter."[12] To a scientist this attempt at the teleology of art is striking. For, surely, a core function of science is precisely to establish some "accessibility," some communication between our minds and the "sheer inhuman otherness of matter." This idea provides a clue in a search for a new and positive narrative for science, for it also resonates with much more ancient themes.

9. Hannah Arendt, *The Human Condition* (Chicago: University of Chicago Press, 1958), 314.

10. Jürgen Habermas, "Religion in the Public Sphere," *European Journal of Philosophy* 14 (2006), 1–25.

11. T. C. B. McLeish, "The Search for Affirming Narratives for the Future Governance of Technology: Reflections from a Science-Theology Perspective on GMFuturos," in *Governing Agricultural Sustainability*, ed. P. Macnaghten and S. Carro-Ripalda (New York: Routledge, 2015).

12. George Steiner, *Real Presences* (Chicago: University of Chicago Press, 1989).

By Job's Ash Heap

If we are looking for ancient tributaries of the cultural stream that in our day is known as "science," then one clue of where to look is already lodged in the slightly older nomenclature of "natural philosophy." This already implies a core of "wisdom" rather than simply "knowledge." So the corpus of ancient wisdom literature constitutes a natural field in which to search. In support of the claim that, within this corpus, the book of Job constitutes the best biblical starting point for a narratology of the human relationship of the mind with physical creation, let us read from the point at which God finally speaks to Job (after 37 chapters of silence) in 38:4–7:[13]

> Where were you when I founded the earth?
>> Tell me, if you have insight.
> Who fixed its dimensions? Surely you know!
>> Who stretched the measuring cord across it?
> Into what were its bases sunk,
>> or who set its capstone,
> when the stars of the morning rejoiced together,
>> and all the sons of God shouted for joy?

The writer delineates a beautiful development of the core creation narrative in Hebrew wisdom poetry (a form found in Psalms, Proverbs, and some Prophets that speaks of creation through "ordering," "bounding," and "setting foundations"[14]), but now in the relentless urgency of the question-form, the voice continues by sharpening its questions, first towards the phenomena of the atmosphere:

> Have you entered the storehouses of the snow?
>> Or have you seen the arsenals of the hail? (Job 38:22)

The voice then directs our gaze upwards to the stars in their constellations, to their motion, and to the laws that govern them:

---

13. We take quotations of the text from the magisterial new translation and commentary by David Clines, *Job 38–42*, Word Biblical Commentary 18B (Nashville: Thomas Nelson, 2011), 1048–52. Additional translation from Clines, *Job 1–20*, World Biblical Commentary 17 (Grand Rapids: Zondervan, 2015); and Clines, *Job 21–37*, World Biblical Commentary 18a (Grand Rapids: Zondervan, 2015).

14. W. H. Brown, *The Seven Pillars of Creation* (Oxford: Oxford University Press, 2010).

Can you bind the cluster of the Pleiades,
    or loose Orion's belt?
Can you bring out Mazzaroth in its season,
    or guide Aldebaran with its train?
Do you determine the laws of the heaven?
    Can you establish its rule upon earth? (Job 38:31–33)

The questing survey next sweeps over the animal kingdom, then finishes with a celebrated "decentralising" text that places humans at the periphery of the world, gazing in wonder at its centrepieces, the great beasts Behemoth and Leviathan. This is an ancient recognition of the unpredictable aspects of the world: the whirlwind, the earthquake, the flood, and unknown great beasts. Even these short extracts from the longer poem give something of the impressive, cosmic sweep of this text. In today's terms, we have, in the Lord's answer to Job, a foundational framing for the primary questions of the fields we now call cosmology, geology, meteorology, astronomy, zoology, and so on. Of course, to use the text in this way is an unwarranted and anachronistic projection of our current programs over a vast gulf of cultures. However, if we are instead alert to the poetic form, we can recognise in this extraordinary wisdom-poem an ancient and questioning view into nature, unsurpassed in its astute attention to detail and sensibility towards the tensions of humanity in confrontation with nature.

There are forces at play behind this text that draw on an energy, recognisable to scientists today, that generates the developing relationship of intellect between the human mind and the inhuman realms of nature. Being alert to the subtle random dynamics underpinning statistical mechanics or of the chaotic phenomena in nonlinear dynamical systems theory, a contemporary scientist will find herself at home in Job's world of incomprehension in the face of cosmic disorder. More is true: there is another reason that scientists find this passage in Job so resonant—and that is its *form*. For we know that the truly essential and imaginative task in scientific discovery is not the finding of answers but the formulation of the fruitful question.[15]

Long recognised as a masterpiece of ancient literature, the book of Job has

---

15. This point has been stressed repeatedly by modern scientists, e.g., Einstein: "If I had an hour to solve a problem and my life depended on the solution, I would spend the first 55 minutes determining the proper question to ask. . . . For once I know the proper question, I could solve the problem in less than five *minutes*."

attracted and perplexed scholars in equal measures for centuries and remains a vibrant field of study today. David Clines, to whom we owe the translation employed here, calls the book of Job "the most intense book theologically and intellectually of the Old Testament."[16] Job has inspired commentators across vistas of centuries and philosophies from Basil the Great to Kant to Levinas. Susan Neiman has recently argued the case that the book of Job constitutes, alongside Plato, a necessary source-text for the foundation of philosophy itself.[17]

However, although readers of the text have long recognised that the cosmological motif within Job is striking and important, it has not received as much comprehensive attention as the legal, moral, and theological strands in the book. There are a few notable exceptions, for example the work of Norman Habel.[18] Arguably the identification of a direct link of Job's subject matter to the human capacity for natural philosophy goes back at least as far as Aquinas, who refers at several points to Aristotle's *Physics* in his extensive commentary on the wisdom book,[19] but these connections are rare in preference to metaphorical readings. This deemphasising of cosmology might partly explain why Job 38, from which we have taken the extracts above and known as "The Lord's Answer," has had such a problematic history of reception and interpretation. Does it really answer Job's two questions about his own innocence and the meaninglessness of his suffering? Does the "Lord" of the creation hymns correspond to the creator Yahweh of the Psalms, the Pentateuch, and the Prophets? Does the text even belong to the rest of the book as originally conceived? Some scholars have found the Lord's Answer spiteful, a petulant put-down that misses the point and avoids the tough questions. For example, David Robertson perceives that this "God" fails utterly to answer Job and finds him to be a charlatan deity.[20] But are these interpretations justified? Even looking at the text through the fresh lens of science today resonates with the *difficulty* of questioning nature, even its painfulness, as well as its *wonder*—that is how scientists respond at a first reading time and again.

---

16. Clines, *Job 1–20*, 22.

17. See Neiman, "The Rationality of the World: A Philosophical Reading of the Book of Job," ABC Religion and Ethics, 19 October 2016, http://http://www.abc.net.au/religion/articles/2016/10/19/4559097.htm.

18. N. C. Habel, *The Book of Job* (Atlanta: John Knox, 1981).

19. Thomas Aquinas, *Expositio super Iob ad litteram*, trans. Brian Mulladay, ed. Joseph Kenny, http://dhspriory.org/thomas/SSJob.htm#382.

20. David Robertson, "The Book of Job: A Literary Study," *Soundings* 56 (1973): 446–68.

To begin to answer the charge, at the textual level, that the "Lord's Answer" isn't an answer, we need to observe that the intense nature imagery of the book is by no means confined to Yahweh's voice. On the contrary, nature imagery is employed from the very outset of the prologue and throughout the disputations between Job and his friends. Indeed, every theme picked up in the Lord's Answer *has already appeared in the cycles of dialogue between Job and his friends.* The entire book is structured around the theme of wild nature. There is, furthermore, an ordered pattern in the realms of creation explored predominantly in the three cycles of speeches:

1. Inanimate nature: earth, winds, waters, springs, stones, sea. For example, see Eliphaz's superlative terms by which he frames the rewards of Job's repentance (5:22–23):

    > At ruin and blight you will mock,
    >> and you will have no fear of the wild beasts.
    > For you will be in covenant with the stones of the field,
    >> and the wild animals will be at peace with you.

2. Animate nature: plants, animals, vines, milk, honey. For example, see Job's final speech of the cycle evidencing the absence of a moral code for nature (21:10, 18, 24):

    > Their bull sires without fail,
    >> their cow gives birth and does not lose her calf . . .
    > How often are they like straw before the wind,
    >> like chaff swept away by the storm? . . .
    > His pails are full of milk,
    >> and the marrow is juicy in his bones.

3. The cosmos: heavens, moon, stars, Sheol, the far extremities of the world. For example, Eliphaz speaks to our first explicit view of a Hebrew cosmology (22:12–14):

    > Is not God in the height of the heavens?
    >> Does he not look down on the topmost stars, high as they are?

> Yet you say, "What does God know?
>> Can he see through thick clouds to govern?
> Thick clouds veil him, and he cannot see
>> as he goes his way on the vault of heaven!"

So the cosmological crescendo matches the ratcheting tension of the drama—it is only in this third cycle that direct accusations of personal wickedness are levelled at Job in a brutal climax where Bildad can only answer Job's searching complaints by an attempt to trump them with their irrelevance. God, all-powerful, may rule with an iron fist if he so desires. Finally, there is no human voice worth hearing in such a world. All voices are crushed into silence.

At this point of impasse, the start of chapter 28, a beautiful and structurally quite new voice enters with the poem sometimes denoted as the "Hymn to Wisdom" (28:1–6):

> Surely there is a mine for silver,
>> and a place for gold that will be refined.
> Iron is taken from the soil,
>> rock that will be poured out as copper.
> An end is put to darkness,
>> and to the furthest bound they seek the ore
>> in gloom and deep darkness.
> A foreign race cuts the shafts;
>> forgotten by travelers,
>> far away from humans they dangle and sway.
> That earth from which food comes forth
>> is underneath changed as if by fire.
> Its rocks are the source of lapis,
>> with its flecks of gold.

The scene is a mineshaft under the ground—we can just make out the miners swaying in the gloom. We also begin to see *with* them; a miner's gaze on the earth from below reveals a very different appearance to that from above. The "transformation as if by fire" is a remarkable insight into one of the processes by which minerals separate out, recombine, and solidify in the rocks below ground. If we look hard in the dim candlelight, we might catch a glimmer of gold. The underground world takes us by surprise—why did either an original author or a later compiler suppose that the next step to take in the book was down a mineshaft? Reading on (28:7–11):

> There is a path no bird of prey knows,
>   unseen by the eye of falcons.
> The proud beasts have not trodden it,
>   no lion has prowled it.
> The men set their hands against the flinty rock,
>   and overturn mountains at their roots.
> They split open channels in the rocks,
>   and their eye lights on any precious object.
> They explore the sources of rivers,
>   bringing to light what has been hidden.

We begin to recognise a theme winding through Job, namely, that there is something unique about the way humans fashion their relationship to the physical world. The metaphor directs us to admire the patient and knowledgeable art of mining seams through hard rock, exploring just those places that yield precious ores or stones. But even more significantly, only human eyes can *see* it from this new viewpoint. It is a sight that asks questions, that directs further exploration, that wonders. No wonder such extraordinary human capacity has been confused with the divine.

The writer reveals the true purpose of the interlude—the poem becomes a search for wisdom—a treasure hidden from the eyes of all living things (humans, presumably, included), and that of which even the deeply buried land of death has only heard enigmatic whispers. So, is the world simply a collection of "the wrong places to look" for wisdom and understanding? The conclusion of the hymn "draws back the curtain" once more (28:23–27):

> But God understands the way to it;
>   it is he who knows its place.
> For he looked to the ends of the earth,
>   and beheld everything under the heavens,
> so as to assign a weight to the wind,

> and determine the waters by measure,
>   when he made a decree for the rain,
>   and a path for the thunderbolt—
>   then he saw and appraised it,
>   established it and fathomed it.

The reason God knows where to find wisdom is precisely because he "looked to the ends of the earth . . . established it and fathomed it." It is, as for the underground miners, a very special sort of looking. In this case the special depth of perception is conveyed by adding a numerical aspect to the visual and tangible—for example, God assigns a value to the force of the wind. God's deep view into the world is capable of assessing the function of physical law (or "decree"), as in the controlled paths of rain and lightning and in the coming together of ordered matter. (There is a blurring here between creating the world, and looking at it once it is created.) This is an extraordinary claim: wisdom can be found in participating with a deep understanding of the world, an intense perception of its structure and dynamics. It is a way of relating to the created world that we may even share with its Creator. Even though God necessarily possesses a deeper understanding of creation than a human creature could ever have, nevertheless, the force of the Hymn to Wisdom is that this is a wisdom in which humans are called to share and uniquely given the ability to enjoy. This is admittedly a very bold interpretation, but one that continues to be reinforced as the book of Job unfolds. Even throughout the early dialogues, a deep relation with nature is held up as a future promise to Job—recall Eliphaz's words in 5:23, "*you will be in covenant with the stones*." This extraordinary notion—that the highest possible status of human relationship might be enjoyed between us and inanimate matter—has proved too shocking for many translators to take at face value, but it reappears here in the relational wisdom of chapter 28.

Looking back at the three cycles of dialogue with this new perspective, we see that they have not only taken us through ascending levels of the natural world itself but also introduced us to a series of interpretations of what a human relationship with nature might look like. Getting this relationship right, as we now understand from the cornerstone passage of the wisdom hymn (Job 28:23–27), offers a route to the precious possession of wisdom, the quality most starkly lacking from the disputations. However, none of the other relational perspectives offered from the other clamouring voices within the book of Job up to this point has succeeded in "finding wisdom," any more than the depths of the oceans or foundations of the earth contained in chapter 28. At least five alternative perspectives on nature and its significance can be discerned in the earlier dialogues:

First is the "simple moral pendulum"—the story of nature as both anthropocentric and driven by a moral law of retribution. This is the central narrative of the first three of Job's friends and fails in the face of Job's demonstration of the equal suffering of the righteous.

Second is the "eternal mystery"—the story that speaks of God's exclusive understanding of nature's workings in ways that humans can never know. The friends attempt to refute this, but its unanswerable critique is encountered in the example of the miner in chapter 28.

Third is the "book of nature"—the story of Elihu's speech, in which nature constitutes a giant message board from its maker for those who have eyes to read it. Job counters this with an appeal to evident randomness in natural events of destruction.

Fourth is the story of the uncontrolled storm, flood, and earthquake. This is uniquely Job's interpretation of his relationship with nature. Job uses cosmological chaos in his discourse because his accusation is that God is as out of control regarding human justice, as is the physical world. It takes the Lord's Answer to Job's myopia for Job to see beyond this view from his enclosed and angry state.

A fifth possible relationship with creation is made explicit only once by Job himself. It is the relationship of nature and worship: humans worshipping nature. It is dismissed straightaway but not without giving away its allure:

> If I have gazed with delight on the Sun when it shone,
>   or the moon moving in splendor,
> and my heart has been secretly enticed,
>   and my mouth has kissed my hand—
> this also would have been a punishable crime. (Job 31:26–28)

A sixth storyline is hinted at throughout the speech cycles but is first heard with clarity in the Hymn to Wisdom. It hints at a balance between order and chaos rather than a domination of either. The stark freshness of the reconciliatory, relational, and participative invitation to engage with nature, advanced in both the Hymn to Wisdom and the Lord's Answer in Job 28 and 38–42, is in part generated by its radical departures from the five grim alternative views of the material world that dominate the cycles of Job's discourse with his friends. Remarkably, the first five perspectives map naturally onto the five "narratives of despair" we met in our first section—and we can see the discussion of the narratives in that section as a background to their prior appearance in *Job*:

1. Nature enshrines retributive moral law—the narrative of *exploitation*. This is an exploitative view of nature, as in the modern sense, because it demands of the natural world a meaning centred on human need, rather than a life of its own.

2. Nature is eternal mystery—the narrative of *alienation*. If nature can never be accommodated to the human, if it must always dwell in hiddenness, then the human condition is alienated from it.

3. Nature is a Holy Book to be read—the narrative of the *sacred*. At first this does not look like the modern "narrative of the sacred," which principally deals with the "untouchability" of nature, but by definition a Holy Book cannot be edited; it is beyond our "writing" by definition and divine decree.

4. Nature is uncontrolled chaos (Job's accusation)—the narrative of *evil*. This is the core narrative of Job. He accuses Yahweh of creating a nature that defies order or control. The destructive harm is the embodiment not of moral law (as 1 above) but of moral evil.

5. Nature is an object of worship (Job's denial)—the narrative of *desire*. The connection between desire and worship is a complex one, but its core is well-articulated in the Psalms of longing for God's presence.

The pattern runs parallel to the current analysis of deeply buried narratives behind social attitudes to the natural world. In the modern case, we found ourselves in search of any positive theologically motivated and informed alternative to these five. The sixth storyline, the search for wisdom through the perceptive, renewed, and reconciliatory relationship with nature, begins to look like a potential source for a "missing narrative" of nature in our own times. It is rooted in a monotheistic understanding of creation and covenant, rather than in a pagan or atheistic tradition; it recognises reasons to despair, but undercuts them with hope; it points away from stagnation to a future of greater knowledge, understanding, and healing.

A Theology of Science

We need to draw some threads together from readings of the sixth narrative of wisdom from the book of Job and from the need for such a relational theology of science for our contemporary troubled technologies. The essential constitutive themes of a new narrative for science are

1. the recognition of its place in a long, linear, and deeply human history,
2. an expectation of remarkable human aptitude for reimagining nature,
3. the need for wisdom to work with knowledge,
4. the anticipation of ambiguity and the experience of pain in working with nature,
5. an appreciation of the delicate balance of order and chaos,
6. the centrality of the question and the questioning mind, and
7. the developing wisdom of an understanding of nature as an expression of love.

Within all these themes, the pattern of relationship has dogged us constantly. Science involves the negotiation of a new relationship between human minds and the physical world. The nature-language of the Bible is consistently employed to describe and develop the relationship of care and of understanding between humans and a world that is both our home and also a frightening field of bewildering complexity.

These patterns are only amplified when refracted through a New Testament lens. Within his most painful correspondence (with Corinth), Paul, for example, rethinks the entire project of God's creation in relational terms, working around and towards the central idea of reconciliation. Arguing that those who have been baptised into life with Christ can already view the world from the perspective of a new creation, he writes (2 Cor 5:17–19):

> Therefore, if anyone is in Christ—new creation;
> The old has gone, the new has come!
> All this is from God, who reconciled himself through Christ and gave
>   us the ministry of reconciliation:
> That God was reconciling the world to himself in Christ.[21]

The "ministry of reconciliation" is a stunningly brief encapsulation of the biblical story of the purpose to which God calls people. I don't know a better three-word definition of Christianity, and it does very well as an entry point for Old Testament temple-based Judaism as well.

There is one relationship that tends to be overlooked in expositions of Christian theology—the one between humankind and nature itself. A theology of science, consistent with the stories we have told up to this point, situates our exploration of nature within that greater task. Science becomes, within a Christian theology, the grounded outworking of the "ministry of reconciliation" between humankind and the world. Far from being a task that threatens to derail the narrative of salvation, it actually participates within it. Science is the name we now give to the deeply human, theological task and ancient story of participating in the mending of our relationship with nature. We might summarise a theology of science as follows:

> Science is the participative, relational, cocreative work within the kingdom of God of healing the fallen relationship of humans with nature.

It is an extraordinary idea at first, especially if we have been used to negotiating ground between "science" and "religion"; as if there were a disputed frontier requiring some sort of disciplinary peacekeeping force to hold the line.

It also makes little sense within a view of history that sees science as an exclusively modern and secular development. But neither of these assumptions stands up to disciplinary analysis on the one hand or history on the other. Far from early modern science overthrowing everything Aristotelian and scholastic, the same narrative of new perception, sharpened by a Reformed theology of fall and redemption, appears in Francis Bacon's motivation for experimental science:

---

21. Original translation.

The glory of God is to conceal a thing, but the glory of the king is to find it out; as if, according to the innocent play of children, the Divine Majesty took delight to hide his works, to the end to have them found out; and as if kings could not obtain a greater honour than to be God's playfellows in that game, considering the great commandment of wits and means, whereby nothing needeth to be hidden from them.[22]

We need a "theology of science" because we need a theology of everything. If we fail, then we have a theology of nothing. Such a theology has to bear in mind the tension that the same is true for science—it has never worked to claim that science can speak of some but not of other topics. Science and theology are not complementary; they are not in combat, they are not just consistent—they are "*of* each other." This is the first ingredient of a theology of science.

Just as there is no boundary to be drawn across the domain of subject, there is no boundary within time that demarks successive reigns of theology and science. It is just not possible to define a moment in the history of thought that marks a temporal boundary between the "prescientific" and the "scientific." The longing to understand, to go beneath the superficies of the world in thought, to reconstruct the workings of the universe in our minds, is a cultural activity as old as any other. Furthermore, it is a human endeavour that is deeply and continually rooted in theological tradition. The conclusion is still surprising to much of the contemporary Western world: far from being necessarily contradictory or threatening to a religious worldview in general or to Christianity in particular, science turns out to be an intensely theological activity. When we do science, we participate in the relational healing work of the Creator. For any broken relationship tends to be characterised by ignorance, giving rise to a mutual fear, which in turn leads to harm. When we understand a little more of nature, we begin the process of healing by replacing ignorance with knowledge, fear with wisdom, so that mutual harm might be turned back towards mutual flourishing. We take a step further in the reconciliation of a broken relationship between human beings and the rest of creation.

Our participation in reconciliation is as strong a theme in the New Testament. There is another surprise awaiting the explorer of this road to a

---

22. Francis Bacon, *Valerius Terminus, Of the Interpretation of Nature* (1610), in *The Works of Lord Bacon*, vol. 1 (London: William Ball, Paternoster Row, 1837), 219.

theology of science. Among the "clamour of voices" contesting the relationship between theology and science, the accusation has been raised that scientists today behave like "priests of a former age."[23] This is meant of course in a pejorative sense; the image projected is the priest as representative of oppressive authority. But the Old Testament notion of priesthood was in many ways the perfect opposite of this dark stereotype. The priests were in charge of the festivals that reenacted the foundational acts of Israel's reconciliation to YHWH. The New Testament transformation of priesthood is actually an amplification of a healthy notion of priest as enabler rather than a negation of it. Scientists are priests in the sense that they are specifically at work on behalf of their fellow human beings, in their case transforming the broken relationship between people and the physical world. Special work is required because the task calls for long training and particular skills, but their work is on behalf of all people and requires regular participative engagement. One might even suggest that this should take the form of celebration.

Consequences

Does a theology of science do meaningful work for us? Does it provide any avenues to resolve the painful cross-currents around science in society? Does it suggest new tasks? These must be the test for any endeavour of this kind. It has taken long enough to climb the hill from which we might see science within a Judeo-Christian worldview and outline a theology *of* science that begins to circumvent a relentless territorial contest between theology *and* science. Let's look at just one example.

One leading contemporary commentator, whose interest in the "politics of nature"[24] has not been marginalized, is the French thinker Bruno Latour. In a recent edited volume,[25] he explores the terrifying observation that environmentalism has become a dull topic—with conclusions that are remarkably resonant with those that I have been drawing in this chapter. They break down into four findings: "*a stifling belief in the existence of Nature to be protected; a particular conception of Science; a limited gamut of emotions in politics; and, finally, the*

---

23. Angela Tilby, *Science and the Soul* (London: SPCK, 1992).

24. Bruno Latour, *Politics of Nature: How to Bring the Sciences into Democracy*, trans. Catherine Porter (Cambridge: Harvard University Press, 2004).

25. Bruno Latour, "'It's development, stupid!' or: How to Modernize Modernization," in *Postenvironmentalism*, ed. Jim Procter (Cambridge, MIT Press, 2008).

direction these give to the arrow of time."[26] This is a grand, overarching critique of the politics of nature, but even so, it homes on to the same narrative analysis as did the specific nanotechnology study we examined at the beginning. For example, Latour points out a movement to withdraw all human corruption from a nature that could be maintained in some pristine condition if this were achieved. He rightly terms such a suggestion as "stifling." We can see, after the comparative study of contemporary public narrative around science with that of the book of Job, that it is none other than the "messing with sacred Nature" narrative by another name. Latour extracts the self-contradictory structure of this story of the Golden Age—for him, nature-reserves are artificial by definition. But the alternative "modernist" trajectory is no less problematic. In it, control overcomes nature. We disengage from our environment, not through an environmentalist dream of withdrawal from the sanctuary but through technological domination. Here, Latour revisits the narrative of Pandora's Box because such a modernist hope is dashed on the rocks of the same increasingly deep and problematic entangling with the world that prevents withdrawal. Nature does not respond mildly to an attempt to control or dominate. So neither narrative works—both start with fundamentally misguided notions of the geometries and constraints of our relationship with nature.

Latour's critique of the conception of science is equally resonant with the flawed view of a "scientific priesthood" we have already explored. Political action on scientific decisions is as paralysed by disagreement as it is by disengagment. Not every expert agrees that blood transfusion might transmit the AIDS virus—so we wait in an inaction that condemns children to infection. There is no uniform view on the future trajectory of global warming and its connection with human release of carbon dioxide—so we meet and talk but do not implement. This is the "kept in the dark" narrative with a twist. The political and public community self-impose ignorance by demanding that scientists behave as a conclave, reading the same script and praying the same prayers, until the white smoke of expert agreement is released. The political lifeblood of a communally possessed and confident debate, widely shared and energised, respecting where specialist knowledge lies but challenged within a participating lay public, is simply not yet flowing in our national and international veins.

26. Bruno Latour, "'It's development, stupid!,'" 4, emphasis mine.

At the close of his contribution to *Postenvironmentalism*, Latour makes an extraordinary move—one that meets our journey head on. He calls for a reexamination of the connection between mastery, technology, and *theology* as a route out of the environmental impasse. We have not yet remarked that the ancient narratives unearthed by the nanotechnology project, and reflected in Latour's, are all implicitly or explicitly pagan, although we have seen how they might be met with and transformed by the more positive themes of a Judeo-Christian ancient narrative of nature. So when he refers to the christological theme of the Creator who takes the responsibility to engage with even an errant creation to the point of crucifixion, the contrast with the disempowering and risk-averse narratives of "being careful what you wish for," Pandora, sacred nature, and the rest, could not be starker.

The theological wisdom tradition we have been following, especially in the way that it entangles with the story of science itself, has brought us to the same point that Latour reaches from the perspective of political philosophy. One identifies the need, the other the motivation and resource, for reengagement with the material world, alongside an acknowledgement that one unavoidable consequence of being human is that we have, in the terms of the book of Job, a "covenant with the rocks." This extraordinarily powerful collision of metaphors surely points to the balanced and responsible sense of mastery that Latour urges us to differentiate from the overtones of exploitative dominance.

Conclusions

If we take, one by one, the strands of the "theology of science" that we teased out of our biblical nature trail, it begins to look as though they might be woven into the story, the missing narrative, that Latour wants to hear told. The task before us is to practice the reconciliatory task that the narrative of wisdom urges and to broadcast the new story itself. In an uncanny parallel to the myth of Pandora as recorded by Hesiod, in letting all the troubles of despair out of the box, we, like Pandora herself, have shut the lid to trap inside the one narrative of hope that might have assisted us. Lifting the lid to let it out once more is our new task.

There are two strong values in the possession of the church that can be deployed to great effect in a practical, political support of a healthy science and technology in society: a desire for truth, and an abhorrence of fear. In a "post-truth society" in which one's opponents' tactics are easily labelled as "Project Fear," it is a wonder that such slogans have not already alerted us to the blatant opposition to Christian thinking, increasingly prevalent in the political sphere. This is particularly true of issues around science and technology. The church is at the very least a network of organisations capable of delivering strong social cohesion, service, and voice. What might the effect be of such an influential voice insisting that its core values of truth and the banishment of fear overcome the deployment of falsehoods and threats so often emblematic of technological politics? Such an outspoken move would release a theologically informed voice to speak with transformational potential into a society that does not uniformly, even in majority, share in its theological foundations. (Witnessing a discussion held by Christian leaders, including strongly opposed parties, over the contentious issue of fracking for shale gas recovery, for example, convinced this author of the practical power of a church community determined to hold difficult discussions together in truth and understanding.)

The wider issue of how theologically generated narratives of hope and care might take hold within a secular society is also addressed within the gospel now, just as it was in the first century by Saint Paul's encapsulation of the (then mysterious to Jews and Gentiles alike) Christian message—the "ministry of reconciliation." A mission statement that sets out to heal broken relationships is one that resonates as strongly in late modern times as in late classical. It is understood as clearly needed by believer and nonbeliever alike. Our task is to translate that thought, and harness the energy of hope that drove Paul as strongly as it must the Christian church today, to engage with the urgent task of discovering, through the work of science and through greater wisdom in its application, how to learn of and care for the natural world. The theology of science I have outlined opens many resources for the project of science and technology within today's social setting. It establishes it deeply and naturally within the human condition, and it prepares us for the painful and error-strewn pathway to expect in its execution. It urges us to accept a humble approach in a duty of care for the created world but not a falsely humble one that turns from our responsibility to invest the gift of science in a work of healing. Finally, it suggests a much less exclusive role for science and the task to develop a healthier participation in it and celebration of it in which the church can take a lead. To take up Eliphaz's metaphor once more, it is our task to work towards creating a covenant with the stones.

Subject Index

Scripture Index

Author Index